Carole de Losada, W.C.R. President
Thank you for your help during
our Centennial Celebration Year.
Your commitment and generosity
greatly assisted the S.J.R.E.B. in
"Stepping Out... Into the Next 100 Years!"

Irea Haas, President 1996

D1601830

Santa Clara County

And its Resources

Historical
Descriptive
Statistical

A Souvenir of

The San Jose Mercury

1896

PRESS OF

ALFRED C. EATON

SAN JOSE, CAL.

ISBN 0-914139-03-7
REPRINTED IN 1986 BY THE SAN JOSE
HISTORICAL MUSEUM ASSOCIATION.

INTRODUCTION.

* * * *

MANY PEOPLE who desired to obtain a copy of the First Edition of this book were unable to do so, owing to the fact that the entire edition was sold in less than thirty days from the time of its issuance from the press.

To supply this existing demand is our excuse for issuing this Second Edition. Repeating the words of introduction used before, it is well known that mental pictures of the appearance and characteristics of a country are usually the result of suggestions and scraps of information which but dimly, and often inaccurately outline its features. Few writers indeed can weave words so ingeniously as to present to the mind, unaided by the engraver's art, pictures that will enable the reader to form conclusions that even approach correctness. There are degrees of excellence, however, and in the preparation of this volume we used care to secure writers that were able, careful and conscientious.

In order that dwellers in other lands might appreciate the beauty of our landscape, form an intelligent estimate of our resources, and be enabled to more fully comprehend the value of our climate, we have supplemented the work of our most talented writers with the best efforts of the most artistic photographers, engravers and printers.

Gathering experience from the preparation of the First Edition we are enabled to correct any errors which may have innocently intruded themselves therein, and furthermore to present to the public new pictures and new facts, and thus make the work in many respects a new one.

For the generous appreciation which the public has shown for the previous publication we desire to make grateful acknowledgement.

Chas. M. Shortridge

. . . CHARACTERISTIC FEATURES . . .

City of San Jose.

FREE mail delivery.

Population 29,370.

Three daily newspapers.

Seven banking institutions.

Forty church organizations.

Ninety-four feet above sea level.

Public Parks aggregating 627 acres.

The first town established in California.

Banking capital aggregates over $3,000,000.

Has the largest fruit cannery in the world.

Has the highest electric light tower on the coast.

An abundant supply of pure mountain water.

A Free Public Library, containing 13,000 volumes.

One hundred and twenty-six miles of graded streets.

The climate of Italy in the latitude of Washington.

Well supplied with electric suburban street railways.

Within fifty miles of one of the best harbors in the world,

The Garden City of the Garden County of the Garden State.

Founded November 29, 1777. Incorporated March 27, 1850.

One of the largest and most elegantly appointed hotels on the coast.

Fare to San Francisco by rail, $1.25; by stage and steamer, 75 cents.

Forty-eight miles from San Francisco. Fifteen trains each way each day.

A massive buff stone Postoffice building, which was erected at a cost of $200,000.

Within seven miles of tide water, where sea-going vessels receive and discharge their cargoes.

Maintains a progressive and enterprising Board of Trade, to promote public improvements and encourage immigration.

Better paved and more beautifully shaded streets than any other city in the United States, excepting Philadelphia and Washington.

A Police Patrol Wagon, constantly on duty, which may be summoned by the Police Department telephones, twenty of which are located at the most available points in the city.

Four steam fire engines, one chemical, and an improved hook and ladder truck. Four hose carts, and one hose wagon, each carrying 800 feet of hose. Sixty-two fire alarm boxes.

Total overland shipment of green, dried, and canned fruits from San Jose in 1895, 87,048,905 pounds. Total shipment over the Broad Gauge from San Jose, in 1895, 111,410,375 pounds.

Santa Clara County.

POPULATION 56,396.

The largest olive orchard in the world.

An abundance of good building stone.

The greatest educational center in the west.

Larger than the entire state of Rhode Island.

Pre-eminently the prune-growing center of the world.

Alfalfa here yields from two to six crops per annum.

Six daily newspapers, twenty weeklies, and one semi-weekly.

There are within the county 42¾ miles of street railways.

Increase of population between 1880 and 1890, 43.71 per cent.

Every month in the year ripens a crop of some kind in the open air.

Snow has fallen in the Santa Clara Valley twice in the last twenty years.

The most richly endowed educational instiution in the world is located at Palo Alto.

For the sprinkling and maintenance of county roads nearly $100,000 is expended annually.

The busy bee that works when the sun shines doesn't have much rest in Santa Clara County.

The average length of the county is forty-one miles, and the average width twenty-five miles.

The only home in the United States for the widows and children of soldiers is situated at Evergreen, in this county.

There is not in the United States outside of California a similar area where such an extended list of products may be raised.

The rainfall of the county varies in different sections, the minimum being seventeen inches, and the maximum thirty-three.

The highest peak in the Santa Cruz range of mountains is Mount Bache, 3,780 feet, and in the Coast Range, Mount Hamilton, 4,250 feet.

The Lick Observatory, upon the summit of Mount Hamilton, is directly east of the center of San Jose, from which it is distant thirteen miles in an air line.

Mount Diablo is almost directly north of San Jose, the meridian line passing through the Fair Grounds, and crossing the railroad a few feet east of the narrow gauge depot at College Park. The Meridian road is upon the meridian line.

Santa Clara County is noted for the size and excellence of its public buildings. Among those which attract particular attention are the Stanford University, the State Asylum for Insane, the State Normal School, the Hall of Records, the Postoffice and the Hotel Vendome.

SANTA THE CLARA VALLEY

God touched the earth in kindness, and, lo, it dimpled where
It felt His mighty finger, and a valley nestled there,
And He told the angel artist to paint a sky more blue,
Than ever dainty violet or airy bluebell knew,
And to stretch it o'er that valley, as a promise from its God
That peace and plenty there should spring like flowers from its sod
And He set the mighty mountains to guard that happy vale
Where the autumns kiss the springtimes and the summers never fail.

Then all the birds came singing to where the valley smiled,
And all the suns came shining, by all its peace beguiled;
And from the hidden canyons the brooklets sparkled down
To cheer the future's exiles from the city or the town;
And the gray earth loved its flowers, as the flowers love the sun
And the glory of the daytime into even's glory run;
And the live oak wore its banners green through all the year [unfurled]
And so was Santa Clara's vale first given to the world.

And then man came from out the East, and lo, the valley smiled,
And she took him to her bosom, and she loved him as her child.
She blessed him with her orchards, and she cheered him with her vine,
She fed him with her bounty, and she gladdened him with wine.
He builded there an alter and a happy home, I ween;
And his temple unto learning on gray Hamilton was seen.
Ah, blest was he by nature past man's allotment here,
In that rarest, fairest valley, in that home of peace and cheer.

Then Gilroy smiled to San Jose, and Saratoga's spring
Called all the happy songsters just to hear the waters sing;
Adown Los Gatos' fairy vale a silver brooklet ran,
And Santa Clara seemed a dream to bless the soul of man,
And Almaden lay smiling, as a babe its mother cheers,
And so peaceful were the moments of the onward-tripping years
That the heart of man was gladdened, and he said: "I love thee best -
And so was Santa Clara's vale by God and nature blessed.

A. J. Waterhouse

Scene on Stevens Creek.
View of Valley from Farm of Harvey Swickard.

View of Santa Clara Valley from road to Mt. Hamilton.

Banana Tree on Farm of C. A. Baldwin.
Cattle Scene on Farm of Mrs. A. Younger.

HISTORY OF THE COUNTY.

PREVIOUS to the advent of Europeans California was considered a portion of Mexico, subject to Spain. The authorities, however, knew very little concerning its geographical features, their knowledge having been founded upon the unreliable reports of bay and shore lines, furnished by adventurous navigators.

DISCOVERY OF MONTEREY BAY. In 1602 the Coast was visited by Sebastian Vizcaino, who anchored in Monterey Bay. The distinguishing features of the vicinity were recorded by Venegas and Cabrera, who, presumably, accompanied him. They pronounced it a famoso puerto. This report eventually fell into the hands of the Spanish authorities, who, ever eager to establish out-posts, decided to occupy the land. No particular effort to forward the plan was made, however, until 1769 In that year orders were sent to the officers in charge of the Pueblo at San Diego to dispatch a party in search of Monterey Bay. In keeping with this order, Captain Gaspar de Portola, civil and military governor, and Captain Fernando Javier Rivera y Moncada, left San Diego, July 14th, 1769, with a company, to search for the famous port. Moncado was in command of twenty-seven soldiers, including Sergeant Joseph Francisco Ortega and Lieutenant Pedro Fages, with six or seven of his Catalan volunteers. Engineer Miguel Costanso, Fathers Juan Crispi and Francisco Gomez, seven muleteers, fifteen Christianized Lower Californians, and two servants for Portola and Rivera were included, the company numbering altogether sixty-four persons. Many hardships were encountered, for the land was a new one and the guides inexperienced.

COURT HOUSE AND HALL OF RECORDS, SAN JOSE.

The party reached the Bay of Monterey on October 1st, but failed to recognize it, and continued up the coast. A week later they crossed the Pajaro River, naming it from a stuffed bird found among the natives. On the 17th they crossed the Rio San Lorenzo, at the sight of the present City of Santa Cruz. Continuing along the coast they reached Point San Pedro October 30th, where they camped, intending to remain several days, as rain was falling, several members of the party were ill, and the supply of food was nearly exhausted.

DISCOVERY OF THE SANTA CLARA VALLEY. While the party was in camp two soldiers, hunting for deer, climbed the northeastern hills, and from the summit saw "a valley like a great inland sea, stretching northward and southeastward as far as the eye could reach." The country was well wooded, they said, and very beautiful.

Thus these two deer-hunters who, on the 2d day of November, 1769, stood on the summit of the western hills and surveyed the beautiful Santa Clara Valley were the first Europeans who ever saw it. Unfortunately, their names were not recorded in connection with the discovery.

Ortega, with a small party, had proceeded along the beach toward the Golden Gate. He learned from natives that at the head of a "brazo de mar" there was a harbor, with a vessel at anchor. The party was looking for the arrival of the ship *San Jose* at the sought for Bay of Monterey, with supplies. The entire company, therefore, on the 4th of November, crossed the San Bruno hills to explore the "brazo de mar," which they thought was Monterey Bay, and search for the ships.

L. Selenger.
W. W. Montague.

REPRESENTATIVE COUNTRY HOMES.

Mrs. Mathilde Portal.
Herman Hoeft.

On the 6th they reached San Francisquito Creek and camped in the vicinity of Searsville, where the main party remained four days, while the sergeant and eight other men went east to explore the bay. They reported a large estero, but no sign of any port at its end. A council was held on the 11th, when it was unanimously decided that it was useless to search any further north for the Bay of Monterey, and they therefore returned to San Diego.

ANOTHER EXPLORING PARTY. After that the county was visited by exploring parties frequently. Monterey Bay having been visited and recognized in May, 1796, by Junipero Serra, Portola, Crespi, Fages, and others, and a Mission established, Fages, with Crespi, twelve soldiers, a muleteer and an Indian, started in March, 1772, from San Diego, on a voyage of exploration.

On the 22d of March they entered the San Bernardino (now Santa Clara) Valley, and encamped a little north of the present Gilroy. Thence they proceeded north-westward and entered the great plain which they called the "Robles del Puerto de San Francisco," which was in reality the northern portion of the Santa Clara Valley. They encamped on the 24th on the banks of a creek which they named Encarnacion—probably Calera Creek. This trip is one to which is attached special interest, because this company was the first to thoroughly explore the great Santa Clara Valley. The section comprising the present counties of Alameda and Contra Costa was also visited. After exploring the bay and river as far as Antioch, they returned, camping, April 2, on a stream near Milpitas, which they named San Francisco de Paula, which was probably Arroyo Coches.

GOVERNMENT BUILDING AND POSTOFFICE, SAN JOSE.

party followed Fages' route of 1772, by the way of where Hollister and Gilroy now stand, until they entered the valley about the bay, when they bore to the left. On the 28th they encamped on San Francisquito Creek, below Searsville. This seemed a suitable site for a mission, and a cross was erected as a sign of their purpose to locate there the Mission San Francisco. Thus, no doubt, originated the name San Francisquito, subsequently applied to the stream. The party pushed on, discovered the Golden Gate, and returned in a few days to Monterey.

DISCOVERY OF GUADALUPE AND COYOTE CREEKS. Captain Anza with Moraga, Font, and eleven soldiers, left Monterey for San Francisco March 23, 1776. They found the cross which Palou had erected on San Francisquito Creek still standing. Returning from San Francisco the 29th, they followed the southern boundary of the bay, and finding three streams, named them respectively Rio Guadalupe, Arroyo Coyote, and Arroyo de San Salvador, or Harina. Returning, the party encamped on Arroyo del Coyote April 6th, reaching Monterey on the 8th.

On June 17, 1776, Moraga, who had assumed command of expeditions in place of Anza, by order of Rivera, left Monterey with a command of soldiers and two friars for San Francisco, halting for a day on Arroyo San Francisco. This trip is mentioned because, in November of the same year, Rivera and Pena, on their way to San Francisco, "visited the proposed site for a mission near the banks of the Guadalupe." This shows that the site had been selected at some previous time, but it is not known by whom.

NAMING OF SAN FRANCISQUITO CREEK. In obedience to orders from the Viceroy, Rivera y Moncada left Monterey with sixteen soldiers, two servants, and a mule train, on November 23, 1773, to to establish a mission on the Bay of San Francisco, then unnamed. The

DEDICATION OF THE SANTA CLARA MISSION. On the 6th of January, 1777, Moraga and Pena left San Francisco for the Guadalupe, and, a cross having been erected, dedicated the Santa Clara Mission on the site called aboriginally Thamien, by the natives also known as Tares, meaning men, and Socoisuka, meaning laurel.

Frank V. Wright.

Judge John Reynolds.

REPRESENTATIVE SAN JOSE HOMES.

Ephriam Hatch.

Charles H. Lux.

Felipe de Neve, residing at Loreto, in Baja California, was at this time Governor of the Californias, though his authority over Upper California had been merely nominal, Rivera Moncada, commandant of the new establishments, being responsible to the Viceroy, and subordinate to the Governor only in being required to report fully to him. On the 16th of August, 1776, the King issued a royal order that Gov. Neve should reside at Monterey, as capital of the province, and that Rivera Moncada be transferred to Loreto, there to rule Baja California as Lieutenant Governor. The order did not reach Neve at Loreto until July 20, 1776. He arrived at Monterey February 3, 1787, bringing with him a "herd of live stock." These were probably the first horses and cattle brought to California. In the same year some of them were brought to Santa Clara County.

FOUNDING OF PUEBLO SAN JOSE. The shipment of grain from San Blas for the military establishments of the Californias was an expensive and uncertain method of supply, and officials had from the first been instructed to suggest some practical means of home production. Neve accordingly kept the matter in view during his trip northward, closely examining the different regions traversed to find land that was best suited to the purpose. The result of his observations was that there were two spots eminently fitted for agricultural operations, one being on the Rio de Porciuncula, at Los Angeles, in the south, and the other on the Rio de Guadalupe in the north, near the Santa Clara Mission. He decided that the best way to utilize the advantages offered was to establish two pueblos, or villages. For this purpose he asked for laborers and some other needed assistance. Without waiting for a reply, however, he selected nine of the Presidio soldiers of Monterey and San Francisco, who knew something of farming, and five settlers who had come to California with Anza, and the fourteen, with their families, sixty-six persons in all, started on November 7th from San Francisco for their new home.

A site was chosen near the eastern bank of the stream, three quarters of a league south-east of the Santa Clara Mission, and here the new pueblo, the first in California, was founded on the 29th of November, 1777, under the name of San Jose de Guadalupe, or San Jose on the Guadalupe. This

THE VALLEY WAS COVERED WITH BIG OAKS.

was the beginning of the present City of San Jose. The first buildings were erected a little more than a mile north of the present center of the city, near the little stream spanned by the first bridge on the road leading from San Jose to Alviso. The houses were built of adobe, and were earth roofed. They were subsequently moved to higher ground on the present site of the city, because the Guadalupe at that time was unimproved, and annually overflowed. The settlers each received a tract of land sufficient for the planting of three bushels of maize, with a house-lot, ten dollars a month, and a soldier's rations. Each also received a yoke of oxen, two horses, two cows, a mule, two sheep and two goats, together with necessary implements and seed, all of which were to be paid for in products of the soil, delivered at the royal warehouses.

The amount of land originally set apart by the government for pueblos (villages) in California was four square leagues in rectangular form, equivalent to thirty-six square miles, or 23,040 acres. This law was subsequently changed so as to permit the enclosure of a much larger tract.

DISTRIBUTION OF THE LAND. The lands were formally distributed to settlers in the pueblo of San Jose in 1783, though no order was received for such distribution until 1791, when such grants were authorized by General Nava. In 1783 no attention had been paid to exterior pueblo limits, save the vague establishment of a boundary line betwen the pueblo of San Jose and the Santa Clara Mission lands.

Previous to the year 1820 the business of the valley was of little importance. Vast herds of horses and cattle were raised by the residents of the pueblo and the friars in charge of the missions, but there was no market for live stock until the year mentioned, when trading vessels arrived, and a demand for hides and tallow was created. Stock had increased so rapidly that the hills and valleys in all directions were covered with grazing herds. In 1806 the great number of horses became troublesome, and on May 11th of that year a meeting was held in San Jose, when the citizens and officers of the city decided that twenty-five good mares were all that any citizen had any use for. This allotment of twenty-five horses to each resident made a total of 800 for the village. The remaining number, over 7,500 head, were accordingly slaughtered. Cattle were allowed to increase.

SAN JOSE FROM THE ELECTRIC LIGHT TOWER.

LOOKING NORTH.

PRIMITIVE MANNER OF LIVING. The manner of living was simple. There was no sawed lumber, and houses were universally built of sun-dried bricks; there was not a vehicle in the country that had wheels with spokes in them; there were no fire-places, and no stoves until a few were brought by immigrants in 1846; and there were no hotels or public houses of entertainment throughout the length and breadth of the land.

It was an easy-going life that was led by the few inhabitants of the State during the mission era. Their wants were few, and easily supplied, and they lived contentedly, raising fruits and vegetables for home consumption, and pasturing their cattle on a thousand hills.

ARRIVAL OF JOHN GILROY. Slowly indeed was the country developed. True, a Scot, John Cameron, commonly called John Gilroy, had arrived in the county in 1814, but he soon fell into the habits of the country, and lived in idle contentment at San Ysidro.

There were in San Jose at that time about twenty houses. Robert Livermore came to San Jose in 1816, but remained only a short time, settling within a few months in the valley subsequently named for him twenty miles northeast. Don Antonio Sunol arrived in 1818, and settled in San Jose.

DECLINE OF THE MISSIONS. The missions by this time had commenced to decline. On January 4, 1813, a decree of Cortes was passed which, while pretending upon the face of its preamble to have been formed principally in the interest and to promote the welfare of the pueblos, was, in fact, made with a view of increasing a royal revenue, without regard to the interests of either pueblos or missions. It reduced to private property all lands, except necessary suburbs of pueblos. This took from the missions whatever titles they held to the lands claimed by them, and as some missions had patented lands, the decree virtually amounted to confiscation. Under these circumstances a spirit of unrest and

VIEW OF VALLEY FROM STRAWBERRY HILL, LOOKING TOWARD GILROY.

uncertainty was developed at the missions, and under its influence herds, crops and buildings were neglected, productions decreased, and the Indian neophytes gradually dispersed.

Philip Doak, having left a whaling vessel at Monterey, wandered into the valley in 1822, and married a daughter of Mariano Castro, but was content to follow the pastoral life of the natives.

In 1821 Mexico passed from under the scepter of the Spanish throne, and become an empire in 1822, only to be merged into a republic in 1824. Such happenings, however, had no effect upon the contented dwellers in California, who pursued the even tenor of their way undisturbed.

In 1830 there were not more than a hundred foreigners in the State. In 1831 San Jose contained a population of 524. The crops that year amounted to 1657 fanegas (a fenega being about two bushels) of wheat, 1560 fanegas of corn, and 191 fanegas of beans. The stock owned included 4443 cattle, 2386 horses, and 134 mules. The average price of a mule or a saddle-horse at that time was $10; a fat ox or cow, $5; a sheep, $2. Wheat sold for $3 a fanega, the principal purchasers being the Russian-American Fur Company, which had, without asking permission, established itself on Bodega Bay, north of San Francisco.

SOME PIONEER RESIDENTS. In 1830 came John Burton and Harry Bee. In 1833 arrived Wm. Gulnac, James A. Forbes, Thomas Doak, James Weeks, William Welch, Nicholas Dodera, Matthew Fallon, William Smith, Ephriam Fravel, and Thomas Pepper. In 1834 Thomas Bowen, William Daily and George Ferguson arrived. In 1835 San Jose did not contain forty houses. The first overland immigration may be said to have commenced in 1841, the voyage even then being one of discovery rather than certainty, the only well known points at that time being the Great Salt Lake and the Humboldt River. Previous to this year immigrants had come almost exclusively by sea. In 1841 Josiah Belden, Charles M. Webber and Grove C. Cook came across the continent, each of

SAN JOSE FROM THE ELECTRIC LIGHT TOWER.

LOOKING NORTHWEST.

hem being subsequently connected prominently with the country's pro-gress. In the same year came Henry Pitts, Peter Springer, William Wiggins and James Rock.

In 1843, S. J. Hensley, Julius Martin, Thomas J. Shadden and Winston Bennett made the trip. With this party came theee ladies, wives of Martin, Shadden and Bennett, they being the first white American women who settled here.

In 1844 the well known Murphy party arrived, and from that time forward the arrivals were too numerous to permit of mention in detail.

The American settlers who had recently arrived noticed the large expanse of level land adjoining town, and realized that, although California was only under a military government by conquest, yet the war with Mexico would probably not close without a treaty, and they deemed it wise to divide the lands outside of the town, and yet within the pueblo limits, among the heads of families. They called the people together to discuss the matter, and as there was no objection, decided that a 500-acre lot for each was a fair distribution. They accordingly so divided the land, each man drawing by lot. Thus originated the grants in the valley which were known as the 500-acre titles. These titles were subsequently declared invalid by the Supreme Court.

ARRIVAL OF THE FREMONT PARTY. In March, 1846, Colonel John C. Fremont, at the head of a scientific exploring party of sixty-two men, Kit Carson among the number, reached the Santa Clara Valley. On March 5th, of that year, while encamped near the Mission of San Juan, he was notified by Don Jose Castro, the Prefect, that he must leave the country. Fremont, early next morning, ascended the Gavilan mountains to the south, and upon the highest peak constructed a rude fort. He then unfurled the stars and stripes, and prepared to defend himself. He was not molested by the doughty Don Jose, however, who, with a force of 200 men, had taken the field, but was rather in the humor of the renowned king of France, who, with twenty thousand men, marched up the hill and then marched down again.

In July of the same year Captain Fallon hoisted the American flag in San Jose. The United States did not by treaty, however, acquire title to California until February 2,

LOOKING ACROSS THE VALLEY FROM THE OBSERVATORY ROAD.

THE CONSTITUTIONAL CONVENTION. In 1849 a Constitutional Convention assembled in Monterey, and adopted articles providing for the division of the State into counties. In accordance with that act the Legislature, the first session of which began at San Jose on December 15, 1849, passed on February 18, 1850, the act which apportioned the State into counties. This act was confirmed April 25, 1851.

The original boundary lines of Santa Clara County, established at that time, were described as follows: "Beginning at the mouth of Alameda Creek, and running up the middle of said creek to its source in the Coast Range; thence in a southeasterly direction, following the summit of the Coast Range to the northeast corner of Monterey county; thence in a westerly direction, following the northern boundary of Monterey county to the southeast corner of Santa Cruz

1848. In 1847 the influx of American population increasing in a progressive ratio, the necessity for properly fixing the limits of the pueblo became apparent, and at the request and by the authority of the Alcalde and the Ayuntimiento, William and Thomas Campbell surveyed a plot of land for building lots. It was then considered a tract of land a mile square would be sufficient for the growing wants of any California town, and the survey made by the Campbell brothers embraced about that quantity. It was bounded by Market, Eighth, Julian and Reed streets.

county; thence in a northwesterly direction, following the summit of the Santa Cruz mountains to the head of San Francisquito Creek; thence down the middle of said creek to its mouth; and thence in a direct line to the mouth of Alameda Creek, the place of beginning."

When the Legislature formed Alameda County, in 1853, it took from Contra Costa County for that purpose the major portion of the land necessary, but took also from Santa Clara County all the land between Alameda Creek on the north, and Lone Tree on the south, and between the Bay of

SAN JOSE FROM THE ELECTRIC LIGHT TOWER.

LOOKING WEST.

San Francisco on the west and the summit of the Coast Range on the east, a tract containing about 39,000 acres. Thus it happens that Mission San Jose, once in this county, is now in Alameda. This mission was once one of the most important in the State, both as to wealth and population. There were at one time connected with it over 3,000 Indians, and the Mission owned over 40,000 head of stock, comprising cattle, horses and sheep; and great warehouses full of wheat and produce.

NAMING OF THE COUNTY. The county was named for the Mission of Santa Clara. In territorial days this section was known in Mexico as California Setentrional, or the Upper Missions. It became customary, in the absence of any established boundaries, to designate localities in regard to their proximity to some certain mission. Such descriptions were necessarily vague, and might refer to a very wide scope of territory. "Santa Clara Mission lands," "San Juan Mission lands," and "Mission San Jose lands," were terms in common use. Eventually the word "lands" was dropped, and thus each mission was made to represent a large territory. When the county was formed it naturally was allowed to retain the name by which for so many years the section had been distinguished. The mission was named in honor of Santa Clara, who was born in Assissi, Italy, in 1193, and who became famous for the austerity and piety of her life. She founded an order of religiosas — named for herself — died in 1253, and was cannonized in 1255. The pueblo of San Jose was named in honor of Saint Joseph.

In 1848 the discovery of gold at Coloma caused the most intense excitement, and nearly every one in San Jose left for the mines. At one time but two male residents remained to care for the flocks and herds. Stores and hotels were all closed, and merchants and judges alike went to seek wealth in the mines. Gold had previously been discovered in small quantities on San Francisquito Creek, and specimens of it, together with its history, are now in the museum at the Santa Clara College. Gold had also previously been discovered in small quantities in Santa Barbara County, and the Franciscan Fathers had sent specimens to Mexico, but these facts were not generally known. The raising of horses and cattle seemed to be the prevailing industry until about 1860, when grain raising became prominent and

the cattle were driven to ranges in the mountains. The valley had been owned in large sections, grants having been given to Mexican subjects prior to American occupation. These were nearly all subsequently subdivided and sold. About 1870 fruit-raising began to assume importance, and rapidly developed into the leading industry. In the great artesian basins the growing of vegetables and berries was shown to be very profitable, and the unexampled fertility of the soil caused Santa Clara to be known as the Garden County of the State. This much concerning the county in the past. What it is at present will be shown in other articles, that an adequate idea may be formed concerning the rapidity with which progress has been made and material prosperity with its accompanying blessings secured.

SCENE ON LOS GATOS CREEK.

SCRAPS OF HISTORY. Each tribe of Indians which inhabited the Santa Clara Valley had a separate and distinct dialect, even though the next tribe lived but five miles away. De Mofra states that among the Indians gathered at Mission San Jose there were forty dialects.

Mission San Jose was formerly in Santa Clara County, but when the Legislature, in 1853, formed Alameda County, it included the Mission site in the land taken to form a new county.

Sheep were first brought to San Jose in 1796. Each settler was required to to keep eleven sheep, and the government advanced means to those who were too poor to purchase.

The first steamer which navigated the Guadalupe river at Alviso was the Sacramento. It was placed on the route between San Francisco and Alviso in 1849. The time consumed was ten hours, and the fare was $30.

The Act to incorporate the City of San Jose was passed by the Legislature, March, 27, 1850.

The first strawberry plants brought to Santa Clara County were imported by Thomas Shelton in 1852, and were purchased by Mr. Kennedy, who set them out on the Stockton Rancho. From him Mr. Peebles procured his first plants in 1853, and started the first strawberry farm in the county. At first strawberries were sold for $2 a pound, but a few years later, by reason of the laws of supply and demand, the price fell to 50 cents a pound, when Kennedy, disgusted, went out of business, an action which would now be looked upon with surprise.

SAN JOSE FROM THE ELECTRIC LIGHT TOWER.

LOOKING SOUTHWEST.

DESCRIPTIVE OF THE COUNTY.

The Garden County of the Garden State. Some of Its Chief Characteristics. Excellency of the Climate and Fertility of the Soil. The County Officers.

SANTA CLARA COUNTY is an empire within itself. Notwithstanding the magnitude of the county's present production, and the position which the county holds as the garden spot of the State, one needs but to visit the various sections of the county to be impressed with the far greater possibilities of the future. Scarcely one-fourth of the area is now under cultivation, though all but about forty thousand acres is owned either by individuals or companies. Thousands upon thousands of acres of rich soil, suitable for vines and various varieties of fruit trees, are yet covered with brush. Other thousands of acres of rolling foothills are devoted to pasturage that would grow fruits and vines; and wheat fields stretch away for miles where trees, vines and vegetables would, with cultivation, flourish as alders by the water-brook. Water flows down every mountain side, and in nearly every instance is allowed to wimple away to the sea, or sink in the gravel of the valley creek-beds. A small per cent is used for irrigation, and a very little for power; but the opportunity to develop immense power, and irrigate vast tracts of land, outlines a future for the county of which few have dared to dream. Great oil and natural gas fields await development, and resources, no doubt, which we know not of. Yet Santa Clara County, with only a tithe of its resources developed, has gained pre-eminence as the greatest prune-growing section in the United States, and is known far and wide as one of the richest garden spots in the State.

SCENE ON FARM OF J. P. DUDLEY, ALMADEN ROAD.

five in width, extending from the summit of the Coast Range on the east to the summit of the Santa Cruz Mountains on the west, and from the Bay of San Francisco on the north to the County of San Benito on the south.

The valley extends southeast and northwest, and has an average width of fifteen miles. It is drained by a number of streams, the principal ones being the Uvas, Los Gatos, Guadalupe and Coyote Creek.

CONTOUR AND ALTITUDES. The topographical features of the county are varied. The valley ranges from sea-level at its northern end to an elevation of about 300 feet at its southern. Encircling the level lands of the valley is a wide region of rolling hills, beyond which rise the mountains, culminating on the west in Loma Prieta, 3,780 feet in height, and on the east in Mount Hamilton, 4,250 feet. Of the total area of the county, about 600,000 acres are suited to the cultivation of fruits and vines. Of this about 210,000 acres are in the valley, and 300,000 in the foothills.

THE VARIOUS SOILS. The soil varies greatly in character, but is everywhere deep except upon a few rocky points in the foothills, and in a small section of the valley. Most of the valley soil has been washed down from the mountains. The rich, black loams consist of sediment and vegetable mold, and are highly prized for vegetables, berries and small fruits. The red foothill soil is porous, and generally carries considerable gravel. Before it was cleared it was covered with chemisal or chaparral, and universally looked upon as poor land. It is, however, rich in plant food; and with proper cultivation and irrigation is one of the best soils we have, especially for stone fruits. It is the best soil that can be found for oranges and lemons. Along water courses the soil is usually a sandy loam, often liberally supplied with gravel, and always rich

SIZE AND LOCATION. The western boundary is about twenty miles from the Pacific Ocean, and the northern about thirty miles south of San Francisco. The county has an area of about 800,000 acres—which is greater, by the way, than that of the entire State of Rhode Island. It averages about fifty miles in length, and twenty-

SAN JOSE FROM THE ELECTRIC LIGHT TOWER.

LOOKING SOUTH.

in desirable elements. The reddish-brown lands carry a large percentage of potash, lime and humus. The higher lands are usually of light loam, generally gravelly, shading into darker loams in the timbered sections.

Along the bay the soil consists of silt and other sediment, with a large proportion of vegetable mold. This soil is very rich.

There are throughout the valley, but especially near the Bay of San Francisco, belts of adobe soil. While it is too heavy and damp to offer the best conditions for the growth of stone fruits, blackberries and raspberries and most vegetables thrive in it. It is largely used for the growth of vegetable and flower seed.

There is within the county very little sandy soil, the nearest approach to it being the lighter gravelly soils of the foothills, composed largely of desiccated rock.

Good water is one of the greatest blessings by which any section can be attended. Santa Clara County possesses it in great abundance. The annual rainfall varies from sixteen inches in some portions of the county to sixty in others. In the Santa Cruz Mountains springs are very plentiful, and there are numerous good-sized streams in different portions of the county, the principal ones being Los Gatos Creek, Coyote Creek, The Guadalupe, The Uvas, Pajaro, Penitencia, Calaveras and Campbell creeks. Good well water may be obtained most anywhere in the county at depths ranging from 10 to 150 feet. Artesian water is found at various places in the county, especially near Gilroy and north of San Jose.

VARIETIES OF TIMBER. Nearly the entire valley was formerly covered with groves of the majestic oak, of which, in some sections, many yet remain. They not only give the land a park like appearance, but present unmistakable evidence of the richness of the soil. The banks of streams are usually covered with sycamore and willow. The mountains to the east are almost bare of timber. In the canyons there is always a dense growth of brush—chemisal and chaparral—and occasionally black oak, manzanita and madrone. White oaks are found in some sections, with some live oak. Along the summit there are scattered groves of pine.

The Santa Cruz Mountains, to the west, are more heavily timbered. Along the lower foothills brush is everywhere plentiful, and in fact the entire range is covered with brush of various varieties. Here the beautiful California mountain

SCENE ON COYOTE CREEK, FARM OF J. H. M. TOWNSEND.

LOCAL CLIMATIC CONDITIONS. All have heard of the excellence of California's climate. All California climate, however, is not excellent. The term is too comprehensive for universal use There are in California mountain heights where the snow never melts, and valleys where snow never falls. There are exposed sections where chilly sea breezes blow every afternoon, and protected valleys that sea-breezes never reach. As a whole, the temperature is much milder than in the East.

In the Santa Clara Valley it is not only mild, but more uniform than in most other sections of the State. Vegetation responds quickly to uniformity of climate, and many deciduous fruit trees that are supposed to be quite hardy, show increased vigor under the influence of gentle breezes and plenty of sunshine. Figures of average temperature, which are often widely published, are misleading. It is not the average, but the extremes, from which men suffer and vegetation dies. In

laurel is plentiful, and attains an unusual size. The madrone, or California mahogany, is also one of the principal trees. Upon the northern hillsides black oak is always found, and the California redwood is scattered nearly everywhere. While there are yet a few groves of value for timber, the best were long ago sawed into lumber. One or two small groves have been saved, in their pristine beauty, by owners of summer resorts, and many most noble specimens are yet scattered throughout the mountains. Some of the forests found in this range present a very beautiful and majestic appearance.

this valley the temperature seldom reaches the freezing point. In winter there are usually a few hard frosts, and in the moist, low lands, numerous light frosts. Upon the other hand, there are sections where frost rarely falls. The temperature seldom rises above 90 degrees in summer. The air here is quite dry, as compared with that of the East, and is peculiarly invigorating. The climate of Santa Clara County is exceptionally healthful. The natural drainage is excellent. We do not use any system of drainage here upon any upland farm, as they do in many sections of the East. The soil is of a

SAN JOSE FROM THE ELECTRIC LIGHT TOWER.

LOOKING SOUTHEAST.

porous nature, and consequently no stagnant, disease-breeding pools of water exist. There is, far beneath creek bottoms, usually a bed of clay, and over this passes the lessened summer flow of streams, below the gravel. Hence the saying so often indulged in by Eastern people, that many of the California streams are upside down.

The contour of the country naturally tends to bring about a circulation of air, the warmer air of the valley being constantly drawn into the cooler canyons and up the mountain sides. Pure fresh air comes in every afternoon from the ocean by way of San Francisco Bay. Deflected from its natural course by the Coast Range of mountains, it is tempered by the warmer air of the bay and the adjacent valley lands. Hence we have pure, fresh air of a moderate temperature, full of the life-giving ozone of the ocean. Fresh air, pure water, an equable temperature, and plenty of sunshine, naturally promote health.

CONDITIONS INFLUENCING CLIMATE. The kinds of fruit that may be raised in a given section depends, aside from care and cultivation, upon the soil, the climate and the water. Climate is a condition which cannot be definitely defined and described. Thermometrical figures furnish no certain indication as to what plants may be grown. Plant life depends upon many conditions, and many mixtures of factors bring about various results. The climate is largely influenced by the contour of the country.

GENERAL CONDITIONS FAVORABLE. In California the Sierra Nevada form a barrier on the east, and prevent tempests and blizzards from reaching us from that direction. On the west is the Pacific ocean, with the Japan current sweeping our shores and spreading over the land a breath so equable that the temperature of the air in winter is much warmer, and in summer much cooler, than it otherwise would be.

Locally, we have the Mount Hamilton range of mountains on the east, and the Santa Cruz Mountains on the west. Thus no cold waves come from the east, and no harsh winds from the west. The ocean breeze comes in

SANTA CLARA VALLEY FROM HENRY MILLER'S CAMP, MOUNT MADONNA.

through the Golden Gate, and over the lower hills south of it, and is tempered by the warm air rising from San Francisco Bay and intervening vales before it reaches the Santa Clara valley.

This mildness and equability of climate has a great effect upon plant life. Trees that upon occasion adapt themselves in a measure to conditions imposed in other climates, here respond quickly to the warmer temperature and more continuous sunshine.

It has been said that in California nearly anything will grow nearly anywhere. This statement should be qualified. There is a great variety of soils, all subject to various influencing conditions. What may grow only moderately well in one section may produce largely in another. Some fruits like the moisture-laden air and heavy soils of the coast; others do better in the lighter soils and hotter climate of the interior.

SPECIAL LOCAL FEATURES. Santa Clara County incorporates more favorable conditions than some other localities, because of a combination of circumstances.

First, it is situated near the coast, and the cool breeze from the ocean lowers the temperature in summer and prevents the ardent rays of the sun from burning the leaves and trunks of trees. The same breeze in winter seems warm, and tends to remove from the atmosphere any crispness caused by winds from snow-covered peaks.

Second, it is protected from any severe trade winds by a high mountain range upreared along the coast, and from any hot and withering summer winds from the interior by the Mount Hamilton range.

Third, a variety of climatic conditions as brought about by elevation, the altitude ranging from sea-level on San Francisco Bay to 4,250 feet upon the summit of Mount Hamilton. Thus snow may cover the summits in winter, and in the valleys a semi-tropical warmth prevail, while flowers bloom everywhere in the open air. In summer the influence of altitude is manifest also, the air being cool and moist along the lowlands adjoining the bay, warm and somewhat drier in the center of the valley, and pleasantly cool in the forests that mantle the mountains. The air, too, may be almost stationary in the valley, and

SAN JOSE FROM THE ELECTRIC LIGHT TOWER.

LOOKING EAST.

moved by gentle zephyrs in the foothills, while a brisk breeze sweeps over the summits.

Fourth, by reason of diversity of soil. The valley soil has nearly all been brought down from the mountains. The great protruding ledges of rock exposed to the action of heat and cold, sunshine and rain, gradually disintegrate and mix with the soil. This, with the various clays and minerals, of which the mountains are composed, is washed into waterways and carried to the valley below. This process has been going on for ages, during which period streams have changed their courses many times. Hence the diversity of soil. In some places it is a fine, black sediment, like a lake bottom. In others it is a black loam, resulting largely from a deposit of vegetable matter, worked, reworked, and enriched by earth-worms.

The soil of the foothills is a red, gravelly soil, composed principally of desiccated rock. It is porous and rich in plant food. Along the streams the land is largely composed of a silt, which is a mixture of various soils, and usually carries some gravel. On the lower plains there are broad belts of adobe land. This is a stiff, sticky, black clay, liable to crack under a drying heat, but peculiarly adapted to the growth of vegetables and flowers. When it contains a sufficient per cent of more pliable soil, it is choice land.

Along the Bay of San Francisco there are thousands of acres of peaty soil, composed largely of silt, slickens and vegetable matter. There are along the foothills occasional fields of chocolate-colored loam, and in the mountains a light, open, pliable soil of a chalky nature. Scattered through the county are the result of a mixture of several varieties. Thus there is scarcely a plant for which a suitable soil and proper altitude may not be found.

VIEW ON ALUM ROCK AVENUE, ADJOINING MRS. STAPLES' PROPERTY.

THE COUNTY OFFICERS. The present County Clerk is Henry A. Pfister. He is a native son of San Jose, and is 36 years of age. He was educated in the public schools of the county and then became an assayer and mining engineer, which occupation he followed for a number of years, subsequently embarking in the business of general merchandising, in which he was engaged at the time of his election, in 1894. The position is a responsible one and Mr. Pfister has shown himself worthy of the trust reposed in him.

THE COUNTY ASSESSOR. There is probably no man who knows Santa Clara County more thoroughly than the Assessor, Mr. Lewis Amiss Spitzer. When a young man he herded cattle in the valley and on the hills; later, he drove teams over all its roads; then he farmed its soil, and lastly has made four successful political campaigns within its limits. Mr. Spitzer was first elected Assessor in 1882, having been a deputy Assessor for four years previously, and has been re-elected repeatedly ever since, the last time being in 1894. Mr. Spitzer is a native of Virginia, and was born in 1840. He came west in 1857, and reached California in the fall of 1858. He engaged in teaming and mining in California and Nevada several years, finally settling upon a farm in this valley.

THE COUNTY AUDITOR. The Auditor is W. F. Parker, who is now serving his second term. He is a native of New York, and came to California in 1884. He engaged in the business of fruit raising, and still has an orchard a few miles west of town. He was Horticultural Commissioner two years prior to his election to the position of Auditor. That he is extremely popular with all classes is evidenced by the fact that at the last election he was elected as an independent candidate.

THE COUNTY TREASURER. Joseph A. Lotz, the Treasurer, has been a faithful public official for many years. He was the Treasurer of the City of San Jose for six years, Deputy County Treasurer for eight years, and is now serving his second term in his present position. Mr. Lotz has been a resident of San Jose since 1871.

THE COUNTY RECORDER. The Recorder, Charles P. Owen, is a son of the late J. J. Owen, a pioneer, and the founder of the Mercury. Charles P. Owen was born in New York, in 1858. In 1861 his parents removed to California. He attended the public schools of San Jose, and graduated in 1877. He then became connected with the Mercury, and served in various departments of that paper, in the composing room, in the business office and upon the editorial staff. In 1885 he became a Deputy County Clerk, and acted as Clerk of the Board of Supervisors. In 1886 he was elected County Recorder, and was re-elected in 1888, 1890, 1892 and 1894.

SAN JOSE FROM THE ELECTRIC LIGHT TOWER.

LOOKING NORTHEAST.

THE DISTRICT ATTORNEY. Bertram A. Herrington, the District Attorney, is a native of Santa Clara, and was born in 1869. He graduated from the Law Department of the University of Michigan in 1891 and, in the same year returned to San Jose, where he associated himself with his father, Judge D. W. Herrington, in the practice of law. In this he has been very successful, and in the conduct of his office has proven himself to be energetic, wide-awake and zealous.

THE SUPERINTENDENT OF SCHOOLS. The official in Santa Clara County longest in continuous public service, is Lemuel J. Chipman, Superintent of Schools. The completion of his present term will round out a full score of years devoted to the duties of this office. Mr. Chipman was born in Plumas County in this State, in 1853. In 1873 he received a diploma from the State Normal School, and immediately adopted the avocation of teacher. He served two terms as principal of the Lincoln Grammar School; two terms in a like position in the Grant Grammar School, and two years as Superintendent of the schools of the City of San Jose.

THE COUNTY SURVEYOR. The County Surveyor acts under the direction of the Board of Supervisors, and surveys new roads, establishes grades, and superintends the erection of bridges and public structures. The duties of this office are performed by John G. McMillan. He is a native of Rhode Island, and was born in 1851. He served from 1877 to 1881 as Surveyor of Sutter County. Later he was engaged in the location and construction department of the Southern Pacific Company and was assistant engineer in the construction of the Market, Valencia, Haight and McAllister streets cable railways. Mr. McMillan was Chief Engineer of the surveys of the Leland Stanford University, and on the completion of that building was elected County Surveyor, and is now serving his third term.

THE TAX COLLECTOR. The Tax-Collector, W. A. January, is one of the pioneers of the State. He followed the profession of journalism for many years, having been one of the founders of the Placerville Democrat, one of the oldest papers in the State. Mr. January is serving his second term as Tax Collector. He was Treasurer of the County from 1875 to 1882.

ROADSIDE SCENE NEAR GILROY.

THE COUNTY CORONER. Dr. J. K. Secord, Coroner and Public Administrator, is serving his third term, having been first elected in 1890. Dr. Secord is a native of Canada, and was born in 1835. He enlisted in the Union Army in 1862 and served three years, rising from the ranks to the position of Captain. After the war he attended Rush Medical College, from which he graduated in 1867. He came to California in 1873.

SUPERINTENDENT OF THE INFIRMARY. Z. L. Orcutt, the Superintendent of the County Infirmary, is a native of Canada, and was born in 1844. He came to the United States in 1866, and to California in 1871. Since 1872 he has been a resident of San Jose, and has been engaged in several mercantile pursuits.

SUPERINTENDENT OF THE ALMS HOUSE. W. J. Wolcott, the Superintendent of the Alms House, was born in Ohio, in 1846, and in 1856 removed to Michigan. He served during the whole war with the armies of the Potomac, and his war record includes the great battle of Gettysburg, with many others. In 1875 he removed to California and settled in San Jose. Mr. Wolcott is a skillful builder, and many of our finest buildings were constructed under his care—among them the City Hall and the new Postoffice. Mr. Wolcott has filled several important positions of trust, among them that of Councilman of the Second Ward.

THE VETERINARY INSPECTOR. This position is filled by Dr. H. A. Spencer. The duties of the office require an inspection of dairies and dairy cows, slaughter houses, all classes of meat, products and the surroundings of the places used for the production of the same. Besides being a licentiate of the Board of Veterinary Medical Examiners, Dr. Spencer is a member, and last year was President of the State Veterinary Medical Association. He has been a resident of San Jose since 1855, having come from Illinois when a child of four years. Dr. Spencer is fearless, active and impartial.

SCRAPS OF HISTORY. The first public school in San Jose was established in 1811. The teacher was Rafael Villavicencio. The first Protestant school was opened in 1851, by Rev. E. Bannister. The first iron stove which reached the county arrived in 1846.

OFFICIALS OF SANTA CLARA COUNTY, CALIFORNIA.

Wilbur F. Parker.   B. A. Herrington.   J. G. McMillan.   Dr. H. A. Spencer.

L. J. Chipman.   Lewis A Spitzer.   William A. January.   Joseph A. Lotz.   Charles P. Owen.

W. J. Wolcott.   H. A. Pfister   Dr. J. K. Secord.   Z. L. Orcutt.

SANTA CLARA COUNTY BOARD OF SUPERVISORS.

A Record Made by the Business Managers of the County, Showing Good Roads Constructed, Public Buildings Erected, Indebtedness Decreased, and Progress in Every Department.

THERE is no chapter in the history of the progress of Santa Clara County more interesting and instructive than that to be found in the records of the Board of Supervisors. It is a history of public improvements, the construction of roads, the erection of public buildings, the refunding and gradual extinguishing of a bonded indebtedness, the improvement of river channels, the management of the county's infirmary, alms house, jails and other institutions. The records tell of large revenues received and expended with rare judgment and a proper consideration of economy.

CONSTRUCTING COUNTY HIGHWAYS. There is no county within the limits of the United States that can with more propriety boast of its substantial and well-kept highways, than this. A few years ago these roads were no better than could be found in most any community, but the Supervisors, who are also Road Commissioners of the County, conceived a policy in the construction of roads, the result of which is a revelation to those who are only familiar with the methods usually in vogue. It was a simple method, and that was to each year select some prominent highway in each district and construct it in a manner that would render it durable, letting all the rest go with only slight repairs. It was only a short time until all of the principal thoroughfares were made substantial and permanent, and the cost of keeping them in repair nominal. Then it was found that by sprinkling them in the dry season, little repairing was necessary, and they would remain hard and smooth the year around.

There are now about two hundred and eighty miles of sprinkled roads in the county, and in the performance of this work fifty water wagons are at work for five months in the year. The water is obtained in every manner possible; sometimes by utilizing springs on hillsides, sometimes by gravita-

VIEW ALONG THE ROAD TO MILPITAS.

tion from the river channels, and again by elevating it by means of rams, or pumps operated by steam or horse power. Very little water is purchased. Tanks have been built wherein the water is kept ready for distribution, and these tanks are located about four thousand feet apart along the sprinkled roads. This system is being enlarged each year, and it is only a question of a few years when every road of consequence in the country will thus be improved.

BEAUTIFUL HALL OF RECORDS. Another of the works which will endure to benefit the people and remain as a monument to the wisdom of the Supervisors is the Hall of Records, a magnificent structure which cost $250,000. This was constructed without the issuance of bonds. Every article that entered into its construction was paid for in cash. Not even an interest-bearing warrant was issued. No indebtedness was incurred until the money was in sight with which to liquidate it upon its maturity. It required four years to do the work, but it was well done, and the result justified the time expended. Besides, the cost was distributed through these years and the tax-payers scarcely realized the expenditure.

EXTINGUISHING THE INDEBTEDNESS. Another matter worthy of notice is the rapidity with which the outstanding bonded indebtedness has been extinguished. From time to time the bonds have been refunded and the rate of interest reduced from six and seven per cent to four and four and one-half per cent. The amount has been reduced in ten years from $360,000 to less than $160,000. In a few years more the county will be wholly free from debt. Furthermore, the records of the Board of Supervisors tell us that the Infirmary and the Alms House have been enlarged and improved, until each institution can accommodate

SANTA CLARA COUNTY BOARD OF SUPERVISORS.

Samuel F. Ayer.

George Elmer Rea.   Adolph Greeinger.   J. S. Selby.

John Roll.

one hundred and fifty persons The inmates are comfortably cared for, and no locality can show two better managed institutions of a similar character. In addition the records show that the rate of taxation for general county purposes has been materially reduced from that which prevailed fifteen years ago, and the burdens of the tax payers greatly lessened.

MULTIFARIOUS DUTIES AND CARES. The Supervisors have many duties and serious responsibilities. They have supervision of the roads and give instructions to the Road Superintendents of the seventeen road districts They are the custodians of the county's property, valued at $800,000. They see that the county officers perform their duties; they equalize the assessments; they provide the revenue, and are charged with its legal and economical expenditure.

It will thus be seen that the proper carrying on of the business of the county, the proper fulfillment of the obligations imposed upon them, requires that the Supervisors should be endowed with superior business capacities; that they should possess more than ordinary sound judgment; that they should be honest, industrious, progressive; and be possessed of originality and fertility of ideas, and above all else, have the welfare of the community as the guiding motive of their actions. Santa Clara County has been fortunately blessed in having secured the services of just such men. Following is a brief sketch of the present Supervisors.

CHAIRMAN OF THE BOARD. The chairman of the Board is Mr. Adolph Greeninger. He has been a resident of San Jose for thirty years, and during that time he has been actively engaged in business. Commencing with a little paint shop, his business has grown, until now he personally conducts one of the largest and most complete wagon and carriage manufactories in the State; in fact it is the largest establishment of the kind in the State presided over by a single individual. Having thus demonstrated his ability as a successful business man, it is natural to find him alike successful in his public career. He has been a member of the Board of Supervisors for eleven years. Preceeding his election to the office of Supervisor, he was a member of the Common Council of San Jose for six years, and prior to

FALLS OF LOS GATOS CREEK.

that he had been a member of the Fire Department for ten years. Mr. Greeninger can justly feel proud of his record, and the public likewise appreciate the services which he has performed for them. Mr. Greeninger has specially interested himself in the financial affairs of the county, and the plan of erecting the Hall of Records without issuing bonds or increasing the rate of taxation is an example of his financial genius.

SAMUEL F. AYER ONE OF THE FIRST MEMBERS. The pioneer member of the Board is Mr. S. F. Ayer. He was first elected in February, 1876. His first official act was to decide the question of building the road to the Lick Observatory on Mount Hamilton, the other members of the Board being evenly divided for and against the proposition. He decided that the county should build the road, and it was built. With the exception of two years, Mr. Ayer has been a member of the Board ever since and has been Chairman thereof for nine years. There is probably no man in the State of California possessing a greater knowledge of the government of a county than Mr. Ayer. This knowledge has been secured through long experience, together with an application of a sound judgment and a desire to apply sound business principles to public affairs. His progressive ideas have been adopted and methods copied by the Supervisors of other counties, and the government of Santa Clara County has been considered as a model worthy of imitation. Mr. Ayer's experience has been frequently sought by legislative committees in the framing of road laws and other matters appertaining to the county government. He was largely instrumental in floating the bonds of the county at a low rate of interest and very much more could be said to his credit, as his record is an honorable one. Mr. Ayer is a descendant of revolutionary patriots, his grandfather having been a soldier in Washington's army. Mr. Ayer is a native of New Brunswick. He has been a resident of this county since 1860, and has a large farm near Milpitas.

J. S. SELBY OF THE THIRD DISTRICT. In 1892 Mr. J. S. Selby was chosen to the office of Supervisor by the electors of the third district. That the choice was a wise one the record made by Mr. Selby during his term fully justifies. He has been very active in the matter of extending the road sprinkling system of his district until nearly every highway is well watered and in splendid condition. He has given much attention to improving the river channels that all danger of floods might be removed, and to this end was instrumental in having a law passed by the Legislature by which a system of improvement could be inaugurated. Mr. Selby has been a careful and conscientious worker, and was Chairman of the Board in 1894. He is a native of Missouri, and came across the plains in 1853. Since his arrival in California he has been engaged in the business of agriculture and horticulture, wherein he has achieved a decided success. He has a beautiful home a few miles from San Jose on the Milpitas road. Mr. Selby is of a genial, generous nature and is respected by all who know him.

JOHN ROLL OF THE FOURTH DISTRICT. Mr. John Roll is the energetic member from the fourth district. He lives in Santa Clara, of which place he has been a resident since 1884. He is a native of Wisconsin, and was born in 1852. He was elected a Supervisor at the last general election, in 1894, and is now serving his first year in that position. There is a school, however, which fits a man to perform the duties of this office, and Mr. Roll is a graduate of this institution. This school is service in some municipal body, managing the affairs of a city. Mr. Roll was a member of the Board of Trustees of the town of Santa Clara for six years, and thus gained a thorough knowledge of local public affairs. Mr Roll is a progressive man, and as evidence of this, it is but necessary to cite the fact that the public water system of the town of Santa Clara was secured largely through his efforts while a member of the Board of Trustees. In fact he may justly be considered the originator of the improvement. While Mr. Roll is one of the new members of the Board, yet from his previous public record, the people confidently expect that before the expiration of his term he will promote many schemes which will advance the public weal. He has materially increased the road sprinkling system of his district, notably along Saratoga Avenue and Santa Clara and Los Gatos road, and expects to do more in this line in the future. His record thus far is highly creditable, and his constituents are much pleased with what he has done for them.

GEORGE E. REA OF THE FIRST DISTRICT. The youngest member of the Board, in fact the youngest man who ever was a member of this Board, is Mr. George E. Rea, who represents the first district, and who resides near Gilroy. Mr. Rea is a native of this county, and is the son of Hon. Thomas Rea, a pioneer and one of the early settlers of the valley. He is thirty-one years of age and his life has been usefully spent at his home and vicinity. He was educated in the private and public schools of Gilroy, and received a good business education. For three years he was in the mercantile business at Gilroy, where he became familiar with the practical affairs of life, and afterwards he engaged in the business of dairying and farming, which has been his occupation for the past twelve years. In this he has been successful in establishing a reputation for integrity and straightforwardness which gives him rank among the substantial citizens of the community.

Mr. Rea is serving his first term in public office, having been elected in 1894. He has shown an aptitude for the work of the office, and has progressive ideas, which makes him a valuable public official. He is paying particular attention to adding to the mileage of sprinkled roads in his district.

RESIDENCE OF HENRY MILLER, BLOOMFIELD FARM.

STATE AND COUNTY TAXES. The county tax levy for the fiscal year of 1895-6 has been fixed by the Supervisors as follows:

State of California Fund	.685
Current Expense Fund	.15
Infirmary Fund	.052
Salary Fund	.101
School Fund	.15
Redemption Bond Fund, 1883	.003
Redemption Bond Fund, 1885 } W. P. R. R. }	.006
Redemption Bond Fund, 1890	.003
	$1.15

In addition to this a levy of 30 cents was made for road purposes, which applies only to property outside of incorporated cities and towns. The levy was based upon an assessed valuation of $55,446,995. The total amount raised by taxation, including special school taxes in several school districts, is $762,673.78. In addition, about $85,000 is collected for poll taxes, licenses and official fees. The rate of taxation has been materially reduced during the past twenty years. The value of taxable property has doubled since 1882.

NATURE'S SERIAL STORY.

How the Seasons Succeed Each Other in the Santa Clara Valley. A Year of Broad Sunshine and Long-Continued Fruitage, where Elements are Gentle and Climate Kind.

IN most countries the year is divided into four seasons, the lines between which are so sharply defined that not only may spring, summer, autumn and winter be definitely distinguished, but they may be outlined by months in the almanac. In California the seasons merge into each other so gently that the lines between them is so dimly defined that it can only be designated as existing between two dates some distance apart. The year, in this State is usually divided into what are known as the wet season, and the dry season. This does not properly designate nor appropriately define them. Summer lingers so long in the lap of winter that set calculations cannot be relied upon. An outline of the weather as it usually occurs in each month may enable readers at a distance to form an approximate idea of a Santa Clara County season.

Still sweet with blossoms is the year's fresh prime;
Her harvests still the ripening summer yields;
Fruit-laden autumn follows in her time,
And rainy winter waters still the fields.—Bryant.

THE FIRST SIGNS OF CHANGE. In September come the first perceptible indications of approaching change from the bright, warm, sunshiny days of summer. The nights become the least bit cooler. From a mean temperature of 60 degrees shown in August the thermometer drops to 58 on an average in September, ranging from 60 to 75 in the daytime. About the only fruit that makes its first appearance in September is the pomgranate. The bulk of the fruit crop has been gathered, though some yet hangs upon the trees. Almonds are almost ripe, and grapes are ready to be picked. All kinds of vegetables are yet in the market, and flowers bloom as usual. Farmers who have grown careless because of long-drawn out summer afternoons have hay uncovered in the field, or

THE FIRST BLOSSOMS—ALMONDS IN FEBRUARY.

perhaps a stack of wheat yet waiting to be thrashed. The days are a shade cooler toward the last of the month, with just a suggestion of haziness. A shower at this time would be very unusual; yet it occasionally occurs that a shower comes in this month, though no harm is done.

FLITTING CLOUDS AND FLUTTERING LEAVES. In October come more prominent signs of change. Yet they are signs which would be almost imperceptible to one not acquainted with the peculiarities of our climate. The air grows hazy and seems oppressive. Smoke rises slowly and hangs over the valley or along the mountain slopes. The winds are no longer constant from any quarter, but become variable, both as to direction and force. Perhaps sudden blasts send leaves fluttering down from the trees or whirl the dust along the road. The days are cooler, and the peculiarly dry feeling which characterizes the air in summer is replaced by one of dampness. Dark lead-colored clouds drift across the valley and clouds may hang over the mountain tops, but it doesn't rain. It is just getting ready. No one is justified in purchasing an umbrella in Santa Clara Valley upon the mere suggestion of a rain cloud. The first clouds that come are evanescent. They go floating lazily over the valley, and their shadows play hide and seek on hill and dale, but it doesn't rain. They are little bits of baby rain clouds, but wouldn't hurt anybody. Dark they are for a time, but the sun soon puts upon their frocks the prettiest white edging imaginable, and at sunset the silvery color turns to gold.

THE FIRST, SOFT, GENTLE SHOWER. Then some day the air feels chilly and the sky is dark. The south wind comes in at the kitchen door and leaves go fluttering about the yard. There is a distant roar in the canyon and a white mist in the air. The atmosphere grows darker, a few scattering drops are heard on the roof, and then comes a soft, gentle shower. No snow with it, of course, no sleet, no wild winds. Just a nice, warm rain. It may rain until 3 o'clock in the morning, when it usually ceases until just before daylight, when another shower may be expected. The clouds then commence to clear away, and by 10 o'clock the sun is shining, and nature looks cheerful and refreshed.

GREEN GRASS AND WILD FLOWERS. This is in the early part of October. Rain may fall every few days until an inch or more has fallen. Then there will probably be a week or more during which the weather will be clear. The sky is a brighter blue and the hills have grown darker. If more rain falls the sunny slopes commence to lose their sober russet and take on a vernal hue. Mushrooms break through the sod and a few wild flowers push up their tiny leaves.

PLOWING AND PRUNING. In November rain usually falls more frequently, and the rainy season is generally established by the latter part of the month. It occasionally happens that it commences late, and but little rain falls previous to the first of December. If the season is an average one, about 3.89 inches of rain will have fallen by the end of November. In the meantime the farmer has been plowing the mellow earth and sowing golden grain. The orchardist commences to prune his trees, and if the season is an early one, the vineyardist his vines. Rain may fall during a period of two or three days at a time, but there are usually during this month a great many sunshiny days, though they may be ushered in with a light fog or a darkened sky. Farmers may work in the sunshine during a greater part of this month, and are seldom inconvenienced by any severe or long-continued rain storms. Blackberries, raspberries and a few strawberries are still in market, and all kinds of vegetables. A few light frosts have fallen along creek bottoms and in the low-lands. No snow has fallen, even upon Mount Hamilton, the tallest peak in the county, and upon its crest, 4,250 feet above the sea, Lick

SUMMER SHADE AND SUNSHINE.

Observatory's great white dome yet frequently reflects the western sun. The rainy season, however, is now fully established.

SNOW ON THE MOUNTAIN TOPS. Along in December, however, a little snow will fall on the mountain tops, and the air will be decidedly crisp. If in the night the wind dies down the warm air will be drawn up on the mountain slopes and frost will settle in the valley. In the lower and most exposed sections delicate flowers will be injured. Many plants that grow by the house or in other protected places will flourish and bloom all winter. Along the foothills, at an elevation of from 400 to 1800 feet, frosts will be very light or altogether absent. In the warmer foothill belts oranges and lemons grow and ripen throughout the winter.

SUNSHINE AND SHADOW. In the valley sunshine and shadow have been alternating. More rain falls here in December than in any other month, and yet there is considerable sunshine. Hail falls occasionally, but no snow, unless it be a few flakes, and they usually melt ere the ground is white. The thermometer has ranged between 34 and 58 degrees above zero except on nights when a frost fell. It seldom registers less than 30 degrees above zero, and the lowest temperature we find recorded for the past decade is 22 degrees above zero.

THE VARIABLE WINDS OF JANUARY. In January the rainfall will not be as great as it was in the preceding month, and the wind will be less vigorous. Yet nothing can be said which will certainly indicate days in which rain will or will not fall. In January, too, the wind bloweth where it listeth. During more than half the year the wind is quite methodical, and compared with those which visit other States, very gentle at all times. On the mountain tops a breeze blows quite steadily from the northwest in the daytime, summer and winter, increasing in force of course during the latter season. In the valley, however, wind currents are influenced by local topographical conditions, and are mild or strong, without regard to conditions prevailing upon the mountain tops. Plowing and sowing continues, trees are being planted, and orchardists are still pruning. Grass is growing rapidly and vegetables are coming in. That residents of other States may better understand the relation of season to product, it may be stated that onions, lettuce, carrots, beets, cabbage, turnips, and radishes we have with us always. In this month, however, new potatoes and green peas are first seen in the market. The mean temperature of the month is 43.3 degrees, with 30 and 56.5 as the extremes. Once during the past ten years the thermometer fell to 25 degrees—above zero, of course. The temperature never reaches zero in Santa Clara Valley

LESS RAIN AND MORE SUNSHINE. In February there will be less rain and more sunshine than in January. The rainfall during this month seldom equals two inches. The weather grows a little warmer, the mean temperature rising to 48.2 degrees, with 35.5 and 60.8 as the extremes. A few orchardists still prune, but the work should end with the month—preferably sooner. There are usually a number of warm, sunshiny days, and these cause a few almond trees to blossom.

WHEN FRUIT TREES BLOOM. March is still warmer, and almonds, peaches, plums and cherries bloom profusely. The mean temperature is 52.3 and the extremes 40.7 and 63.9. In this month the winds are variable, and more rain falls than in any other month in the year except December. The average rainfall for March is 3.77, but the rain is warm, and trees, vines and vegetables grow with increased and remarkable vigor. Every orchard is a sea of flowers, and the air is full of perfume. Bees have been gathering honey from scattered flowers all winter, but it took a long time to secure a small quantity. Now there are myriads of bees around every blooming tree and in every field of flowers. We do not have to put our bees in the cellar here in the winter, nor feed them.

WINTER MASQUERADES AS SPRING. In February and March spring hides its face behind an occasional cloud and masquerades as winter. It approaches so quietly that one scarcely knows when it came. It has been lurking about all winter, and now, in April, abandons its mask and smiles continually. Wild flowers tint the hillsides, birds fill the air with melody, and the gentle breezes go laughing o'er the wheat. The sun shines more frequently, vegetation is more luxurious, and cherries are blushing a deeper red. Sometimes during the latter part of this month

HARVEST SCENE ON THE FARM OF M. M. CAHALAN.

it seems like summer had stepped over into spring. The average rainfall for the month is 1.85 inches, and the mean temperature 50.1. The thermometer has indicated as low as 37.4 degrees, and as high as 64.8. Winter dropped asleep amid the flowers.

FRUITS AND FLOWERS. The season for plowing, planting and sowing passed away with April. Spring is preparing to leave and summer is approaching. Strawberries are here, and will be seen in the markets until the latter part of November. Cherries red and ripe hang thick upon the trees, and every field is brilliant with wildflowers. Flowers everywhere—in the gardens, along the roads; in the meadows, on the hillsides—ubiquitous, luxurious, rampant. Great beds of flowers, a yellow acre here, a blue acre there, a white acre yonder, and flowers everywhere. Acres of bouquets and bouquets of acres.

In May there is usually very little if any rain. The average for this month is .53 of an inch. It occasionally happens that the season is late and a number of heavy showers fall in May. Haying commences in this month, and as a rule there is very little danger of injury by rain. The average daily temperature is 57.9 degrees, the lowest being 42.2, and the highest 73.6 degrees.

OUR AMOROUS JUNE. June is one of the warmest months in the year, the average daily temperature being 58.7 degrees, with a mean minimum of 41.4, and a mean maximum of 76. During this month the thermometer upon rare occasions registers 85, 90 or 95. The highest figure reached during the past ten years was 104. Such a temperature, it should be understood, does not create the physical discomfort here that it would in the East. In the New England States many would succumb in such a temperature because the air is there so humid. Here it is arid, and heat does not bring the smothering sensation which characterizes the heated term in the East. In some of the interior counties of California men work in the harvest field in a temperature of 95 and 100 degrees without any pronounced discomfort, and even work when the thermometer indicates 115 in the shade. In the Santa Clara Valley a cool breeze usually comes up in the afternoon from the ocean. It comes in through the Golden Gate, and is deflected south by the Coast Range. Harsh when it leaves the ocean, it is warmed by the air of intervening vales, and is soft and mild by the time it reaches San Jose.

BERRIES AND CHERRIES. Apricots now come into market. A few ripen in May, but they are now plentiful. The earlier varieties of peaches are ripe, and prunes are ripening. Raspberries and currants are ripe, and it is the height of the cherry season. Strawberries and all kinds of vegetables plentiful. The sun shines almost uninterruptedly during this month, and there is never any rain. Haying is about completed, and the grain is ripe. Headers are seen in the fields before the month is ended.

JULY'S UNINTERRUPTED SUNSHINE. July is here the hottest month in the year. The mean daily temperature is 63.3 degrees, the lowest mean 45.6, and the highest mean 81. The temperature may, upon occasions, reach 90, 95 or 100, the latter figures being unusual. No rain falls in July, none in August, and very little, if any, in September. To this fact is due, in a great measure, the horticultural advantages we possess. Summer rains would injure our fruits, berries, grapes, hay and grain, and greatly interfere with the harvesting, curing and packing process.

HEADERS AND HAY BALERS. Melons are coming in, and apples, pears and figs are ripening. Some varieties of grapes are ripe. A few headers are yet gleaning in the fields, and hay-baling still progresses. The continued sunshine has ripened the grasses and the grain, and the fields take on a lighter yellow, while the hills assume a darker brown. The hum of the thresher is heard in the land, and long lines of teams haul the golden grain to the warehouses.

CANNERIES AND FRUIT DRIERS. With the ushering in of August the heat of summer is gradually superceded by the coolness of autumn. So slowly does the change come that the mean daily average temperature of August is but 3.2 degrees less than that of July. In this month the minimum temperature is 46.9 degrees, and the maximum 70.30. Nearly all kinds of fruits are being harvested. Water melons and

musk melons are plentiful, and nectarines are getting ripe. Full forces are at work in the canneries and driers.

SUMMER SHADES TO AUTUMN. Then August merges into September, the latter month bringing weather so similar that the thermometer indicates a difference of less than two degrees in the mean temperature. Thus summer shades into autumn, and another round is commenced. The seasons are separated by very fine lines, and it is difficult indeed to tell when a Santa Clara County winter ends and spring begins, or when spring ends and summer commences. It may be always said that the elements are gentle and climate kind. In this valley it is a year without snow, without tornadoes, without blizzards, and with equable temperature, much sunshine, and long-continued fruitage.

THE AVERAGE RAINFALL. The figures quoted relating to rainfall apply more particularly to San Jose, where the average annual fall is 19.85 inches. In most other sections of the county the rainfall is greater, the figures ranging from 30 inches in the northern portion of the valley to 40, and even 65 inches in some of the mountain districts. The heaviest rainfall occurs along the summits of the Santa Cruz Mountains. The temperature is a little lower on the mountain tops than in the valley, as the upper currents of air are always the coolest. This makes the climate of the mountains a little cooler and more humid than that of the valley. Always mild and exceedingly equable, the climate of Santa Clara County makes it the home of the olive, the orange, the vine, and the fig; the land of sunshine, fruit and flowers.

A NOVEMBER SCENE—PUMPKINS AMONG FRUIT TREES.

HERBS AND PLANTS. Among the herbs, plants and grasses which grow wild in the Santa Clara Valley are: Buttercup, wild barley, coffee berry, pimpernel, wild radish, shepherd's purse, mustard, thistle, tansy, wild oats, wild lettuce, nettle, wild pea, wild yellow heliotrope, the poppy, plantain, fennel, rushes, tule, blue-eyed grass, morning glory, yellow dock, alfilaria, lupine, ronchus, centurea, wild grapes, etc.

THE CITY OF SAN JOSE.

Widely known as the Garden City. Its Massive and Magnificent Public Buildings and Costly Private Residences. Beautifully Paved Streets and Handsome Flower Gardens. Municipal Improvements.

SAN JOSE is one of the largest and most important cities in the State. Situated in the center of one of the richest horticultural districts in the world, its commerce naturally keeps pace with the production of the country by which it is surrounded. The constancy and certainty of income enables our orchardists to pay cash for supplies, and in turn insures the prosperity of merchants. It is, as a result, a city of substantial business blocks, magnificent residences and beautiful gardens.

MODEL AND MODERN. It is not only a city which presents much that is beautiful and substantial architecturally, but it is a center of art and music, culture and Christianity, noted for its atmosphere of elegance and refinement. Its streets are wide and most of them beautifully paved with asphaltum. Electric cars glide along the streets and far into the suburbs. It is brilliantly lighted, has magnificent and costly public and private buildings, and is furnished with all the improvements which assist in forwarding the interests of its inhabitants. It may properly be called a model, modern city.

THE CITY LIMITS. The corporate limits of the city cover an area of about five square miles. The extension of street car lines into the suburbs within the past few years, however, has caused the building of residences along streets miles outside of the corporate lines, so that the city limits do not longer limit the city. In fact a very large per cent. of the present population reside outside of the boundaries of what is technically the municipality. The present population of

the city and its suburbs, based upon the last census and the ratio of increase which applied for the period between 1880 and 1890, is 29,370. This is a low estimate, as the ratio of increase in population here is a progressive one.

STREETS AND PAVEMENTS. The streets of the city present an appearance which is always noted by strangers. The business blocks are as a rule handsome architecturally, and all the public buildings are both massive and imposing. Beautiful residences are so numerous that they always form a subject for remark among visitors from other localities. The streets are not paved with cobble stones, but with smooth and yielding asphaltum, over which vehicles roll almost noiselessly. As the streets are smooth, they are more easily swept than those paved with cobble stones and consequently present a neater appearance. The sidewalks are laid with cement or asphaltum, and the streets are sprinkled in summer, and cared for in winter.

Flowers grow here so luxuriously and with so little care that nearly every residence, however humble, has a flower garden. So numerous and beautiful are they that San Jose is everywhere known as the Garden City. Every month in the year some varieties of flowers may be found in bloom.

OUR UNRIVALLED ROADWAYS. Another prominent feature is the opportunity presented for driving. Not only are asphaltum streets smooth, level, and pleasant to drive upon, but in every direction stretch away broad, hard, well-kept roads. Roads leading through

THE CITY HALL, SAN JOSE.

Santa Clara Street—Looking West from First Street.

First Street—Looking North from Santa Clara Street.

SAN JOSE STREET SCENES.

San Fernando Street—Looking East from First Street.

First Street—Looking North from San Fernado Street.

shady lanes, by handsome villas and beautiful gardens, out by converging lines of fruit trees, under spreading oaks and by fields where gentle zephyrs go laughing o'er the wheat. Roads lead in every direction, and in summer nearly every road is sprinkled. Roads lead up and down and across the valley, and one may drive in sunshine or shade, among orchards, by open fields, or ascend to summits overlooking the valley. There is in our roads a variety that never fails to interest, and a beauty that always charms. There is probably no other city in the world which presents such inducements for bicycling, as there are in the city and its suburbs hundreds of miles of roads that can scarcely be approached for excellence.

MASSIVE PUBLIC BUILDINGS. San Jose has a number of handsome and costly public buildings. Most all of them have been constructed within the past few years, and are furnished with the latest improvements in methods of heating, lighting and ventilating.

The City Hall, situated in the center of Market Street Plaza, was built at a cost of $150,000. It is two stories high with a basement, is built of brick and stone and finished with pressed brick and stone trimmings. It is well heated, and lighted with both gas and electricity. Besides furnishing abundant room for city officers, it contains a very large, light and well-ventilated room in which is located the Public Library.

The Santa Clara Court House is a massive and imposing structure of Corinthian architecture, and cost $225,000. Although one of the oldest of our public buildings, its substantial character and excellent plan of structure, as well as the size of its rooms, makes it an ideal building. The County Jail, located in the rear of the Court House, was built on a liberal plan, and cost $90,000.

The Hall of Records is one of the most massive buildings in the city, and its architecture is very beautiful. It is built of marble, granite and steel, and is an enduring testimony of the prosperity and artistic taste of our people. It was built on a scale which insures ample room and protection

EARLY MORNING SCENE ON MARKET STREET, SAN JOSE.

for the county's documents for many years. It was built at a cost of $200,000.

The Postoffice Building, completed last year, is also an imposing structure, substantially built, and of modern architecture. It is built of grey stone from the Goodrich quarries, and cost $140,696. Is contains two stories and a basement, and has apartments not only for the postoffice and its officers, but for other government officials. One of its features is a handsome tower containing a costly clock with four dials. The city maintains a public library, to which is constantly being added the latest and best literature. The library now contains over 13,000 volumes, of which 450 were added during the past year. The total number of books circulated for home use during the year 1895 was 56,511. The library occupies light and comfortable rooms on the second floor of the City Hall, and is open every day from 9 in the morning until 9 in the evening except on legal holidays. Students find here a valuable aid in their studies, the reference library being very complete.

The officers of the Free Public Library are: Board of Trustees— E. J. Wilcox, President; J. L. Bothwell, Secretary; Frank Stock, J. J. McLaurin and Frank Montgomery. Librarian, Miss Agnes Barry; Assistant Librarian, Miss Nellie Egan.

THE FIRE DEPARTMENT. In keeping with the spirit of enterprise and progress which characterizes our citizens, San Jose has been provided with a Fire Department equipped with the latest and most efficient appliances.

There are three engine houses, located with a view of serving in the best possible manner the different districts. All of the buildings and appliances are owned by the city. There are four steamers, three of which, one Silsby and two Amoskeags, are in service. The Clapp & Jones engine is held in reserve. It is, however, kept in perfect condition, ready for instant service, a man being employed for that especial purpose. The Chemical engine is a double eighty-gallon Champion. The hook and ladder truck

The Alice Building, South Second Street.
The Louise Building, Second and San Fernando Streets.
The Martin Block, North First Street.

THE PHELAN ESTATE BUSINESS BLOCKS, SAN JOSE.

The New York Exchange Block, North First Street.
The Phelan Block, Eldorado and First Streets.
The Rucker Building, North First Street.

is also one of the latest, and carries an extension ladder seventy feet in length, which can be raised and extended in a few moments. There are four hose carts and one hose wagon, each carrying 800 feet of hose. Hose amounting to 5,500 feet is held in reserve. This makes a total of 9,500 feet, which is enough to cover an extended territory. The Gamewell system of fire alarm is in use, and works perfectly. The force numbers fifty three, seventeen of whom are full-paid men, and thirty-six call men. The full-paid men are uniformed. The apartments are very neatly and comfortably furnished, and located directly over the engine rooms, connected with which are steel rods down which the members of the department slide.

THE SALARIES OF THE FIREMEN. The salaries paid are not large, and the remarkable efficiency of the department is due largely to the interest evinced by the Chief, J. F. Dwyer, and the prompt service given by the members, who take pride in forwarding the interests of the city.

The Chief Engineer is paid $50 per month. The city furnishes the buggy, and the Chief provides his own horse. The assistant receives $20 per month. The engine drivers receives $100 per month, each one furnishing two horses. Drivers of hose carts receive $75 per month, and have to furnish a horse. Engineers are paid $80 per month, foreman $20 per month, while the captain of the Chemical receives $75, and the fireman $70. The Superintendent of the fire alarm system gets $75 per month, and extramen $15.

The efficiency of the department, and its real practical value as a part of the municipal machinery, is very clearly and most forcibly illustrated by the fact that during the year ending Jan. 1, 1895, the loss by fire within the city limits, where property is highly valued and fire risks the greatest, was but $43,840, while the loss in the suburbs, beyond the jurisdiction of the fire department, was $238.500.

J. F. DWYER.

THE CHIEF OF THE DEPARTMENT. The Chief Engineer, J. F. Dwyer, although but 32 years of age, has been in the department fourteen years. He served five years as foreman of Empire Engine Company, and is now nearing the completion of his third term as Chief of the Department. His extended period of service has made him thoroughly acquainted with the city's need, and to him is due to a great degree the present efficiency of the department, as he is deeply interested in its success, and ever alert to test and recommend the adoption of every improvement calculated to save time and promote the interests of the city. In

this he has the hearty co-operation of other members of the department and the support of the tax-payers.

The previous Chief was R. Hoelbe, who joined the Department as a volunteer in 1870. In 1877 he was elected foreman of the Alert Hose Company. In 1882 he was elected Assistant Chief, and as such served four years. In 1888 he was elected Chief of the Department, and served until 1893.

SOURCES OF WATER SUPPLY. San Jose is peculiarly fortunate in regard to the facilities for obtaining an abundant water supply. The mountains which surround the valley abound with streams and springs, the water from which flows through the valley to the Bay of San Francisco. Some of it is used for power, some for irrigation, and some flows away unhindered to the sea. A portion follows down the rock strata which bend down and outward under the valley, to rise as life-giving streams of artesian water when the rock is pierced by the drills of the industrious well-borer.

R. HOELBE.

DEMAND AND SUPPLY. Water may be obtained anywhere in the city at a depth varying from ten to ninety feet, and in portions of the city artesian water may be secured at depths varying from ninety-five to four hundred feet. The water supplied by the San Jose Water Company, however, is brought from reservoirs in the Santa Cruz Mountains. The first water company was organized in 1866, with a capital of $100,000. Water was obtained from artesian wells for about two years, when, owing to the growth of population, it was found necessary to have a more abundant supply, and the right to use the waters of Los Gatos Creek was purchased. In 1868 a new company was organized, and the capital stock increased to $300,000. This company at once set to work to develop the system which now exists. The capital stock was subsequently increased to $1,000,000, great reservoirs were built in the mountains, and other extensive and costly improvements were made.

THE MOUNTAIN RESERVOIRS. All of the mountain reservoirs were natural lakes, which were enlarged, cleansed, riprapped with rock, and made secure with masonry and earthwork. The largest reservoir is situated at Lake Ranch, on the divide between the Saratoga and Los Gatos Canyons, at an elevation of sixteen hundred feet. This covers an area of about twenty five acres. It is supplied by several mountain streams, and the water is allowed to overflow into Lyndon Creek, where it follows the shaded gravelly bed down the mountain until it reaches a

Chemical Engine Company, No. 1
Franklin Engine Company, No. 3

THE SAN JOSE FIRE DEPARTMENT—ENGINES, TRUCKS AND HOUSES

Hook and Ladder Company, No. 1.
Torrent Engine Company, No. 2.

Relief Hose Company, No. 2.
Empire Engine Company, No. 1.
Eureka Hose Company, No. 1.

point just above Lexington, when it is taken up in pipes and carried across Los Gatos Creek, and emptied into a conduit leading to San Jose.

Upon the Santa Cruz Mountains, at an elevation of about twelve hundred feet above San Jose, there are two other reservoirs, one of which covers an area of about fifteen acres, with an average depth of twenty feet, and the other seven acres, having an average depth of fifteen feet. These are known as the Howell reservoirs. Into them water flows from other mountain streams and springs, and overflows into the Rundel, and thence to Los Gatos Creek.

PIPES AND PRESSURE. The water is conducted in pipes from Los Gatos Creek to a reservoir seven miles from San Jose, and 218 feet above the level of the city, having a capacity of 5,000,-000 gallons. It is thence led into another reservoir three miles from and ninety-five feet above the city, with a capacity of 2,500,000 gallons. These

SAN JOSE WATER COMPANY'S RESERVOIR, ON LAKE RANCH.

two latter reservoirs answer a two-fold purpose, as they reduce the pressure in the pipes, and hold sufficient water to supply the town for some time in case of accident to pipe lines in the mountains. The Water Company also has nine

wells in San Jose, varying in depth from 450 to 800 feet. The Knowles pump, which had a capacity of 2,500,000 gallons per day, has been replaced by a Holley pump, having a far greater capacity. This is only used in case of

SAN JOSE WATER COMPANY'S RESERVOIR, NEAR LEXINGTON.

accident, or when heavy rainfall in winter causes the water in the mountain lakes to become badly discolored.

EXTENT OF SERVICE. The Company now supplies San Jose, Santa Clara and Saratoga, and is laying pipes to supply Los Gatos. There are now in use ninety-two miles, and 3,640 feet of piping. In addition to the present plant, the company is planning to build another large reservoir on Hooker Creek, a few miles above Los Gatos, not only to provide for the growing necessities of the service, but to secure a greater supply to be held in reserve. There are other sources of supply which can at any time be drawn upon, and there is no danger that San Jose, though it should become a city as large as San Francisco, will ever grow beyond the capacity of the resources which may be drawn upon for water supply. Furthermore the water is free from all organic matter and disease germs and is perfectly healthy. Few cities are more fortunate in this respect than San Jose.

The officers of San Jose Water Company are : President, W. D. Tisdale; Vice President, E. Williams ; Secretary, A. S. Williams.

In California towns grow so fast and the price of lots increase so rapidly that municipalities often find it impossible to purchase the land necessary for park purposes. San Jose was laid out when land was cheap, more than a hundred years ago, and large areas were early set aside for parks. The land was allotted in keeping with the value that was then placed upon the land, however, rather than in anticipation of the country's future greatness. Even the most sanguine failed to anticipate the growth and development of the past decade, and the greater portion of the princely domain once included within the city limits was sold. Thus it became necessary a few years ago to add by purchase to the city's breathing places.

San Jose now has five public parks, with a total area of 627.75 acres. They consist of the Alum Rock Park, Washington Square, St. James Park, Market Street Plaza and Cadwallader Park.

THE ALUMN ROCK PARK. This is one of the handsomest natural parks owned by any municipality in the State. It is situated in a canyon in the Coast Range of mountains, seven miles northeast of the city, and has an area of 580 acres. Extending through the tract lengthwise a distance of several miles is the beautiful mountain stream now known as La Penitencia. It rises well up towards the summit of the mountains, and is augmented by water from springs and brooks flowing into it until it becomes a good-sized stream. It goes rushing through a rough canyon, over rocky rapids, and through narrow gorges and deep pools. In a narrow place in a defile the water falls about seventy-five feet. Mountains rise on either side, and the canyon is rich in vine and verdure.

DERIVATION OF THE NAME. The park derived its name from a rocky bluff which juts out into the canyon above a narrow gorge through which flows the Creek Penitencia. In the crevices of the rock is found a substance which is said to be alum in its natural state.

The Creek Penitencia was so called because during the earlier history of the Missions at San Jose and Santa Clara, the priests regularly met under the shady oaks aligning its banks and confessed to one another their sins. The true Creek Penitencia, however, is the little stream which rises on the Murphy farm and flows north to Milpitas. The proper name of the Alum Rock Creek is Aguage.

THE MINERAL SPRINGS. There are numerous springs within the park, some furnishing pure, and others mineral water. These are scattered along the canyon for a distance of several miles, but the majority of them are in the vicinity of the bath house. Sulphur and soda springs are the most prominent. These usually contain other ingredients such as chloride of magnesium, carbonate of soda, iron, or lime, and other carbonates and sulphates. But one hot spring has been discovered. The water of this has a temperature of 98 degrees as it trickles from the hillside, and is probably much warmer a few feet beneath the surface.

THE CAMPING GROUNDS. Below the pagoda a few hundred yards the canyon widens, and a broad, level plot of ground is covered with spreading oaks. Here picnics are held, and campers are allowed to pitch their tents. On the north abruptly rise steep hills almost devoid of timber. To the south the mountain slopes are thickly covered with trees and tangled wildwood. Through the center of the tract meanders the mountain stream. The scenery is naturally beautiful and beautifully natural.

ALUM ROCK PARK COMMISSIONERS. The Alum Rock Park Commission was organized by an Ordinance of the City Council on June 22d, 1891. The commissioners have devoted themselves to the improvement of the city's pleasure grounds and to them is due the credit of having made wonderful changes and important accessions to the attractiveness of the place. Their work in the space of five years can be summarized as follows:

THE RECORD OF IMPROVEMENTS. There has been built a gentlemen's bath house and a ladies' bath house, the baths of the latter being constructed of tiles; a large swimming pool and dressing houses have been constructed; a new restaurant building has been erected; the roads throughout have been practically rebuilt; the banks of the creek have been protected from the washings of floods; a concrete dam for a water

THE PARK HOTEL, SAN JOSE.

Beneath the Alders on Penitencia Creek.
The Road in Penitencia Creek Canyon.

SCENES IN ALUM ROCK PARK.

Smiling Nymphs and Purling Streams
A Bend in the Road along the Creek.

A View of the Camp Ground.
Fountain and Plunge Bath.

A Picnic Party.
The Lower Penitencia Falls.

SCENES IN ALUM ROCK PARK.

The Pagoda.
The Upper Penitencia Falls.

Camping among the Oaks.
Scene on Penitencia Creek.

supply has been constructed and water pipes laid; a brick reservoir constructed wherein to store water needed to supply the camping grounds; the esplanade lying between the swimming bath and the creek has been filled in and new ground made thereby; additional supplies of fresh water have been obtained, and the supply of sulphur water enlarged; a kiosk has been erected, supplied with fountains and surrounded with a garden of flowers: trees have been planted; the grounds have been cleared of poison oak, and paths have been laid out from the depot to the baths, and from the forks of the road to the falls. In this work and in the care of the grounds about $25,000 has been expended. This is a splendid record of progress, and too much praise can not be given to the members of the Board. It is rare that the services of such prominent men can be obtained in connection with public affairs.

THE ALUM ROCK ROAD. The road from San Jose to Alum Rock Park is for several miles perfectly straight, and the grade is not more than a few feet per mile. About half way the road commences to ascend almost imperceptibly toward the foothills. Here it is flanked with towering eucalypti, which in summer furnish to the traveler grateful shade. The road gradually winds up the foothills in graceful curves, and at such a light grade that in most places teams may trot comfortably.

The view from the summit of the grade is very beautiful, as it incorporates a comprehensive view of the valley with its orchards, and farms, San Jose and its smoking chimneys, and the western foothills.

The San Jose and Santa Clara electric line extends to East San Jose, connecting there with a motor road which extends to the Alum Rock bluff, from whence a footpath leads to the bath houses, a few rods distant.

THE ST. JAMES PARK. The most beautiful park in the city is the Saint James. It is near the commercial center, and is therefore largely resorted to. The magnificent buildings by which it is surrounded add to its attractiveness, as the broad, open lawn is thereby

ST CLAIRE CLUB BUILDING, FACING ST. JAMES PARK.

brought into contrast with the entire utilization of adjoining space. There has been a charming negligence, or a careful simulation of such, in the arrangement of trees and shrubs, and as a result the park presents the appearance of a natural grove, the trees in which seem to have been most fortunately distributed. There is a greater variety than is usually found, the list including eucalyptus, pepper, sycamore, pine, cork elm, cypress, palm, willow, maple, umbrella, orange, birch, yew, locust, oak, and a variety of flowering trees and shrubs.

Saint James Park was surveyed in 1848, by C. S. Lyman, under instruction from the Mexican government. It is 1,005 feet in length and 610 in width, and contains two blocks. It is bordered on all sides by a cement sidewalk, and walks of like material converge in the center around a pool where the fountain plays.

The outside walks of Saint James Park are bordered by rows of fan palms. Drooping pepper trees also add beauty to the scene, the bunches of red berries contrasting with the green of the waxy leaves. There are everywhere wide stretches of greensward, and flowers bloom there every day in the year. Seats are provided in sunshine and shade, and a gardener is employed to care for the trees and flowers.

THE NORMAL SCHOOL PARK. Washington Square contains nearly thirty acres, and is situated within five blocks of the center of San Jose. The ground slopes gradually in all directions from the center, and upon the highest point is situated the handsome State Normal School building. An oblong driveway extends around the park, and it is kept in such excellent condition that it makes a good road for bicycling, as it is sufficiently long to test speed and endurance. There are here very few trees, most of the land being devoted to open lawns, with occasional beds of flowers. In front of the building which crowns the center plays a fountain. Beds of flowers are scattered about, and a few ornamental trees, including fan palms. The State expends more than $2,500 annually in the care and improvement of the grounds.

VIEWS IN ST. JAMES PARK, SAN JOSE.

THE MARKET STREET PLAZA. The Market Street Plaza contains about two blocks, and is 1160 feet long by 229 in width. It was laid out in 1848, by C. S. Lyman. It is peculiar in that it occupies the center of one of the principal streets in the city, streets curving into adjacent blocks to form an oblong plaza. In the center of it stands the City Hall building, and upon a gore to the northeast, created by reason of the survey for the plaza, is the massive postoffice building. The Plaza contains no tall trees, the space being devoted largely to lawns, beautified by a great variety and profusion of roses.

THE CADWALLADER PARK. Cadwallader Park is a triangular plot of small size at the junction of First and Second streets. When the adjoining property is covered with business blocks, this little plot of green will be very attractive. This park was willed to San Jose by N. Cadwallader, who was noted for his generosity.

THE POLICE FORCE. The City of San Jose has a well drilled and efficient police force. There are twenty officers, and the chief. The city also has a patrol wagon, which is on duty day and night within the city limits. The Chief o' Police is paid $125 per month. Two patrol officers receive each $115 per month, and each furnishes two horses, which they provide for at their own expense. All other police officers receive $75 per month. All officers have to furnish their own uniforms, clubs, pistols, hand-cuffs, etc., and, like the members of the Fire Department, are appointed for but one year. A feature which adds greatly to the efficiency of the Police Department is a system of telephones. There are now twenty of them, located at points which are available to the largest number of people.

THE SEWERAGE SYSTEM. The city is located on a plain which slopes gently toward the Bay of San Francisco, the fall being about ten feet to the mile. This is sufficient to insure a rapid flow of water and the thorough drainage of sewers, which extend to tidewater on the Bay of San Francisco, nine miles north of the city. There are forty miles of main and branch sewers. The principal drainway is through the center of the city. It is thirty feet below the surface, and is built of brick. Within the city it is of oval shape, with an aperture three feet wide by four and a half feet high. Outside of the city it is of circular form, with an aperture of five feet in diameter. Subsidary brick sewers, with an aperture of twenty-five by forty-two inches encircle the city, emptying into the main drain just outside the city limits on the north. With these

MARGARET PRATT HOME FOR AGED WOMEN, SAN JOSE.

are connected branch sewers, constructed of vitrified pipe, and running along the center of each street. The extent and solidity of the system are indicated by the fact that the cost of the system as first introduced, not counting the improvements now being made, was $285,000.

THE BOARD OF TRADE. San Jose has a Board of Trade which was organized in 1886. It has proved a powerful factor in promoting the interests of the county by initiating new industries and by advertising the resources of Santa Clara Valley. The present members are active, energetic business men, identified with the best interests of the community and have devoted themselves to the work of progress.

CHARITABLE AND BENEVOLENT SOCIETIES. The oldest society organized for charitable purposes in San Jose is the Ladies' Benevolent Society, which was organized twenty-three years ago. A few years later it received an endowment of $25,000 as a gift of the late James Lick, and in 1877 a Home of Benevolence was established. In 1878, as the proceeds of an Authors' Carnival, the sum of $3,000 was realized with which a substantial building was erected for the purposes of a Home, at the corner of Eleventh and Martha streets, on a tract of six acres which had been willed to the society by Mr. Morey. The building was dedicated in 1880, and since then several additions have been made to the edifice. The purpose of the Home

OFFICERS OF THE SANTA CLARA COUNTY BOARD OF TRADE.

William Moir, Director.   R. Summers, Vice President.   C. J. Steeple, Treasurer.

J. P. Fay, Secretary.   C. M. Wooster, President.   A. C. Darby, Second Vice President

A. Greeninger, Director.   T. R. Weaver, Director.   Frank Stock, Director.   W. C. Andrews, Director.

is to provide shelter for orphans, half orphans and abandoned children. At present there are ninety-one children within its hospitable walls. It is supported partly by the State, the interest on the Lick Fund and by donations— the latter being thankfully received at any time. The first president of the Society was Mrs. Dr. Cobb and the present officers are: Honorary President, Mrs. P. D. Hale ; President, Mrs. Benjamin Cory ; First Vice-President, Mrs. S. J. Churchill ; Second Vice-President, Mrs. G. B. McKee ; Secretary, Mrs. Mary McCullock ; Financial Secretary, Mrs. M. T. McCall ; Treasurer, Mrs F. D. S. Williams. Board of Directors—Mrs. E. R. Stone, Mrs. A. H. Cochran, Mrs. E. H. Guppy and Mrs. D. M. Barker.

The Pratt Home is an institution founded by Mrs. Margaret Pratt as a home for aged women. A beautiful building on South First street is devoted to the purposes of the trust and has a number of inmates who find health and comfort therein during their declining years.

Among the other charitable associations are the Ladies' Catholic Aid Society, the Sheltering Arms Society and the Bureau of Associated Charities.

A CITY OF CHURCHES. Nothing more certainly shapes the destiny of a community than the moral tone by which it is characterized. There is scarcely a section of Santa Clara County, however remote, in which there is not a church building of some kind. In every town in the county which is more than two years of age a number of church societies are represented, while in San Jose there is a great variety, and many handsome and costly buildings. Some of the congregations are comparatively small, but most of them are large, ranging from 200 to 900

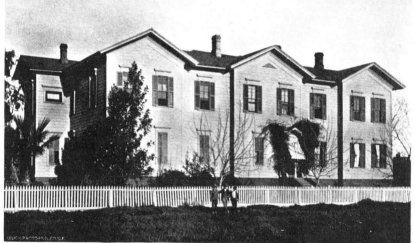

HOME OF BENEVOLENCE, SAN JOSE.

people, and in the aggregate form a religious influence which enters into, and to a very great extent regulates business and society. The list of church organizations in San Jose is so large that there are few people who may not in some of them find pleasant associations and a satisfactory church home. There are forty one organizations, and twenty-nine church edifices. The cost of the buildings range from $1,300 to $90,000, and San Jose numbers among its ministers some of the most prominent in the State.

A LIST OF THE CHURCHES. The Franciscan Fathers established a church in San Jose as early as 1803. They had established one at the Santa Clara Mission in 1777. The first Protestant

sermon ever preached in the county of which there is any record was delivered by Rev. Elihu Anthony, a Methodist, on the corner of First and Santa Clara streets, in November, 1846. In December, 1849, the First M. E. Church was organized by Bishop William Taylor. The present church building cost $25,000. The pastor is Rev. Romaine S. Cantine.

In 1849 the First Presbyterian Church was organized. The present building, which is of brick, cost $22,000. The pastor is Rev. John W. Dinsmore.

The Baptist Church was organized in 1850. The building was erected at a cost of $10,000. The present pastor is Frank M. Mitchell The M. E. Church South was organized in 1851. The brick building cost about $10,000, and the pastor is Rev. J. M. Weems.

The Episcopal Church building was erected in 1863. The rector is Rev. J. B. Wakefield.

The Congregational Bickur Cholim was incorporated in 1862, and the Synagogue was erected in 1870. The Rabbi is Rev. A. Brown.

The A. M. E. Church, was organized in 1864. The pastor is Rev. D. S. White.

The German M. E. Church was organized in 1868, and the building was erected in 1879, at a cost of $8,000. The pastor is Rev. O. Wilke.

The Cumberland Presbyterian was organized in 1875, and the building was erected in 1876. The pastor is Rev. James W. Mount.

The First Christian Church was organized in 1874, and the building was erected in 1885. The pastor is Rev. B. B. Burton.

The Congregational Church was organized in 1875. The building was erected in 1888, and cost $7,000. The pastor is Rev H. M. Tenney.

The Centella M. E. Church was organized in 1884, and the chapel was built in 1886. The pastor is Rev. A. H. Briggs.

The Free Methodist Church building was erected in 1888. The pastor is Rev. G. W. Griffith.

The Friends organized in 1867. The building was erected in 1886. The pastors are B. H. Jones and Rev. William Butler.

The Emmanuel Baptist Church was organized in 1884, and the building was erected in 1889. The pastor is Rev. J. Barr.

The Swedish Lutheran was organized in 1884, and the building was erected in 1886, at a cost of $3,000. The pastor is Rev. A. M. L. Herenius.

The Unitarian Society was organized in 1888. The building cost $17,000.

SAN JOSE CHURCH EDIFICES.

Swedish Lutheran Emmanuel.

St. Patrick's Church

Trinity Episcopal.

The Christian.

Cumberland Presbyterian.

The First Christian.

Congregational Church.

German Evangelical Lutheran Emmanuel.

The Pastor is Rev. N. A. Haskell. St. Joseph's Church was founded by the Franciscan Fathers in 1803. The building cost $90,590. The pastor is Father D. J. Mahoney.

St. Patrick's church was erected in 1878, at a cost of about $15,000. The pastor is Rev. P. McGuire.

The United Presbyterian Church was organized in 1874, and in 1876 the building was erected at a cost of $4,000. The pastor is Rev. J. C. Lynn.

The Seventh Day Adventists organized in 1893, and the building was erected at a cost of $1,375. The pastor is Rev. G. K. Owen.

The Central Christian Church was organized in 1891, and the building was erected at a cost of $4,000. The pastor is Rev. J. H. Hughes.

In East San Jose is located the Bowman M. E. Church, of which Rev. W. B. Priddy is pastor.

At College Park there is an M. E. Church of which Rev. Seneca Jones is pastor.

On Union Avenue, near Minnesota, is the Union Methodist Church, of which Rev. C. G. Milnes is pastor.

Of the Second Presbyterian Church Rev. R. F. Maclaren is pastor.

St. Mary's Church, on Third street, near Reed, is a very handsome and costly building. Rev. Father Melchers is the priest in charge.

The Bethel German Church is on the corner of Orchard and San Carlos. Rev. G. Denninger is pastor.

The Episcopal Mission is located on South First street. Rev. F. H. Smith is pastor.

The Emmanuel Baptist Church is located on the corner of Crandall and East streets. Rev. Mr. Thompson is pastor.

The Grace English Lutheran Church has recently erected a handsome edifice on the corner of Second and Julian streets. The pastor is Rev. V. G. A. Tressler.

Numerous other church organizations, not yet having erected edifices, hold services in rented halls. Christ's Episcopal Church services are held in Druids' Hall. The pastor is Rev. J. A. O'Meara. The Reorganized Church of Latter Day Saints have services at 162 South First street. The presiding elder is J. B. Carmichael. The Advent Christian Church meets in Odd Fellows' Building. The pastor is Rev. H. F. Carpenter. The

SAN JOSE Y. M. C. A. BUILDING.

Swedish Mission Church, J. Osborn, pastor, holds services in Pythian Hall. The Swedish Baptist holds services in the Bethel German Church. Of the Cottage Grove Union Chapel, Mrs. M. F. Williams is Superintendent. The Florence Night Mission holds services in a hall on Fountain Alley. The Superintendent is W. Chappel. Of the Swedish Mission, Rev. N. J. Linquist is pastor. The pastor of the Japanese M. E. Mission is T. Maeajume.

The Salvation Army, commanded by Captain Armstrong, holds services in a hall on North First street. New Church services are held in Rutherford Hall. The Antioch Baptist Church, Rev. T. S. Smith, pastor, holds services in a new church on Julian street, near Sixth. The Y. M. C. A. building was erected at a cost of $25,000. The Secretary is W. H. Baugh.

POSTOFFICE AND POSTMASTER. The San Jose Postoffice is a handsome and commodious structure, which was completed in 1894. The building and site cost $250,000. John W. Ryland, the Postmaster, was appointed in August, 1894, and took charge of the office on the first day of October following. Mr. Ryland is a native of San Jose, and is a son of Hon. C. T. Ryland, one of the prominent citizens of the State. In the conduct of the office Mr. Ryland has displayed an aptitude for the work, and by his genial manner has won the appreciation and confidence of the public.

THE GROWTH OF AN ESTABLISHMENT. In 1865 there was a little paint shop in the rear of a blacksmith shop on Santa Clara street opposite the Auzerais House. Adolph Greeninger was the proprietor. He was a practical carriage painter. He was gifted with foresight and clearly saw with his mind's eye the marvelous growth of a city. He also saw that if he wished to master his business he must control every department in the manufacture of vehicles. With this idea he enlarged his business, purchased a lot on San Fernando street, and in 1878 erected the two-story block known as the Globe Building. Here in partnership with Hugh Youug the business of the Globe Wagon and Carriage Works was conducted. Here he at once undertook the entire manufacture of wagons and carriages. The business thus established thrived and in the

SAN JOSE CHURCH EDIFICES.

German Methodist Episcopal.

United Presbyterian
Centella Methodist Episcopal.

The First Presbyterian.

The Unitarian

The Hebrew Synagogue.

course of a few years became so extensive that the removal to more commodious quarters was made necessary. So four years ago a two-story building ninety by ninety-seven feet was erected and is now occupied by the firm, for, in the meantime a son, Mr. A. J. Greeninger, had succeeded to the interest of Mr. Young. The lower floor of this building, together with an extensive yard in the rear, is devoted to iron and wood working departments and also used as a repository for completed vehicles, bicycles and harness. The upper floor is exclusively used by the painting and trimming department. Fiteen men find employment in the establishment, which is complete in every particular. Any kind of a vehicle can here be made. Besides supplying the local demand for home-produced goods, there is kept on hand a large line of wagons, carriages, harness, and bicycles manufactured by Eastern concerns of high repute. Besides establishing himself as a successful and reliable business man, Mr. A. Greeninger has been entrusted with the duties of public offices. At present he is one of the Supervisors of the County.

and many dainty articles of adornment of unique and elaborate design are products of his workshop. There is a constant demand for medals, badges, and souvenirs of various kinds, which, he supplies upon the shortest notice. Being also a practical optician, he makes a specialty of optical goods.

GREENINGER & SON'S GLOBE CARRIAGE WORKS, SAN JOSE.

THE SAN JOSE
BALATA
PAINT WORKS.

Among the various manufacturing enterprises of San Jose the Balata Paint Works occupies an important position. The members of the firm are George B. McKee and A. DeRochebrune, Jr., who transact business under the firm name of George B. McKee & Co. Both are practical men, understanding the business in every detail. Mr. DeRochebrune has been in the business twenty-five years, and Mr. McKee thirty years. They have been engaged in manufacturing paint in San Jose during the past seventeen years, and know exactly what qualities are necessary to make a paint that will withstand the long continued sunshine of this locality.

The firm first rented a building, but increasing business made it necessary that quarters should be obtained offering needed facilities for the rapid and economical handling of the trade. The property at the southeast corner of second and San Fernando streets was purchased by them, and the two-story brick building which now adorns the site was erected by them at a cost of over $21,000. The factory is located at 70 to 84 East San Fernando, a few doors east of the salesroom. The power for propelling the paint mill is supplied by an eight-horse power gas engine. The white lead and zinc are ground and thoroughly mixed by the mill, and led thence to various tanks, where the coloring matter is added.

The Balata paint contains no acids or alkalies, but is composed of pure white lead, pure oxide zinc, pure linseed oil, and pure Balata gum. The

GEORGE W. RYDER'S JEWELRY STORE, SAN JOSE.

RYDER'S
JEWELRY
STORE.

In 1875 Mr. Geo. W. Ryder came to San Jose, established himself in the jewelry business. The present store has been occupied since 1876. During this time the business has increased largely. He manufactures jewelry to order, and has built up a large business in this line. He has a corps of experienced and artistic workmen,

SAN JOSE CHURCH EDIFICES.

Second Presbyterian, South Second Street, near William.
St. Joseph's, Market and San Fernando.

First Methodist Episcopal, North Second, near Santa Clara.

St. Mary's, South Third, near Reed
Baptist Tabernacle, Second and San Antonio.

gum gives to the Balata paint the peculiar gloss which causes it to appear as if the object had been varnished after having been painted. It makes the paint more durable, also, and dries with a smooth, hard and elastic finish, which does not crack, peel or blister.

Not only house paint, but the finest carriage paints are manufactured, and all are ready for use, so that there is no loss in mixing, and anyone can apply it. The house paint is put up in barrels, and in 5 gallon, 1 gallon, 2 quarts, 1 pint, and 1 gill cans. All the carriage paint is put up in patent, easily-opened cans.

The Balata paint flows freely from the brush, and sets promptly. It will, by reason of the rubber it contains, resist the action of water more successfully than ordinary paint, and covers a greater area per gallon. One gallon of Balata paint covers 200 square feet of space. To ascertain the amount of paint required to cover a certain surface with two coats, add the number of feet in width of the front and rear walls to the feet in length of both side walls. This multiplied by the average height will give the whole number of square feet to be painted. Divide it by 200, which is the number of square feet one gallon will cover, and the quotient will be the total number of gallons required to paint the room.

McKee & Co. sell oil, glass, brushes, paper hangings, etc., as well as paint, and have a beautiful and well-stocked store.

THE FLATS OF W. H. GREEN. The six flats on the corner of Fourth and Julian streets, San Jose, were erected in 1893 at a cost of $10,000, and the building is owned by William H. Green. It is a commodious three-story structure, admirably planned, and supplied with all modern conveniences and sanitary appliances. The flats are arranged in sets of six and seven rooms.

THE EVOLUTION OF A BUSINESS. When San Jose was yet called a pueblo, Frank Stock opened a little tin shop on Market street. In 1854 his brother, John, became associated with him under the firm name of F. & J. Stock. Early in the sixties John Stock purchased the interest of his brother and continued in trade until 1884, when he retired from active business and was succeeded by his three sons, John L., Frank

and Peter H. Stock. They adopted as the name of the firm. The John Stock Sons. In 1869 a building 22x60 feet was erected, which now forms a portion of the store. Adjoining property was afterwards purchased and the size of the main store is now 45x100 feet. In addition to this is a second story of the same size, and in the rear are the workshops and store rooms. Besides this there is a warehouse near the depot, 50x100 feet, two stories high and a basement. In their plumbing, tinning and sheet iron departments from twenty-five to forty men are employed. The salesrooms of the firm contain an artistic display of mantles, the equal of which can not be found in any other town of the size of San Jose, which it is worth the while of anyone to behold.

THE DOERR BLOCKS. One of the handsomest of the business buildings presenting modern architectural features in San Jose is the Minna Block, on San Fernando street, erected recently by Charles Doerr. He also owns the Doerr Block on South First street, in which is located the New York Bakery, and which consists of three buildings, which were remodeled, improved, and connected by a massive front. Mr. Doerr has retired from active business life, and the bakery business is now carried on by his son, Henry Doerr.

THE BUSINESS OF W. W. MONTAGUE CO. The main store of W. W. Montague Company is in San Francisco, where it is one of the oldest business houses. Mr. Montague in 1890 established a branch in San Jose. The store occupies nearly the entire lower floor and basement of the large building on the southwest corner of First and St. John streets. Here can be seen a complete stock of stoves and ranges, embracing every variety, from the tiny coal-oil heater to the massive range of latest design. Particular attention is paid to plumbing and tin roofing. They are prepared to put in irrigating plants, including pipes, pumps and any desired power for elevating the water. The business is under the management of C. W. Morris. Mr. Montague, the founder of the business, has a large ranch at Agnews Station, where he has a beautiful residence, which he occupies when he desires to escape from the turmoil of the city, and surrounded by trees and flowers finds sweet repose.

W. H. GREEN'S FLATS, FOURTH AND JULIAN STREETS, SAN JOSE.

SAN JOSE BUSINESS HOUSES.

George B. McKee & Co.'s. Building.
The John Stock Sons Store.

Doerr's New York Bakery.
Doerr's Minna Block.

TREANOR'S CARRIAGE REPOSITORY. Fifteen years ago an agency was established in San Jose for the sale of Studebaker wagons, and the firm has since been continuously represented here. In January, 1893, the business was purchased

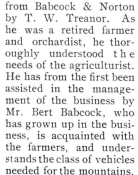

from Babcock & Norton by T. W. Treanor. As he was a retired farmer and orchardist, he thoroughly understood the needs of the agriculturist. He has from the first been assisted in the management of the business by Mr. Bert Babcock, who has grown up in the business, is acquainted with the farmers, and understands the class of vehicles needed for the mountains,

T. W. TREANOR'S CARRIAGE REPOSITORY, SAN JOSE.

the valley, the orchard, the vineyards, and the city. Mr. Treanor's repository and warerooms, on the corner of Market and San Fernando streets, San Jose, are the finest and most extensive retail warerooms in the State. The building is entirely of brick, and is hard-finished throughout. It has a frontage on Market street of sixty-five feet, and a depth of 200 feet, running the entire depth of the block, thus giving a rear entrance on San Pedro street. This entire space of 13,000 square feet is occupied by vehicles, in great variety, from carriages to labor-saving agricultural implements. Mr. Treanor buys in carload lots directly from Eastern factories, and as San Jose is a terminal point, and rents are cheaper than in San Francisco, he is enabled to sell goods cheaper than they could be purchased in San Francisco. The wisdom of the original owners of the establishment in selecting the Studebaker wagons is daily apparent, as the sales are constantly increasing, and the Studebaker vehicles are recognized as the best which are in the market. Mr. Treanor has also one of the largest stocks of agricultural implements and orchard machinery that can be found in the State. Among other specialties is the Forbes cultivator, a home-made orchard implement which has commended itself wherever it has been introduced. Other specialties are bicycles and harness.

SAN JOSE ARCHITECTURAL FEATURES. San Jose is noted for the architectural beauty of its buildings, a number of which are shown in this

THEODORE LENZEN.

book. No one firm has more largely contributed to the appearance of our dwellings and business houses than Theodore Lenzen, the architect. Among those which he designed may be mentioned the City Hall, O'Connor Sanitarium, the Fredericksburg Brewery, the Oak Street School, the Franklin Engine House, the George B. McKee & Co building, The Union Savings Bank Building, the Santa Clara College, the College of Notre Dame, the Centella Chapel, the H. Lux residence, F. C. Franck residence, the D. Henderson residence and the Booksin residence, all of which are shown in this book.

PFAU'S LIVERY STABLE. Louis J. Pfau owns the livery stables on Vine street near Santa Clara. To accommodate his patrons he has been obliged to increase his stock. The secret of his success in business is the fact that he thoroughly understands it. He has been educated in it. Mr. Pfau is a native of New York. He came to California when two years of age and has resided here thirty-six years. He has been honored by the citizens of San Jose, having been elected a member of the Board of Education and served two terms, and was also elected a member of the Common Council, recently completing his term of office. In public and private life Mr. Pfau has earned the reputation of being honorable and just in all things.

RESIDENCES OF MODERN ARCHITECTURE—BY THEODORE LENZEN.

Mrs. M. A. Mabury, First and Julian Streets, San Jose
H. Lux, East San Jose.

F. C. Franck, Santa Clara.

D. Henderson, Santa Clara.
H. Booksin, Second and Reed Sts., San Jose.

SPRING & SON'S CLOTHING ESTABLISHMENT. In March, 1892, the reopening of an old establishment, that of T. W. Spring & Son, was one of the most important commercial events in the history of San Jose. The building that the firm had occupied for twenty-two years had gone through a general overhauling from cellar to roof. The entire lower front and interior was remodeled and transformed into one of the most convenient and imposing clothing houses of the West. The partition between the old store and what was known as the California Restaurant was removed, and the whole building thrown into one vast emporium.

There are two central entrances on Santa Clara street, and one on Market. Three large show windows, sixteen feet in length, give a handsome and attractive appearance to the Santa Clara street front, while one window ten feet in width, and three, six feet in width, makes a handsome display on Market street. The first entrance from the corner is a central entrance into the clothing department. The second entrance is a central entrance into the furnishing department. To the right of this is the hat department. From the Market street entrance you go directly into the shoe department, at the rear of which is a wing where the tailoring department is located. At the right of this is the stairway leading to the stock rooms and the trunk and manufacturing rooms, which are on the second floor. The office is situated near the center of the store, overlooking all the different departments of the first floor.

The interior finish is of oak and the different departments are all supplied with handsome show cases of modern make and style. The building covers an area of 70 feet on Santa Clara street by 110 on Market, with an ell in the rear 30 by 60. The building is two stories in height, with a large and commodious basement, and is on the corner of two of the city's main thoroughfares. Each department is under the capable management of an experienced manager, and all the departments are supplied with full stocks of goods.

The energies of the proprietors are devoted strictly to men's goods. Handling no other lines of goods but these, due consideration is given to all the minute details that go to make it the successful house that it is, and as it enjoys a very large patronage, it is safe to say that Messrs. Spring & Son are well adapted to the clothing and furnishing business.

Clothing may be purchased as cheaply in San Jose as in Chicago. The cost for freight from manufacturing centers in the East to California amounts to very little upon a single suit of clothes, while the difference between rents in the business center in Chicago and the business center of San Jose is considerable. Our merchants, therefore, are enabled to sell goods as cheaply as do Eastern merchants.

HALE'S LIVERY STABLE. L. M. Hale conducts a livery stable on South Second street, San Jose, which is noted for the elegance of its turnouts, and the style and speed of the horses. There are few stables in the State, and certainly none between San Francisco and Los Angeles, where there are more highly-bred or speedy animals in the livery than Mr. Hale has. He operates, also, the Lick Observatory stage line, which carries the United States mails. At Morgan Hill Mr. Hale has an orchard of 90 acres, and owns the system of water works which supplies the town. He is also a Director of the Union Savings Bank, and a large stockholder in the Home Union, an extensive mercantile establishment.

HALE'S LIVERY STABLE, SAN JOSE.

SANTA CLARA COUNTY'S PUBLIC ROADS. Marsden Manson, the chairman of the State Highway Commission, in an address recently delivered upon roads, spoke as follows concerning the roads in Santa Clara County:

"Santa Clara County has the best roads in the State, and it is a quarter of a century ahead of any other section of the State. It spends $90,000 a year, one-half in the building and repairing of roads, and the other half in economically sprinkling 270 miles of graded and graveled roadway. The county officials are judiciously constructing culverts of masonry, thereby doing away with expensive repairs. I believe that the mass of the people realize that one of the principal problems confronting the owner of every home in the State, is, how can I most cheaply take away from my home my products, and get to it what I need? This becomes apparent when a Santa Clara farmer can load thirty-four bales of hay on a wagon, and with a single span of horses trot to market and trot back with an equivalent load, which in many counties two or three span could no more than haul."

The letter "j," in the Spanish language, has the sound of "h," and "e" the sound of "a." The name San Jose, therefore, is pronounced as if spelled San Hosay.

T. W. SPRING & COMPANY'S SAN JOSE CLOTHING HOUSE.

Furnishing Goods Department
Display Window.

Clothing Department.
Display Window.

Children's Department.
Display Window.

SAN JOSE TO SANTA CLARA.

Electric Cars that Glide Along Santa Clara Street and the Alameda, Connecting the Two Cities. Value of Cheap and Quick Communication. Service Urban and Suburban.

ONE of the grandest factors in the development of either city or country is rapid communication. The ideal location for a residence is one sufficiently removed from the business center to secure fresh air and other benefits of a country life, while yet within easy reach of the business center. Distance is seldom considered of as much importance as time. Property that can be reached in ten minutes is usually more valuable than that which cannot be reached in less than twenty minutes, even if the latter be nearer the business center.

Electric cars give a more satisfactory service than horse cars, because of the speed attained, and the personal comfort derived from riding upon cars that are moved by machinery, and that may be easily stopped and started.

CALIFORNIA'S FIRST ELECTRIC. The first electric street car line ever built in California was built in San Jose, and the San Jose and Santa Clara Electric Company was the first company on the coast to adopt the overhead trolley system. Cars on the Santa Clara line pass along the celebrated Alameda, a wide and beautiful street, adorned with ornamental trees and many handsome and costly residences. It was laid out by the Franciscan Fathers more than a century ago. It is one of the most fashionable residence streets of the city, and is in summer time a most beautiful driveway.

TIME, DISTANCE, FARE. As to speed attained, one may now take an electric car at First and Santa Clara streets, for instance, and in nine minutes land opposite the Fair Grounds on the Alameda. In sixteen minutes more he can reach our sister city of Santa Clara, nearly four miles from the starting point. But eleven minutes are required to reach East San Jose from First street. Considering that cars run every seven and one-half minutes, this is remarkable service. The entire distance from East San Jose to Santa Clara is made in forty-five minutes, including the time consumed in receiving and discharging passengers, and an intermission of five minutes at the termini. Thus

ON THE ALAMEDA, SANTA CLARA TO SAN JOSE.

the actual running time is about thirty-five minutes. Connection is made at East San Jose with the motor line for Alum Rock Park, the great pleasure resort on Penitencia Creek.

The fare between East San Jose and the Fair Grounds, on the Alameda, is but five cents, or to Santa Clara, ten cents. This is at the rate of but two cents a mile. A branch line extends south on Tenth street, and is owned by the same company, the fare from Tenth and Reed to Hedding street being five cents.

The first car for East San Jose leaves First street at 6:08 in the morning, and the first car leaves East San Jose for San Jose proper at 6:24. The first car leaves San Jose for Santa Clara at 6:20 a. m. The last car leaves Santa Clara for San Jose at 11:25 p. m., and the last car which leaves East San Jose for Santa Clara starts at 11:09 p. m.

One may live two miles from the city, and yet have a car passing his door every seven and one-half minutes that will take him to the center of the city in less than fifteen minutes. These daily trips give to business men fresh air and an enjoyable change from business routine.

The record of the Santa Clara line is remarkable, in that while the new road has now been in operation over five years, there has never been an interruption of service to exceed one hour, and but one serious accident has occurred.

This company built the celebrated cement bicycle track at the Fair Grounds, where so many records have been lowered. It also built the large pavilion, adorned the picnic grounds, and has recently completed arrangements with the Southern Pacific Company, by the terms of which all the week-day excursion parties are to be brought here.

OFFICERS OF THE COMPANY. The officers of the San Jose and Santa Clara road are: Directors—J. H. Henry, J. P. Burke, B. D. Murphy, C. M. Wooster, and J. T. McGeoghegan. President, J. H. Henry; Vice-President and Manager, J. P. Burke.

REPRESENTATIVE RESIDENCES OF SAN JOSE.

C. T. Ryland   Mrs. Nigel D'Oyly.   Abram King.   B. D. Murphy.

SANTA CLARA.

A City of Colleges, Manufacturing Establishments, Beautiful Homes and Thrifty Flower Gardens. The Mission Established in 1777. The Great Seed Farms.

SANTA CLARA is situated in the center of one of the richest valleys in the world. It is one of the choicest places of residence in the county, its location with relation to San Jose making it in this regard especially desirable, as electric cars run between the two cities every few moments from early in the morning until late at night. It is noted also for the number and luxuriance of its flower gardens. The soil is exceedingly fertile and climate mild, and it is in this vicinity that most of the great seed farms are located. The conditions greatly favor the growth of all sorts of vegetation, and every lot and plot may be easily transformed into a garden. The streets are shaded with ornamental trees, and as the avenues are broad and level, the vistas are very enchanting, showing between great rows of trees against the sky the towering mountains in the distance—south, east and west. Nine miles north stretches away the Bay of San Francisco.

HISTORY OF SETTLEMENT. The settlement of the town dates from 1777, in which year the Santa Clara Mission was founded by the Franciscan Fathers. The first frame building, however, was not erected until 1847. In 1850, when California was admitted, the town site was surveyed, lots were sold, and a number of residences erected. A tannery, flouring mill, machine shop and other enterprises soon followed, and the town is now an important manufacturing center. The Pacific Manufacturing Company has an extensive sash, door and blind trade which calls for the employment of 100 men the year round and the expenditure of $60,000 per annum for wages alone. The tannery, too, has been constantly increasing its output, until it now employs seventy men, and pays out

STREET SCENE IN SANTA CLARA.

$50,000 per annum for wages. The monthly disbursement of this money adds much to the city's prosperity by placing in circulation money for prompt payment.

Approaching the town from San Jose one passes along the Alameda, a magnificent highway, bordered with handsome villas and palatial residences. Along the center glide the electric cars which connect the town with San Jose. The road is well cared for, and is a popular driveway, where may always be seen passing vehicles of all kinds from English dog-carts and fashionable surreys to lilliputian carts with Shetland ponies. It is the main highway between the two cities, and is usually alive with foaming chargers and high-steppers.

PUBLIC AND PRIVATE SCHOOLS. Santa Clara is noted for its educational advantages, and pupils are sent here from nearly all the Pacific Coast States, and occasionally from Mexico and Central America. Many families of liberal means have located here in order that their children may enjoy these educational privileges while living at home. The Santa Clara College is remarkably well equipped, both as to faculty and apparatus. The Academy of our Lady of Angels is a boarding school for girls. Notwithstanding the presence of these vast institutions of learning, the public school system is remarkably complete. The school house is a handsome structure eighty feet square, and contains eight rooms, each thirty-six by forty feet, all well lighted and ventilated. In addition to this there is an annex two stories high containing five rooms. The building stands in a shaded park of two and a half acres in extent. There are enrolled 329 pupils.

VIEW OF SANTA CLARA FROM WATERWORKS TOWER.

The Principal of the school, Prof. John Manzer, teaches the High School, assisted by the Vice-Principal, Miss Mina Cole, and Nettie Knowles and Mrs. A. H. Post. The teachers of the eight grades in the grammar school are: Eighth grade, Ella L. Glendenning; seventh grade, Carrie M. Thompson; sixth grade, Loma E. Jordan; fifth grade, Nannie W. Teaford; fourth grade, Kate Doyle; third grade, Minnie L. Mackay; second grade, Miss Nettie Knowles; first grade, Mrs. A. H. Post. There are also three special teachers, as follows: Latin, Lorenzo Offield; penmanship, Bertha Warren; music, Laura Linville.

The school Trustees are: S. Oberdeener, D. Henderson, C. C. Morse, George H. Worrell and A. A. Harris; and the School Superintendent, A. L. Kellogg. The Santa Clara school is known as one of the best in the county.

CHURCHES AND PASTORS. Santa Clara has six church organizations, the ratio of churches to the population being much greater than in most towns of similar size. All of the church organizations have edifices.

The Methodist Episcopal Church building was erected in 1866, and contains a pipe organ which cost $1,500. The parsonage was built at a cost of $2,000, and the entire property is valued at $15,000. The pastor is Rev. H. B. Heacock.

The Presbyterian Church was organized in 1863. The parsonage and church building cost $6,000. The pastor is Rev. W. B. Cumming.

The Christian Church was organized in 1851. The Advent Church edifice was erected at a cost of $2150. The members of these two organizations recently united, under the name of the Church of Christ. Their pastor is Rev. T. H. Lawson.

The Baptist Church building was erected in 1863. Pastor, Rev. C. S. Medhurst.

The Episcopal Church was constructed in 1873. Pastor, Rev. A. P. Anderson.

The Catholic Church is the oldest. Rev. Father Raggio officiates, and is assisted by the priests connected with the college.

BOARD OF TRADE. A Board of Trade was incorporated in December, 1895, and has already done much in advancing the interests of the town. Its Directors are wide awake and progressive and under their leadership many new ideas will develop into material improvements which will add to the prosperity of the community.

The Directors of the Board are E. H. Smith, F. F. Percival, J. W. Hyde, W. E. Higgins, D. Henderson and L. L. Morse. O. A. R. Saunders is the Secretary.

THE SANTA CLARA PUBLIC SCHOOL.

THE MUNICIPAL WATER WORKS. That Santa Clara is an enterprising and progressive town is evidenced by the fact that the municipality has just completed a system of water works which is regarded as a model one by all who have inspected it. Nearly unanimously the voters of the town consented to the issuance of bonds to the amount of $60,000. These were sold at a premium of $3,040.80. The works were commenced in the Spring of 1895 and were completed in March, 1896. The water is obtained from four artesian wells, each having a depth of about 225 feet. These are connected together and again connected with the pumps in the power house. The water is very clear, pure and wholesome and the supply is sufficient to meet all requirements for many years, but can be increased at any time by the sinking of new wells. There are two Worthington pumps, each having a capacity of 50,000 gallons per hour. The water is forced directly into the mains and at the same time into tanks. There are four tanks placed upon a steel tower, and each with a capacity of 45,000 gallons. The tower is eighty feet high, and to the top of the tanks the distance is ninety-eight feet. With the tanks full and the pumps not working the pressure of water in the mains is between 45 and 50 pounds. At any time, as in case of fire, the flow of water to the tanks can be cut off and a pressure of from 125 to 200 pounds to the square inch may be obtained. This affords the best possible protection from fire.

SANTA CLARA CHURCH EDIFICES.

Advent Christian   *The Presbyterian*   *The Roman Catholic.*   *The Episcopal.*
The Baptist.   *Church of Christ.*   *Methodist Episcopal.*

There are sixteen miles of mains, the size of the pipe varying from 12 to 2 inches. The town is supplied with fifty-three hydrants, fifteen of which are double, that is, two lines of hose can be attached to each hydrant.

The cost of the work was about $56,000, which was slightly under the estimates furnished by C. E. Moore, the engineer. There are now over five hundred connections to the mains and a sufficient revenue is insured to pay all expenses and the interest and principal of the bonds as the same become due.

With the surplus remaining from the proceeds of the bonds, the town will purchase an engine and dynamos and operate an electric lighting plant, there being sufficient boiler capacity to operate it already provided.

SUPERINTENDENT OF CONSTRUCTION. The successful construction of the water system is largely due to the eminent services which the Town Board were able to secure in the person of C. E. Moore, who was selected to superintend the construction. Thus honest and faithful work was secured in every detail. Mr. Moore is a graduate of Union College, State of New York, having completed the engineering course therein in 1870. He at once connected himself with railroad work and soon had charge of the construction of a division of the four-track road of the N. Y. Central R. R. Thereafter, for several years, he was the Bridge Engineer of the Wabash System and constructed hundred of bridges throughout the middle Western States, his largest work being the construction of the bridge over the Missouri river at St. Charles. He then came West and for some time he was on the location and construction department of the Southern Pacific Co. Besides his railroad work, Mr. Moore has been connected with rolling mills in the East, has had a varied experience in inspecting iron and steel and has constructed a furnace for manufacturing wrought iron pipe. In every department of engineering he has a practical knowledge and there are few who can outrank him in his profession.

THE SANTA CLARA WATER WORKS AND C. E. MOORE, SUPERINTENDENT OF CONSTRUCTION.

OPPORTUNITIES FOR INVESTMENT. The State institution for the care of feeble-minded was formerly located in Santa Clara, and here were erected some costly buildings upon a plot of sixty acres. Through some political maneuvering the inmates were removed to Glen Ellen, Sonoma County. The buildings are in good condition, the soil is exceedingly fertile and water plentiful, offering an excellent opportunity for the establishment of some great enterprise.

There is an opportunity also for the establishment of a boot and shoe factory, as the Santa Clara Tannery furnishes all kinds of leather, which is now largely shipped East, there to be manufactured into shoes and reshipped to California.

THE WEATHER BUREAU. R. L. Higgins is the Voluntary Observer of the Weather Bureau, and he has the most thoroughly equipped private office in the United States except one in Philadelphia. He has a large number of instruments, the most important being a Frieze sun recorder, a Robinson self recording anemometer, a Frieze recording barometer, a Howard raingauge, a Draper recording thermomete , and maximum and minimum thermometers. These keep a complete and reliable record, showing the exact temperature at any moment in the day, the sunshine each minute, the rain fall and the wind velocity. Telegrams are received daily from the Weather Bureau in San Francisco giving forecasts, and signals are displayed.

A comparison of these records with those kept elsewhere, show that we have here less monthly range in temperature, less hours of fog, less miles of wind velocity, and more sunshine, than any other section of the Pacific Coast. The records may be examined by any one who may be inclined to doubt the assertion.

The Santa Clara Fire Department is very thoroughly equipped for a town of 3,000 inhabitants, as there are four companies; Hope Hose Company, Hook and Ladder Company, Hose Brigade Company, and the Tanner Hose

H. G. BOND'S HOME, SANTA CLARA

A Glimpse of the Grounds.
The Conservatory.

The Residence.
The Grapevine Arbor.

Company. The fact that the loss by fire has not averaged more than $500 per year during the past twenty-five years, speaks well for the efficiency of the Department. The officers of the Fire Department are: Chief Engineer, J. P. Menton; First Assistant, Henry Menzel; Second Assistant, George Wanderer; President, E. S. Wright; Secretary, George Gebhardt; Treasurer, John Eberhard.

THE LOCAL NEWSPAPERS. Santa Clara has two newspapers, one a weekly and the other a semi-weekly. The pioneer publication, the Santa Clara Journal, is a semi-weekly, and is published by Downing & Haman. The policy of the paper is characterized by a dignity and a spirit of enterprise that has greatly aided in forwarding the interests of the city. The News, although but about a year old, is a creditable publication, and pays particular attention to local news. It is published by McKenney & Son.

HOME FINANCIAL INSTITUTIONS. Santa Clara has a bank with a paid-up capital stock of $125,000. Its officers are: President, D. Henderson; Vice-President, A Block; Cashier, William M. Burnop.

Santa Clara also has a prosperous Building and Loan Association, in which some of the most prominent citizens are interested.

Another home institution is the Santa Clara County Mutual Life Insurance Association.

THE PUBLIC OFFICIALS. The city officials are: City Trustees —Mayor, J. B. O'Brien; John Roll, D. O. Druffel, W. O. Watson, and J. J. Miller. Clerk, O. A. R. Saunders; Treasurer, R. B. Roll; Marshal, J. A. Lovell; Surveyor, C. E. Moore; Watchman, J. P. Menton.

PACIFIC MANUFACTURING COMPANY. The Pacific Manufacturing Company, of Santa Clara, owns one of the largest planing mills on the Coast. The buildings and lumber yard occupy several acres. From 90 to 100 men are employed the year round, and the pay roll ranges from $60,000 to $70,000 per annum. The monthly distribution of this money adds greatly to the prosperity of Santa Clara.

The company makes a specialty of furnishing sash, doors, blinds, mouldings and trimmings for the interior finish and decoration of residences, and in this line has an extensive trade, shipping material throughout the State. Another specialty is the manufacture of redwood wine and water tanks. The lumber business of the company is also extensive. The celebrated Cyclone windmill, seen all over the coast from Mexico to British Columbia, is manufactured here.

Most of the lumber used by the establishment is sawed by mills in the Santa Cruz Mountains, twenty miles south, from whence it is hauled by teams to Santa Clara. The officers of the company are: President, George P. Thurston; Vice-President, James H. Pierce; Secretary, R. T. Pierce.

THE HOME OF MRS. H. H. HEADEN. In the western suburbs of Santa Clara, on the San Francisco road, rises a row of majestic redwoods. They never fail to attract the attention of travelers along the road, as they were evidently planted by the hand of man, and yet seem too tall to have grown in a lifetime. They were planted by Dr. B. F. Headen, who, in 1864, brought from the Santa Cruz Mountains some tiny trees in sacks and planted them along the fence. They grew so rapidly that in 1867 he brought others, and the enormous growth which has taken place since that time is indicated by their height which is now between eighty and ninety feet.

Dr. B. F. Headen with his wife came to California from Indiana across the plains in 1852, arriving in Santa Clara in October of that year. Here he purchased a tract of about sixty-one acres, and at once commenced to improve it. Dr. Headen died in 1875, and the farm has since been carried on by his wife, Mrs. H. H. Headen, who has greatly beautified and improved it. Of the 61 acres the house, barn and flower gardens occupy about 2 acres, the pasture 14 acres, and the remaining 45 acres are in orchard.

Mr. Headen probably did more than any other one person toward the establishment of the University of the Pacific, in which he took a great interest, and was elected a trustee in 1853, and served as such twenty years.

MILLS OF PACIFIC MANUFACTURING COMPANY, SANTA CLARA.

REPRESENTATIVE RESIDENCES OF SANTA CLARA AND VICINITY.

Mrs H. H. Headen.
Captain James Sennett.

C. C. Morse.
Francis Smith.

SANTA CLARA SEED FARMS.

Fields of Vegetables and Seas of Flowers. Rich Soil, Uninterrupted Sunshine and Plenty of Water for Irrigation. Vegetables that Grow in Winter. Care and Cultivation.

THE fame of California as a fruit-growing section is world-wide. Few know, however, that while Santa Clara County is the greatest prune-growing center of the United States, it has also one of the largest seed farms in the world. Our growers supply only the great wholesale houses, who in turn supply the retailing establishments. The latter sell seed under their own labels, and the purchaser has no means of knowing where the seeds were grown.

OUR FAVORABLE CLIMATE. As we have the climate and soil best adapted to their development, we grow the best garden and flower seeds that can be produced. Perhaps the most important among the many favorable features here presented is the extended summer season, with its almost uninterrupted sunshine. This permits the seed to most thoroughly ripen. In localities where the season is short, seed must reach maturity quickly, and they do so at the expense of proper development. In California, however, the season is longer, and the warm climate insures thorough ripening. Upon C. C. Morse & Co.'s seed farm, near Santa Clara, for instance, lettuce planted in December grows through the winter and spring, but does not run to seed until along in June or July, or about the same time that lettuce planted in April goes to seed in Rochester, New York. This lengthened period of ripening is very favorable to the character of both plant and seed, especially as regards cabbage and lettuce. There is no plant which does not respond to the warm climate, broad sunshine and rich soil, where there is no rain in summer to bruise flower petals or dampen seed, and where water from artesian wells may be applied just where and just when it is needed. A more favorable combination of circumstances can scarcely be imagined. Seed growers have searched in vain for similar features in other states and countries.

Here are sweet peas, on tiptoe for a flight,
With wings of gentle flush o'er delicate white,
And taper fingers, catching at all things,
To bind them all about with tiny rings.
—KEETS.

SANTA CLARA'S FIRST SEED FARM. Seeds were first grown in California for the trade by R. W. Wilson, of Rochester, New York, who came here for his health, and who had grown seeds to some extent in the East. He began with a few acres of onions and lettuce and after a few years sold to Kellogg & Morse. This firm was subsequently succeeded by C. C. Morse & Co , who now have one of the largest seed farms in the world. More than 200 acres are devoted to sweet peas alone, while a total of more than 2,000 acres are in garden and vegetable seed. Their main warehouse is located in Santa Clara.

FLOWERS IN PROFUSION. When the flowers are in bloom the view presented is grand beyond description. Nearly all the common varieties of vegetable seed are grown, and hundreds of varieties of flowers. There are fields of onions and lettuce hundreds of acres in extent, and there are acres of bouquets and bouquets of acres.

Acres of pansies, pinks, dahlias, nasturtiums, heliotrope, hollyhocks, larkspurs, marigolds, forget-me-nots, verbena, petunias, poppies, and many other flowers, with from two to seventeen varieties of each. Particular attention is given to the culture of the sweet pea, one of the most popular of all flowers. Of these they aim to grow every variety the sweet pea specialist can name, and more than ninety varieties are now cultivated. The greatest novelty in this line is a dwarf white pea, originated here, known as "Cupid."

From the top of any of Morse & Co.'s farm buildings one may look down upon acres and acres of flowers and vegetables. There are green and golden lawns of lettuce, bordered perhaps with pink, maroon, or scarlet peas, beyond which is a great sea of silvery green, which one scarce can believe is a field of onions in blossom. Great forests of parsnip, standing higher than a man's head, and looking like a young forest. Leeks, with spikes

SCENES ON C. C. MORSE & CO.'S GREAT SANTA CLARA SEED FARM.

A wilderness of Radish, showing height.
The Dwarf White Sweet Pea, "Cupid."
Other Sweet Peas on either side showing comparative size.

Part of a Hundred and Fifty Acre Field of Onions.
A Field of Parsley showing Men and House in the distance.

Glimpse of a Fifty Acre Field of Leeks.
Sweet Peas—Portion of a Ten Acre Patch.
A world of Beauty and a Sea of Blossoms.

equally as tall, bursting into purple blossoms. Great fields of golden cabbage stretching away, with turnips, kale and kohl rabi —masses of blossoms and seas of flowers. Everything blooms in its time, and many of the common vegetables bear beautiful flowers. Fifteen sorts of carrots, as many of cabbage, twenty varieties of onions, and seventy-five of lettuce, of odd shapes, odd sizes, and various shades of green and yellow.

ELEMENTS OF SUCCESS. The principal farm contains 1200 acres, and is supplied with water from four artesian wells. The soil is a rich, dark loam, and the land slopes gently toward the bay, furnishing ideal conditions for cultivation and irrigation. The elements of successful growth are probably not present elsewhere in such a wonderful combination, and the thoroughly ripened seed grown here germinates freely. This is now well understood, and many eastern dealers send seed to be grown here, contracting to pay so much per pound, the grower insuring separate grounds and perfect classification.

VEGETABLES THAT GROW IN WINTER. A matter which, while it attracts no particular notice among residents of the county, never fails to challenge the attention of visitors from the East, is that many of the most tender vegetables are grown throughout the winter and are, except in occasional instances, uninjured by frost. The varieties which are carried through the winter are cabbage, salsify, beets, carrots, parsnips, parsley, leek, celery, lettuce and kale. Thus the land produces more than twice as much as the same soil could produce were it under the influence of a climate such as characterizes any of the Eastern States, and most foreign countries.

MORSE AND CO.'S SWEET PEA FARM NEAR GILROY.

HOW SEEDS ARE HARVESTED. All the seeds are gathered by hand, and spread on canvas sheets to dry, after which they are thrashed with flails by hand, or with machines made especially for the purpose. The seed are marketed in strong, closely-woven sacks. To avoid possible waste of valuable seed, two sacks are used, one inside the other. A sack of seed weighs from 38 to 165 pounds, according to variety. Beet seed are the lightest and sweet pea seed the heaviest. It is a business which demands the closest care and attention, not only in cultivation, but in classification. On an average 130 men are employed the year round. Planting and harvesting are carried on nearly every month in the year, the time of sowing, however, being arranged so that no seeds are harvested during the winter rains. The seed-grower here claims nearly all seasons for his own.

MRS. CARROLL'S PROPERTY. Martin Murphy willed to each of his children 820 acres of land. That portion of the grant between the Southern Pacific Railroad and San Francisco Bay, and between Alviso and Mountain View, fell to Mrs. Mary C. Carroll. Most of this immense tract is in the artesian belt, and the greater portion of it is a black, heavy loam, shading from adobe into a light, clay soil. The darker and heavier soil is all choice land for vegetables and flowers, and several hundred acres of it were leased by C. C. Morse & Co., of Santa Clara, who raised vegetables and flower seeds.

Mrs. Carroll's land extends from a short distance south of the Southern Pacific Railroad, to the Guadalupe Slough, which puts in from San Francisco Bay on the north. Thus there is both river and rail communication with San Francisco, which is but about forty miles distant. All produce can be shipped by schooner very cheaply, and San Francisco is a good market for fruit, vegetables, and all farm produce. Strawberries are always grown here profitably, and much of Mrs. Carroll's property is choice berry land. There are very few places in the world where such a variety of crops may be raised, so near a good market.

The seed farm occupies perhaps a thousand acres of Mrs. Carroll's land, and most of the remainder is rented. It is a vast tract, the management of which necessarily involves great care. Mrs. Carroll has important interests elsewhere, also, as she owns 250 acres of land near Milpitas; owns the Jefferson block in San Jose, is interested in the Murphy block of San Jose, and owns a number of city lots.

Mrs. Carroll's land fronts on the San Francisco road on the south, and the road from Alviso to Mountain View passes through the centre of the tract. The freight rate to San Francisco, by schooner, for produce, is $1 per ton. The price of land in the vicinity averages about $200 per acre.

The opposite page gives a number of pretty scenes from the lands of Mrs. Carroll, and her sister Mrs. Arques.

THE ARQUES AND CARROLL PROPERTIES.

The Old Murphy Homestead, near Mountain View.
Gathering Flower and Vegetable Seed.

Among the Oaks, on Mrs. Nellie Arques' Farm.
A Glimpse of the Cabbage Field, Seed farm.

Residence of Mrs. Nellie Arques, near Lawrence Station.
View on the Seed Farm—Land owned by Mrs. M. A. Carroll.

LOS GATOS.

The Beautiful and Thrifty City at the Base of the Santa Cruz Mountains. Its Magnificent Business Blocks, Costly Residences and Delightful Climate.

MOST delightfully situated is Los Gatos upon low, rolling foothills at the mouth of a canyon at the base of the Santa Cruz Mountains. The evergreen heights above shield it from the winds and fogs which might otherwise come in from the ocean, and its altitude causes it to be bathed in a warm, dry and invigorating air which nightly rises from the lower levels. The moisture is largely removed by contact with cooler strata on its way, and the atmosphere of the foothills is remarkable for its purity and uniformity of temperature. It is characterized by a brightness and balminess that is quickly noted by one coming from any other locality.

BEAUTY OF LOCATION. The site is one of picturesque beauty, and combines the loveliness of the valley, the varied charm of the rolling hills, and the grandeur of the mountains. The town sits upon the edge of the plain, and south of it the mountains rise in ramparts a thousand feet in height. The various terraces and jutting points command a view of almost unparalleled beauty, incorporating a broad valley covered with orchards and vineyards, and the mountains rising beyond to a height of over 4,000 feet, crowned with the white dome of the great Lick Observatory.

THE LOS GATOS CREEK. The natural beauty of the town and its surroundings is what first attracts. Through a wide canyon a stream of water flows from the mountains, passing directly through the town. The banks are heavily wooded, and the scenery is very beautiful. The stream rises well up toward the summit of Loma Prieta, over three thousand feet above Los Gatos, and nearly twelve miles distant. It is augmented by other streams flowing in from both sides of the canyon until it becomes a large body of water, having a fall of over six hundred feet in seven miles. Perhaps a tenth part of the flow is used to furnish power for the Los Gatos Ice Manufacturing Company, and for the Electric Company, but power enough could be developed for extensive manufacturing plants. In fact, by piping water from the San Jose Water Company's reservoirs, which are located at an elevation of about seven hundred and fifty feet above Los Gatos, power of great magnitude could be developed. The water could subsequently be used for supplying the cities of the plain.

PICTURESQUE SITES FOR RESIDENCES. The business portion of the town is centered about this stream, which the principal street crosses by a noble bridge, spanning the canyon with a single wide and lofty arch forty-five feet in height. The residences are scattered over the hills, the valley and the mountain terraces surrounding the town. The picturesque sites afforded by this diversity of levels are the most charming imaginable, and many of the most commanding peaks and plateaus are adorned with villas of great architectural beauty. The beautiful sites are not all owned by the rich, however, and there are hundreds of handsome cottages commanding views equally as beautiful.

The soil and climate are peculiarly favorable to the growth of vegetation, and nearly every home in the city is surrounded by a garden of its own.

VIEW OF LOS GATOS—LOOKING NORTHWEST.

LOS GATOS.

(LOOKING NORTHEAST.)

Many of these are perennially green with orange trees and fan palms, and sweet with the fragrance of flowers. The climate is so mild that not only do fruits of the temperate zone thrive, but some of the semi-tropical as well. It is not an uncommon thing to see the banana spreading its broad leaves in the open air in gardens where golden oranges hang thick upon trees surrounded by banks of flowers and beds of vegetation. In the suburbs, many of the houses in addition to their lawns and gardens, are surrounded by orchards and vineyards, and the hills are covered with oaks, madrones and shrubbery. The town, therefore, is garlanded with green trees, bright blossoms, delicious fruits and trailing vines. The charm of the place grows upon the mind, too, as one drives about the city, coming upon new and unexpected scenes of beauty.

HOW THE TOWN WAS FOUNDED. The redwood timber in the mountains very early attracted the attention of settlers in the valley, and mills were established in the canyon, Los Gatos being made a station on the road. Its growth, however, dates from the completion of the railroad in 1877, and has been in many ways marvelous. Not only on account of remarkable increase in population, but because of the substantial character of the business blocks, the architectural beauty and cost of many of the residences, and the horticultural development which has been brought about. That such a beautiful and thriving city, surrounded by orchards and vineyards, and embowered in trees and flowers, should have sprung up within the past few years, seems like a dream.

but the remarkable growth of these orange trees commanded attention, and resulted in a rapid development of the fruit industry. Grapes were planted, and these flourished as vigorously as the trees. The profits of both orchard and vineyard were large, and a large number of acres was planted. The crops soon increased, and driers were needed to handle the fruit. These brought with them an increase of population and trade. Homes were established, more stores erected, and a general spirit of progress has since pervaded the town and the country by which it is surrounded.

The wheat fields which furnished the mill with grain have long since been converted into orchards, and the building is now used as an ice factory, twenty-five tons being manufactured daily. The great dynamos which furnish the electric power for the city are also located here. The tract which was planted as an orange orchard was years ago divided by streets and cut up into town lots. Every year large farms are being divided and planted with trees and vines, and the small farms in the edge of town are constantly being encroached upon by cottages, villas and gardens. In fact there are but few large tracts remaining, ten and twenty-acre orchards being in the ascendency.

BUSINESS BLOCKS AND HOTELS. In 1884 there were about 600 inhabitants and in 1888 about 1500. In the latter year the town was incorporated. The population is now about 2,800, and it is one of the most prosperous cities in the county, and, indeed in the State. The Hofstra block, recently erected, would attract attention in a city of twice the size, and the Theresa block, the property of J. W. Lyndon, is equally as costly and im-

VIEW IN CANYON ABOVE LOS GATOS

THE OLD STONE MILL. In 1854 James A. Forbes erected upon the bank of the creek a stone flouring mill, at a cost of $40,000. It eventually passed into the possession of the Los Gatos Manufacturing Company, which improved the property in many ways. The grounds were planted with ornamental trees, including about four hundred orange trees. It was known that the soil was suitable for fruit growing, as fruit trees had been growing in the valley many years,

posing, while there are many others of almost equal importance, ranging in cost from $7,000 to $17,000. The El Monte Hotel is palatial in size and appointments, and the Los Gatos and The Merritt are both large, first-class hotels.

The importance and extent of the fruit interests in the vicinity has brought about the establishment of a number of related industries, such as canneries, fruit driers, and wineries. The Los Gatos Canning Company

VIEWS IN LOS GATOS

Scene near the Depot—Looking North.
Santa Clara Avenue—Looking North.

The High School.

The Novitiate.
Main Street—Looking East.

packs an average of about 50,000 cases of fruit per annum, employing during the season from 275 to 300 persons. The fruit consists principally of peaches, apples, apricots, cherries, currants, grapes, gooseberries, quinces, tomatoes, nectarines, pears. plums, raspberries and strawberries. Most of this is shipped East and to England. The fruit drying companies also employ several hundred hands, drying peaches, prunes, and apricots almost exclusively.

The winery of W. B. Rankin is one of the largest in the county and consumes in the manufacture of fine wines the largest portion of the vineyard product of Los Gatos and the immediate vicinity. An extended description of this institution, accompanied by illustrations, will be found in another portion of this book.

FACTORIES, MILLS AND BANKS. Numerous other enterprises add to the prosperity of the place, such as box factories, and planing mills, of which there are three, an agricultural implement factory, a machine shop, a piano factory, a foundry, stores of all kinds, hotels and livery stables. Los Gatos has a wide reputation also as the home of institutions for the cure of dipsomnia. The virtue of a course of treatment is here greatly enhanced by the climate, which recuperates the patient, and the scenery, which uplifts and interests. The municipality, appreciating the benefit conferred upon mankind by these institutions, attaches a penalty to the selling of liquor to those undergoing treatment at the institutes.

One of the first evidences of the prosperity of a new town is usually the establishment of a bank, and Los Gatos had a bank as early as 1883. The Bank of Los Gatos, with a capital stock of $50,000, has as its officers: President, G. L. Turner; Vice-President, J. W. Lyndon; Cashier, Eben C. Farley; Assistant Cashier; James J. Stanfield; Directors, G. L. Turner, J. J. Stanfield, Grant Moore, John W. Lyndon, and A. Berryman.

The Commercial Bank of Los Gatos has a paid-up capital of $60,000, and the officers are: President, J. R. Ryland; Vice-President, Magnus Tait; Cashier, L. C. Trailer; Directors—Noah G. Rogers, Magnus Tait, L. C. Trailer, J. R. Ryland, and A. Berryman.

THE CITY COUNCIL. The municipal affairs are in the hands of a council, the members of which are: Mayor, Fen Massol; Councilmen, B. F. Williams, Fen Massol, T. J. Davis, E.

THE LOS GATOS CREEK BRIDGE.

N. Davis, and Henry Schomberg. Other city officials are: Clerk, George A. Butler; Marshal, M. F. Blank; Treasurer, B. W. Peace. That they are enterprising and awake to the best interests of the city is shown by the sewer system recently introduced, and the various street improvements.

Los Gatos has a Board of Trade, of which the officers are: President, R. R. Bell; Vice-President, C. W. Gertridge; Secretary, G. H. Adams, Treasurer, J. W. Riddle; Trustees—R. R. Bell, B. M. Hewett, F. M. Jackson and Lee Darneal.

THE TWO NEWSPAPERS. Los Gatos supports two weekly newspapers, which have largely aided in the upbuilding of the city. The Los Gatos News, an eight-column folio, is published by W. H. B. Trantham and W. R. L. Jenks. The Mail, a six-column quarto, is published by D. D. Bowman.

SCHOOLS AND CHURCHES. The public school system comprises the eight primary grades of the county system, the grammar grade and the High School. Instruction was given last year by ten teachers. Los Gatos has a large High School building, and the manner in which it was erected shows in an unmistakable way the interest taken in educational matters. A few years ago a law was passed providing for the levying of a tax for the construction of High School buildings. Under its provisions the Los Gatos district voted bonds for $6,000. The law was subsequently declared unconstitutional, but the citizens came forward and signed bonds, and completed the building. The grammar school building cost $8,000, and the High School building $6,000. A building is rented also in the eastern portion of the city for school purposes. In addition to the public schools there are two private schools

The teachers of the public schools are: High School, Principal, A. M. Kelly, and D. H. Temple; eighth grade, Belle Phelps; seventh grade, Jennie A. Cilker; sixth grade, Gertie Black; fifth grade, Ethel C. Ayer; fourth and fifth grades, Martha E. Cilker; fourth grade, Blanch Starkweather; third grade, Hannah Buckley; second grade, Grace M. Blank; first and second grade, Rena B. Ott; first grade, Louise Van Meter. In 1889 there were six teachers, and the public schools were carried on at an expense of $3,575. In 1890 the cost was $4,891. There are now ten teachers, and the annual cost of maintaining the Los Gatos school is $10,000. Los Gatos has six church organizations, each one of which owns a building. Several of

The Christian

The Ca*tholic*

LOS GATOS CHURCH EDIFICES.

The Presbyterian.

The Episcopal.

The Baptist.

Methodist Episcopal.

them are beautiful and commodious edifices, and speak well for the moral tone of the community and the liberality of its citizens. The pastor of the M. E. Church is Rev. Wesley Dennett; of the Baptist church, Rev. S. B. Randall; of the First Presbyterian church, Rev. S. Conn; of St. Luke's Episcopal, Rev. H. H. Clapham; of the Catholic church, Father Connelly; the Christian church, Rev. C. W. Jopson. The Salvation Army holds meetings regularly also, the corps now being in charge of Lieut. Wright and Lieut. Jungbeck.

THE CATHOLIC NOVITIATE. Upon a bench of land on the east side of Los Gatos Creek, several hundred feet above the center of the city, stands a massive brick building three stories in height. It is a Catholic institution, known as the Novitiate of Sacred Heart, and is a training and boarding school, where young men are educated and trained for priesthood. In 1886 the Society of Jesus purchased here two hundred acres of land, and erected the building, which cost $33,000. About fifty acres have been planted with trees and vines, and the orchard and vineyard now produce almost enough to pay the running expenses of the institution.

The system of training adopted here is very severe. Pupils are required to possess a good grammar school education before they are admitted. They then go through a two-years' course of training and examination, pursuing in the meantime a course of study. If at the end of that time their general demeanor and progress has been satisfactory, they are allowed to take the three vows of poverty, obedience and chastity They then take a four years' course in grammar, Latin, Greek and English. This is followed by one year of poetry and a year of rhetoric, after which they take three years of philosophy at the College at Santa Clara. They are then sent to some college, where they teach from five to six years, when they return to a four years' course in theology. They are then ordained as priests. There are now thirty young men in the novitiate class, and twenty have finished the course. The Superior of the Novitiate is Rev. D. Giacobbi, and his Assistant is Rev. N. Congiato.

The view from the Novitiate is very grand, and the surroundings very beautiful. The hill in the rear is covered with vines, and orange trees all around are in season loaded with fruit. Trees everywhere bend with fruit,

RESIDENCE OF JOHN W. LYNDON, LOS GATOS.

and the air is filled with the perfume of flowers. Los Gatos Creek rushes through the canyon beneath overhanging sycamores and alders. The town nestles near at hand, and rows of trees and vines stretch across the valley toward the great mass of steeples, chimneys, streets, and smoke which indicates the busy city of San Jose, nine miles away. In the blue distance the bay of San Francisco, shining in the sunlight. The accessories are such as would naturally make poets, rather than priests.

In keeping with the progressive spirit evinced by the citizens of Los Gatos along the line of public improvements a Town Improvement Association was recently formed. The members will improve the depot grounds and lay out a depot park and garden, erect a public band stand, plant shade trees along the city and city property. The officers of the Association are: President, G. H. Adams; Vice-President, Mrs. R. A. Urquhart; Secretary, F. F. Watkins; Treasurer, J. J. Stanfield. Directors— Mrs. R. A. Urquhart, Mrs. E. F. Pierce, Dr. Sarah Hughes Graves. Dr. R. A. Urquhart, George H. Adams, G. S. McMurty and J. R. Ryland.

Los Gatos has two mails per day from San Francisco and the East, and two from Santa Cruz, Monterey, and points south. The postmistress is Miss Josephine Gaffney.

The city is supplied with incandescent electric lights, the power for which is generated by water from Los Gatos Creek, which propels a 600-light machine, furnishing at this time 450 lights. The city is also supplied with gas.

A PIONEER RESIDENT. One of the first settlers of Los Gatos is J. W. Lyndon. He owned large property interests in the town and by careful attention to business his resources rapidly increased in value. He is a director in the local banking institutions and has a number of business blocks in the town; also in San Jose. His residence in Los Gatos is one of the most beautiful among the many handsome residences for which the town is noted.

The freight shipments from Los Gatos aggregate about 20,000,000 pounds annually. Last year a third rail was laid along the track of the narrow gauge railroad and shipments can now be made to all parts of the country without the expense of reloading.

REPRESENTATIVE RESIDENCES OF LOS GATOS AND VICINITY

William P. Veuve.

J. H. Lyndon.

H. D. Postlethwaite, Los Gatos and Saratoga Road.

William P. Veuve's Flower Embowered Porch.

CITY OF GILROY.

The Metropolis of Southern Santa Clara. Its Great Dairy Interests. The Artesian Well Basin. Rich Orchards and Gardens. Municipal Waterworks. Prominent Citizens.

GILROY is the metropolis of Southern Santa Clara. It is situated in the center of a valley about eight by twenty miles in extent, for which it is the natural trading center and main shipping point. Its growth was for many years retarded because a greater proportion of the land was held in large tracts, which were used for pasture and grain raising. When these grants were subdivided and sold, and fruit-growing was inaugurated, a new era dawned. Pastures were converted into grain fields, into orchards and gardens. Hundreds of families settled where there had been but one. This brought about more and better cultivation, with an increased product of the soil, and gave a new impulse to all lines of trade.

THE PICTURESQUE SURROUNDINGS. East and northeast of Gilroy rise the foothills of the Coast Range. To the north, the level valley as far as the eye can see, wheat fields, alternating with young orchards and groves of oaks. To the northwest rise the high peaks of a spur of the Santa Cruz Range, low foothills nearer at hand dividing the Uvas from the Santa Clara Valley. Several miles west rise wooded slopes of laurel, live oak and madrone, with tall redwoods reaching far up towards the sky on the summit. The Uvas enters the valley a few miles west of Gilroy, flowing along the western side of the valley, and discharging into the Pajaro, the waters of which flow through a low gap in the mountains to the Bay of Monterey. In a southeasterly direction the valley widens, presenting a magnificent scope of level land, most of which, though now used for grain raising, is the richest kind of garden soil, as is demonstrated by the gardens recently planted on the farms of Samuel Rea and Henry Miller.

STREET SCENE IN GILROY.

RIVERS AND ARTESIAN WELLS. The Llagas flows down the center of the valley from the north, the San Felipe enters from the Coast Range on the east, and the San Benito flows in from the south, all of them eventually emptying into the Pajaro. In the great district where these various streams converge, within a radius of several miles, there is a great artesian basin, where flowing water may be obtained at depths varying from 39 to 313 feet. There are several hundred wells, one of the strongest of which furnishes over 125,000 gallons per hour. Heretofore only a small per cent of the water has been utilized, and this was used to irrigate pastures with—this being Gilroy's noted dairy section. Most of the precious fluid was allowed to flow unheeded away to the sea. Within the past few years, however, much of the land has been used for garden purposes, and the water has been more thoroughly utilized. An artesian well, with the rich soil and semi-tropic climate of the Santa Clara Valley, enables the farmer to make gardens rivalling in richness those of the Hesperides. The extended and rainless summer season greatly increases the producing capacity of the land, as the soil is so rich that vines and vegetables may be, and usually are, grown, between rows of young fruit trees, and often two crops of vegetables are grown in one season.

THE GREAT DAIRY SECTION. Gilroy's principal product is cheese, the succulent grasses which flourish along the creeks and in the low lands at the confluence of the several streams in the center of the valley, having early brought about the development of the industry. Gilroy now produces 1,300,000 pounds of cheese per annum, which is about one-fifth of the entire product of the State. The price

GILROY CHURCH EDIFICES.

Episcopal Church.

Christian Church.

Catholic Church.

Presbyterian Church.

M. E. Church South.

First M. E. Church.

received ranges from 6 to 10 cents per pound. The principal cheese manufacturers are J. P. Sargent, J. C. Zuck, George E. Rea, A. Forni, S. M. Maze, R Eschenberg, Walter Doan, Albert Dexter, Jacob Doan, A. Lester, J. H. Ellis, C. B. Cruze, W. N. Furlong, C. Wentz, A. Watson, F. Sargenti, and Albert Wilson.

HISTORICAL AND DESCRIPTIVE. The town was named after John Gilroy, who, arriving in Monterey from England in 1813, settled at San Ysidro, now known as Old Gilroy. The district in which Gilroy is situated was formerly known as Pleasant Valley. In 1850 James Houck erected a hotel and a stable on the old stage road between San Jose and Monterey, and here sprang up, when the railroad was built, a town which developed into the present thriving city of Gilroy.

The land was formerly covered with groves of magnificent oak trees, many of which yet remain, giving to the locality a natural park-like appearance. In addition to this, there are numerous lawns and flower gardens. It is a city of neat cottages and home-like residences. The streets are broad, and the natural drainage, owing to the porosity of the soil, is excellent, so that the streets are neither muddy or sticky in the winter, and in summer they are kept well sprinkled.

THE CITY OFFICIALS. Gilroy is governed by a Mayor and Common Council, elected biennially. That the city is wisely and economically governed is indicated by the low tax rate, which is but seventy five cents on the hundred dollars, and by the general appearance of the city. The streets are kept clean and thoroughly sprinkled. A few years ago the city voted to own the waterworks and gas works. The citizens are thus assured of having water and gas at reasonable rates. The present city officials are: Mayor, M. Casey; Clerk, W. R. Pyle; Treasurer, Henry Hecker; Marshal, John Rive; Councilmen—Levi Mayock, Geo. A. Wentz, Valentine Grodhaus, Geo. T. Dunlap, J. W. Thayer, and W. A. Whitehurst. Superintendent of Waterworks, J. W. Norris.

STREET SCENE IN GILROY.

THE CITY WATER WORKS. It was a wise stroke of policy that prompted the purchase of the waterworks by the city. It is a grand system, and the original cost was more than $50,000. The plant was put in by William Hall, in 1871, and was purchased by the city in 1873. Since then bonds to the amount of $50,000 have been voted, for the purpose of extending and improving the system. The dam is on the Uvas river, nine miles northwest of town, from which the water is transferred in a flume to the reservoir about three miles from the city. Thence the water is distributed in pipes. The water is pure and soft, being supplied largely by springs in the mountains, and there is an abundance for all public and private uses.

THE FIRE DEPARTMENT. Gilroy is better supplied with means for extinguishing fire than nearly any other town of similar size in the State. The citizens are proud of their Fire Department, and the members evince a lively interest in assuring promptness and efficiency of service. The Chief of the Fire Department is James McElroy; First Assistant, J. A. Laird; Second Assistant, O. M. Giles. The Board of Fire Delegates consist of: President, John Hoesch, Secretary, Will Blake; Geo. Keaton, C. M. Hoover and R. G. Einfalt.

CHURCHES AND SCHOOLS. Gilroy is well supplied with church organizations, nearly all of which own handsome edifices.

The First Methodist Church building cost $4,500, and the parsonage $2,000. The pastor is Rev. W. D. Crabb.

The South Methodist Church edifice is valued at $2,000, and the pastor is Rev. Mr. Green.

The Presbyterian Church building was erected at a cost of $6,000, and parsonage at a cost of $4,000. The pastor is Rev. John E. Stuchell.

St. Stephen's Episcopal Church building cost $4,000. This organization has no regular pastor.

St. Mary's Church building cost $4,000, and Father T. F. Hudson is in charge.

REPRESENTATIVE RESIDENCES OF GILROY AND VICINITY.

P. F. Hodges.

Samuel Rea

Mayor M. Casey.

Thomas Rea.

The Christian Church building cost $4,000, and the pastor is Rev. Thos. Edwards.

The Free Methodists have no building, but services are regularly held by Rev. J. A. Cothran.

The Latter Day Saints also hold services, Elder J. M. Putney preaching.

Gilroy has a grand public school building, which contains eight rooms and was erected at a cost of $13,790. There are, including the High School department, eight grades. The Principal is Prof. W. W. Pettit, who, with J. A. Lightall, teaches the High School. Other teachers are: First grade, Helen Strange; second grade, Hanna Sorrenson; third grade, Lida Lennon; fourth grade, Nellie Baillaige; fifth grade, Grace Hoover; sixth grade, Irene Hankenson; seventh grade, Fanny Morey; eighth grade, Clara Eckhart. The school trustees are: L. A. Whitehurst, A. P. Baillaige and C. P. Weldon. There are within the district 789 children between 5 and 17 years of age. School graduates are received at universities without further examination.

THE THREE NEWSPAPERS. Newspapers are prime factors in promoting the growth and prosperity of a town, if they are the proper kind, and there are within the county none more enterprising than those of Gilroy. They are creditable representatives of the town and its resources, and in point of local news are far ahead of papers published in Eastern cities of similar size. The oldest paper is the Advocate, which was established in 1867. It is a weekly, and is published by F. W. Blake. The Gazette, established in 1881, is also a weekly, and is published by B. A. Wardell. The Telegram is a weekly, which was established in 1894, and is published by Mrs. R. G. Einfalt.

BOARD OF TRADE. This organization is composed of a number of well-known business men, and has been an important factor in the growth and development of the town. It was organized October 1, 1875; and reorganized July 17, 1891. The present officers are: President, O. M. Welborn; Vice-President, J. W. Thayer; Secretary, F. C. Staniford; Treasurer, M. Lennon. Directors—O. M. Welborn, L. A. Whitehurst, J. W. Thayer, A. Robinson, J. M. Einfalt, S. W. Kilpatrick, S. T. Moore and H. C. Holloway.

VIEW OF VALLEY FROM GLEN RANCH, LOOKING TOWARD GILROY.

SAMUEL REA'S FARM NEAR GILROY. The history of the transformation of the willow patches and bare land into veritable gardens gives intimations of the changes which will certainly take place within the coming years. There are thousands of acres in the valley that, while they are now more productive than much land in the East, may yet be transformed into gardens as fair as any in the Orient; for the land is very fertile, and only awaits the care and cultivation which man can give, to make it blossom as the rose.

CLEARING THE WILLOW LAND. Samuel Rea came to California in 1852, from Illinois, and went to work in the gold mines near Downieville. He sought the yellow metal with varying success there and at Nevada City until 1856, when, hearing of the beauty and fertility of the Santa Clara Valley, he removed hither. In 1863 he purchased from the Las Animas grant 275 acres of the rich delta land at the mouth of Carnadero Creek, near Gilroy, to which he subsequently added enough to make 322 acres. The land was at that time covered with a dense growth of willows. Mr. Rea cleared the land and opened a channel for Carnadero Creek at a cost of $20,000. He thus reclaimed and brought under cultivation one of the richest tracts of garden land in the county.

In 1869 he went East on a visit, and in Jefferson County, New York, married Miss Kate Vincent, returning with her to visit the East in 1873 and in 1883.

DAIRYING AND GARDENING. As Mr. Rea's land was moist, and furnished an abundant supply of native meadow grasses, he went into the dairy business, which he followed with success and profit until a few years ago, when he found it more profitable to lease his land to Chinese who pay a fair price per acre rental, cash in advance. There are four artesian wells on the farm, ranging in depth from 150 to 345 feet, which furnish an abundant supply of water for irrigation.

The lessees raise onions, potatoes, corn, pumpkins and strawberries. They raised last year 125 bushels of corn to the acre, and took ten tons of pumpkins per acre from the same land, the pumpkins having been planted between the rows of corn. They also planted onions between the rows of young strawberry vines, and harvested 300 sacks of onions per acre. The sacks average 115 pounds in weight, and the onions had been contracted for at fifty cents per hundred.

FINELY BRED HORSES Mr. Rea has a number of finely-bred horses, in which he takes great pride. He has not, however, gone into the business extensively. Last year he allowed Johnny Bury (sired by Antinous) to be taken on a circuit. He was in twelve races and took money out of every one. This year he competed in Portland, Oregon, and won in 2:20¾, and won in several other races.

THOROUGHBREDS ON FARM OF SAMUEL REA, NEAR GILROY.

Mr. Rea has a magnificently furnished residence, where he enjoys life with his wife and two daughters, Florence Viola and Lillian Etta.

THE MAYOR OF GILROY. Mayor Michael Casey of Gilroy located in that city twenty-three years ago, and has since continuously resided there. He served as Chief of the Fire Department three consecutive terms. The confidence which the people repose in him is shown by the fact that he served four terms, or eight years, in the Common Council, and was in May, 1894, elected Mayor of the city, and re-elected in 1896.

THE REA-SARGENT PARTY IN CAMP.

Samuel Rea was elected Supervisor in 1879, took office in 1880 and served two years and ten months, the term having been shortened by the new State Constitution.

SAN FELIPE TOBACCO. Tobacco has for many years been raised at San Felipe, in the southern part of the county. The climate there is quite warm, and tobacco grows very thriftily, acquiring a flavor that is highly praised by consumers. There is more sunshine and much warmer weather in San Felipe than in the choicest tobacco sections of Virginia. A fair minimum crop is 1200 pounds per acre. The lowest price received is 10 cents per pound, and the average price for good tobacco is 25 cents. Several years ago a large cigar factory was established in Gilroy, but owing to improper methods of curing, the business did not prove profitable. A movement is now being made to establish another. There is no

MAYOR CASEY, OF GILROY.

question about the quality of the tobacco. The United States census report for 1890 gives the average value of ten leading crops, per acre, throughout the country, as follows: Corn, $9.47 per acre; wheat, $9.90; oats, $8.16; rye, $8.27; barley, $12.76; buckwheat, $8.24; potatoes, $38.34; cotton, $15.69; hay, $11.08. Tobacco ranges from $44.24 to $204.18 per acre, $61.57 being the average. The highest yield and prices are for seed-leaf tobacco, used exclusively for cigars. The average yield per acre in New York is given at 1339 pounds; in Connecticut, 1417 pounds; in Pennsylvania, 1205 pounds. It costs to produce tobacco about as follows: lowest cost, $2.70 per hundred pounds; highest, $10 per hundred. In 1889 the crop in Pennsylvania cost the grower, when ready for market, $8.12 per hundred pounds; in Connecticut, $9.85 per hundred; in New York, $8.00 per hundred.

ONE OF GILROY'S PIONEERS. Thomas Rea, of Gilroy, was born near Gallopolis, Ohio, November 22, 1820. In 1833 he went with his parents to Hancock County, where he resided five years. In

J. D. CULP'S TOBACCO PLANTATION, SAN FELIPE.

1838 the family removed to Macon County, Illinois. Having attained his majority Mr. Rea separated from the family circle in 1842 to commence life

for himself, going to Grant County, Wisconsin, where he worked in the lead mines until November, 1894, when, hearing of the new El Dorado in California, he left for the gold fields. En route, he passed down the Mississippi

DAIRY SCENE ON FARM OF GEORGE ELMER REA, NEAR GILROY.

to New Orleans, thence by steamer to Panama, and across the Isthmus, reaching San Francisco on the 2d day of February, 1850. He went first to Auburn, Placer County, and thence to Downieville, Sierra County, where he remained until March, 1852. Leaving there in 1853, he crossed the plains, arriving in Gilroy the 3d of September. In 1873 and 1874 he represented his district in the Assembly. From 1872 to 1876 he served Gilroy in its City Council, and was Mayor of Gilroy from 1886 to 1888, and has held other important positions.

MILLER AND LUX. Miller & Lux formed their partnership in 1858, commencing business with 1,000 cattle. They purchased land when opportunity offered, usually paying prices which now seem insignificant. The land now owned by the firm aggregates 14,539,180 acres. Mr. Lux died several years ago, and the property is now being divided and sold for the benefit of the heirs. The Bloomfield Farm near Gilroy, in this county, belongs to Henry Miller, who purchased it in 1863.

FACTS CONCERNING CHEESE. During the past year the manufacture of cheese in Santa Clara County has not been very profitable, as the price has been but about six cents per pound, and has fallen as low as four cents. During the month of November, however, the price rose to 9 cents per pound. The great cheese-making district is Gilroy and vicinity, from whence nearly 125,000,000 pounds of cheese are exported annually. Most of it is made of milk from which the cream has not been extracted. There is in California, however, no law prohibiting the manufacture of filled cheese. It is contrary to law, however, to sell skimmed milk for milk which is supposed to contain its natural quota of cream. Santa Clara County has a Veterinary Inspector who sees that the law is enforced.

FACTS CONCERNING WHEAT. From sixty to seventy pounds of wheat are usually sown per acre in Santa Clara County when the crop is to be cut for grain, and from ninety to a hundred pounds

HENRY MILLER'S BLOOMFIELD FARM, NEAR GILROY.

when it is to be cut for hay. On unirrigated land the crop varies from ten to twelve sacks containing from 135 to 140 pounds each, per acre, equal to from

1350 to 1680 pounds, or from 22½ to 28 bushels. Wheat is now from 97½ cents to $1.05 per cental. On irrigated land the crop may be doubled. In Santa Clara County, however, wheat is never irrigated, as more profitable crops may be grown with the same amount of labor.

HENRY MILLER PARTY IN CAMP

THE ALMS HOUSE. The county owns, near Milpitas, a farm of one hundred acres, with extensive buildings, where the indigent are well cared for. The soil is rich, and a very few acres in trees suffice to supply the inmates with fruit. Three artesian wells supply the ground with an abundance of water for irrigation, and vegetables are raised in great abundance. Fifty acres in pasture and forty acres in hay serve to supply the stock with food. Nineteen head of cows furnish plenty of butter and milk, and poultry, fresh eggs, so that the table is more attractive than it could be made elsewhere, even at far greater expense.

The Alms House is visited three times per week by the county physician, Dr. H. C. Brown, and oftener when necessary. There are now one hundred and twenty-eight inmates, which are kept at a cost of twenty-five cents per day per capita for food, clothing being purchased separately. W. J. Wolcott is superintendent; Frank A. Rounds, stewart; and David Maloney, farmer. An illustration of the Alms House will be found on page 105.

91

PALO ALTO.

The Park-like Village on the Banks of the San Francisquito. Near the Great Stanford University. Young, but Attractive and Enterprising.

PALO ALTO is one of the youngest, and yet one of the most enterprising and attractive towns in the county. The town is most beautifully located in a grove of oaks, and this gives to the landscape a beautiful park-like appearance, while the buildings are all new and bright, most of them being of modern architecture. The townsite was owned by Timothy Hopkins, and was platted by him when, in December, 1891, the opening of the Stanford University made the establishment of a depot a necessity. In the following February J. F. Parkinson established a lumber yard, and as the town was near the University there was a demand for accommodation for both professors and pupils, and houses sprang up as if by magic. Since then the growth of the town has progressed very steadily, and many buildings have been recently erected and many more are in course of construction.

Among those completed is one owned by Westall & Boyce, designed for the Sigma Alpha Epsilon Cub, costing $10,000. Manzanita Hall, recently completed, at Alba Park, will accommodate the training school for boys and cost $7,000. A system of town waterworks has just been completed by C. W. Jones, consisting of two tanks holding 30,000 gallons each, elevated seventy feet, with wells from 100 to 300 feet in depth, pumps and other requisite paraphernalia. The recent decision in favor of Mrs. Stanford, and therefore in favor of the Stanford University, in the case in which the Government sought to hold the estate responsible for railroad bonds, has given the town a new impetus, and revived the proposition to build an electric road to the Bay of San Francisco. Palo Alto has no saloons, all deeds containing a clause which provides that liquor shall not be sold. This was inserted by Mr. Hopkins, and is so firmly upheld by the citizens that all effort to evade its provisions have ended in failure.

THE PALO ALTO—TALL TREE.

CHURCHES AND SCHOOLS. When the town was started, a little more than three years ago, steps were taken to form a school district, and a school was opened with forty-two scholars. The place now boasts of a $15,000 school house, which is a model structure, incorporating all necessary improvements for the securing of heat, light and proper ventilation. The Principal is Prof. S. W. Charles; Miss Ethel Ormonde teaches the intermediate, Miss Grace Wasson the third and fourth grades, Mrs. E. H. Powers the primary, and Miss Gardner is in charge of the kindergarten. The trustees of the public school are: Major W. E. Norris, Wm. Pluns and C. D. Marx; and Mrs. A. P. Zschokke, B. L. Sloan and C. D. Marx are trustees of the High School. The Stanford University, that greatest of all educational institutions, is but a scant mile away, the grounds adjoining the town. In the way of private schools there is a preparatory school for boys, known as Manzanita Hall, and one for girls, known as Castilleja Hall. Pupils are here prepared for entrance to the Stanford University. Thus Palo Alto is well supplied with schools, both public and private.

There are four church organizations, the Methodist, the Baptist, the Presbyterian and the Episcopal. All of them own sites, and the Methodists and Presbyterians have beautiful buildings. Rev. M. H. Alexander is pastor of the Methodist church, Rev. W. D. Nicholas of the Presbyterian, and Rev. R. B. Peet of the Episcopalian. The Baptists have at this time no regular pastor. There is also a Young Men's Christian Association, which has a very creditable reading room. The Secretary is Burton Palmer.

PALO ALTO'S IMPROVEMENT SOCIETY. Palo Alto has a Progressive League, which was organized for the promotion of public improvements, and which has already accomplished considerable along this line, which is made evident by the clean and attractive appearance of the town. Through its instrumentality extensive improvements have been made in street work, and in the laying of sidewalks. Through its efforts the school district was formed and the erection of the handsome school building insured. The incorporation of the town was due also in a great measure to the efforts of this club. The result of recent efforts toward the improvement of the town are noticeable in the beautiful palms along University Avenue, and the improvement of the little plat of ground by the depot. The officers of the Progressive League are: President, Judge E. L. Campbell; Vice-President, J. F. Bixby; Treasurer, B. F. Hall; Secretary, C. W. Decker.

It is not surprising that in a town whose citizens have shown so much business enterprise and activity in other matters, a Mutual Building and Loan Association should be found. Many of the homes of the town have been built by loans made through this association; among its stockholders are some of the most prominent citizens. The officers are: President, J. S. Butler; Secretary, F. A. Raney; Treasurer, Bank of Palo Alto.

VIEWS IN PALO ALTO.

Alpha Sigma Epsilon Club House.
Presbyterian Church.

Street Scene.

Episcopal Church.
Public School.

As regards secret societies, Palo Alto has the Ancient, and the Independent Order of Foresters. There are in addition a number of college societies.

GOOD TRANSPORTATION FACILITIES. Palo Alto is peculiarly fortunate in the matter of transportation facilities, as there are nine trains per day to and from San Francisco, with an extra train on Saturday. A train leaves Palo Alto for San Francisco every morning at 5 o'clock, followed by another at 6:40, one at 7:30, and one at 8:30. Afternoon trains leave at 12:14, 2:05, 3:37, 5:37. This gives ideal service, and many rich people who transact business in San Francisco have homes in Palo Alto or in the vicinity. Every evening a theater train leaves Palo Alto at 6:20 o'clock. Returning, it leaves San Francisco at 11:30. Carryalls connect with every train to take passengers to the University. Much produce is shipped by schooner from Clark's Landing, a few miles north of town.

THE GROVES OF OAKS. The scenery at Palo Alto and vicinity is attractive. The town is located on ground which slopes very gently toward the bay. All about are groves of beautiful live oaks, and where uncultivated is covered in spring with a rich carpet of grass, adorned with myriads of wild flowers. Along the creeks there is a tangled mass of undergrowth and wildwood, with trailing vines and blossoming plants. The bay can be seen to the north and east, and south and west, but a few miles distant, are the mountains.

Crossing the town at the southwest corner, near the San Francisquito Creek, is the road which leads to the grounds and gardens of Mrs. Leland Stanford. Following the creek and winding along beneath the sheltering trees a splendid avenue leads to the mansion. It is an ideal homestead, where every comfort, every ornament and every luxury that culture and refinement could suggest and money procure, has been provided. The great Palo Alto stock farm is near, where have been reared some of the fastest horses the world has ever known.

Immediately west of Palo Alto lies the splendid estate of Timothy Hopkins. It is just outside the county, San Francisquito Creek being the dividing

RESIDENCE OF MRS. JANE L. STANFORD, NEAR PALO ALTO.

line. The road which winds along the creek, in Palo Alto, which was laid out and beautified by Timothy Hopkins, has recently been presented to the town. Palo Alto is just in the edge of the artesian well belt, and flowing wells may be had but a short distance east of town, where there are extensive vegetable gardens. Just north and less than a mile from Palo Alto, but in San Mateo County, a great Catholic University has been built, at a cost of $300,000. A depot has just been completed at Palo Alto, at a cost of $5,500.

The broad avenue which leads to the University is bordered by wide walks and long rows of palms. In fields on either side are forests of eucalyptus and other ornamental trees, where flowers bloom and bees and birds ever make melody. The name is of Spanish origin, and means "tall tree," the tree from which the name was derived being a majestic redwood, which stands on the banks of the stream near the railroad.

THE PALO ALTO TIMES. Palo Alto is represented by the Palo Alto Times, a clean and creditable daily and weekly now in its third volume, which is published by Thomas W. Kemp. The Daily Palo Alto is published for and in the interest of students of the University, as is also The Sequoia, a weekly. Of the latter, W. J. Neidig is editor, and J. M. Switzer, Business Manager. Of the former, Sherrill B. Osborne is editor, and F. W. Morrison Business Manager.

OFFICIALS PUBLIC AND PRIVATE. The Town Trustees are: Joseph Hutchinson, J. S. Butler, Prof. Charles D. Marx, D. L. Sloan and W. C. Lund, and Joseph Hutchinson is President of the Board; H. W. Simkins, Clerk; H. M. Kingore, Recorder; John S. Squire, Treasurer; W. W. Truesdale, Town Marshal.

Mrs. Matilda Yesle is Postmistress, and Rob Danneberg is the railroad company's agent, and also Wells, Fargo & Co.'s agent.

Palo Alto has a bank, of which B. Parkinson is President, J. Hutchinson, Vice-President, and G. R. Parkinson, Cashier.

Palo Alto has a Woman's Club, the officers of which are: President, Mrs. E. L. Campbell; Secretary, Mrs. Southard; Treasurer, Mrs. Mitchell.

The freight shipments from Palo Alto amount to about one million pounds annually, and promise to increase largely in the future.

SANTA CLARA COUNTY HOMES.

John A Hicks, Los Gatos.
Mrs W. J. Parr, Los Gatos

Jacob Eberhard, Santa Clara.
Mrs. L. Heidt, 607 Orchard St., San Jose.

MOUNTAIN VIEW.

The Interesting Town Between the Mountains and the Bay. The Thermal Fruit Belt and the Garden Lands in the Artesian Basin. The County's Greatest Vineyard District.

BETWEEN the mountains and the bay, eleven miles from San Jose, is situated the interesting town of Mountain View. Most of the land in the vicinity was formerly covered with immense groves of noble oaks. Many of these remain, giving to the landscape a charm which is unique in the extreme. The trees are covered with a peculiar light-colored moss, which hangs from the limbs in pendants, and greatly adds to their beauty and unique appearance.

THE THERMAL BELT. Mountain View is within the thermal belt which, commencing in the extreme northwest corner of the county, covers a strip of land several miles in width from San Francisco Bay to the foothills near Saratoga, and thence to the mouth of the canyon at Los Gatos. The climate of the entire Santa Clara Valley is mild, even for California; but within this belt it is peculiarly so, and fruits not only acquire a very rich flavor, but ripen early. Where the ground is silty, apricots and peaches attract particular attention.

THE VINEYARD DISTRICT. Some of the most profitable orchards in the county are near Mountain View. In view of this, it seems strange that the contiguous territory has been so largely devoted to the growing of vines. True, the soil is suitable for grapes especially in the foothills. The lower valley soils are almost too rich for grapes, resulting in the production of large crops and large berries, which are not considered as choice for wine-making purposes as those grown in the foothills. However, the vineyards are here, by the score, and most of them of sufficient area to make a dozen vineyards of the size usually found in other states. There are twenty-two wineries in the vicinity, and in the season as many as seventeen car-loads of wine per day are shipped. It is claimed by residents of the village that, regarding the amounts of freight shipped, Mountain View is in importance fourth on the list of stations in the county. North of Mountain View the Bay of San Francisco spreads away. Several arms or sloughs wind through the marsh lands to within two miles of town. Schooners and small sailing craft can come up to the mainland, and here wharves have been built and warehouses established. Henry Rengstorff owns one, George Jagles another, and the third is the Captain Guth landing. Several years ago, when the wine shipments first began to attract attention, several parties, seeking to reduce the cost of transportation, established a line of schooners, and commenced to ship wine from the landings. The Southern Pacific Company had in previous years freely given for publication figures regarding the shipment of freight. After that they refused to give any statistics, lest competition should be invited. As long ago as 1890, however, the freight shipments for August were 2,251,856 lbs.; for September, 4,284,054 lbs.; and for October, 3,794,655 lbs., making a total for three months only of 11,796,841 lbs. The average monthly ticket sales during that year was in round numbers, $1,000.

STREET SCENE, MOUNTAIN VIEW.

THE ARTESIAN BELT. North of Mountain View there are very few vineyards, and but few orchards. The soil is quite heavy, and more suitable for gardening purposes, to which it is largely devoted. The artesian belt all lies north of the railroad. If the road had been surveyed with a view of defining the artesian belt, it could not have more closely outlined it. From the limit of the basin in the northwestern edge of the county, near Palo Alto, to San Jose, there are no artesian wells south of the railroad, except two weak ones between Santa Clara and San Jose. Although most of the land north of Mountain View is devoted to grain-raising, nearly all of it is suitable for gardening, the rich soil, artesian water and mild climate forming a very favorable combination of circumstances.

BUSINESS AND PLEASURE. A few miles southwest from Mountain View there is a tract of land which has attracted a number of San Francisco business men, who, while they transact business in the city, have here established homes. Among them are John I. Sabin, President of the Sunset Telephone Company; G. C. Morgan, D. M. Delmas, G. T. Sanborn, Joseph Sladky, A. J. Robinson, J. T. Dunn, Wm. Castello, D. F. Farnsworth and others. Their homes are, in many instances, connected by telephone with Mountain View, and therefore with nearly every important city in the State. A great many prominent orchardists throughout the county have telephones.

HISTORY OF SETTLEMENT. Mountain View was formerly a station on the old stage road between San Francisco and San Jose, and there were established a hotel, stable, store, church, school, and various shops. When, in 1864, the railroad was built, it passed about a mile north of the stage station and much of the business naturally drifted to the new town on the railroad. The two settlements are now connected by a long street, on either side of which are city lots and small plots, with cosy homes. Upon nearly every lot, no matter how small, there are fruit trees, and usually a wealth of flowers. The settlements are referred to in a general way as Mountain View, but are often distinguished locally as Mountain View and Old Mountain View. It is now a community of about 900 population, and is well supplied with hotels, stores, livery stables,

MOUNTAIN VIEW CHURCH EDIFICES.

and shops of all kinds, and has a very promising future.

CHURCHES AND SCHOOLS. The more prominent Christian organizations are represented, and most of them own edifices. The Cumberland Presbyterian Church was organized in 1864 and the pastor is Rev. B. F. Whitemore. The M. E. Church South was organized in 1872, in which year the building was erected. The pastor now in charge is Rev. B. F. Green. The Memorial Baptist Church was organized in 1890. It now has no regular pastor. The Catholic Church, of which the building was one of the first erected, is in charge of Rev. Father Raggio.

The school house is a four-roomed building, two stories in height, and cost $6,500. It is situated in the center of a four-acre tract, which is covered with many magnificent oak trees. The average attendance is about 250, and there are six teachers: E. E. Brownell, principal and teacher of seventh and eighth grades; Miss Jeannette Cutter, fifth and sixth grades; Miss Eugenie Gairaud, fourth grade; Miss E. Mabel Scott, third grade; Miss Clara Halsey, second grade; Miss Sallie Cox, first grade.

Board of School Trustees—J. S. Mockbee, J. S. Bailey, and James Showers.

The public spirit of the people is evidenced by the support of a free library and reading room, which contains about eight hundred volumes, with most of the principal magazines and papers. It was established in 1890, is maintained by contributions, and is run in connection with Woman's Exchange, under charge of W. C. T. U. Miss Jessie Huff is librarian.

The Mountain View Register, a seven-column folio, is published weekly by P. H. Millbery, editor and manager. It has aided greatly in developing the town, and placing before the public its resources and attractions.

Mountain View, like most other towns in the county, has a Bicycle Club, the Mountain View Cyclers, which has a membership of fifty, and which incorporated for $10,000, owns its own building, billiard tables, furniture, real estate, etc.

The length of the rainy season, and the amount of rain-fall, is shown by the record kept by J. S. Mockbee. The season of 1894-5 commenced September 30th, upon which date the first shower fell, and ended May 30th, rain having fallen this season ususually late. The total rain-fall for the season was 22.36 inches.

Mountain View has a small park, planted with umbrella trees and fan palms, which will, within a few years, be an attractive feature of the town. This village is eleven miles from San Jose, six miles from Stanford University, and forty from San Francisco, with all of which places it is connected by rail, with five passenger trains per day each way. Its elevation above the sea level is seventy three feet.

The postmistress is Miss Rose A. South, and clerk, Miss Maggie Haverty. Miss Julia Martin is agent of the Sunset Telephone Company, and F. J. Fackrell agent of the Southern Pacific Company.

The total shipments from this point for the fiscal year ending June

THE MOUNTAIN VIEW PUBLIC SCHOOL.

30, 1895, were as follows: Wine, 13,023,785 pounds; hay, 1,543,615 pounds; merchandise, (including green and dried fruits, now classed as merchandise,) 1,598,580 pounds; dried fruit (shipped prior to new classification), 52,805 pounds; green fruit, 171,600 pounds; grapes, 63,870 pounds; mixed fruits, 78,200 pounds; prunes, 69,400 pounds; nuts, 3,025 pounds.

RESIDENCE OF D. M. DELMAS, NEAR MOUNTAIN VIEW.

According to the Assessor's returns there are within the county 4,457,761 fruit trees. Allowing 108 trees to the acre, this makes the area in fruit 41,276 acres divided about as follows: almonds, 226 acres; apples, 415; apricot, 4,954 acres; cherries, 1,472 acres; figs, 20 acres; nectarines, 8 acres; olives, 165 acres; oranges, 17 acres; peaches, 4,682 acres; pears, 1,341 acres; prunes, 27,417 acres; plums, 422 acres; lemons, 15 acres; walnuts, 108 acres.

The etymology of the word Californiais indoubt. There are two Latin words, "calida fornax," meaning "hot furnace," which might easily be corrupted into California. Calidus fornus and Califoria are expressions of the same root. Another possible source of derivation may be found in "cala y fornix," Spanish and Latin for vaulted cove. From the Greek we have kala phor neia, and kalos phornia, variously translated "beautiful woman," "moonshine," "fertile land," or "new country." From the Spanish we have "colofonia," or resin. The California Indians used the term "kali forno," meaning "mountains, or high hills."

REPRESENTATIVE SAN JOSE RESIDENCES.

F. P. Russell.
W. A. Bowden.

E. C. Flagg.
Dr. Elizabeth Gallimore.

MAYFIELD.

Near the Great Stanford University, Between the Mountains and the Bay. Rich Garden Lands in the Artesian Belt. Fruit and Vine Land in the Thermal Belt.

MAYFIELD is situated in the northwestern portion of the county, about sixteen miles from San Jose, and within a mile and a quarter of the great Stanford University. It is in the noted thermal belt, which skirts the foothills, in which flowers bloom perennially. Fruit trees thrive also to a greater degree than in sections affected with frost. South and southeast of Mayfield the land is largely devoted to agriculture, and here may be found some of the largest vineyards in the county. North of the village, in the artesian basin, is the garden district, where vegetables and vegetable seed are grown. Much of this fine land is still used for grain-growing, but as San Francisco reaches further and further to the south, will be used for supplying the metropolis with vegetables and berries. Orchards have not been extensively planted in the vicinity of Mayfield, but the soil along the base of the foothills is especially well suited to peaches, prunes and apricots. The great mountain slopes to the south, now covered with a dense growth of brush, will, within a few years, be covered with orchards and vineyards.

ADJACENT TO THE UNIVERSITY. The soil is in every direction fertile, and the crops large. Mayfield is known, however, in connection with its proximity to the Stanford University, rather than as a great shipping point. The town proper is but a little more than a mile from the University, while the tract upon which it is located most of the cottages rented by students, is less than a mile. Omnibuses connect with every train, and run between the town and the University every few moments during the day. These will no doubt be replaced within a few years by an electric street railway, as the travel increases in a direct ratio with the increasing attendance at the University.

In 1853 E.O. Crosby took up a piece of land and named it the Mayfield farm. When a postoffice was established in the vicinity it was called May-

CACTUS GARDENS, STANFORD UNIVERSITY GROUNDS.

field, and the name was retained as the town grew. The town was platted by William Paul, March 20, 1876, and surveyed by J. J. Bowen, at that time County Surveyor.

Mayfield now contains all the requirements of a modern village, and has a population of about 1,000. The residences are as a rule surrounded by flower gardens, which give to the place a home-like appearance, very pleasant to those who have resided where flowers cannot be so easily cultivated. Many of the houses are beautiful examples of the modern architecture which has within the past decade so beautified California homes.

Lincoln Avenue, one of the main thoroughfares of the town, extends 3,500 feet through the tract known as College Terrace, and affords direct communication with the University over the splendid driveway, sixty-three feet in width.

Land in the vicinity of Mayfield, unimproved, commands from $185 to $250 per acre. Land in the foothills, a few miles south, may be had much cheaper.

SCHOOLS AND CHURCHES. The Methodist Episcopal Church was erected in 1872, and cost $3,500. The pastor is M. H. Alexander.

The Catholic Church was erected in 1871, and services are held by Father Riordan.

Mayfield has a commodious school house, which cost $4,000. The average attendance is about 150. There are four teachers, as follows: Seventh and eighth grades, Adam Maxwell, Principal; fifth and sixth grades, H. B. Welsh; third and fourth grades, Bertha de Laguna; first and second grades, Mrs. J. Albee.

The postmistress is Mrs. A. E. Deitrick. The agent of the Southern Pacific Company is F. G. Wetzel.

A weekly paper, the Mayfield Palo Alto, is published by F. M. Tyrrell.

Mayfield, although principally a village of homes, and a source of supply for the Stanford University, is not an unimportant shipping point.

VIEWS IN MAYFIELD.

Street Scene.
Mayfield Hotel

M. E. Church.

Catholic Church.
Public School House.

THE TOWN OF CAMPBELL.

The Thriving Village in the Midst of the Orchards. The Largest Fruit Drying Plant in the County. A Town in Which there are no Saloons.

CAMPBELL is situated in the center of one of the richest fruit growing districts in the county. Here is situated the largest fruit-drying plant in the county, owned by the Campbell Fruit Growers' Union, and an extensive fruit cannery, owned by J. C. Ainsley & Co. It is a thriving village, the fruit crops being uniformly large, and the farmers and merchants accordingly prosperous. It is on the line of the South Pacific Coast Railway, five miles from San Jose and but fifty-one from San Francisco. The soil is composed largely of silt and gravel washed down from the mountains in ages past by Los Gatos Creek, whose shifting course spread the rich deposit over an extended territory. This is the richest soil known for stone fruits, and Campbell orchards are among the thriftiest in the county.

FOUNDED BY BENJ. CAMPBELL. The town was the result of the increased growth and development which followed the planting of orchards. The necessity for a trading center in this section was evident from the first, and in 1887 the townsite was laid off on land owned by Benjamin Campbell. He came to California from Kentucky, in 1846, and in 1851 selected the homestead where he now resides and commenced to raise grain and stock. When the railroad was constructed and a town sprang up, Mr. Campbell refused to sell land except with a proviso in each deed that no liquor should be sold. As a result there are in Campbell no saloons.

ENTERPRISE AND IMPROVEMENT. During the past year many buildings have been erected and new enterprises established. One of the most important has been the establishement of a bank, by Cooper & Reinig. It at once commanded a fair patronage. Samuel T. Cooper is its President, and Frederick W. Reinig is Cashier.

The new water company was formed during the past year, for the purpose of supplying water not only for domestic use, but for the irrigation of surrounding orchards, and the sprinkling of roads and streets. The plant was put in at a cost of $10,000. The officers are: President, Benjamin Campbell; Secretary, F. M. Righter. A number of very handsome and costly residences have recently been built, and a number of new enterprises established, such as a harness shop, a restaurant, a bakery, a hardware store, a feed and livery stable, a paint shop, laundry, etc. Campbell is connected with other towns in the state by telephone and telegraph, and a movement is now being made to have the town supplied with electric lights.

CHURCHES AND SCHOOLS. Campbell has two flourishing church organizations, the Methodist Episcopal and the Congregational. The Methodist Episcopal was organized in 1887, and now has a large membership and a handsome edifice, which cost $2,800. The pastor is Rev. William Anguin. The Congregational Church was organized in 1889, and in 1891 built a neat house of worship at a cost of $2,000. The pastor is Rev. William Windsor.

Campbell has also a handsome school building, completely furnished. A. C. Ross teaches the grammar grade, and Lillian Mason the primary and intermediate grades. A new schoolhouse will be built the coming year to cost $5,500 to accommodate the increasing school population.

BENJAMIN CAMPBELL.

ORGANIZATIONS AND OFFICIALS. An association for the improvement of the town and called the Campbell Town Council has been doing efficient work, and is officered as follows: B. Campbell, Chairman; J. F. Duncan, Secretary; S. F. Cooper, Treasurer; J. C. Ainsley, F. M. Righter, W. W. Turney, O. N. Bagwell, Mrs. B. Campbell, Mrs. J. C. Ainsley, Mrs. S. A. Foote and Mrs. Poor, Directors.

Campbell has a Young Men's Christian Association, which owns a building with a large auditorium, furnished with a gymnasium and a small library. The President is John F. Duncan, and the Secretary, John Blaine, Jr. There is also an energetic Woman's Christian Temperance Union.

There are three trains per day to and from San Francisco. Trains leave Campbell for San Jose and San Francisco at 7:45 a. m., 9:06 a. m., and 3:29 p. m., and leave San Francisco for Campbell at 10:34 a. m., 4:29 p. m., and 7:00 p. m. Campbell was greatly benefited by the change from narrow to broad gauge, as reshipment at San Jose is no longer necessary.

THE LOCAL PAPER. A weekly paper run by Blaine & Williams, called the Campbell Weekly Visitor, is a very bright, clean and creditable publication, calculated to greatly advance the interests not only of Campbell, but of the county.

SHIPMENTS DURING FISCAL YEAR. During the fiscal year ending January 1, 1896, the following amounts of fruit have been exported: Dried fruit, 2,430,750 pounds; green fruit, 364,570 pounds; canned fruit, 1,205,885 pounds; merchandise, 280,000 pounds.

VIEWS IN CAMPBELL.

Row of Cottages, Central Avenue.
Central Avenue, Looking North.

Methodist Episcopal Church.
Congregational Church

Campbell Avenue.
J. C. Ainsley & Co.'s Cannery.

MILPITAS.

The Land of a Thousand Gardens. How it Became Celebrated in Song and Story. Its Exceedingly Rich Soil and Artesian Wells. Where Peas and Potatoes Grow.

MILPITAS, though one of the smallest towns in the county, occupies an important position commercially, by reason of the rich garden land by which it is surrounded. It is also well known throughout the State as a result of a popular political shibboleth which originated in the early history of the town, and which has ever since been quoted. In 1863 the Rev. Starr King addressed the people at San Jose upon the political issues of the day, and a number of Milpitas citizens attended, one of whom carried a transparency upon which he had painted the words: "As goes Milpitas, so goes the State." The assurance of "the man from Milpitas" attracted attention, and the saying spread until it was quoted from one end of the State to the other.

THE FIESTAS OF EARLY DAYS. Milpitas was also known in early days as a sporting center. The Mexicans who then resided there and in the surrounding hills gathered once a year for fiestas, of which horse-racing, dancing, bull fighting, and other Mexican sports were attending features. The games were often continued several days.

ERAS OF DEVELOPMENT. Milpitas was early selected as a portion of a tract of land granted to a subject of the Mexican government. The first white settler was Michael Hughes, who, in 1852, erected the first frame building. Joseph R. Weller, who is still a resident, arrived in 1853. Land in the vicinity was first used upon which to pasture herds of horses and cattle. When the grain-growing era was inaugurated, the town commenced to assume importance. Subsequently the planting of fruits, berries, and vegetables demonstrated the great fertility of the soil, and the discovery of artesian water made it one of the richest garden sections in the State. Much of the soil is a sediment which has been deposited by inflowing streams, and which is extremely fertile. This shades into a deep, black loam, peculiarly suited to the growing of vegetables and strawberries. It is equally suitable for pears.

THE THERMAL BELT. A few miles east of Milpitas rise the foothills of the Mount Hamilton Range. Along the face of these extends a thermal belt which is seldom visited by frost. It is on the leeward side of San Francisco Bay, and the warm breath of the waters, wafted by gentle breezes along the hillsides, tend to prevent the settling of frost even in the coldest winters we have. Here peas may be planted early, and they early mature. The soil is especially well suited to the growth of potatoes, also, and in the busiest part of the season from twelve to fifteen carloads of potatoes and green peas are shipped from Milpitas daily.

ASPARAGUS GROWING CENTER. Milpitas is also the great asparagus-growing center. Cutting commences in the earlier part of April, and continues until the latter part of June or early part of July. The price obtained by the grower varies from $7.50 per box early in the season to 75 cents per box later on. The average crop is about one hundred boxes per acre, with one hundred and twenty-five boxes as an exceptional crop. The profit per acre varies from $100 to $300 per acre.

STREET SCENE IN MILPITAS.

PROFITABLE STRAWBERRY RAISING. Strawberry culture in the vicinity of Milpitas is also very profitable. The Longworth is in best demand, and always brings a little more than the Cheney or Sharpless. The two latter are more generally raised, however, as the berries are larger, and the plants are more easily cultivated. Comparatively few white men engage in the business, because of the necessity for detail and care, and the difficulty of obtaining white laborers. White men who own

SCENES IN MILPITAS AND VICINITY.

The County Alms House.
The Catholic Church.

The Presbyterian Church.
The Public School House.

soil suitable for strawberry culture usually rent their land to Chinamen, who willingly pay a rental of $20 per annum per acre. It is more profitable, however, to raise berries on shares. The usual plan is for the owner to prepare the land for planting, after which the Chinese put in the plants, cultivate, and care for them. The Chinese pick the berries and the proprietor markets them, giving the former one-half of the net proceeds. Strawberries are sold in chests which contain twenty five pound drawers. Sharpless berries command from $2.50 to $4 per chest, and Longworth from $4 to $6. The profits vary greatly in different seasons, and under the present system depend in a great measure upon the Chinamen, who are often unreliable. The gross income from strawberries range from $75 to $500 per acre.

THE HAY AND GRAIN CROP. East of Milpitas there is a broad expanse of valley land upon which are raised large crops of wheat and hay. As Milpitas is near the great hay-markets of San Francisco, hay can be raised more profitably than in many of the interior valleys of the State. There are in Milpitas several large warehouses where hay is stored in summer to await the better prices which prevail in winter. There are also large warehouses on a slough which puts in from the Bay of San Francisco, a few miles away, and hay and grain are shipped from the landing to San Francisco by schooner.

Milpitas is a Spanish word, derived from "mil," meaning one thousand, and "pitas," flowers, or garden. The name is variously translated "a thousand gardens," "many gardens," and "land of a thousand flowers."

SCHOOLS AND CHURCHES. Milpitas has the usual number of stores, hotels, shops, stables and other business houses ordinarily found in a village of four hundred population. There are six trains per day each way, connecting with San Jose, six miles south, and

with San Francisco forty-two miles northwest. The main school-building cost $6,000. There are three teachers: D. H. Chaplin, principal; Miss Osee E. Ashley, intermediate; and Miss Kate Bellew, primary. The attendance varies from one hundred and twenty to one hundred and forty. The school is provided with a library containing over six hundred volumes. The Presbyterian Church building was erected in 1872. Of this, Rev. J. A. Mitchell is pastor. The Catholic Church building was constructed about the same time. The pulpit is filled by Father Maguire.

SOUTHERN PORTION OF SAN FRANCISCO BAY FROM PROSPECT PEAK.

AS A SHIPPING POINT. Milpitas is one of the most important shipping points in the county, as it is the depot not only for the product of the many orchards and gardens along the bottom lands, but the rich grain lands to the east, the garden lands on the hillsides, and the extended territory further back in the foothills, where there are many rich valleys, notably the Calaveras. Much of the hay crop is shipped by schooner to San Francisco, and considerable is consumed in San Jose, amounting, perhaps, to one-half the crop. A large per cent of the berry crop is also sold in San Jose.

THE ROAD TO PROSPECT PEAK. The road leading east from Milpitas winds along the Arroyo Coches a distance of several miles. A branch from this road ascends a spur of the mountain leading north to Mission Peak. The grade does not seem to be very steep, yet rises 1600 feet in seven miles. No one who has not witnessed it can appreciate the grandeur of the view which is presented as one ascends the grade. At the point known as Cape Horn the valley may be seen spread out as a map, each farm a little square, and each house a little dot upon the plain.

The grandest view, however, is obtained from Prospect Peak, upon the upper portion of J. R. Weller's farm. The elevation above the valley is 1900 feet, and the mountains at this point are so steep that the orchards and farms beneath seem to nestle almost at our feet. Westward is presented one of the most unique views that may be seen in the world. The great Bay of San Francisco stretches away toward the Golden Gate, its bright waters shimmering in the sunlight as it is fanned by the morning breeze. A long, black line of smoke, with a white dot at one end, serves to call attention to a steamboat, which, in the distance, seems to move along most tediously. Long trains, likewise, creep over the plains, followed by a white line of steam and smoke.

SPREAD OUT AS A MAP. Milpitas, surrounded by its gardens, sits upon the plain but a few miles away. Orchards seem like lilliputian squares in a great checkerboard. The large, white barns at the foot of the mountain are so nearly beneath us that they seem to have no walls, but sit flat upon the ground. Away beyond the miles upon miles of farms to the west Mountain View stands upon the plain, with Mayfield, Palo Alto and Stanford University beyond, distinguishable only as nuclei of numerous white spots among great groves of trees. The towering mountains of the range beyond seem more clearly outlined, as the angle of vision is not so acute, and the redwood trees are clearly distinguishable, fringed against the western sky.

THE CELEBRATED SPRING ON THE FARM OF J. R. WELLER.

extended view. As early as 1858 a man named Taggart was impressed with the utility of the spring and the beauty of the surroundings, and settled there. In the same year John Dooly paid him $8,000 for his squatter's right. Subsequently a handsome barn was erected at a cost of $3,000, and a dwelling which cost $1,500. Subsequently Mr. Weller purchased the tract of 160 acres and fenced it. He has since farmed a portion of it, using the remainder for pasturage. He put out fruit trees and otherwise improved it, and eventually purchased adjoining farms, until he now owns tracts aggregating 640 acres. Upon these there are nine springs, furnishing sufficient water to irrigate several hundred acres.

SCENE ON J. R. WELLER'S FARM, NEAR MISSION PEAK.

One is surprised, when on the way to this point, after riding along the summit of a ridge for a half hour, to find that the road leads into a widening valley through which, beneath oaks and alders, flows a beautiful stream of water. Surprise to wonder grows when one follows the stream to its source and learns that the water emerges from a spring in the side of the mountain, a full-grown brook at the start, the water bubbling up clear as crystal from beneath the granite rock. This spring, which is probably not approached in volume of water by any other in the State except that which flows from the noted Gold Spring in Tuolumne County, is upon the farm of J. R. Weller, at an altitude of 1600 feet, and a few hundred feet below the peak which commands such an

THE HOME AT MILPITAS. Mr. Weller owns also 360 acres at Milpitas, where he has a home, with most pleasant surroundings. The soil is very fertile, and Mr. Weller leases a number of acres for strawberry culture, to which it is especially well suited. He pays most attention, however, to the dairy business, keeping about eighty head of graded Durham cows, and selling the milk to San Jose creameries. He plants about twenty acres of beets and corn for the milch cows, and upon the remainder of the farm raises hay. Mr. Weller is one of the pioneer residents of the county, having arrived in the valley in 1851.

SARATOGA ON CAMPBELL CREEK.

The Orchard-Crowned Village of the Foothills. The Celebrated Saratoga Springs. In the Thermal Belt. Orchards and Canneries. The Water Power.

WHERE the waters of Campbell Creek emerge from the Santa Cruz Mountains sits a beautiful village. With a railroad to San Jose it will be a second Los Gatos, as it is one of the richest fruit-growing districts in the county, and is in the foothill thermal belt. Situated at the mouth of the canyon, on the road to the rich fruit and vine-growing sections above, the great lumber regions over the summit in Santa Cruz County, and near one of the most wonderful mineral springs in the United States, it is a natural trading center, and with a railroad, will be an important town.

As early as 1849 Martin McCarthy, realizing the beauty and future commercial importance which the place would probably assume, took up a quarter section of land where Saratoga is now located. In 1855 the postoffice was established and in 1863 the town was surveyed by C. W. Healey.

WATER POWER AND MANUFACTORIES. In 1868 E. T. and W. T. King established a paper mill. A. Pfister shortly thereafter entered into partnership with them, and the firm became known as E. T. King & Co. In 1874 the establishment was amalgamated with the Lick Mills property. When Blake, Robbins & Co. of San Francisco were taken into the firm the association was converted into a joint stock company, and both concerns conducted it until 1878 as the Saratoga and Lick Mills Paper Manufacturing Company. As other mills were established in the State, profits diminished, and the mill was closed. The use of steam power, when plenty of water could have been secured, was not calculated to insure permanent success. In 1868 Peter Somerville established a mill for the manufacture of pasteboard, and conducted it until 1878. These enterprises are mentioned to more forcibly illustrate the fact that Saratoga possesses a water power that is of great practical value.

THE LUMBER MILLS. In 1851 a saw mill was established in the redwoods above Saratoga and the lumber was all hauled out through the village. All of the available timber on this side of the summit has been sawed, and the mills were recently removed to a

YUCCA PALM, SANTA CLARA COLLEGE.

point about five miles below the summit, toward the ocean. The lumber is hauled to the summit on cars with a wire cable, operated by steam. It is then hauled with teams to Santa Clara. The daily output of the mills is about 5,000 feet, and the lumbermen claim that they own enough available timber to keep the mill running for ten years. The Santa Clara Mills obtain their lumber here.

SCHOOLS AND CHURCHES. The first school was established in 1860. The present school-house contains three rooms and cost $2,000. There are three teachers, the principal being Prof. E. A. Loosemore. Mrs. T. W. Whitehurst has charge of the intermediate, and Miss Eliza Cross of the primary department.

Saratoga is well supplied with church organizations, having five, all of which, except the Episcopal, recently organized, own buildings. The Methodist Church, of which Rev. J H. Wythe is pastor, erected a building during the past year. The Christian Church owns a neat edifice, and their pastor is Rev. Henry Shadle. The pastor of the Congregational Church is Rev. W. H. Cross. Rev. Gassman is the Episcopal minister, and the Catholic Church is supplied from Santa Clara. There is an active Women's Christian Temperance Union and a Chautauqua Circle.

ORCHARDS AND CANNERIES. About one mile east of Saratoga is the extensive F. G. Hume fruit-canning establishment. There are also some large fruit-drying plants in the vicinity, notably Gordon's, Beardsley's and the Sorosis Packing Company's.

The foothills produce fruit of very excellent flavor. Prunes and apricots, particularly, thrive. In the higher altitudes, where the elevation and heavy forests bring about a lower temperature, apples and cherries reach their greatest development. Saratoga is one of the best cultivated sections in the county. The size of the town affords no indication of the number, extent and wealth of the orchards in the vicinity. New orchards are being planted, and every year the vineyards reach further up onto the hillsides.

VIEWS IN SARATOGA.

A Street Scene.

The Public School.
Catholic Church

Congregational Church.
Christian Church.

VIEWS OF CONGRESS SPRINGS, NEAR SARATOGA. CALIFORNIA.

The Hotel and Cottages Behind the Trees.
The D. O. Mills Cottage.

A Black Oak Above the Spring.

The Alvinza Hayward and L. P. Sage Cottages and Hotel.
General View of Hotel and Cottages, Looking Northwest.

VIEW OF CONGRESS SPRINGS, SARATOGA, CALIFORNIA.

Approach to Hotel Grounds.
Rustic Bridge over the Brook on the way to the Springs

Fishing in the Brook.
One of the Springs.

PACIFIC CONGRESS SPRINGS.

A Noted Health Resort of the State. Mineral Waters Possessing Rare Medical Properties. A Well-Kept Hotel with Romantic Surroundings Conducted by J. F. Pfetch.

ART may imitate nature, but can never equal it. This is most forcibly illustrated in the case of mineral springs. Chemists may by analysis discover approximately what natural mineral water contains, but a mixture of chemicals in like proportions does not produce a compound having the same properties that were possessed by the natural product. Nature in her laboratory may have been thousands of years preparing by slow processes the chemicals which combine to produce the peculiar waters of a mineral spring, and the result cannot be duplicated, either instantaneously or otherwise. Natural mineral waters, therefore, have a peculiar value.

LOCATION OF CONGRESS SPRINGS. Among the most valuable mineral springs in the United States are those located in the canyon a mile above Saratoga, and known as the Pacific Congress Springs. They were discovered in 1862, or earlier, and in 1866 were purchased by a syndicate of wealthy men composed of D. O. Mills, Alvinza Hayward, A. J. Easton, E. W. Knight, O. F. Griffin, Louis McLane, John O. Earl and George R. Spinney. They improved the spring and built a hotel and several private cottages. In 1872 the property was purchased by L. P. Sage, who subsequently expended about $40,000 in improving it. There are three springs, the water in all three being identical in composition.

LEASED BY J. F. PFETCH. Recently Congress Springs were leased for a term of twenty years, with privilege of purchase, by J. F. Pfetch, a gentleman who has for many years been a promoter of large enterprises in the East, where he expended for capitalists

in one instance in the improvement of electric railways and hotel property more than a million dollars. In nearly every instance Mr. Pfetch's dealings have involved the purchase of hotel properties and the development of trade by the construction of electric railways.

Mr. Pfetch visited Santa Clara County several years ago, and was deeply impressed with the wonderful properties of the water at Congress Springs, as well as the natural beauty of the surroundings, the mild and equable climate, and the opportunity to make it the leading resort in the State. When he had disposed of his business interests in the East, he returned to California and visited every mineral spring in the State, of importance. He concluded that there were none offering equal advantages, considering medicinal qualities, climate, and natural attractions, and accordingly entered into negotiations with a view of leasing them.

AN ELECTRIC RAILWAY. As soon as Mr. Pfetch secured the lease he took steps to secure the right of way for an electric railway from San Jose. Its construction will greatly enhance the interests not only of Saratoga and San Jose, but of the entire territory along the line. Other extensive improvements are contemplated, including the construction of a handsome club house, a new dining room, an addition to the hotel, new stables, etc. The grounds about the house will be laid out in lawns and flower gardens, and paths will be made through the forests which cover the mountains above the springs.

The property contains 720 acres, and besides the extensive forest there is an abundance of land for orchard, vineyard and pasture lands. Fifty acres are now in vines, 20 acres in fruit trees, and 160 acres are used for raising

GENERAL VIEW OF CONGRESS SPRINGS HOTEL—SHOWING VALLEY BEYOND.

hay. A herd of Jersey cows will be kept in order that guests may be supplied with plenty of fresh milk and butter; gardens will supply them with fresh vegetables, and orchards with fruit. Everything will be kept neat and clean, and the wants of every guest assiduously attended to. The table will be made especially attractive.

The hotel is one of the finest and most thoroughly equipped in California. It has a frontage of 450 feet facing south. It contains all the modern improvements and the hotel and cottages are specially designed for health, comfort and enjoyment. It has telegraphic and telephonic communication with the outside world. One of the attractive features is a new Natatarium where all kinds of mineral and fresh water, plunge and shower baths can be enjoyed. The individual bath rooms are furnished with the latest improved porcelain tubs.

CLIMATE AND SURROUNDINGS. The climate is pleasant in the extreme. The hotel is located on the hillside in a canyon in the Coast Range of mountains, one mile above Saratoga, amidst most enchanting scenery, 800 feet above the level of the sea, and is seldom reached by the fog. It is protected from strong winds, and the air is always clear, bright and invigorating. It is one of the best hunting and fishing resorts in the county, the surrounding hills being well supplied with quail, doves, rabbits and squirrels; and Campbell Creek, which runs through the place, is a fine trout stream.

There are in numerous directions good roads, offering opportunity for riding and driving among the orchards and vineyards of the valley on the one hand, and through forests and up mountain grades on the other.

ORANGE GROVE, SOROSIS ORCHARD

bladder, rheumatism, gout and cutaneous affections. It simply, yet effectually, cleanses the system.

It is very grateful to the stomach of febrile patients, lessening nausea and gastric irritability, rendering the fluids in the body alkaline, and promoting a more copious secretion of the urinary organs.

In biliary calculi it has been found very beneficial. An acid which dissolves feldspathic and micaceous rock must also have some action on urate of lime and biliary salts.

Vesical calculi are also influenced, as in catarrhal affections of the bladder, chronic cystitis, etc. It is especially good for Bright's disease of the kidneys, the chalybeate carbonated water being much more valuable in such cases than simple alko-carbonated water.

The iron tends to raise the temperature of the body by creating more red blood corpuscles, producing a healthier glow and rosier cheek.

ANALYSIS OF THE WATER. An analysis by B. B. Thayer, State Assayer, and Winslow Anderson, assayer at the State University, shows that the Pacific Congress Springs water contains:

U. S. GALLONS CONTAINS.

Mineral ingredients	Grains.
Sodium Chloride	119.15
Sodium Carbonate	123.35
Sodium Sulphate	12.95
Potassium Carbonate	2.06
Magnesium Carbonate	26.34
Magnesium Sulphate	4.19
Calcium Carbonate	16.03
Ferrous Carbonate	14.03
Calcium Sulphate	14.19
Alumina	4.50
Silica	3.98
Total Solids	340.77
Free Carbonic Acid	44.17

THE WATER AND THERAUEPTICS. Water from Congress Springs has for years been sold all over the Coast. A receiver is placed over the main spring in which to collect the gas, and the water is bottled in its natural state. It belongs to the alkalo-chalybeate class, which is so valuable for table purposes. Its action is mildly aperient, from the presence of Glauber and Epsom salts, diuretic from the large amounts of carbonates, and antacid from carbonic acid gas, which forms alkaline carbonates with metallic bases. The water is also largely tonic and ferruginous from the large quantity of iron salts. It has obtained considerable celebrity in the treatment of anæmia, dyspepsia, liver and kidney troubles, irritability of the

Water may often be rapidly assimilated by absorption as well as when introduced into the stomach. The Congress Spring water is very delicious for bathing purposes, and facilities are provided for its use in this manner.

ADDITIONAL SARATOGA ITEMS. Saratoga is represented by a weekly paper, the Saratoga Item, published by Claude Pollard. It is a clean paper, with a moral tone.

Oranges flourish in the vicinity of Saratoga and are seldom injured by frost.

NEW ALMADEN ON THE HILLTOP.

Where the Great Quicksilver Mines are Located.   History of their Discovery and Development.   Details of the Industry.   The Output, Prices and Profits.

AT New Almaden, twelve miles south of San Jose, are located the richest and most productive quicksilver mines in the world, excepting only the Almaden mines in Spain. The location of the ledge was known to the Indians, who used the vermilion for face paint, at least three-quarters of a century ago In 1822 they told Luis Chabolla and the Robles family concerning the ore, and in 1824 Senor Robles showed it to Don Antonio Sunol. The latter, supposing that the bright globules in the ore were silver, spent a year and $400 in trying to extract it. During the succeeding twenty years no efforts were made toward its development.

On November 12, 1845, Andres Castillero, a Mexican officer sojourning at the Mission Santa Clara, examined the ore, and pronounced it cinnabar. He filed a claim upon the ledge on November 22, 1845, and formed a company with a view of development. The property in 1864 passed into the hands of The Quicksilver Mining Company, of New York, by whom it has since been operated. They paid for the mine $1,700,000. Up to March 6, 1891, the product amounted to $14,939,055.41. The land owned by the Company aggregates 8,500 acres.

From these extend drifts. The mercurial ores are mingled in a series of beds and laminations of great number and extent, so that the whole workings are very irregular and contorted.

GENERAL VIEW OF FURNACES AND CONDENSERS, HACIENDA.

THE THREE SETTLEMENTS. There are three sections to the settlement. The reduction works are located in the canyon on the banks of the Alamitos. Here are also about fifty dwellings, an hotel, a public hall, a store, the superintendent's residence, and other buildings. This part of the village is known as the Hacienda. The word is of Spanish origin, and means the headquarters on a large farm, or other estate. Here is located the postoffice, and there is also a telegraph and express office. The population of Hacienda is about 250.

Upon the hill, where the main shafts are located, is another settlement, known as New Almaden, containing a store, offices, a public hall, a public school, and two church edifices. All of the buildings except churches and schoolhouses are owned by the company, which rents them to employes at very low rates, ranging from $3 to $5 a month. Water is piped to the town from springs several miles away, and is supplied to families for 50 cents a month. The settlement at Hacienda is supplied with water taken from Los Alamitos Creek, and is furnished free of charge.

SHAFTS AND REDUCTION WORKS. The reduction works are situated in a canyon, on Alamitos Creek. The ledge outcrops on the ridge of a hill about a mile distant, and 475 feet higher. The outcrop is 1,700 feet above the sea level. There are four shafts, from each of which, at levels varying from 50 to 100 feet apart, horizontal drifts have been run upon the vein The deepest shaft is 2,450 feet, the bottom being 750 feet below the level of the sea The second shaft is 1,800 feet in depth, the third 1,000 feet, the fourth 600 feet, and the fifth 310 feet.

SCHOOLS AND CHURCHES. There is a public school at Hacienda, taught by George W. Bishop and Miss Lottie Bulmore. There is a postoffice, express and telegraph office. George Carson is the Postmaster and express agent. The public school at New Almaden has three teachers. F. M Chaplin is principal; Lillie Hopkins teaches the

SCENES AT THE GREAT NEW ALMADEN QUICKSILVER MINES.

grammar grade, and Miss Jennie W. Roberts the primary. The average attendance is 197. The Methodist Church building cost $4,000, and the pastor is Rev. J. W. Peters. The Catholic Church is in charge of Father Picardo.

There is a third settlement, containing 300 people, known as Spanishtown, located at a still greater elevation. There is here a public school also, taught by Marcella Barry.

THE HELPING HAND. At Hacienda there is a building containing a library and a commodious hall. This was erected by a Society known as the Helping Hand. Employes of the company contribute $1 per month each toward a fund for the employment of a resident physician, surgeon and dentist, and for benevolent purposes. The Helping Hand Society also owns a building at New Almaden, containing a hall and reading room. There are other societies, including the Sons of St. George, Knights of Pythias, and three local benevolent societies, known as the Hidalgo, the Philanthropic and the Guadalupe.

HOW THE VEIN IS WORKED. Most of the work performed underground is done by contract, including the sinking of shafts, running of drifts, and extraction of ore. The tunnels are seven feet high and five feet wide, and cost the company from $20 to $35 a yard, according to the nature of the rock passed through. There is very little earthwork, except in the running of tunnels to intercept veins for the removal of ore.

The ore body is from fifteen to thirty feet in width, the hanging wall being clay slate and the foot wall serpentine. The hills rise abruptly in the shape of an inverted V, and the vein outcrops on the highest point. This enables the company to work the mine very advantageously, as tunnels can be driven in from the hillsides, intercepting the shafts several hundred feet below the surface. Through these the ore is taken out. At the mouth of each tunnel is built a large platform and a series of sheds. Here the ore is screened and assorted.

Where the ore is exceedingly rich, men have to work short shifts, relieving each other every few hours, as constant handling of the ore causes considerable of it to be absorbed by the body. It is volatile at any tempera-

GENERAL VIEW OF SPANISHTOWN, NEW ALAMADEN.

ture above 40 degrees. Its presence in the system in large quantities causes the appetite to fail, the digestion to become impaired, the secretions to become thin and copious, and the skin to have an earthy paleness. If salivation results, a copious flow of watery saliva follows, accompanied with soreness and swelling of the gums, and a peculiar fetor of the breath.

PROCESS OF DISTILLATION. Quicksilver is freed from the ore by distillation. The ore is burned in furnaces. The quicksilver passes off in the form of vapor, which is led by iron flues into condensers. After passing through eight condensing chambers, the vapors are conducted into a tank, where they are sprinkled with water. There are at New Almaden eight furnaces, all but one being continuous. From twenty-four to thirty-six tons of ore are passed through a perpetual furnace daily, every ton remaining in the furnace about nine hours above the fire bridge, and about four hours below in the hottest portion of the furnace, where the last particles of silver are extracted.

The ore is assorted into two sizes, known as granza and tierras. There are four tierras furnaces One is charged with 72,000 pounds of ore every twenty-four hours; two each receive 48,000 pounds in twenty-four hours, and the other, 24,000. There are two granza furnaces, each having a capacity of 20,000 pounds in twenty-four hours The heavier the ore is when it is placed in the furnace, the lighter the rock is after the mercury has been extracted, as it is then porous.

THE ELUSIVE METAL. The great subtlety with which the vapors of the metal penetrate the minutest openings is remarkable. It forces itself through imperceptible cracks and pores. When the old intermittent furnaces were removed, 2,000 flasks, or 153,000 pounds, were recovered by washing out the ground to a depth of thirty feet. The present furnaces are as impervious as they could well be made.

The company employs from 230 to 245 men the year round besides those who work by contract. The wages depend largely upon the locality of the work, its importance, and the degree of skill required for its performance. Laborers earn from $1.50 to $2.50 per day; mechanics, from $2 to $3 60; underground foremen, from $2 75 to $4.50 per day.

PRODUCT AND PRICES. The total product of the mines from June, 1850, to December 31, 1895, was 930,269 flasks of 76½ pounds each, or 71,165,578½ pounds, equal to 35,582 tons and 1578½ pounds. The average price per flask for that period was $36.32. This and rentals made the income $14,939,055.41, up to December 31, 1892, since when no public reports of the output have been made. The highest price per flask was $120. The lowest was $25.25. The present price, which has prevailed with slight variations for several years, is $32 per flask. The average output is now about 600 flasks of 76½ pounds each, per month. Quicksilver becomes solid at 40 degrees below zero, when it becomes malleable, and resembles lead. Its boiling point is 662 degrees Fahrenheit, when it forms an invisible, transparent vapor. It is volatile, however, at any temperature above 40 degrees.

THE COMPANY'S REPRESENTATIVE. The Quicksilver Mining Company's manager and sole representative in California is Robert R. Bulmore. He took a position with the Company eighteen years ago as accountant and cashier. During the many years which have since elapsed he has become familiar with every detail of the business. His expert knowledge not only of the processes of mining but of the market and the means of properly supplying it, makes him an invaluable man. The Company furnishes for his use a most elegant residence, with handsome grounds.

JAMES HARRY, THE LATE SUPERINTENDENT. James Harry, until his death in December, 1895, was the Superintendent of the mine. He came from Cornwall, England, twenty-five

ROBERT R. BULMORE.

years ago, and went to work at the Almaden mine. The knowledge gained of mining in Cornwall enabled him to more quickly master the details of quicksilver mining, and he was promoted from one position to another until 1891, when he was appointed Superintendent of the entire mine. His expert knowledge of every detail, and especially of the peculiar local conditions which characterize California ore deposits, eminently fitted him for the position. He had the reputation of being one of the most expert quicksilver miners in the United States. His death, in December, 1895, took from the service of the mining company a faithful and efficient servant, who was respected and beloved by his employers and also by his fellow workers.

The surface foreman is C. F. O'Brion, the underground foremen are Richard Harry and W. Gilbert, the civil engineer and office clerk is C. C Derby, and the chief engineer is James Harrower.

NATURAL CARBONIC ACID GAS. A new industry at Almaden is the extraction from the mine of carbonic acid gas. A number of years ago several miners were overcome in one of the drifts by a deadly gas. The drift was walled up and deserted. Last year experiments were made, when it was learned that it was natural carbonic acid gas. A company was formed, and the gas is compressed in steel tubes under a pressure of 1650 pounds to the square inch, and sold throughout the State to manufacturers of soda and other carbonated water. It is, with the exception of the supply at Saratoga, New York, the only deposit of natural carbonic acid gas of consequence in the United States. A trade of considerable importance is being built up which is liable to expand year after year, as the demand will surely increase and the use of this gas prevail to a larger extent

BOHLMAN'S LIVERY STABLE. For sixteen years past the transportation of freight and passengers to the New Almaden Quicksilver Mines has been under the control of Mr. F. Bohlman. Besides this, however, Mr. Bohlman tilled the lands of the mining company, comprising 2,500 acres. He also had an interest in the butcher business. Four years ago he enlarged his business by purchasing and stocking a livery stable in San Jose. His establishment is located on Santa Clara street, and is popularly known as the City Stables. Here are kept vehicles and conveyances of all kinds ready for public use. His stock is first-class and Mr. Bohlman prides himself on keeping it in good condition. He is attentive to his business and courteous to his patrons. He absolutely controls the livery business at New Almaden

JAMES HARRY.

and Hacienda, and his San Jose patronage is quite extensive and growing larger each year.

MINERAL PRODUCTS IN 1894. The report of the State Mining Bureau for 1894 states that Santa Clara County produced that year: 7,235 flasks of 72½ pounds each of quicksilver, worth $222,189; 5,000 gallons of mineral water; 80,000 cubic feet of natural carbonic acid gas, worth $79,072; 3,500 barrels of petroleum; 52 725,000 brick; and 24,000 cubic feet of building stone, worth $9,120.

FACTS CONCERNING ALFALFA. Alfalfa cannot be grown profitably except in sections where it can be irrigated. In this county its culture is confined almost exclusively to the artesian districts. It is cut six times per year. If it is cut less frequently the stalks grow too rank. The average profit per acre is about $37.50.

BEATIFUL ALMA.

ALMA is most beautifully situated in a grove of oaks on a bench by the side of Los Gatos Creek, three miles above Los Gatos, and twelve from San Jose. The village is not large, containing only a store, hotel, blacksmith shop, depot, postoffice, and a few smaller shops, but there are a number of charming residences, and it is an attractive place in which to reside. It is an important shipping point, as there are in the mountains above extensive fruit-growing districts. The climate is very pleasant. Alma escapes the fogs which visit the western slopes of the mountains to the west, and as the elevation is 560 feet, the weather is not so warm as it is in the valley in the daytime, and the warm air draws up the canyon in the night, making the temperature very equable.

FRUIT GROWING AND AGRICULTURE. Grapes are most largely grown in the vicinity, as even the steepest hillsides are suitable for their culture. Prunes, however, bear heavily, and in fact most kinds of fruit, the soil here, as in all the great mountain districts, being rich in plant food. The great forests which cover the mountains west and south, with the attending growth of vegetation and flowers, furnish a rare opportunity for bee-raising, as the honey made here is of excellent quality. Bees are never without food, because the weather is

GENERAL VIEW OF ALMA.

MAKING HOMES ON THE HILLSIDES. Within the past few years men have extended roads up the canyons to the east, along the ridges, and to the very summit. Springs have been sought out, brush cleared away, houses built, and trees planted. The soil is rich, and it only needed persistent labor to transform the brushy hillsides into orchards and vineyards. There is often less frost upon exposed knolls where the wind blows than in more sheltered localities in the valley, and in the years to come the great mountain section east of Alma will produce some of the best fruit in the county.

THE SODA SPRING. On the Mount Pleasant road, about three-quarters of a mile east of Alma, there is a strong soda spring, which contains iron and magnesia. The water flows from a small pool by the side of a stream which comes from the hill above. The carbonic acid gas comes up in silvery bubbles through the clear water, which is alive with ebullition. The sides of the spring are covered with the familiar snuff brown of oxydized iron. The water has gained quite a reputation for its medicinal qualities, which, of course, are confined to the minerals, the so called soda water taste being imparted solely by the carbonic acid gas.

The Moody Gulch oil wells are

never cold enough to prevent them from working. It is never necessary to store bees in the cellar here in winter, as it is in the East. They gather honey all winter. Flowers of some sort are blooming every day in the year. It is one of the choicest sections in the State for apiculture, as there are few other localities which furnish such a constant supply of food, and the honey is very white, has a delightful flavor, and commands a good price.

situated but a short distance from Alma. The school teacher is Miss S. M. Whitehurst. The Methodists have a church, of which Rev. Wythe is pastor. The agent of the Southern Pacific Company is C. A. Stice.

The shipments from Alma station during the past fiscal year amounted to about 800 tons.

There is good trout fishing and hunting in the vicinity of Alma.

WRIGHTS STATION.

The Rich Fruit-growing Section in the Surrounding Mountains. Fertile Soil and Grand Scenery. Private Residences and Summer Resorts. Natural Gas and Mineral Springs.

WRIGHTS Station, though a small village, is an important shipping point, as it is the depot for the extensive fruit-growing sections in the surrounding mountains. Travelers on the cars receive little intimation from what they see along the route or at the station, concerning the rich and beautiful section which crowns the mountain above the heavy belt of timber which covers the hillside, and reaches down into the stream which rushes through the canyon. The roads which leave the little space of open ground by the depot to enter the leafy tunnels through the woods furnish no suggestion of the vine-clad slopes, the towering redwoods, the green fields, the cozy homes and bending fruit trees which adorn the great territory above and beyond. The beauty of this section can scarcely be described. There is a wealth of resource, a grandeur of scenery, and a fertility of soil that challenges description.

THE GREAT MOUNTAIN FRUIT REGION. The amount of fruit shipped indicates in a manner the horticultural wealth of the county. There are in the vicinity about 3,200 acres of trees and vines now in bearing. Of this area about 1,000 acres are in French prunes, about 1,000 acres in vines, the remaining 1,200 acres being of various varieties. The fruit raised in this section takes on a richness of flavor which is always noticeable. It is firm in texture, also, and its keeping qualities, therefore, pronounced. In the season, about two carloads of green fruit are shipped daily. The brush is being cleared from the northern side of the canyon, and the land planted to vines. When these come into bearing the output of the vicinity will be very materially increased.

SOILS AND SPRINGS. The body of the soil consists largely of disintegrated sandstone and clay, and has the appearance, particularly on the hilltops, of the "white ash" soil of the Fresno raisin district. It is rich in plant food, and never lacks moisture, as the rainfall in this section is always sufficient for all needs. Springs emerge from the mountain sides in numerous places, some of which are mineral, and from every steep ravine rushes a sparkling stream. The atmosphere is always cool, influenced as it is by breezes from the coast.

THE FLOW OF NATURAL GAS. Wrights Station has a resource which may yet prove to be of great importance. When the great tunnel was being driven through the mountain by the railway company a strong flow of natural gas was encountered, and an explosion followed, which resulted in the death of thirty-two Chinamen. The main leak was subsequently stopped, but gas still escapes in small quantities. The extent of the supply is unknown, but is probably great enough to warrant development.

GRAND SCENERY AND PICTURESQUE HOMES. The scenery is everywhere beautiful, and within the past few years people in search of sites for homes have climbed the mountain sides, searched out the springs, and made winding roads around the knolls, up the canyons, and to the very summits. The brush has in many places been cut away, and trees and vines cover knolls and hillsides White houses stand on projecting points far above deep canyons, or nestle in groves of trees on the benches.

GENERAL VIEW OF WRIGHTS STATION.

MORGAN HILL AND SAN MARTIN.

Localities Where May be Found a Fertile Soil, Mild Climate, Good Water, Adjacent Market, Cheap Communication, Schools, Churches, and Other Advantages.

MORGAN HILL is one of the youngest towns in the county, but it is one of the brightest and most enterprising. It is situated in the midst of a beautiful grove of oaks, and there are many beautiful sites for homes, both in the valley and on the eminences. A wooded hill rises several hundred feet above and within a few blocks of the center of the city. This will undoubtedly be entirely occupied within a few years by residences, as it affords extended views of the valley, north, east and south. Great groves of oaks dot the plain, and wheat fields stretch away in the open. The many new orchards that have been planted within the past two years look like spots on a checker-board, and rows of vines converge in the distance as they reach up onto the hillsides.

The growth of Morgan Hill dates from about three years ago, when the great land grants in the vicinity were subdivided and placed on the market. Most of the land in the northern part of the valley is now held in small tracts, and the opportunity presented to purchase unimproved land for orchard purposes brought into the vicinity many families. Thus Morgan Hill grew rapidly.

HOW THE NAME ORIGINATED. This tract of land was included in the rancho formerly owned by Daniel Murphy. He willed it to one of his daughters, Diana Murphy, who subsequently married Morgan Hill. The grant was then sold to C. H. Phillips and designated the Morgan Hill Rancho, and a town sprung up, which was named Morgan Hill. It is now a thriving village of about 250 inhabitants, with a depot, postoffice, telephone station, express office, two hotels, a restaurant, three stores, a livery stable, lumber yard, and several small shops, with a number of very comfortable

GENERAL VIEW OF MORGAN HILL.

residences. It will soon be the principal town between San Jose and Gilroy.

CHURCHES AND SCHOOLS. The Methodists have erected a very comfortable church building, and services are held regularly by the pastor, Rev. S. E. Crowe. The Baptists have just completed a very neat building also, and their pastor is Rev. W. V. Gray.

A school house, one of the most beautiful, architecturally, in the county, was erected last year at a cost of about $4,000. There is at present but one teacher, Miss Carrie Wooster.

IMPROVEMENTS AND INSTITUTIONS. Within the past year a number of houses have been erected, including, besides several residences, the Home Union Store, the Baptist Church, a restaurant, a public hall and the Morgan Hill Sun building.

The town is supplied with a system of water works, owned by L. M. Hale, the water being piped to all parts of the town from springs in the mountains several miles northeast.

Unimproved orchard land in the vicinity is being sold for from $100 to $125 per acre. The fruit trees planted within the past few years seem very thrifty. Corn is largely planted between the rows, with a view of securing an income until the trees come into bearing. The soil of the foothills east and west of the valley is choice vine land, and at suitable elevations, when water can be supplied, oranges thrive.

THE MORGAN HILL SUN. Morgan Hill has a weekly newspaper, now three years old, which has performed good service in making known to the people of the East the beauties and resources of

MORGAN HILL

Street Scene, showing Groves of Oaks.   S. P. R. R. Depot.   Public School House.
Methodist Church.   Baptist Church.

Morgan Hill and the valley in which it is located. Mr. Edes came from South Dakota, and never wearies of telling about the sun-kissed land where blizzards never come, and flowers bloom every month in the year.

SAN MARTIN AND ITS SURROUNDINGS. Land generally acquires value in proportion to its money-earning capacity. In cities this is usually determined by the location of the land. In the country it more largely depends upon the adaptability of the soil for the growing of valuable crops; but it is influenced to some extent by its location in regard to markets. The productive power of the land is in turn made available in direct ratio as the climate is favorable or unfavorable. One of the most important factors in estimating land values—its value as a site for a home—is often overlooked. The ideal conditions include a fertile soil, a mild climate, the presence of schools and churches, means of cheap and rapid communication, and an adjacent market. If the surroundings are such as to make the location attractive as a site for a home, and the soil will produce crops sufficiently renumerative to insure the possession of all the comforts of home and some of the luxuries of life, the conditions are as near perfect as are likely to be found in any portion of the world. There are many locations in Santa Clara County where such conditions exist, and the result is being made evident in the rapid increase of the value of land.

VALUES REAL AND STATED. Inasmuch as the value of land does not depend entirely upon what it now produces, but rather upon what it may be made to produce, it is evident that there is very little land in the county but what is worth much more than the figure at which it is held. A peculiar fact concerning land in the Santa Clara Valley is, that it is always worth more than the price which even sanguine men place upon it. Its full possibilities have not yet been demonstrated. Each year new crops are introduced, the adaptability of certain soils to certain crops is demonstrated, and as the horticultural possibilities are brought to light, values are increased accordingly.

WHAT MIGHT HAVE BEEN. It is a common thing to hear old residents of California remark that they knew Fresno County when it was a sheep pasture, and a poor one at that, and that if they had only known that it would eventually be the great raisin center they could have acquired great wealth. Likewise Pomona, Ontario and Riverside soil was classed as desert land, and is now known as choicest orange

THE TOWN OF SAN MARTIN, ONE YEAR OLD.

land. The Santa Clara Valley was used many years as pasture land for cattle, and it is now known as the Garden Spot of California. There are many men now living here who have witnessed the transformation, and there is not one of them who could not have acquired great wealth by the investment in land of comparatively small sums.

THE SIGNS OF THE TIMES. Another strange fact is, that many now refuse to read the signs of the times, just as they did in the past. In the past, development progressed slowly, primarily because there was no means of communication with the business centers of the East except by ox-team. Then New York was within six months of San Francisco. Now it is within six days. Then we obtained most of our supplies from the East. Now the East obtains many of its supplies from California. Methods of communication are constantly increasing, and California is rapidly becoming the Mecca of all who seek health, climate, and opportunities for profitable investment. The population, and therefore land values, will necessarily increase in a progressive ratio.

THE LARGE GRANTS SUBDIVIDED. Most of the land in Santa Clara Valley has been divided and sold in small lots. The price at which land may be obtained, therefore, varies with the ideas of owners, and there is often a wide difference in the price of two lots of land which are in every particular similar. The only instances in which prices are uniform are those in which land is offered by those who have purchased large grants, and are offering it for sale in small lots. Most of these grants have been sold. Among the few which remain are the great San Martin and Morgan Hill ranches, in the southern part of the valley, comprising about 19,000 acres. Most of it is suitable for fruit-raising, and is situated on the line of the Southern Pacific railroad, between San Jose and Gilroy. Upon one tract is situated the town of Morgan Hill, and upon the other the town of San Martin. Hundreds of acres have been purchased and planted to fruit trees during the past year, and within a few years it will be one of the most important orchard districts in the county. The proprietor of the tracts, which are being offered in lots of five, ten, and twenty acres, is C. H. Phillips, and the manager of the office in San Jose is T. S. Montgomery. The land is being sold at from $100 to $125 per acre, with terms of payment which enables buyers to pay much of the purchase price from the profits earned from crops, a condition to be appreciated by men of moderate means.

SCENES ON THE SAN MARTIN RANCH—NEAR MORGAN HILL.

SARGENTS STATION.

The Great Picnic Resort on the Pajaro, and its Attractions. Hunting, Boating and Fishing. Stock-Raising Farming and Cheese-making. Brea Deposits and Mineral Springs.

SARGENTS is most beautifully located in a grove of oaks, upon the banks of the softly-flowing Pajaro. It is a place of much natural beauty, as the banks of the river are covered with alders and willows, and the scenery along the river is charming. The hotel has been surrounded with ornamental trees, and the grounds are provided with platforms and rural seats. It has thus become a prominent picnic resort, merry parties gathering there in the summer season from every direction. Bicycle and other clubs often hold annual meetings here, of which barbecues are usual features.

THE HUNTER'S PARADISE. It is also a great gathering point for hunters, parties from San Francisco, San Jose and other points meeting here for annual outings. The wooded canyons are full of quail and pigeons, and deer are yet quite plentiful in the adjacent mountains. Wildcats, coons and coyotes are plentiful, as well as smaller game. The river teems with catfish and other varieties, and salmon comes up the river from the ocean in the spawning season.

ENTERPRISES AND RESOURCES. The village is comparatively small, containing only a depot, express office, postoffice, a hotel, kept by Alexander Graham, and a livery stable. Yet there is considerable travel, and it is the shipping point for an extensive territory. There are a number of large dairies in the vicinity, and cheese forms one of the principal exports. There are several large cattle ranges in the vicinity, notably those of Henry Miller and J. P. Sargent. Considerable grain is shipped from Sargents, and at times the shipments of brea are important. The brea deposits on the farm of J. P. Sargent, three miles from the station, are extensive. The demand for asphaltum for street paving will no doubt result in the upbuilding here of an important enterprise. Sargents is the shipping point for San Juan and the contiguous territory in

SCENE ON PAJARO RIVER, NEAR SARGENTS.

San Benito county. Much travel centers here, as the only bridge which spans the Pajaro for many miles is located here.

LEGENDS AND LECTURES. A stage runs between Sargents and San Juan, making several trips a day. It is driven by the veteran Mark Reagan, who was one of the drivers on the old overland in early days, and who has been driving here seventeen years. He has an inexhaustible store of legends concerning the people who lived here in territorial days, and tells them in a remarkably entertaining manner. One of the features of a trip to the Mission at San Juan is the historical and descriptive lecture given by the gifted Reagan.

THOROUGHBRED HORSES AND CATTLE. Some very fine stock is owned in the vicinity. Upon the Sargent farm there is a fine herd of Durhams, and included in the Sargent string of horses is the Nutwood stallion Sevenoaks, whose sire was sold for $23,000; also Jim Mulvaney, with a record of 2:19¼. Mr. Sargent also has some fancy-bred Berkshire and Poland hogs. Four miles from Sargents Station, upon land belonging to Mr. Sargent, is a white sulphur spring, which is largely resorted to in summer by camping parties. It is a very attractive resort, in a deep, wooded canyon, where the scenery is uplifting.

The Pajaro is the dividing line between Santa Clara and San Benito Counties, and is spanned at Sargents by a handsome bridge. The river at this point flows very gently, and the overhanging trees and windings of the river make the river scenery very beautiful. The river can be navigated with row boats a distance of two miles below the station, and this feature is an attractive one to the campers. Fish are usually very plentiful, as the stream flows into the ocean, and the supply of certain varieties is

SCENES AT SARGENTS STATION.

The Grove at Sargent's Residence.

In the Picnic Grounds.

In front of Sargent's Station Hotel.

Hon. J. P. Sargent and Family at the Old Homestead.

inexhaustible. There is more game in the vicinity than in any other portion of the county that is easily accessible, and parties frequently come from a distance to hunt coyotes, kill quail, deer, and other game, larger and smaller. The Pajaro River is fed by Carnadero Creek, San Benito, the Uvas and Llagas, and empties into the bay of Monterey at a point near the town of Watsonville.

PRODUCTS AND SHIPMENTS. The shipments from Sargents consist principally of hay, grain, fruit, cheese, butter and eggs. The shipments for the year ending July 1, 1895, were: Hay, 1,302,500 pounds; grain, 852,300; fruit, 809,200; cheese, 139,200; butter, 93,900; eggs, 77,400; poultry, 24,500; and miscellaneous, 136,600, making a total of 3,435,300 pounds.

SARGENT'S JURISTAC RANCHO. One of the largest stock ranges in the county is that known as the Juristac Rancho, consisting of about 10,000 acres, and located in the extreme southwestern portion of the county. The proprietor, Hon. J. P. Sargent, is widely known, as he came to California in 1849. In that year in company with three brothers he established a store in Weavertown, El Dorado County. In 1850 they commenced to purchase stock, and in 1851 closed out their store and turned their attention to stock-raising. In 1853 Mr. Sargent came to Santa Clara County, and in 1850 purchased the Juristac Rancho, where he has since resided. He has retired from active business life, having placed the management of his interests in the hands of his sons. Upon his range he keeps about 1,200 head of graded cattle. He has always been an ardent admirer of good stock, and as early as 1862 purchased some Durham or Shorthorn cattle with which to improve his herds. He purchased some finely-bred horses, also, and now owns Seven Oaks and Jim Mulvaney, the record of the latter being 2:19¼. He owns also some fine Berkshire and Poland China hogs. Mr. Sargent's sons inherit their father's love for stock in a marked degree. In addition to other animals, James Sargent owns some thoroughbred fox terriers, which were awarded the first prize at the Los Angeles bench show, and second prize in San Francisco.

James Sargent carries on a dairy, where about 206 head of cows are milked. The output of the cheese factory is about seventeen flats a day,

A BULL'S HEAD BREAKFAST—SAINT CLAIRE CLUB.

of twenty-five pounds each. J. P. Sargent was elected by the Republicans in 1872 to represent his district in the Legislature. During the past few years he has lived very quietly upon his farm, enjoying the fortune which he years ago accumulated. Mr. Sargent married, November 4, 1864, Miss Agnes Bowie, of San Juan, and they have five children—James, Ross, Agnes, Ida and Ouida. Recently bereavement came upon them and death took from them their son, Ross, a most estimable young man.

CATTLE ON RANGES. There are within Santa Clara County, according to the annual report of L. A. Spitzer, County Assessor, 25,097 head of cattle. The ranges are nearly all located in the Mount Hamilton range of mountains in the eastern portion of the county. Following is a list of a few of the stock-owners, with the number of cattle owned and running on ranges within the county: C. M. Weber estate, 1200; Robert F. Morrow, 2,000; Charles F. McDermott, 1,200; Joseph Grant, 600; Thomas E. Snell, 400; David Williams & Bros., 500; DeForest & Bowman, 400; Frank Hubbard, 800; F. A. Hyde, 1,500; H. W. Coe and Charles Coe, 500; Mahoney Bros., 350; Harry Dowdy & Sons, 600; Horace Wilson, 800; J. P. Sargent, 1,200; Henry Miller, 3,000; Williams, 400; C. Beverson, 500; J. Rogge, 150; Henry Manser, 150; Frank Hubbard, 650; J. A. Green, 1,250. David Murphy, O. D. Arnold, E. Thomas, Fenley Bros., George Smith, John Corcoran, J. R. Parker, Mrs. Corcoran, and Cole Bros. also own cattle.

FACTS FROM THE RANGES. Cattle in Santa Clara County vary in price according to the kind of season experienced upon the ranges in Oregon and Nevada. If the winter there has been a disastrous one, it causes an advance in the price of beef cattle. On the other hand, if the rainfall is deficient upon the ranges in the southern part of California, prices are likely to be low, as in such cases owners in the south are compelled to throw their stock on the market without regard to the demand. Last fall, cattle sold here as low as from $11 to $14 per head. In Santa Barbara County yearling steers were bought for $10 per head and shipped to Santa Clara County at a cost of freight of $1.80 per head. Average two-year-old steers here are now worth $14 per head. The price of cattle is increasing, as the area available for pasture is each year decreasing.

A Group of Vaqueros
Branding the Mavericks.

RODEO SCENES ON THE GREAT J. P. SARGENT CATTLE RANGE.
Throwing a Steer,

A Corner in the Cattle Corral.
Marking the Mavericks.

THE GREAT PINE RIDGE SECTION.

Vast Stock Ranges Where Cattle Gain Their Own Livelihood Throughout the Year. The Pine Forests and Healthful Climate. Coe Brothers' Range and the Noted Soda Spring.

ONE of the grandest districts in the county, and one concerning which the public at large knows very little, is that which lies along the summit of the Coast Range of mountains on the eastern boundary of the county. The higher mountain land is used almost exclusively as range for stock, and is seldom visited except by hunters and stockmen. A great proportion of the area consists of steep and rocky canyons and brushy hillsides, suitable only for pasturage purposes, but there are many sections where orchards and vineyards thrive and fruit acquires an excellent flavor.

THE GREAT PINE FORESTS. Of this vast mountain territory Pine Ridge is one of the most attractive sections. Here is a grand forest of the magnificent long-leafed southern pine—the only one on the Pacific Coast. These stately trees grow over a hundred feet high, scattering themselves in picturesque irregularity from rivulet to mountain top, and covering the table like summit—nearly 3,000 feet above the level of the sea. Scientists tell us that 2,200 feet is about the correct altitude for weak lungs. Pine Ridge is far above the fog line, and here asthmatics may rest and breathe air that is not only absolutely free from deleterious substances, but is pervaded with the ever present essence of the pine—which, though sometimes imperceptible to the senses, has a definite medicinal effect to check or destroy the germs of disease in the lungs.

THE MILD WINTER WEATHER. Pine Ridge is comparatively free from frost. The tomato, one of the tenderest of all vegetables, grows and bears often as late as the 1st of January. Robins and wild pigeons driven from the Sierra Nevada by the storms of winter, come here to wait until spring removes the snow from their summer home. Snow seldom falls here, and does not usually remain on the ground longer than a day at Coe Brothers' Camp, 2760 feet above the level of the sea, though it often falls on Mount Hamilton, at an elevation of 4,250 feet, as early as the 1st of November.

The scenery on Pine Ridge is superb. The snow-capped Sierra and Mount Whitney—the highest mountain in the United States—mingle their magnificence with the sunrise above the valleys. The view of the setting sun, incorporating much of the Santa Clara Valley, with its thousands o semi-tropic orchard homes spread out below, is a marvel of poetry the pen cannot describe, and of beauty no artists can portray. To appreciate the wildness and grandeur of the surroundings one needs to see Pine Ridge in sunshine and shadow. It is beautiful when the fog is in the valley and the sun shines on the mountain top. It is grand when the murmur of the pines enters into sympathy with the storm which rages without, and the pine-log roars and crackles in the old fashioned fireplace within.

FAUNA AND FLORA. The native grasses include wild oats, alfilaria, bunch grass and burr clover. Grass does not decay here in summer as it does in the East where it is subjected to winter rains, but cures into hay as it stands, and in most places on the mountain ranges is from six inches to a foot and a half high when the first winter rains come.

The hills are covered with scattering pines, black oak, white oak, madrone, manzanita, silver-leafed maple, chaparral, jamisel and deer brush. The whole region is well watered, springs breaking forth from the hillsides even to within less than a hundred feet of the summit, never more than half a mile apart, insuring plenty of water for stock. In every valley there is a trout stream, and the woods are full of deer, wild cats, coons, coyotes, quail and pigeons. Coe Brothers employ upon their range one of the most noted riders of the West—D. B. Gruwell—whose feats of horsemanship are a revelation to all except those who ride the ranges.

PINE RIDGE MINERAL SPRING. Upon Coe Brothers' range there is a valuable mineral spring, the water of which contains lithia, iron, magnesia and various carbonates and sulphates, and is highly charged with carbonic acid gas. The water is mildly aperient and diuretic, and is a very delicious drink. It is similar to carbonated water from other springs, except that the large percentage of lithia makes it especially useful in affections of the kidney and for rheumatism. It is a very valuable natural medical water, and the local firms which deal in mineral water will no doubt purchase the right to sell it.

VIEW ON M. M. CAHALAN'S FARM.

VIEWS FROM THE GREAT PINE RIDGE SECTION.

Twin Lakes, on C. M. Weber's Range.

Cow Boys—Coe Brothers' Corral.

A Glimpse of the Great Pines, Pine Ridge.

A View of San Felipe Valley.

Above the Clouds, on Pine Ridge—Coe Brothers' Range.

A Cow Boys' Mid-day Camp.

THE PORT OF ALVISO.

ALVISO is the county's greatest port, and is destined to become a great shipping center. Situated at the head of navigation on Steamboat Slough, in the center of one of the richest garden districts in the world, but three miles from the Bay of San Francisco, and within eight miles of San Jose, its growing importance as a shipping point impresses the most casual observer. San Francisco is less than thirty-five miles distant by water, and but forty by rail and ferry. Thus even the most perishable fruit may be shipped at small cost, and reaches San Francisco in the freshest possible condition.

EXTENSIVE BRICK WAREHOUSES. Alviso is noted for its shipping facilities and the volume of business transacted in that line, rather than for its size. It contains, however, besides stores and hotels, a number of very large brick warehouses, used principally for the storing of hay, of which from 5,000 to 8,000 tons are shipped annually. The hay is hauled from the valley and foothills, about one-third of the crop being shipped during the harvest season, the remainder being stored.

HARBOR SCENE, PORT ALVISO.

FRUITS AND BERRIES. The peculiar nature of the soil makes it suitable for the growth of a large list of products, and it cannot be said that any one of the plants to the growth of which the soil is adapted grows better than another. The conditions elsewhere, however, cause the demand to be greater for one product than another, and the perishable nature of berries gives Alviso a great advantage over more distant points. More than one-half of the strawberries consumed in San Francisco are grown in the vicinity of Alviso. The varieties usually grown are the Longworth and the Sharpless. The price received varies from $2.50 to $6.00 per chest, and the profit from $75 to $500 per acre.

THE PROFITABLE APPLE. Apples do not acquire the flavor nor possess the keeping qualities which characterize those grown in the mountains, but attain a greater size, and as the market is near, they are grown very profitably. The crops are larger than are usually obtained elsewhere. Fred Burrell secures from 500 to 1,300 boxes per acre, and receives from 50 c. to $1.00 per box.

FERTILITY OF THE SOIL. The soil in the vicinity is a heavy, black loam, formed of silt brought down from the mountains by the Guadalupe river and Coyote Creek, and peat formed by the decomposition of vegetable matter. This makes one of the richest combinations possible, and seems inexhaustible. It is one of the best in the world for vegetables, berries and small fruits, and it is safe to say that in the years to come the Alviso district will be one of the most noted berry-growing sections in the United States. It is not improbable that this will also be the principal vegetable district for supplying San Francisco, as the rich soil, cheap freights, and artesian water plainly indicate.

PROFITS OF PEAR CULTURE. Pears thrive also in an unusual manner, and are generally profitable. They seem to assimilate any unusual amount of moisture in the soil to better advantage than most other fruit trees. The price of pears varies more than the price of some other fruits, however, and for this reason they are not always highly profitable. The residents of the vicinity are fond of telling how Charles Ogier rented for three years a tract of land containing 130 acres upon which was a large pear orchard, and cleared enough money within that time to purchase a $25,000 farm. It was an exceptional instance, as the crops are not always as large or the price so great. A Bartlett pear orchard is generally profitable.

THE ASPARAGUS FIELDS. This bottom land is the very best for asparagus, and more than two-thirds of the amount consumed in San Francisco is grown at Alviso. The crop varies from seventy-five to a hundred and twenty-five fifty-pounds boxes per acre. The price ranges from 75 cents to $3 per box, and the gross income is from $37.50 to $225 per acre.

THE YIELD OF TOMATOES. Tomatoes are almost twice as profitable here as in the East, as the season is twice as long, the fruit is twice as large, and the output per acre more than twice as great. The average wholesale price is about 20 cents per box of fifty pounds. The largest contracts last year were made on a basis of 38 cents per hundred. The crop averages about 400 boxes per acre per annum. The land is rich and tomatoes are usually grown between rows of fruit trees, thus utilizing the land to the fullest extent.

RASPBERRIES AND BLACKBERRIES. Raspberries and blackberries are grown extensively as they are at home in the silty, peaty soil of the low lands, and bear prodigious crops. Raspberries usually sell for from $5 to $8 per chest of 100 pounds. The income ranges from $175 to $500 per acre.

Alfalfa, grain and nearly all fruits and vegetables grow thriftily. Sugar beets are now being grown to some extent, as the refinery at Alvarado is but fourteen miles distant. The price per ton ranges from 4.50 to $5, and the product per acre from twenty to forty tons.

THE LUMBER PORT. Alviso is a great lumber port, nearly all of the lumber which is used south of this point being brought direct from the great lumber regions of Mendocino and Humboldt direct to Alviso by sailing vessels. From 6,000,000 to 17,000,000 feet of lumber are landed at the Alviso wharves annually.

SCHOOLS, CHURCHES, ETC. Alviso has three stores, an hotel, and the usual number of shops. The public school has an average attendance of about forty. The principal is James Carson, and

Miss Selina Burston is in charge of the primary department. There is a neat Methodist Church, in which Rev. C. G. Milnes holds services every alternate Sabbath.

RIVER AND RAIL. In addition to the three trains per day each way connecting with San Francisco and San Jose, a steamer plies between Alviso and San Francisco daily. Freight per ton is $1.00, while the fare is 50 cents. The freight on berries and small fruits is 22½ cents per chest. A stage connects with the steamer, the fare from Alviso to San Jose being 25 cents. San Francisco capitalists are now securing rights of way for another broad-gauge road from Alviso to San Jose, which will connect with another line of steamers which will ply between Alviso and San Francisco. The steamer Alviso leaves Alviso every evening at 7:30 o'clock for San Francisco, and returning, leaves Washington street wharf in the latter city at 10 o'clock in the forenoon.

THE OYSTER BEDS. Along the edge of the bay a few miles northwest of Alviso the Morgan Oyster Company has extensive oyster beds. Fresh oysters are put up in cans and packed in ice. They are thus shipped to all parts of the West. The business has in the past few years reached vast proportions, and the demand is still increasing. Natural clam beds exist also along the shores, and many men find employment in gathering and selling them. Another industry has sprung up within the past few years which has already assumed importance. The Morgan Company raise Eastern oysters almost exclusively, and these are protected; the bay is full of small California oysters, however, and upon these the sturgeon, stingarees and other fish prey to such an extent that thousands of tons of rejected shells are annually washed up on the shores. The shells are composed principally of lime, which is in great demand as shell-forming food for poultry. The shells are shoveled into sacks and shipped to all portions of the State. The wholesaler receives 15 cents per sack of 60 pounds.

Artesian wells can be obtained anywhere in Alviso and vicinity at depths ranging from 240 to 400 feet.

A GLIMPSE OF ALVISO.

SOME OF THE SMALLER TOWNS.

Villages and Hamlets in the Valley and Mountains. Important Shipping Points, Trading Centers and Future Cities. Berryessa, Lawrence, Lexington, West Side, Rucker and Madrone.

HERE are within the county several villages which, while they do not call for extended notice, warrant mention. Among them are the following :

Berryessa is a small village about four miles northeast of San Jose. It is in the center of a rich fruit region, and consists of school-house, church, store, blacksmith shop, and a number of residences. There is also a postoffice and telephone office, and in the vicinity are a number of fruit drying plants, besides the J. H. Flickinger Company cannery. The pastor of the M. E. Church is Rev. H. C. Langley; the teachers of the public school are Annie Bose, Maggie Munn and Gertie Abel; the postmaster is N. Bacoch. J. W. Shaw conducts a general merchandise store and acts as assistant postmaster.

Lawrence Station is on the Southern Pacific railroad, about seven miles northeast of San Jose. There is nothing at the station except the depot and a hay and grain warehouse, but near at hand there is a Presby-

SHAW'S STORE AT BERRYESSA.

terian Church, a Methodist Church, and a schoolhouse. The land in the vicinity is very rich, the artesian well district commencing but a short distance north. The postmaster, express agent and agent of the Southern Pacific Company is Arthur F. Purdy.

Lexington is situated on the narrow gauge in the canyon about three miles south of Los Gatos. When lumbering was the main industry in the Santa Cruz Mountains, Lexington was a thriving village. The road from Los Gatos to Santa Cruz was at that time a toll-road, and the gate keeper resided in Lexington. R. S. Swain conducted a hotel and a man named Josephs had a store. When the railroad was built business naturally went to Alma, where a postoffice was established. There is still in Lexington, however, a hotel, a livery stable and a blacksmith shop.

THE VILLAGE OF WEST SIDE.

West Side is a small village among the vineyards and orchards on the west side of the valley, about eight miles from San Jose. It contains a general merchandise store, a town hall, a church, a blacksmith shop, postoffice, cooper shop and telephone office. The postmaster is Alexander Montgomery. Rev. William Windsor is pastor of the M. E. Church, and the Collins District school, a short distance from the village, is taught by Miss T. E. Wheeler.

In 1893 the great Dunne ranch was thrown on the market, in small subdivisions, which found ready purchasers. To this circumstance the town of Rucker owes its existence. It is situated three miles from Gilroy and the surrounding land is very fertile. In and near the town are one hundred farmers who have places of from five to seventy-five acres. The dryer of the Santa Cruz Fruit Company is located here, besides which is a store, blacksmith shop, etc. A new $5,000 school house was erected last year. The postmaster is S. C. Richter.

Madrone is a station on the Southern Pacific Railroad, about eighteen miles south of San Jose, where there is a hotel, store, depot and blacksmith shop. Grain growing and stock-raising are the principal industries, though much of the land is suitable for fruit-growing, and with irrigation would be very productive. The Postmaster, Express Agent and Agent for the Southern Pacific Company is L. J. Pinard, who is also proprietor of the hotel.

Evergreen is situated about eight miles southeast of San Jose, near the foothills. Here is located the Women's Relief Corps Home for the care of the dependent widows and children of veterans—the only institution of the kind in the United States. There is also a postoffice, store, butcher shop, blacksmith shop, church, and public school. Rev. C. G. Milnes is pastor of the M. E. Church, James E. Preston, the principal, and Mamie F. Chew and Bessie G. Wyman teachers in the public school. The postmaster is Francis J. Smith, and the Matron of the W. R. C. Home, Mrs. Bayington.

Coyote Station is on the Southern Pacific Railroad, twelve miles southeast of San

THE RUCKER SCHOOL HOUSE.

WOMEN'S RELIEF CORPS HOME AT EVERGREEN.

Jose. Near here is the great Laguna Seca, or lake, from which water is to be taken for the extensive system of irrigating canals now being constructed through the orchard districts by the Citizens' Water Company.

The sum of $111,600 was paid for the 526 acres of land including the lake, and vast sums are now being expended for canals and impounding dams. The postmaster is Emil F. Heple; and the teachers in the public school are Mrs. Stella Harding and Miss Minnie Nikirk.

Gubserville is a postoffice and stage station on the road between Santa Clara and Saratoga about five miles from Santa Clara and seven from San Jose. A handsome two-story school house has been erected near within the past year, and a short distance north of it there is a Methodist Church. Gubserville has also a manufactory of agricultural implements. The Postmaster is Frank Gubser.

Agnews is a station on the line of the narrow gauge railroad between Santa Clara and Alviso. At this point is located the Agnews Insane Asylum. The business houses consist of a hotel, blacksmith shop, etc. It is in the center of the strawberry district and large quantities of this fruit are shipped from here.

At one time Guadalupe was a thriving village. This was when the Guadalupe quicksilver mines were in operation. These mines were and are yet rich, but litigation over land titles compelled the suspension of operations a number of years ago and the village became deserted. At some time work will probably be resumed and old-time prosperity be revived. Guadalupe is situated four miles southeast of Los Gatos.

Besides at the towns enumerated herein additional postoffices have been established in the country at points where no village exists. These postoffices are named as follows: Bell's Station, College Park, De Forest, Frohm, Gilroy Hot Springs, Hillsdale, Kensington, Mount Hamilton, Patchen, San Felipe, Stanford University.

The incorporated cities of the county are San Jose, Santa Clara, Gilroy, Los Gatos and Palo Alto.

AS AN EDUCATIONAL CENTER.

The Many Magnificent Institutions in Santa Clara County which are Devoted to Educational Interests. One of the Grandest in the World. Schools, Public and Private.

NOTHING more certainly indicates the intellectual status of a community than the interest of its citizens in educational matters. The centers of education are centers of art, refinement and progress. San Jose was the first town estab- in the State, and here was opened very early in the century a public school. The prestige gained by age and location made the city an important commercial center, and educational facilities more than kept pace with its growth commercially. In 1851 the University of the Pacific was established, and in the same year the Santa Clara College. The common school system was organized in 1853, and since then the development of institutions of learning has been marvelous.

COLLEGES AND UNIVERSITIES. Santa Clara County now contains not only one of the grandest and most richly endowed universities in the world, the Stanford, but a number of other institutions of magnificent proportions and great scope. Among the number may be mentioned the State Normal, the University of the Pacific, the College of Notre Dame, Santa Clara College, Academy of Our Lady of Angels, St. Joseph's College, the San Jose Business College, the Garden City Business College, the Wash-

THE CAMPBELL PUBLIC SCHOOL

burn School, the San Jose Institute and the San Jose Academy. Santa Clara County's educational institutions have attracted world-wide attention, and in the lists of scholars nearly every prominent country on the globe is represented.

DESCRIPTIVE AND STATISTICAL. There are within Santa Clara County eighty-six school districts, and 13,738 children between 5 and 17 years of age. Total number of children in the county under 17 years of age, 18,649. There are 154 primary schools, 104 grammar schools, and 4 high schools, making 262 public schools. The number of months in which school is maintained varies from 6 to 10½ months, and

average 9.65 months. The percentage of women among those employed as teachers is remarkable. Within the county there are 280 teachers in the public schools, 32 of whom are males and 248 are females. In the city of Jose there are 99 teachers in the public schools, 10 being males and 89 females. Another noticeable fact is, that of the teachers in the public schools, two-thirds of the number are graduates of the California State Normal School. During the fiscal year ending June 30, 1896, five school houses have been erected, making the total number of public school houses in the county ninety-one.

The total value of public school property in the county is $563,377. The county assessment roll of taxable property amounts to $56,512,650. The rate of taxation for school purposes is 15 cents per $100. The amount received during the fiscal year for the support of public schools was $107,619.64.

There are within the county 14 private schools, and the number of scholars attending private schools, 2,685. Number of teachers in private schools, 203. Total number of teachers employed in public and private schools, 483.

SALARIES AND RECEIPTS. The average wages per month paid to male teachers in primary and grammar grades, $87.12; in high schools, $158. Average wages per month paid to female teachers in primary and grammar grades, $65.35; in high schools, $110.

The total receipts for the support of public schools in the city of San Jose during the fiscal year was $112,004.26. Total valuation of public school property in San Jose, $300,000. Number of primary schools, 47; number of high schools, 1. Average monthly wages paid to male teachers in primary and grammar grades, in San Jose, $75; in high schools, $190; average monthly wages paid to females in primary and grammar grades, $75; in high schools, $114. Total number of teachers in San Jose public schools, 99; number who are graduates of the California State Normal School, 71.

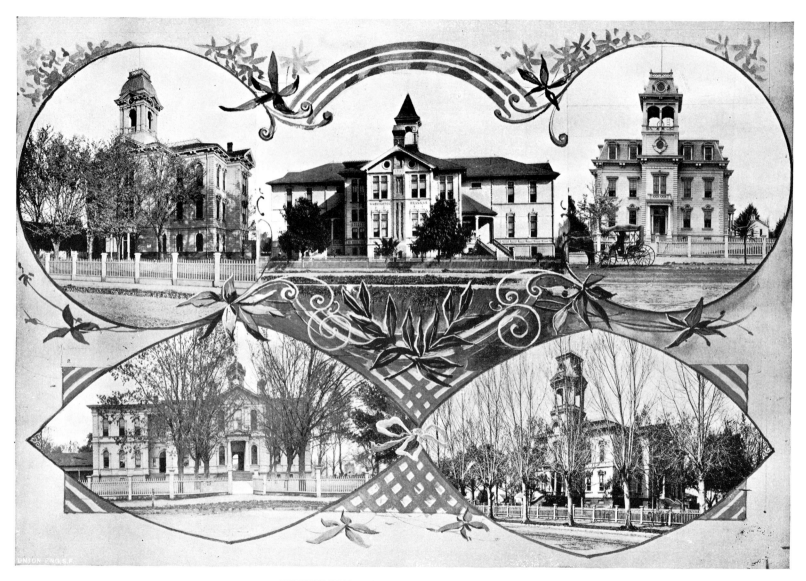

Longfellow School.

Lowell School.

REPRESENTATIVE SAN JOSE SCHOOL HOUSES

Washington Grammar School

Horace Mann Grammar School.

Grant School.

School census children in San Jose, not including East San Jose, College Park, The Willows, or other suburbs, 4,733. The County Superintendent of Schools is L. J. Chipman. The members of the County Board of Education are: President, Cornelia M. Farley; Secretary, L. J. Chipman; Elmer E. Brownell, W. W. Pettit and H. M. Bland.

THE STATE NORMAL SCHOOL.

In its particular line the State Normal School at San Jose is beyond question one of the best, and as to faculty and equipment is probably not excelled anywhere.

It presents to scholars who seek to become teachers opportunities almost unapproachable. The building, which cost 148,936, is situated in the center of the city. The annex, or training department, cost $45,000, and was built in 1893. The training department is one of the most practical and useful features, and one in which the principal, Prof. C. W. Childs, takes especial interest, as it was secured principally through his efforts. He first visited nearly all the Normal School buildings in the United States in search of knowledge concerning the advantages presented by each, and then drew plans incorporating all the valuable features noted. As a result a model building was secured.

A library of several thousand volumes is accessible, besides the ordinary reference books found in well-equipped schools. The museum is a workshop. Regular instruction is given to classes by the Curator, Mrs. A. E. Bush, in the preparing and labeling of specimens for study with the microscope. Other features of especial interest

THE STATE NORMAL SCHOOL, SAN JOSE.

are: the training room, well supplied with wood and iron working machinery; the clay modeling room, the chemical and the physical laboratories. The regular attendants of the Normal number 625, and of the training department 275, making a total of 900.

The present principal of the State Normal School at San Jose is Charles W. Childs, who has held the office since 1889. He has been a teacher in the Normal School for eighteen years and has filled almost every position in the school, from teacher of drawing in the junior class up to and including the office of Vice principal and Principal. He was born in 1844, in Genesee,

New York, and in 1860 graduated at the Wauwatosa High School, Wisconsin. At the outbreak of the Rebellion he served a short time in the army, and subsequently came to California, and began his life work teaching a public school at Cold Springs, El Dorado county. Though not at that time of age, he achieved marked success at the very commencement of his career as

PROF. CHILDS.

teacher. After teaching several years he entered the State Normal School and graduated in 1867. Finally he took a course in a commercial college in San Francisco, and thus equipped returned to his work, assuming the principalship of the High School at Suisun, which position he held eight years. He served as County Superintendent of Schools of Solano county for two successive terms, and as a sequence of the reputation gained by his capable administration at the close of his term of office was elected to the position of teacher in the State Normal School. In 1889 he was elected principal. The principal is a practical, progressive man; to him the Normal School owes its lecture course, its manual training work, its newspaper study, its training school building, and its present progressive influence He is the author of several excellent text-books now in use in the schools of this State. A man having extended experience in teaching and supervision in the schools of the State, he knows its spirit and history.

The Normal School is managed by a Board of Trustees appointed by the Governor; the Governor and Superintendent of Public Instruction being ex-officio members.

REPRESENTATIVE SANTA CLARA COUNTY COUNTRY SCHOOL HOUSES

Valley View School.

The Hamilton School.

Julian School.

The Lincoln School.

The Collins School.

The San Tomas School.

LELAND STANFORD UNIVERSITY.

LELAND STANFORD

THE LARGE number of institutions of learning located in Santa Clara County has caused it to become known far and wide as the educational center of the West. Each of these presents advantages which attract students, according to opportunities offered for certain lines of study. The most noted is the great Leland Stanford University, located near Palo Alto. This was presented to the people by Senator Stanford and wife, who, for the purpose of endowing it executed a grant conveying to the trustees the estates known as the Palo Alto farm in Santa Clara County, the Gridley farm in Butte County, and the Vina farm in Tehama County.

The Palo Alto property was the Senator's country home, and is one of the finest private properties in the United States It lies along the Southern Pacific Railroad, between Menlo Park and Mayfield, and contains 7,200 acres. The parks, gardens, orchards and vineyards which surround the mansion occupy 300 acres. The University buildings and lawns occupy a similar area, and the remainder is used as a stock farm. It is the most complete establishment of the kind in the State, and here have been sired many of the fastest horses in the world.

The Gridley farm contains 22,000 acres and is one of California's great wheat farms.

The Vina property, which is the largest of the three estates contains 59,000 acres. It cost the Senator, it is stated, $1,000,000. After it came into his possession he planted upon it 3,000,000 vines, making it by far the largest vineyard in the world. These three estates contain in the aggregate 88,200 acres. Upon all of them there are costly buildings and improvements. At the time the grant was made the estimated value of the Palo Alto farm was $1,200,000, the Gridley farm $1,600,000 and the Vina property $2,500,000. In addition to the real estate there were cash benefits and endowments, money for the erection of buildings, libraries and equipments, making the total value of the gift at that time about $12,000,000 and the land has since increased greatly in value. Such munificence is unparalleled in history. Since that time the death of Senator Stanford occurred. By the terms of his will the University is to receive $2,500,000 in cash. This bequest is not yet available, as the estate has not been distributed.

The University comprises a series of buildings grouped around a quadrangle 586 feet long and 246 feet wide. The enclosed space is laid with bituminous pavement except where the soil has been devoted to the growth of tropical plants and flowers. Opening from the arcade are the various

A GLIMPSE OF STANFORD UNIVERSITY FROM THE HILLS

class rooms, laboratories, draughting rooms, and rooms for scientific investigation and instruction.

The dormitories are east and west of the quadrangle. Encina Hall, for young men, is at the east, and occupies a ground area of 312x150 feet. It is four stories high, decorated with end arcades, a central arched porch, and mosaic work. It is provided with electric lights, hot and cold water, steam heat, suitable furniture, bath rooms on each floor, and has accommo-

THE LELAND STANFORD UNIVERSITY

Roble Hall, the Ladies' Dormitory.

The Stanford Museum.

The East Entrance to the Quadrangle.

Encina Hall, the Boys' Dormitory.

dations for 315 students. Roble Hall, for young women, is west. It is of concrete, about one-third the size of Encina Hall and accommodates 100 students. Higher up on the terrace and southeast of the University buildings proper are the residences of the professors, at present thirty in number. These houses are of modern architecture, elegantly furnished, and occupy a commanding location. The museum is north of the main buildings, and is 313x156 feet including wings. In the rear of the main buildings the mechanical laboratories, workshops, power houses, etc., are located. There are numerous other buildings also, such as gymnasiums, etc. The architecture of all the buildings is Moorish, and is based upon that of the old missions founded in California by the Franciscan Fathers. The main structures are built of Santa Clara County brown stone, obtained at the quarries south of San Jose. The roofs are of red tiles, which give a warm tone that is very cheerful and attractive. The University is thirty-four miles from San Francisco and seventeen from San Jose. The number of students last year was 1,100. This semester there will be a few over 1,200.

The faculty of Stanford University comprises of some of the most noted instructors the world has produced. David Starr Jordan, who has a world wide reputation as an educator and writer, is President of this institution.

THE SANTA CLARA COLLEGE. The Santa Clara College is the pioneer college of California. It was founded by the Fathers of the Society of Jesus, March 19, 1851, and on April 28th, 1855, was chartered with all the rights and privileges of a university. From the first it has steadily grown, adding new buildings, until now there are several large structures, besides others of less importance, enclosed in a quadrangle of nearly ten acres, laid out in lawns, flower gardens, vineyard, orchard and play grounds.

The college is in reality a combination of three schools—one for boarders, one for day scholars, and a preparatory department, and offers three courses of study—one leading to the degree of A. B., one to the degree of B. S., and a Commercial Course.

Aside from the usual features common to all colleges, this college is remarkable for its completeness of equipment in several special departments. The physical laboratory is almost unrivalled in the United States. There

GLIMPSE OF A CORRIDOR, STANFORD UNVERSITY.

is a collection of more than 450 instruments and machines, electrical, mechanical, optical and astronomical, as well as all others necessary for the demonstration of the laws of heat, light, sound and electricity. The cabinet of paleontology, the chemical laboratory and the museum, are all equipped with everything that can aid the student in his research for knowledge.

There are nine sectional libraries, devoted to the needs of special departments, and a main library which contains 12,000 volumes, many of which are very rare, some being nearly four centuries old. There are a number of societies devoted to the cultivation of oratory and debate, and an auditorium. This has a very large stage, and will seat 2,000 persons, and is remarkable for its acoustic properties.

The corps of professors and teachers is highly efficient, and numbers over thirty. The average yearly attendance is about 200, while the number who have received their Bachelor's degree from the college is about two hundred and fifty.

Among the alumni of Santa Clara College may be found many distinguished names—names of men who have reached eminence in the profession of law, medicine, engineering and in scientific pursuits; names of men who have been honored in politics and have been, or who are now, Senators, Members of Congress, Judges and officials of State. The record made by this college as a factor in educating the people of the great State of California is an enviable one and the institution is one to which Californians point with pride.

ANNUAL EXPENDITURE PER SCHOLAR. The average annual expenditure in the United States for each scholar attending public school is $17.62; the average annual expenditure in the north Central States is $19.96; in the north Atlantic States, $23.65; in the south Atlantic States, $8.25; in the South Central States, $7.59; in Santa Clara County, Cal., $26.07.

RATIO OF SCHOOL POPULATION. The ratio of school population (children between the ages of 5 and 17 years), to the total population in the United States as a whole is 29.61 per cent. The average monthly salary paid to male teachers in the United States is $44.89 per month, and for female teachers $36.65 per month; while in California the average for male teachers is $80.70 per month, and for female teachers $66.20.

The Great Swimming Pool, Supplied by an Artesian Well.

Scientific Department Building.

SCENES AT THE SANTA CLARA COLLEGE.

An Aged Date Palm.

The Teachers' Residence and Old Mission Church.

A Glimpse of the Garden.

UNIVERSITY OF THE PACIFIC.

A Pioneer Institution of Higher Learning, comprising the San Jose College and Conservatory of Music at College Park, and Napa College, at Napa.

THE University of the Pacific had its beginning in a school which was opened by Rev. Edward Bannister in 1851 in San Jose, at the corner of San Fernando and Second streets, in a building which was afterwards used as the Court House, and was known later as the "What Cheer House." In the same year a charter was granted locating the institution at Santa Clara, under the name of the California Wesleyan College. In the following year the name was changed by an Act of the Legislature to the University of the Pacific. Two buildings were erected in Santa Clara, a three-story brick structure, for the gentlemen's college, and a frame building for the Collegiate Institute for females.

In 1866 two tracts of land lying about half way between San Jose and Santa Clara, and containing about 432 acres, were purchased by the trustees of the University at a cost of about $72,000. A portion of this land was set apart for the University campus, the remainder being divided into lots, which were put on the market.

The first building on the new grounds, now known as West Hall, was erected during the presidency of Rev. T. H. Sinex, D. D., and was ready for occupation early in 1871. Under President A. S. Gibbons the Ladies' Hall was built. In the administration of Rev. C. C. Stratton, D. D., three new buildings were added, the commodious brick edifice known as East Hall, Central Hall, and the Jacks-Goodall Astronomical Observatory. Under President C. Hirst, D. D., the Conservatory of Music, a superb structure, containing a spacious auditorium and numerous other rooms, was erected, the Ladies' Conservatory Association having assumed the responsibility of defraying one-half of the entire cost. The building was inaugurated with a grand concert during commencement week in 1890.

CONSERVATORY OF MUSIC, UNIVERSITY OF THE PACIFIC.

The Napa Collegiate Institute, at Napa, California, was incorporated in 1871, and in 1886 it was re-incorporated as Napa College. In September, 1894, the California Conference of the Methodist Episcopal Church, which had held control of these institutions from their incipiency, authorized the consolidation of the University of the Pacific with Napa College, and it was later decided by the trustees, that these united institutions should be jointly known as the University of the Pacific. Rev. F. F. Jewell, D. D., was elected Chancellor, and Rev. J. N. Beard, D. D., President. As reorganized the University comprises three institutions: San Jose College, at College Park, Cal.; Napa College, at Napa, Cal., and the Conservatory of Music, at College Park. Each of these has a separate Dean and Faculty. Prof. M. S. Cross is Dean of the San Jose College, and Leon Driver is Dean of the Conservatory of Music.

During the 44 years of its existence the University of the Pacific has graduated about four hundred students. The facilities of the institution have increased and improved from time to time, and now its museums, libraries, astronomical observatories, and chemical and physiological laboratories, together with its beautiful grounds and commodious buildings, afford excellent advantages for the education of young people of both sexes, under Christian influences. At both colleges four regular courses of study are offered, classical, philosophical, literary and scientific, leading to corresponding baccalaureate degrees. Both have academic departments, with courses which prepare for the regular college courses, and both provide superior instruction in art, music, elocution and oratory, and in commercial branches. The Conservatory of Music is also equipped for the most thorough study of music, both vocal and instrumental.

West Hall.

Conservatory of Music.

SAN JOSE COLLEGE–UNIVERSITY OF THE PACIFIC.

East Hall.

Ladies' Dormitory

COLLEGE OF NOTRE DAME.

The Great Educational Institution where so many of our Young Ladies have Graduated. The System of Teaching Objectively. The Department of Music and the Janko Keyboard.

ONE of the grandest of the many grand educational institutions which are situated in Santa Clara County is the College of Notre Dame, which was founded in 1851, by Sister Mary Cornelia, of the Order of Notre Dame, members of which Order have labored on the Pacific coast during the past fifty years. It is remarkably complete as regards equipment, each department being supplied with the latest and most practical aids to education. Most all principles are illustrated objectively, and in this way the pupil gains a practical knowledge that could not otherwise be obtained.

The buildings are situated upon a plot containing about ten acres, enclosed by a high brick wall, near the business center of the city. They are all large, well lighted and ventilated, and arranged so as to facilitate communication and insure seclusion for scholars in each department. As it is one of the oldest colleges in the State it has graduates all over the coast, and is so well known as an institution offering exceptional advantages, that pupils are sent not only from this and adjoining States, but from Mexico, Central America, and elsewhere.

There are several features of the college worthy of special mention. The physical laboratory is unusually complete, and contains many expensive instruments not usually found in educational institutions. The natural history cabinets are also both extensive and costly, being supplied with many rare ethnological, geological, paleontological and entomological specimens. Notre Dame is supplied with a full set of Trouvelot's reproductions of astronomical photographs, which are very useful adjuncts in the teaching of astronomy; and there are numerous maps and charts in every department.

This college is divided into three departments. The primary is devoted almost exclusively to day pupils. The academic and collegiate courses include both day pupils and boarders. In addition to the regular curriculum there are departments in which music, drawing, painting and other useful and ornamental branches are taught, notably plain and fancy needlework, embroidery, Irish point lace, and artificial and wax flower making.

Music is taught in all its branches, and for this the college is well equipped, both as to instruments and teachers. Lessons are given on the piano, harp, guitar, mandolin, violin, banjo and zither, and there are twenty-three separate music rooms, in each of which there is a piano. An improvement of great merit in the musical line, the Janko piano keyboard, has recently been introduced, this being the only one now owned by any educational institution in the West. There are six rows of keys, arranged in a step-like manner, so that the same note may be struck in whichever line is the handiest. This gives great compass of execution. The eminent advantages are the stretching of cords and the resulting combinations. Chromatic glissandos and glissandos in thirds and other intervals can be played, and extended chords of orchestral grandeur are within the reach of one performer which could formerly only be encompassed by two. Runs become as dainty and rippling as if played on the harp, and legato effects, which are impossible on the old keyboard, can be produced with ease. The peculiarity of being able to produce the same tone in three different places gives the performer far greater freedom and convenience of action.

Connected with the college is a large and beautiful chapel, handsomely finished and furnished, where scholars and teachers gather daily for worship. While mental and moral training is attended to, no less care is bestowed upon physical culture. The assembly hall of the institution, a spacious and beautiful structure in Corinthian style of architecture, offers

THE SAN JOSE NOTRE DAME INSTITUTE—A HOME FOR ORPHANS.

COLLEGE OF NOTRE DAME, SAN JOSE, CALIFORNIA.

Front View of Main Entrance.

A Glimpse of the Grounds.

Notre Dame College from the East.

West Wing of College, Showing rear of Chapel.

Notre Dame Hall.

ages for the calisthenic classes regularly trained during the scholastic year. Though not yet a century old, the Institute of Notre Dame educates annually upwards of one hundred and fifty thousand pupils, has fifty-four flourishing schools on the European continent, twenty-one in England and Scotland, and forty in the United States. The most important of the Notre Dame English schools is the Government Liverpool Normal College, where thousands of teachers are ably fitted to assume the responsible duties of their sacred charge, so far-reaching and uplifting in its influence for good, on the sadly neglected masses of the down-trodden children of the poor. The latest branch of Notre Dame is a foundation in Congo, Africa, where the Sisters are already doing good work among the natives.

COOPER KINDERGARTEN, SAN JOSE.

SAINT JOSEPH'S COLLEGE.

SAINT JOSEPH'S COLLEGE. This College was established in 1850. It is conducted by the Fathers of the Society of Jesus in charge of St. Joseph's Church and is intended for day scholars only. The building is a handsome three-story structure on San Fernando street, and was erected in 1891-2. It has accommodation for 200 pupils and the demand for desks is frequently in excess of the supply. Three distinct departments are maintained in the College, the preparatory, commercial and classical, each being in charge of a separate corps of professors and instructors. The preparatory department has two divisions, one to prepare the young pupil for the commercial course, and the other to prepare him for the classical. The commercial course aims to give the student a thorough business education, which comprehends mathematics, English, history and the special branches of penmanship, bookkeeping, stenography, etc. The classical course is designed to furnish a broad and liberal education of a University character, and embraces higher mathematics, language, history, literature, the principles of the Christian Doctrine—in a word, an ample and advanced education.

Rev. Father D. J. Mahoney, S. J., is President of the College, and takes active charge of all departments. To his executive ability is due the high standing and efficiency of the institution.

SANTA CLARA COUNTY SCHOOLHOUSES.

The Lincoln Grammar School, San Jose.

Peabody Kindergarten, San Jose.

Second Street Kindergarten, San Jose.

The Alameda School.

The Moreland School.

THE LICK OBSERVATORY.

The Great White Dome on the Summit of Mount Hamilton.   Lick's Gift to the People.   The Noted Road and the Magnificent View of the Valley.

THE fame of the great Lick Observatory on Mount Hamilton is now world-wide, and thousands of people visit it annually, each one of whom assists in heralding to the world the delights of the trip and the

JAMES LICK.

intense interest which attaches to the Observatory and its unique attractions. The trip from beginning to end is calculated to create impressions that will be stamped indelibly upon the mind.

The observatory is twenty-eight miles from San Jose by stage road and thirteen miles in an air line. It is one of the grandest roads in the State—wide, and of easy grade. It leads eastward from San Jose on the Alum Rock road five miles to the foothills, along a wide avenue, bordered a distance of several miles on either side with rows of eucalyptus and cypress trees; thence winding up and over foothills graceful with undulating vineyards and rows of fruit trees that converge and diverge, crowning knolls and reaching far up onto the mountains.

The road bends into ravines and rounds jutting points, ever rising, the view growing constantly grander and more extended. The valley begins to appear like a map, each orchard with its rows of trees distinctly out-

THE LICK OBSERVATORY IN WINTER—ALTITUDE, 4,209 FEET.

lined; white houses everywhere dotting the plain. Then around hillsides where black oaks and mountain laurel bend over the road, and wild flowers bloom in profusion amid luxurious grasses that everywhere cover the hills, the ravines and the roadside. Hall's Valley, rich with grainfields, and rolling hills covered with green oaks greet the view, making a picture of great beauty. Over another range and Smith's Creek is reached, where the hungry traveler finds a good hotel and a good meal awaiting him. The excellence of the water is noted by all, and the ranch butter and thick cream are remembered ever after.

The mountain climb really commences here, the road zig-zagging up the hill with hundreds of curves in order to insure a lighter grade. As one rounds the turn a glimpse of the observatory is caught, apparently just above, yet it can only be reached by a long, round-about climb. Hidden from view one moment, it seems to stand out more boldly as the stage rounds the next jutting point. The view rapidly broadens until the summit is reached. Here the scene is indescribably grand—a poem without words. The great Bay of San Francisco stretches away to the north, while the Santa Clara Valley is spread out like a map from Palo Alto on the north to Sargents on the south. Across the valley the Santa Cruz Range with its blue mountains uprears against the ocean, its redwood forests fringing against the western sky. Through a gap in the Coast Range to the east the Sierra Nevada may be seen, snow-capped and dim in the distance, overhung with the fleecy clouds which characterize that region in summer. Lower down may be seen upon clear days a wide stretch of the great San Joaquin Valley. Nearer, the pine-clad hills are deep, steep canyons, where the buzzards soar on tireless wing above abysses awful in their grandeur. The Observatory was given to the world by James Lick, who left an estate of $3,000,000, nearly all of which was devoted to public

148

THE GREAT LICK OBSERVATORY.

A Glimpse of the Moon.

The Observatory in Winter.

The Summit in Summer.

The Eye End of the Thirty-six Inch Equatorial.

The Great Telescope and its Mountings.

uses, $700,000 being given to provide for the construction of the largest telescope in the world and its installation on Mount Hamilton. The whole cost of the establishment was $610,000. The remaining $90,000 is invested as an endowment fund. The interest upon this is insufficient for the support of the Observatory, and the deficiency is made up by annual appropriations from the income of the California State University. Congress originally granted as a site for the Observatory 1,350 acres. Other tracts have since been purchased by the State and by private parties, making the total area of the reservation 2,581 acres. The road to the summit of Mount Hamilton was built by the county at a cost of $78,000.

The Observatory consists of a main building containing computing rooms, library and the domes of the 36-inch equatorial and the 12-inch equatorial, and detached buildings for the meridian circle, the transit, the horizontal photo-heliograph, the portable equatorial and the Crocker photographic telescope. On the grounds are dwelling houses for the astronomers, students and employes, and shops for the workmen. The Observatory is fully provided with instruments, the most important of which are the 36-inch equatorial, the Crossley reflector, the 12-inch equatorial, the 6½ inch meridian circle, the Bruce spectroscope, a 4-inch transit, a 4-inch comet-seeker, a 5-inch horizontal photo-heliograph, and the Crocker photographic telescope. There are, besides many minor pieces of astronomical, physical, meteorological and photographic apparatus, including spectroscopes, seismometers, photometers, micrometers, clocks, chronographs, etc.

Students who are graduates of the University of California or any college of like standing are received at the Lick Observatory to pursue a higher course of instruction in astronomy. Quarters are assigned to them at Mount Hamilton, and in return they are required to execute such computations as may be assigned to them. They must furnish their own text-books, food, etc., but no fees or charges of any sort for instruction are required from students in the University.

The Observatory buildings are open during office hours every day in the year. The various instruments can be seen at any time during office hours when not in use, and when the work of the Observatory will allow; they are also at the disposition of visitors from 7 to 10 o'clock on Saturday evenings. This gives freer access than is allowed to any other observatory

in the world. The uniform courtesy and attention extended to visitors by the Professors here is the subject of wide comment. Those visitors who come in the daytime are personally conducted through the various buildings and the uses of the instruments are explained to them. On Saturday evenings each visitor is shown the most interesting celestial objects through the 36-inch and 12-inch equatorials. Some of the professors are usually present, and no pains are spared by them to make these visits pleasant and profitable. Lectures are given by the astronomers at different times and places, and all specially interesting observations and discoveries are described in the magazines and the daily press. In these and other ways the Observatory is made directly useful to the public, and it is an important factor in the intellectual advancement of the nation.

It is impossible to describe in detail the scientific work which has been and is being carried on. Much of it is of a technical nature and uninteresting to the general public. It may be said in a general way that ten new comets, a great number of double stars, and Jupiter's fifth satellite were discovered here. The photographs of solar eclipses have put a new face on the constitution of the solar corona, and the photographs of sunspots awaken the most intense interest. The photographs of the moon's surface, taken at short intervals during its entire age, are the most interesting and satisfactory that have ever been taken. By enlarging the photographs the mountains and their shadows, with the tremendous craters that scar the surface, can be seen with great detail, and the heights of the mountains can be determined with nicety. With the great Lick Telescope any object upon the moon 200 feet high can be seen.

STAGE STATION, HALL'S VALLEY, MOUNT HAMILTON ROAD.

The altitude of the various points along the road between San Jose and the Observatory is as follows: Broad-gauge depot at San Jose, 88 7 feet, Junction House, 399 feet; Grand View House, 1,500 feet; summit between Hall's Valley and Grand View, 1,838 feet; Hall's Valley, 1,543.5 feet; Smith Creek Hotel, 2,146.2 feet; marble floor of the Lick Observatory, 4,209.46 feet; top of the cover of the Kepler reservoir, 4,246.20 feet.

The astronomers engaged at the Lick Observatory are: Prof. E. S. Holden, Director; Prof. J. M. Schaeberle, Prof. W. W. Campbell, Prof. Allen L. Colton, Prof. R. H. Tucker, Jr., William J. Hussey and D. G. Aitken. Secretary, Chas. D. Perrine.

TROPICAL PLANTS AND FLOWERS. The immense acreage of land throughout the county which is now planted to fruit-producing trees has given rise to an extensive and profitable nursery business, in which a large number of men are given occupation. In addition to the mere growing of trees for planting, however, the esthetic natures of the people which leads them to ornament and beautify their grounds with tropical plants, shrubs and flowers, has resulted in the establishment of gardens and hot houses where tender plants and tropical flowers are grown exclusively.

THE DEMAND FOR CUT FLOWERS. In California the trade in fresh cut flowers is an extensive one. Flowers grow here so freely and luxuriantly that all may indulge in their possession. They are largely used for the decoration of dining tables and parlors. At the flower stands in San Jose may be seen choice flowers in profusion every day in the year. Many of these are grown in the Bourguignon gardens.

SCRAPS OF HISTORY. The first census or enumeration of which we have any knowledge regarding San Jose was taken in 1631. At that time there were at the pueblo 166 men, 145 women, 103 boys, and 110 girls, a total of 524. There were 4,443 head of cattle, 2,386 head of horses, and 134 mules. The average price of a mule or saddle horse at that time was $10; an ox or a cow, $5; a sheep, $2. Cattle were raised only for their hides and tallow. Grain was sold to the Russian Fur Company. The market price was $2.25 per bushel.

The word "vara" is frequently heard in connection with Santa Clara County land measurements. It is a Spanish unit of measurement, and is equal to 33.38676 inches.

The first telegraph line between San Jose and San Francisco was built in 1853.

The railroad from San Francisco to San Jose was built in 1863.

ORCHARD, NURSERY

In 1882, Emile Bourguignon, realizing the demand for this class of nursery products, located on Moorpark Avenue, about half a mile south of the San Jose narrow-gauge depot, and made arrangements to supply all the demand called for.

GARDENS AND HOT HOUSES. On three acres of ground are nine large hot-houses, in which the tender young shoots are matured sufficiently to allow of outdoor cultivation. Upon the ground not occupied by the hot-house is grown nearly all varieties of tropical plants, shrubs and flowers. A specialty is made of growing rare roses and carnations, of which the nursery contains a great many species. Hot houses in the Santa Clara Valley, it may be stated, are made more for the purpose of protecting the delicate leaves of plants from winds, than a protection from cold. Frame buildings made of open lattice work are often used in summer, and glass houses in winter.

AND HOT-HOUSES.

THE HOTEL VENDOME.

The Great Summer and Winter Resort which is Visited Annually by Thousands of Tourists, and its Commercial Value to the City and County. Its Beautiful and Park-like Grounds.

THE degree of eminence attained by a locality depends primarily upon its resources, and their intelligent utilization. The importance which some enterprises bear to a city and its growth, however, often escapes notice. Occasions have arisen in the history of nearly every city when many of its most important commercial institutions have been tided over seasons of financial depression and threatened disaster by banks and bankers, and business interests thereby greatly advanced and conserved. Yet we often fail to extend to them the consideration to which their importance entitles them.

In other and scarcely less important ways a magnificent hotel often largely shapes the destiny of the city in which it is located. Men of wealth and leisure demand the elegance and luxury which can only be furnished by hotels of great size and cost. Such men are often attracted to a city by the superior advantages offered by such an establishment, and subsequently invest large sums in the community which first commended itself to them through the air of refinement, elegance and wealth reflected by the hotel. As a principle, it may be stated that while a good hotel may exist where there is no city, a good city can scarcely exist where there is no hotel.

The citizens of San Jose early recognized the necessity for providing proper hotel accommodations, and our hostleries have kept pace with the growth of the city. The new era which came in with the horticultural development of the county called for the establishment of something far in advance of anything previously attempted, and the demand found realization and expression in the construction of the Hotel Vendome. The building was projected upon such a magnificent plan, and the specifications were so carefully executed that the completed structure is an ornament to the city, an evidence of unusual enterprise, and an object of world-wide fame. In grace of architecture, beauty of location, and magnificence of appointments, it has no superior on the Coast. It was built at a cost of $285,000.

By reason of its beautiful grounds, its accessibility, its location and surroundings, it has attracted the class of tourists which, while being exacting, appreciates the best, and will pay liberally for first-class entertainment. The Raymond & Whitcomb Company at once made arrangements to bring their wealthiest patrons to the Vendome, as did Thomas Cook & Son. The Golden Gate Tours, under the management of the Pennsylvania Central, also include the Vendome in their itinerary. The wealthier class of those who travel independently, likewise make the Vendome their headquarters.

HOTEL VENDOME PARK.

The building is four stories high, of the Queen Anne style of architecture, presenting a handsome and imposing appearance. Wide verandas furnish opportunity for the out-door existence which our climate invites. Broad and richly carpeted halls, one of which is three hundred feet in length, terminate on wide verandas. Every room has sunlight, and each is connected with the other in such a way that suites of rooms may be had in great number and variety of arrangement. The furnishings are rich and expensive, and the whole building presents an air of quiet, home-like elegance that is attractive in the extreme. In every department arrangements have been made with a view of securing convenience. An Otis elevator furnishes easy and quick communication between the various floors. The stairways are broad, and everywhere are parlors, closets, and every needed appliance for pleasure, for comfort, and for safety.

One of the most charming features of the Vendome is its sun-parlor, which crowns the building. It commands an extended panoramic view of the valley, and the mountains beyond, which travelers say is seldom equaled.

The classical music which is furnished by the Vendome quartette, is an attractive feature, each musician being a specialist in his line. Concerts, for which a printed programme is furnished, are given every evening during the dinner hour, and later on the veranda. The table is supplied with everything the market affords, and no other market affords the variety which may be secured in this, the Garden City of the State.

The manager, Mr. Geo. P. Snell, has, by reason of his energetic and liberal policy, greatly forwarded the interests of the city.

HOTEL VENDOME, SAN JOSE, CALIFORNIA.

SAN JOSE AS A MUSICAL CENTER.

A Musical Atmosphere, the Influence of Which is as Wide as the West. The Advantages Presented for the Acquirement of a Classical Education.

F. LOUI KING.

PEOPLE of wealth, refinement and education are naturally attracted to those communities in which there is an atmosphere of art and culture congenial to thier tastes and where the greatest facilities are offered for the acquirement of a complete classical education by their children. To this fact San Jose owes much of its prosperity, music as a science having here been elevated to a standard hitherto unknown in the history of the West. Pupils are sent not only from Oregon, Washington, Idaho, Nevada, Arizona and Colorado, but from many other States west of the Mississippi, while a number of wealthy people have disposed of their interests elsewhere in order that members of the family might, to the fullest extent, enjoy the privileges here presented.

This condition was foreshadowed by the great teacher and composer F. Loui King, when years ago he said: "I am convinced that at San Jose or at Stanford University there is a possibility of building up the greatest musical center in America, if not in the world; a center that in a few years can be made not less illustrious than Bayreuth, and that will attract to this valley the best artists and the most ardent students of music of all nations. To effect this we have the climate, the location, the cultured community, the native talent, and all the elements out of which a musical center must be made. There needs nothing to realize the result but the money and

the men." No one was better qualified to express such an opinion than F. Loui King, as he had, fifteen years previously, come to take charge of the musical department of the University of the Pacific, where he set the standard of musical culture high, educated the people up to it, and raised the musical department to a distinct branch of the University work. As Dean of the Conservatory, therefore, where under his guidance pupils had been trained that were subsequently accepted by the greatest masters in Europe, he was well advised as to the conditions which would naturally lead to the predicted result.

At the time he made the prophecy, Prof. King had been called to take charge of the Conservatory of Music connected with the University of Oregon, and doubtless failed to realize that he was to be so largely instrumental in bringing about the result which he had so clearly foreseen. Our best citizens, however, realized the necessity for furthering the musical interests of the city, and inaugurated a movement which subsequently resulted in the return of F. Loui King, and the establishment in our city of a grand Conservatory of Music, with appropriate buildings, and the great master and composer as its Dean.

Around such a master it is but natural that others should gather, such as Earl Brown the Professor of Voice Culture, who studied under the best masters in Italy, France and Germany, and has a certificate from Signor Lamperti; John Haraden Pratt, Fellow of the American College of Musicians, who has a certificate from the Leipzig Conservatory; Hermann Brandt, the great violinist; Frederick S. Gutterson and others. San Jose, therefore, offers advantages in the musical world which are exceptional. Its musical atmosphere, also, attracts to our city the best solo artists. We have as a result, been enabled to enjoy the performances of the masters of music.

A series of piano recitals have been given also at the Conservatory by F. Loui King and his pupils, embracing some of the best works of the old classical and modern composers, executed with such a degree of artistic finish that they have been sources of both pleasure and profit.

THE KING CONSERVATORY OF MUSIC.

INTERIOR VIEWS OF THE KING CONSERVATORY OF MUSIC.

Theorg Room.

Glimpse of the Hall and Gallery.

Library.

Prof. King's Study

Vestibule and Concert Hall.

Auditorium.

MANUFACTURING INDUSTRIES.

Santa Clara County as a Producer of a Variety of Finished Products. Large Quantities of Leather, Paper, Woolen Goods and Building Materials Produced Every Year.

THE SPERRY FLOUR COMPANY. The little old brown mill by the brook, with its picturesque water-wheel, and the dusty miller standing in the doorway, is gone. The mill of to-day is a gigantic structure of brick and iron, and stands by the side of the steel tracks that stretch away to the grainfields on one hand, and toward the great deep water port of San Francisco on the other. The old burr stones have been discarded, and the roller process has been substituted. Thus more flour is extracted from the grain, it is better dressed, it is finer and whiter, and the impurities are more carefully removed. A modern and a model mill is that operated by the Sperry Flour Com-

pany, the San Jose manager of which is William G. Alexander. It is this company which manufactures the Drifted Snow Flour. The reputation of this brand has been secured by care and effort to produce the best. The grain is selected with the utmost care, by an experienced judge of the qualities of wheat, who is constantly in the field, buying that which is superior for milling purposes. Much of the grain used comes from King City, Paso Robles and Templeton. The flour is exported in large quantities to Central America, Mexico, Chili, Japan, China and the Sandwich Islands. Ten thousand barrels in one shipment is not an unusual consignment. The Sperry Flour Company also makes a specialty of rolled barley. The barley is thoroughly steamed before it is rolled. The grain is thus cured and sweetened. The steaming process makes it more easily digested, and causes it to be more easily assimilated. The Sperry Flour Company supply only the wholesale trade, and Drifted Snow Flour finds its way into thousands of families where its superior quality is appreciated.

THE SPERRY FLOUR COMPANY MILLS, SAN JOSE.

GLENWOOD LUMBER COMPANY. The Glenwood Lumber Company is one of the corporations posing as a leader in one of the industries not only of Santa Clara Valley, but of the Pacific Coast. It was not brought into existence by idle capital looking for an investment, but by the enterprise of its promoters, who, starting with a small capital, have pushed themselves to the front, backed by the good will and patronage of an appreciative public, which never fails to recognize the true merit of a concern grown from its infancy in their midst, which strives to gain and appreciate their support. They engage in the manufacture of lumber on a large scale, with mills located at Rockport, Mendocino County, where they have the responsibility and interest of the town resting upon them, operating a hotel, store, post office, mill and other business ventures, all of which are tributary to the support of a large area of country. They have their own steamer line running to all coast ports, with principal yards at San Jose and Port of Alviso, the latter place being the wholesale distributing point for Santa Clara Valley and interior places south on the line of the Southern Pacific Railroad, among which is the branch yard of the Glenwood Lumber Company at Morgan Hill, being one of the first business enterprises to locate at that thriving place, which has grown up within five years from a flag station to one of the most thriving towns in Santa Clara Valley. The town was built of Glenwood lumber, to which they refer with pardonable pride. Their principal offices and places of busi-

THE GLENWOOD LUMBER COMPANY'S PLANT.

Glenwood Lumber Company's Steamer.

Planing Mill at San Jose.

Lumber Yard and Wharf at Alviso.

Lumber Yard at San Jose.

ness are in San Jose, at 34 North Third street, and planing mills at San Jose, corner St. James and San Pedro streets. Theirs is the only steam freighting vessel running into the port of Alviso from outside ports, and they can claim for the future the title and the honor of being the pioneers in showing the possibilities of this waterway, which has for a quarter of a century laid dormant amidst a farming population of thousands, and almost within the shadow of San Francisco, the metropolis of the Pacific Coast. They employ upwards of 150 men in saw mills, planing mills, yards and offices, and their interests are so firmly cemented with those of the public that they invite investigation in all their undertakings, knowing that patronage will follow.

PROPRIETOR OF THE EAGLE BREWERY. George Scherrer, proprietor of the Eagle Brewery of San Jose, was born in Alsace, France, April 8, 1832. Early in youth he formed a desire to come to the United States, and as soon as he was 21 he embarked for New York. He resided there until 1858, when he removed to San Francisco. In 1860 he came to San Jose, remaining with his employer, Joseph Hartman, nineteen years, and finally succeeded him in business

H. DREISCHMEYER'S BRICK YARD, SAN JOSE.

He now employs twenty-two men, and occasionally more, none of whom receive less than $60 per month. Mr. Scherrer is an exempt fireman, having served as a volunteer in San Jose Fire Department nine years.

SAN JOSE AGRICULTURAL WORKS. The extensive fruit-growing interest in Santa Clara County creates a demand for implements especially suited to the business, such as low-set wagons that will easily pass under the branches of the fruit trees; special forms of cultivators, etc. The San Jose Agricultural Works is especially prepared for manufacturing implements of this kind.

DREISCHMEYER'S BRICK MANUFACTORY. Henry Dreischmeyer, Jr., owns a brick yard in San Jose, occupying 2 acres of land at the intersection of Thirteenth and William streets. The plant has been in operation six years, having been established by the present owner in 1889. The capacity per annum is 6,000,000 brick, and the output is something over 2,000,000, the daily product being 16,000. A force of twenty-five men is employed. The average depth of the clay beds is twenty feet, so that the supply is practically inexhaustible. The establishment turns

GEORGE SCHERRER'S EAGLE BREWERY, SAN JOSE.

Carriage Repository.

General View from Street.

SAN JOSE AGRICULTURAL WORKS.

Implement Wareroom.

Glimpse of a Workroom.

out common building brick, stock brick, pressed brick, and all kinds of ornamental work. The proprietor, Mr. Dreischmeyer, is but 29 years of age, and was born and raised in this county.

THE LICK PAPER MILLS. In a county where there is so much fruit grown, there is naturally a great demand for paper in which to wrap it for transportation. It was discovered early in the history or transportation that fruit kept better when wrapped in paper than when allowed to come in contact with other fruit. Most of the better quality of fruits that are now shipped green, such as peaches, pears, oranges and apricots, are wrapped in paper, and this is nearly all furnished by the Lick Paper Mill, which is one of the largest paper manufacturing plants on the coast.

The mills were originally built by James Lick, who gave to the world the great Lick Observatory, and were used by him for manufacturing flour. They were eventually purchased and transformed into paper mills. In 1882 the principal buildings were burned, and the present more extensive and commodious buildings were erected. A spur track was also built from the main line at Agnews Station to the mill, for the shipment of the product.

The property is now owned by the Lick Paper Company, the majority of the stock being held by A. D. Remington, who owns the great paper mills at Watertown, New York; and the remainder by J. G. Scott, and other officers of the company.

Over a million pounds of the fruit paper are manufactured per annum, besides thirteen other varieties, such as manilla, red express, gray express, druggists' wrapping papers, etc. The output per month is about two hundred tons, worth about $12,000. About forty men are employed, and the mill runs night and day.

Newspaper is made of wood, such as poplar, spruce or hemlock. Paper for wrapping fruit is made of cotton and wood pulp, red express of burlaps and wood pulp, and druggists' paper of chemical fiber.

The mill is located on the Guadalupe, a stream which flows through San Jose, and into an artificial lake on the Lick property, where the water furnishes part of the power necessary to propel the machinery. In addition to this, there are three steam engines, the entire plant representing an investment of about $500,000. The buildings are three stories in height. The foreman's residence, formerly the private residence of Mr. Lick, was

built with marvelous care and at great cost. The grounds are laid out very handsomely, being ornamented with rows of fan palms and fruit trees, and beds and banks and flowers, which, it is scarcely necessary to state, grow here in great profusion and with remarkable vigor. The property is within the artesian basin, and there are upon the property several artesian wells. These furnish an abundance of water for irrigating orchards, gardens and lawns.

THE SAN JOSE BOX FACTORY. The development of the fruit industry creates a demand for boxes in which to market the product. The requirements called for a box that would be light, strong, and free from any odor that might be imparted to its contents.

These conditions were most completely met by the use of white pine and spruce. The extent to which the business has grown is shown by the fact that A. Lake, of San Jose, who commenced a few years ago to manufacture fruit boxes on a small scale, now uses 1,500,000 feet of lumber per annum. Of this, 1,000,000 feet is spruce, and 500,000 feet white pine.

The style of box and the material from which it is manufactured has much to do with the sale of its contents. Fruit growers early learned that it didn't pay to put first-class fruit in second-class boxes. This season Mr. Lake commenced to manufacture a dovetailed box, of clear, white spruce neatly sandpapered and finished, which at once commended itself as the handsomest and best box offered. The demand for this style as a 25 pound prune box has been so great that the mill, even with an increased force, could not keep up with the orders. The principal packing firms have given orders for a large supply for next season, and the mill is now running to its full capacity.

Apple boxes vary in size from 40 to 50 pounds capacity. They sell in shooks for from 9 to 12 cents; boxes made up, 11 @ 14 cents. Asparagus boxes, 50 pounds capacity, 12 @ 14 cents for shooks, and 14 @ 16 cents for boxes. Blackberry, raspberry and strawberry baskets, $3.50 per thousand. Berry chests, slatted, with twenty-five pound drawers, $1.75. Cherry boxes of 10 pounds capacity, for Eastern shipment, in shooks, 4 @ 5 cents; boxes, 5 @ 6 cents; for local use, shooks, 3 @ 4 cents; boxes, 4 @ 5 cents. Grape boxes for packing purposes, 40 pounds capacity, 10 @ 12 cents; for shipping, capacity 20 pounds, in shooks, 4 @ 5 cents; boxes 5 @ 6 cents.

THE LICK PAPER MILLS AT AGNEWS STATION.

Interior View, Showing Machinery.

Glimpse of the Superintendent's Residence and Grounds.

General View of the Mills.

The Old Mill Dam.

Prune boxes, capacity 25 pounds, in shooks, 5 @ 7 cents; boxes, 6½ @ 8½ cents; dovetailed, 9 @ 11 cents. Tomato boxes, capacity 50 pounds, in shooks, 12 @ 14 cents; boxes, 14 @ 16 cents. The brand is printed on all boxes free of charge, except that the customer furnishes the stencil.

THE EBERHARD TANNERY. One of the largest tanneries in the State is that located at Santa Clara and owned by Jacob Eberhard. It now handles 29,000 hides annually, besides 3,000 calf skins and 100,000 sheep skins. Over 900,000 pounds of leather are shipped annually. Jacob Eberhard, the proprietor, is very popular, having earned the admiration of his employes by his generous treatment of them. He distributes annually among them a share of his profits, besides paying them good wages He frequently gives banquets, also, to his men, and, as a result, his employes, as well as the people at large, feel very friendly toward him.

THE RED STAR LAUNDRY. In this age but few women attempt to do laundry work, the inventor's genius having produced machines that perform work that is far superior to any that can be done by hand. In laundry work, as in other lines, the best results can only be obtained by close attention to the minutest details. The Red Star Laundry, for instance, manufactures its own soap, using only the best refined tallow and pure chemicals. In this way all harmful elements are eliminated and a soap is secured which removes dirt without injuring the fabric.

The garments are first placed in a wooden cylinder containing tepid water, where they are rolled back and forth as the cylinder revolves. There are no paddles or washboards. Hot water and soap are added, fresh water constantly flows in through a central pipe, from whence it is forced through the clothes and passes out through small apertures on the periphery. From this bath the clothes emerge in an hour and twenty minutes, perfectly clean.

The moisture is abstracted from the clothes by placing them in an enclosed iron tub, which is revolved at a high rate of speed by machinery. The rim of the tub contains small openings, and the speed causes the water

THE RED STAR LAUNDRY, SAN JOSE.

to be thrown out. The moisture is in this way much more successfully removed than it could be by hand. Some of the garments are starched and hung up in a steam-heated drying room. Others are passed directly to the mangle, a series of large steam-heated iron cylinders, between which they are passed, under pressure. The heat removes all moisture and the pressure causes the garments to emerge perfectly smooth.

Collars, cuffs and white shirts are ironed by machinery, and the beautiful gloss obtained is the result largely of heat and pressure. Nearly all work is performed by machinery. The care taken with the work and the success achieved in having garments present an immaculate appearance, has given the Red Star Laundry a widespread reputation. Nearly all the laundry work for the 1,200 students and professors at Stanford University is done here, in competition with San Francisco laundries. Work is sent also from Los Gatos, Gilroy, Hollister, Monterey and Santa Cruz and from interior towns as far away as Red Bluff, 247 miles from San Jose. The Red Star Laundry is an incorporation, of which J. B. Leaman is President and Manager. The Foreman is John McGinnis.

AN IMPROVED ROTARY ENGINE. There have been many rotary engines invented, but until a San Jose inventor, A. W. R. Berr, perfected his new engine there have been none which proved to be satisfactory for general work. There were weak points in them somewhere; they could not use steam with economy, they would wear in certain parts and could not be adjusted or they could not stand a continued strain. Mr. Berr has overcome all difficulties and has constructed a piece of machinery that is simplicity itself and is adjustable in all its parts, which are few in number. It is a double-acting engine, the pistons being fulcrumed in the center, the fulcrum block adjustable from the outside of the case, so that the engine need not be taken apart to raise or lower this fulcrum block. The small blocks in the ends of the pistons are self-adjusting, and in case they wear out can be replaced at trifling cost. The pistons working in a rotating drum, the drum forming a steam-tight joint in an eccentric chamber, which is also adjustable, makes this a practically noiseless machine. It uses steam expansively and economically. It can be run at a very high rate of speed and can be built

SANTA CLARA COUNTY MANUFACTORIES.

Jacob Eberhard's Tannery.

The Fredericksburg Brewery.

Western Marble and Granite Yards.

Steiger & Sons' San Jose Pottery.

The Lick Paper Mills.

In the San Jose Woolen Mills.

to reverse instantly. All movable parts being encased, it is perfectly dust proof. It being also adapted as a pump, both engine and pump can be put on the same shaft and thus constructed it makes undoubtedly the simplest and best pump or engine that can be devised for the use of the farmer for irrigating or other purposes. It requires no expensive engineer—any boy or man of ordinary intelligence can run this engine. The weight and space required for these engines are about one-fourth of that of the ordinary piston type. Mr. Berr is the machinist in charge of the San Jose Woolen Mills and his residence is 470 North Third street, San Jose, where he may be addressed by those who may desire more particulars concerning his engine.

THE REMILLARD BRICK COMPANY. One of the largest concerns for the manufacture of brick in the Western States is the Remillard Brick Company. In California they have three establishments for the manufacture of brick, one at Pleasanton with a capacity of 17,000,000 annually, one at San Jose with a capacity of 12,000,000 and one near San Rafael with a capacity of 8,000,000 a year.

SANTA CLARA VALLEY MILL AND LUMBER COMPANY'S YARD, SAN JOSE.

It was in the fall of 1891 that the company purchased the Ashworth place of 173 acres, located on the east bank of the Coyote creek at the termination of Keyes street and just without the corporate limits of the city of San Jose. It was here that after investigation they found an extensive deposit of clay of the highest quality, comprising the entire tract and extending from the surface to a depth of over thirty feet. This gives sufficient raw material to keep the present works running for the next century. In the beginning of 1892 the works were constructed and the most improved machinery was procured and the latest approved methods were adopted for the manufacture of all kinds of brick. The process of manufacture is as follows: By means of a donkey engine the moist clay is dredged and hoisted directly into large cars standing on a railroad track; thence a dummy locomotive hauls the cars a distance of two hundred and fifty yards to the mixing and moulding machines, into which the clay is dumped. The clay needs no special preparation. It contains just the right quantity of sand to make perfect brick. From the moulding machines the "green" brick are spread on the drying ground, and from there they go to the kiln. The kiln is of the "continuous" type, so called because the brick can be burned continually in it, that is, in one portion the green brick are placed in position for burning while in another portion the burning process is completed and the brick are ready to take out. When running to its full capacity the establishment gives employment to 125 men.

The principal office of the company is at Oakland, corner of Second and Clay streets. The San Francisco office is on Berry street near Fifth. P. N. Remillard is President and P. H. Lamoureux is Secretary of the company.

The products of the several establishments of this company are shipped all over the State of California. Besides, at the head office, in Oakland, the company deals in fire brick, cement and other builders' material.

BERR'S IMPROVED ROTARY ENGINE.

THE WORKS OF THE REMILLARD BRICK COMPANY.

The Great Kiln and Drying Grounds.

The Clay Pit.

View of Drying Grounds and Mixing Houses.

OUR FINANCIAL INSTITUTIONS.

The National, Commercial and Savings Banks of the City of San Jose. Bankers Who Are Interested in the Welfare of the City and County.

THE history of financial institutions of San Jose presents a similar and in some ways a more marvelous growth than has marked the progress of other industries in this valley. Less than thirty years ago two men with a capital of $100,000 came down from the mines and engaged in the business of banking. These two men were W. J. Knox (now deceased) and T. E. Beans, now president of the Bank of San Jose. Since that time the number engaged in banking has increased from two to six hundred and sixty-seven, considering, as it is proper to do, that each stockholder in a banking institution is a partner in the business. The capital invested has increased from $100,000 to nearly $2,000,000. In like ratio the amount of deposits has increased from a nominal sum to nearly $4,000,000. And during all of this time no depositor has lost a cent by reason of failures or mismanagement.

COMMERCIAL AND SAVINGS BANK. On each of the four corners formed by the intersection of First and Santa Clara streets, in San Jose, there is a bank. On the northwest corner is the Commercial and Savings Bank. As its name indicates, it transacts a general commercial business and also has a savings department. It was the second banking institution organized in San Jose and was the outgrowth of the firm of McLaughlin & Ryland, private bankers. The firm was in business in 1869 and the bank was incorporated in 1874. Among the first stockholders were C. T. Ryland, E. McLaughlin, B. D. Murphy, M. Malarin and Herman Hoffman. L. Lion, the president of the bank, is a careful, thorough business man, and can tell you just what investments are safe and what are not. James W. Find-

THE HAYES-CHYNOWETH MANSION, NEAR EDEN VALE.

ley is Vice-President, John T. McGeoghegan is Cashier, and Henry Phillips is Secretary. The capital stock paid up is $500,000. The reserve fund is $165,000. The bank is very careful as to its loans and investments and is very particular to see that there is a sufficient margin to amply protect the depositors.

FIRST NATIONAL BANK. On the southwest corner of First and Santa Clara streets is the First National Bank. L. G. Nesmith, the Cashier, has been connected with the bank since its infancy, and knows its history. In July, 1874, the Farmers' National Gold Bank was chartered. It did business under favorable auspices until 1879, when, by the resumption of specie payments the distinction between gold and other forms of currency was abolished. It was then converted into a regular national bank and the name was changed to that which it now bears. Last year it was rechartered for an additional term of twenty years. In order to secure a renewal it had to submit to an examination as to its condition and management. It was proven to be worthy of a long and useful life. The officers of the bank are: President, George M. Bowman; Vice-President, Cyrus Jones; Cashier, L. G. Nesmith. Besides the above-named gentlemen the directors are: W. D. Tisdale, F. Brassy, J. E. Crocket, James D. Phelan and E. C. Flagg—names which are synonymous with honor, business capacity and financial worth. The capital stock, paid up in gold coin, is $500,000; reserve and surplus, $170,273.59; total assets, $957,463.48; deposits, $258,388.69. The comparatively small amount of deposits is due to the fact that it pays no interest on deposits. The business of the bank is conducted in accordance with

SAN JOSE BANKING INSTITUTIONS.

Commercial and Savings Bank.

Union Savings Bank.

The First National Bank and Security Savings Bank.

The Bank of San Jose.

Garden City Bank.

Safe Deposit Bank of Savings.

the laws and regulations of the United States, which are very strict and which are a sufficient guarantee that the interests of the public are adequately protected.

SAFE DEPOSIT BANK. On the southeast corner of First and Santa Clara streets is the San Jose Safe Deposit Bank of Savings. In addition to transacting a general commercial and savings business, it has provided for the accommodation of the public a complete outfit of steel deposit safes, contained in a fire and burglar proof vault. The bank was incorporated in 1885. The president and manager is E. McLaughlin, who has been in the banking business in San Jose for nearly thirty years, first as a member of the banking firm of McLaughlin & Ryland, later as manager of the Commercial and Savings bank, and last in his present position. The Vice-President is E. A. Wilder, and J. E. Auzerais is Cashier. The banks of San Jose always show up well in the reports of the Bank Commissioners, and the Safe Deposit is no exception to the rule. According to the latest report, this bank has a paid-up capital of $300,000 and a reserve fund of $261,971.80. Its total assets aggregate the large sum of $2,410,618 61. The large amount of deposits, viz: $1,827,245.05, indicates that it enjoys a large share of the public confidence. Its administration has been wise and prudent and it is entitled to receive all the confidence bestowed. At the same time its policy has been a liberal one and the interest of both depositors and borrowers have been carefully guarded.

THE BANK OF SAN JOSE. On the northeast corner of First and Santa Clara streets the Bank of San Jose is located. The officers are: President, T. Ellard Beans; Vice-President, William Knox Beans; Cashier, C. T. Park; Assistant Cashier, John T. Colahan.

UNION SAVINGS BANK. On the corner of Fountain and First streets is located the Union Savings Bank. It is a commercial as well as a savings institution and is also supplied with a safe deposit department for the reception of valuables. It is managed by an energetic and progressive set of men. The Board of Directors is composed of

RESIDENCE OF O. A HALE, SAN JOSE.

H. Ward Wright, President; Henry W. Edwards, Vice-President; L. M. Hale, H. C. Morrell, William H. Wright, E. A. Wheeler and T. E. Johnson. Mr. A. Friant is Cashier and F. V. Wright assistant. Considering the fact that it was not incorporated until 1889, it has had a wonderful growth. It has a paid-up capital of $300,000 and a surplus of nearly $50,000. According to its monthly statement made in October, 1895, its total assets were $1,232,491.17. At the same time its deposits were $880,919, an increase since the preceding June of more than $170,000. In its savings department it has over two thousand depositors with an average deposit of $250 to each depositor.

GARDEN CITY BANK. Half a block further south, on the corner of First and San Fernando streets and near the new postoffice building, is situated the Garden City Bank and Trust Company. It is the successor to the Garden City National Bank, which was incorporated in 1887. It did a successful business until 1893, when it was deemed best to convert it from a National to a State bank. At the same time its capital was enlarged from $100,000 to $200,000, which is fully paid up. It has nearly a hundred stockholders, among them being merchants, farmers, fruit growers and professional men. The Directors are: George M. Bowman, C. C. Morse, H. Mabury, A. McDonald, T. S. Montgomery, S. B. Hunkins, J. W. Blauer, J. J. Miller, Uriah Wood, Thomas F. Morrison and Rush McComas. Mr. McComas is the President. E. F. Jordan and A. B. Post occupy the responsible position of Tellers. This financial institution has established itself in the confidence of the public and has acquired a large patronage.

SECURITY SAVINGS BANK. On First street next to the First National Bank is located the Security Savings Bank. It is the youngest of our banking institutions, having been incorporated in July, 1891. It has a paid-up capital of $50,000; reserve, $4,167.73; total assets, $387,773.39, deposits, $326,256.46. There are 1,100 depositors, each with an average deposit of about $300. The officers are: F. Stock, President; L. G. Nesmith, Vice President; Paul P. Austin, Secretary and Manager; Board of Directors, H. Booksin, W. S. Clayton and H. Curtner. Last year this bank divided among its depositors the sum of $13,259.44.

REPRESENTATIVE RESIDENCES OF SAN JOSE.

James A. Clayton

Lawn on James A. Clayton's Grounds.

H. Ward Wright.

C. H. Phillips.

CYCLING INTERESTS.

The Large Number of Wheels Owned in the City and County. Large Clubs and Magnificent Club Rooms. The Cement Track and World's Records.

*S*ANTA CLARA COUNTY offers to wheelmen, attractions seldom found elsewhere, the climate and roads forming a combination which cannot be duplicated anywhere in the East. As regards climate, there are very few days indeed when wheelmen may not ride in comfort except for short periods during the rainy season. Roads aggregating hundreds of miles in extent extend to nearly every section of the county. The system of small farms has resulted in the construction of a netwoak of roads and cross-roads, and all roads in the valley are practically as level as a floor. More than a hundred miles of the main county roads are sprinkled, and there are no heavy stretches of sand. Within the city of San Jose there are miles upon miles of level streets paved with asphaltum, and shaded avenues extend in some cases miles into the country.

The road from San Jose to Gilroy is thirty miles in length, and the grade on an average is but sixteen feet to the mile. which is practically unnoticeable. The greatest elevation is about half way between the two cities, the land sloping gradually each way. A good wheelman, riding leisurely, can reach Gilroy in three hours. Comfortable riding will take one from San Jose to Los Gatos, a distance of nine miles, up a grade aggregating 320 feet, within an hour. San Francisco, fifty five miles by wagon-road, can be reached from San Jose in from four and a half to six hours. Oakland, forty-five miles, is but three and a half or four hours away. Ten miles an hour over any of the Santa Clara Valley roads is a pace easily within the compass of the average wheelman.

LUXURIOUS CLUB APARTMENTS. The interest taken in cycling matters here is widespread. Its influence seems to reach to the uttermost parts of the county and affects all classes of people. The clubs include among their members some of the most prominent citizens. The Garden City Cyclers occupy the entire upper story of a handsome building on San Fernando street, near the center of the city. There is a room for the Directors, a parlor, a billiard room, a reading room, a gymnasium, bath

RESIDENCE OF MRS. MARY MURPHY COLOMBET, SAN JOSE.

rooms, and a wheel room. All of these apartments are large, and most luxuriously furnished. The furniture, carpets, tables and chandeliers cost $2,500. The members occupy fifty-dollar chairs and recline on one hundred-dollar lounges.

CEMENT BICYCLE TRACK. San Jose has a cement bicycle track, upon which a number of world's records have been made. It is an ellipse, and very curiously constructed. Various methods have been tried in the East, and the San Jose track was built with a view of incorporating all the points favorable to speed. It is just one-third of a mile in circumference. It was built for a two minute track. That is to say, it was so constructed that the wheels will stand at right angles with the track when traveling at a speed of a mile in two minutes. The combined cost of track and grand stands is given as $9,000.

WHEELS IN THE COUNTY. The twenty-eight bicycle agencies in San Jose have sold 1,061 wheels during the past year, and some of them cannot secure wheels fast enough to supply the demand. The number of wheels owned in the city has just about doubled within the past year. There are nine bicycle clubs in San Jose, with memberships ranging from 24 to 325. There are clubs also in Mayfield, Mountain View, Palo Alto, Saratoga, Gilroy and Campbell, with large numbers of wheelmen in every town and throughout the county that are not attached to clubs. Clubmen figure that there are three unattached wheelmen for every member of a club. A number of estimates have been made by wheelmen concerning the number of wheels now owned in the county, the lowest estimate being 1,500 and the highest 6,000. The average of all estimates given is 2,681, though some of the best informed cyclists think 3,000 is more nearly correct. Upon this basis, and assuming the average purchase price to be $100, the investment represented is $300,000. A century round trip from San Jose to San Francisco by way of Oakland, returning by way of Palo Alto, is 100 miles.

THE GARDEN CITY CEMENT BICYCLE TRACK.

Waiting for the Pistol Shot,

Coming Down the Home Stretch.

A Glimpse of the Wheels.

A View of the Grand Stand.

Crossing the Tape.

THE OLIVE OIL INDUSTRY.

How the Oil is Extracted, the Price it Brings, and the Profit per Acre. Soils best Suited to the Culture of the Tree. Methods of Planting and Pruning. The Choicest Varieties.

Where Olive Branches Spread and Thrushes Trill.

THE olive is one of the fruits first mentioned in ancient history. It yet occupies an important position in horticulture, and is destined to reach a place of still greater importance, especially in California, where the soil and climate are exceptionally favorable for its cutiva-tion. Experiment has shown that the tree reaches its greatest development in calcareous soils rich in potash, and in climates which, while tempered by breezes from the sea, are not seriously affected by fogs. These conditions are met to a remarkable degree in some portions of Santa Clara County, and it is here that, with one exception, the business of making olive oil has reached its greatest development. It would be more correct to say ' the business of extracting olive oil,'' as the oil exists in the berry exactly as it does in the bottle, and is not manufactured, but simply separated from the solid portion of the berry by the application of pressure.

OUTLINE OF HABITAT. The olive tree will grow in any soil not exceedingly moist, and will endure extreme arid-ity of soil and long seasons of drought. It responds quickly, however, to more favorable conditions. It thrives best in a deep, open, porous soil, of a light character. It does not succeed well in heavy bottom lands, nor yet upon land that is too dry or stony. It is, however, the most hardy and durable of all fruit-bearing trees, specimens now growing in Europe antedating all record. It may be planted in consocation with vines or fruit trees, and the farmer thus secures an income from the more rapidly growing fruits while his olives are coming into bearing. One of the greatest features of the olive industry is that the fruit does not ripen until nearly all the other fruits are gathered. This gives winter work for those who handle the summer fruit, many of whom would otherwise be without employment.

WHEN INTRODUCED HERE. Olive trees were first planted in this county by the Franciscian Fathers, at the Santa Clara Mission. The first grove of importance, however, was planted by Don Jose Arguello, on his Quito rancho, now owned by E. E. Good-

A green olive tree, fair and of goodly fruit.—JEREMIAH II, 16.

AN OLIVE TREE AT EL QUITO.

rich. Some of these trees are now thirty years of age. They were of the Mission variety, and were subsequently grafted with scions from the better varieties from Italy.

THE BEST VARIETIES. The Mission is one of the hardiest varieties, but from sixty to seventy-five pounds of olives are required to make one gallon of oil, while the best Italian varieties, such as the Corregiolo, Infrantoia, Grossaia, Moriello and Razza, which were engrafted at El Quito, will produce a gallon of oil to every fifty or sixty pounds of fruit.

Pickled olives, when the proper varieties are used, properly prepared, are very delicious. Few can learn to love the Spanish product, which is put up in a very crude manner. It does not take long, however, to cultivate a taste for the California product, and a large industry is growing up here in the preparation of olives for table use.

The most modern system of pruning, which has been adopted in France and Italy as well as in California, is to cut out the inside branches, and leave the tree in the shape of a goblet. The method is most beautifully illustrated by the engraving, which, by the shadow, shows the sunlight coming down through the centre of the tree. The particular benefit is, that the advent of sunshine prevents the development of scale.

The trees occasionally come into bearing the fifth or sixth year, but usually not until the seventh. The smallest crop produced by the youngest trees is one-half a box, while the older trees produce from five to six fifty-pound boxes. The more aged trees of Palestine and Italy produce as high as a thousand pounds of olives per tree, which product will of course be equalled here when our trees reach an age as great.

PROCESS OF MANUFACTURE. The fruit is gathered before it is ripe, and allowed to dry in the shade for from two to three weeks, when it is crushed in a mill by a heavy stone wheel, revolved by a whim. The pulp is then placed in a flexible mat or basket, about eighteen inches in width, and six inches in depth technically known as a

THE QUITO OLIVE FARM—OWNED BY E. E. GOODRICH.

View of Olive Orchard, Showing Vines Between the Trees.

A Great Cherry Tree.

A General View of the Olive Farm, Showing House in the Distance.

View Toward Los Gatos, Showing Peach Trees and Vines.

The Grape Vine Arbor, Vines Just Coming Into Foliage.

bruscol. The oil is allowed to run into a tank, the dregs and water of vegetation falling to the bottom, and the oil rising to the top. It is then skimmed off. The oil is subsequently filtered through a prepared paper, when it is ready for market. It can also be kept indefinitely in a cool cellar. The best quality is expressed from fruit picked before it has attained a full state of ripeness.

Virgin oil, rarely sold even in Italy, is the very small amount which runs of from the sacks (bruscole) after they are placed in position for pressure, but before the pressure is applied. No virgin oil is sold in California.

TESTS FOR PURITY. Olive oil is of a delicate yellow, and has very little odor. Even experts cannot detect slight adulteration, either by by taste or smell. Olive oil is most largely adulterated with cotton seed oil. Oil of mustard and sesamum seed are also used. The medicinal qualities of olive oil are only freely imparted by that which is pure, and very little pure oil is found in the market, except that from California. The so-called Italian oil, which may be obtained at wholesale in the United States, is of course spurious, as good oil costs $2.00 in Italy, and cannot, therefore, be sold here for $1.75.

QUALITIES OF OLIVE OIL. Pure olive oil is very nutritious, and is often prescribed in lieu of cod liver oil. The latter is obtained from the liver of cod fish, the livers often being thrown into a heap, and allowed to partially decay before the oil is extracted. Animal oils are especially liable to become rancid when kept, and it is very desirable to avoid this effect, for, instead of having the mild, demulcent properties which constitute their chief value, they become irritant, and unfit, even as vehicles for other substances, to be applied to the skin or taken internally. Olive oil is, in addition to being nutritious, mildly laxative. It is valuable also as a vermifuge. Taken into the stomach in large quantities it serves to involve acid and poisonous substances, and mitigate their action. It is valuable both as food and medicine. The recent increase in the demand is due largely to the fact that physicians have learned that pure olive oil may be obtained here. The cheaper grades of oil are now also used largely in cooking, instead of lard and cotton-seed oil, and is always preferred, as it never imparts the rancid taste which characterizes lard, and which is made most prominent in pies and cakes.

VIEW ON COYOTE CREEK, NEAR FARM OF J. H. M. TOWNSEND.

DEBIT AND CREDIT. It costs to produce olive oil in Santa Clara County, on the most valuable lands, about $1.75 per gallon. The cost is less where the trees are raised on the cheaper lands of the mountains and foot-hills. It sells here for $8.00 when packed in bottles, twelve of which contain a gallon; per case of two dozen bottles; twelves or twenty-fours, $10; in gallon tins, $3.60; per quart bottle, $1.00, per pint, 65 cents; and sample bottles, 20 cents. The Mission oil sells for from $3.00 to $4.00 per gallon, according to how it is put up.

The value of the product per acre where olives are planted is indicated by the fact that upon the El Quito farm, which contains but eighty-one acres in orchard, there are 3,800 olive trees, 1,600 peach trees, 30,000 vines in bearing and 20,000 not in bearing, making an average of more than 681 plants per acre. This will be better understood when we state that the land is unusually fertile, and that trees and vines are planted between the rows of olives.

Great care is used here in the manufacture of olive oil, and the product is delicate as cream.

VALUE OF PUBLIC BUILDINGS. The value of public buildings, land and machinery owned by Santa Clara County is given by the Auditor as follows: Court House and Jail, $400,000; Hall of Records, $285,000; Infirmary and 45 acres of land, $60,000; Alms House and 100 acres of land, $40,000; Jail at Santa Clara, $3,000; Quarry Jail and 10 acres of land, $2,000; Jail and lot at Mayfield, $250; Jail and lot at Saratoga, $300; Jail and lot at Madrone, $100; land, engines, pumps, tanks pipe, etc., used for sprinkling roads, $45,000; value of school lots, houses and furniture, $487,-000; total, $1,322,650.

CULTIVATED AND UNCULTIVATED. The future greatness of Santa Clara County is in a measure indicated by the development which has already taken place. The county contains, according to the most careful measurement of the county map, 836,200 acres. Of this amount, 595,773.82 acres are assessed, and 113,928 acres cultivated. Thus it will be seen that less than one-seventh of the entire area is now under cultivation. Much of the land that is cultivated is not made to produce as largely as it might. There are 48,207 acres the title to which still vests in the government It will thus be seen that the present product is insignificant in comparison with what will naturally characterize the coming years.

REPRESENTATIVE RESIDENCES OF SAN JOSE.

Mrs. E. J. Cadwallader,

Edward Williams.

Mrs. W. P. Dougherty.

Abram King.

AN OLD SPANISH GRANT.

How William Fisher Astonished the Natives by Bidding Six Thousand Dollars for Twenty-Three Thousand Acres. Mrs. Mary Murphy Colombet's Farm.

IN 1820 two New England lads shipped as cabin boys on clipper ships bound for California for hides and tallow. Both ships came to anchor in Monterey Bay, and there the boys became acquainted. One was William Fisher and the other Roland Gilson. Fisher admired the country and left the ship with a view of remaining. He soon became tired of living in a strange land among a strange people, however, and again went to sea. In 1845 he returned, and, visiting the Santa Clara Valley, was so infatuated with its fertility and natural beauty that he decided to secure some land. Shortly after his arrival the Rancho Laguna Seca was ordered sold by the Court. It consisted of four square leagues in the shape of a rectangle and contained 23,040 acres. Charles Weber, John Gilroy and a number of other Americans were present, and Fisher astonished them by his bidding. He first bid $1,000 and some one offered a slight advance. Fisher bid $2,000.

Weber nudged Gilroy and Gilroy said to Weber: "The man is crazy." The other bidders held a consultation and offered a few hundred dollars more. Fisher promptly bid $3,000, and his competitors retired to talk it over. The result was an offer of a few hundred dollars in advance, followed by a bid of $4,000 by Fisher. Then there was a lull. The stockmen wanted the land, as it was a most magnificent tract, covering the entire width of the valley and was well wooded and watered. They decided to make one more bid, advancing the price $300. Fisher, in a louder tone, bid $6,000. Then the Americanos and Mexicanos turned away in disgust, saying that no sane man would pay $6,000 for a paltry four league grant of land while there was more land than any one knew what to do with. The purchaser, however, was satisfied with his bargain. Mr. Fisher's judgment was good and he builded wiser than he knew. Even the most sanguine dared not dream of the developments that would accompany the coming years.

Mr. Fisher made several trading trips to Mexico, bringing on return trips in 1846 his family and household goods. In 1847 he anchored in San Francisco Bay, and there met Roland Gibson, who, like himself, had, during the interim of twenty-seven years, become the master of a vessel. Fisher sent East by Gilson for a double-seated carriage, which arrived in 1848. It was one of the first that had ever been seen in California and excited considerable interest, the only vehicle then in general use being the two-wheeled Mexican carts, the wheels of which were sawed from oak trees.

COMBINED HARVESTING MACHINE, RANCHO LAGUNA SECA.

THE GREAT GRANT SUBDIVIDED. Mr. Fisher bought stock and soon had horses and cattle on every hill and in every hollow. He held his tract intact, and prior to his death willed it to his wife and children. It has since been divided into many tracts, most of which have been sold. The land has so rapidly increased in value that it has brought wealth to a large number of his children and grand children. Sixty acres of most any of the valley land would now bring as much as Mr. Fisher paid for the entire 23,040 acres in 1845.

MRS. COLOMBET'S FARM. Mrs. Mary Murphy Colombet, one of his daughters, still retains 4,480 acres near Madrone, which is a magnificent tract, nearly all of it being the richest garden soil. Water may be obtained anywhere within a few feet, as there is a strong under-current, flowing, apparently from Coyote Creek to the great laguna near Coyote Station. Many of the grand old oaks yet remain in the valley and smaller varieties dot the foothills.

Four hundred and thirty acres have recently been planted to orchard, divided as follows: Apricots, 25 acres; Bartlett pears, 25 acres; Royal Anne and Napoleon Bigarreau cherries, 65 acres; peaches and olives, 90 acres; prunes, 225 acres. Great avenues have been laid out and planted on either side with fan palms and other ornamental trees, and in a few years they will be magnificent driveways.

Mr. and Mrs. Colombet have a handsome residence on the corner of Fifth and William streets, in San Jose, where they entertain friends in the hospitable manner which prevailed in California in its pastoral days.

SCENES ON THE RANCHO LAGUNA SECA—PROPERTY OF MRS. MARY MURPHY COLOMBET.

FOREST HOME FARM.

The Coleman Younger Property on Alviso Road. Garden Land in the Artesian Belt, and the Actual Income per Acre. Artistically Planted Groves of Trees.

ONE of the oldest and best known properties in the county is the Younger farm, or Forest Home, on the Alviso road, about a mile and a half north of San Jose. It was selected in 1850, by Coleman Younger, from among the many choice sections of land at that time available for settlement. Mr. Younger arrived in Monterey in that year, and hearing marvelous stories of the beauty and fertility of the Santa Clara Valley, at once made arrangements with a Mexican cart-driver to furnish transportation hither for himself, his luggage and his servant, paying therefor the sum of $150. He soon selected the farm mentioned, and in 1852 returned to Liberty, Missouri, where, in March of 1853, he married Mrs. Augusta, and with an emigrant train of five wagons and 500 head of cattle, started on the 1st day of May for California, arriving on the 1st day of November.

ARTISTIC TREE PLANTING. In 1856 Mr. Younger planted an orchard, consisting of apples, peaches, and pears. In that year he also planted maple, weeping and black willows, elm and other ornamental trees. The beautiful arrangement and grouping of them never fails to attract attention from passers-by, the skill and taste shown being worthy of an artistic gardener. Some of these trees are now as tall as forest trees, and add much to the natural beauty and attractiveness of the farm and its surroundings.

THE DAIRY BUSINESS. As Mr. Younger succeeded in bringing nearly his entire band of cattle through safely, he naturally drifted into the stock business. Oliver Reeves, who came in the same year, lost most of his cattle while attempting to cross the mountains. Mr. Younger, therefore, entered into an arrangement with him whereby Mr. Reeves should care for his cattle on shares. Together they carried on the dairying business at Gilroy for many years, the business proving quite profitable, as cheese at first commanded fifty cents per pound, and the price fell slowly.

SHARPLESS STRAWBERRIES, ED. YOUNGER'S FARM.

THE HERD OF DURHAMS. Mr. Younger was a great lover of fine stock, especially cattle, and in 1858 he imported from Kentucky the finest herd of thoroughbred Durhams that could be purchased. They were his special pride, and he used every effort to improve them. The Younger herd became so noted that he sold cattle nearly all over the United States, and in Central America, British Columbia and Japan. He often exhibited them at fairs, and from one cow alone, "Sprightly," took over a thousand dollars in premiums. Of the greater number he ordered pictures to be painted by the artist, A. P. Hill, and these yet adorn the Younger residence. From 1861 to 1895, over $250,000 worth of cattle have been sold from the Younger herd.

THE YOUNGER ESTATE. Coleman Younger died six years ago last April, at the ripe age of 81 years, Previous to his demise he divided his property between his wife and children. The farm contained at that time 211 acres. Mrs. Coleman Younger now owns 80 acres, Edward Younger 32½ acres, Miss Augusta Younger 30¼ acres, Mrs. Rosalie Clemishire 28½ acres, and Mrs. Alice Gally 20 acres. The soil is exceedingly fertile, as it is composed largely of a silt deposited by overflow from the Guadalupe in early days, prior to the time when the city inaugurated its system of river improvement. Mr. Younger also fertilized the farm with sewage from the city for many years before the present sewer system was constructed to the bay. The land, therefore, is unusually rich, and crops of every kind flourish accordingly. The main sewer from San Jose runs through the farm, furnishing excellent drainage.

ARTESIAN WATER IN ABUNDANCE. The land is in the artesian belt, and flowing wells may be obtained upon any portion of the farm. There are now fourteen wells upon the property, five of them being upon Mrs. Coleman Younger's farm, three upon Edward Younger's,

THE FOREST HOME FARM.

The Driveway.

A Peek-a-boo from the Little Tots

One of the Artesian Wells.

The Coleman Younger Residence.

three upon Mrs. Alice Gally's, two upon Miss Augusta Younger's and one upon Mrs. Rosalie Clemishire's. The average depth is about 250 feet, and all of the wells furnish strong flows. The wells upon Mrs. Coleman Younger's farm are seven inches in diameter and water flows in a stream from two and a half inches to four inches in depth over the seven inch pipe. The flow is about the same, year in and year out, and will probably never be affected by the sinking of other wells, as it is on the southern boundary of the artesian belt. As the flow comes from the south, wells to the north cannot affect it, and but few more wells can ever be obtained further south.

PRODUCTS AND PROFITS. Not all of our farmers are willing to impart information concerning the output of their orchards or farms. The members of the Younger family, however, all have other resources, and do not attempt to make the land produce to its greatest capacity, being content with a reasonable and certain income. Mrs. Coleman Younger raises Australian rye grass upon a portion of her land, which is sold to the Fredericksburg Brewery at a uniform price of $10 per ton. They use it for packing bottles. The grass is a perennial, and the land has not been plowed since the seed was sown, several years ago. Three crops per annum are harvested, and the average income is $70 per acre. Mrs. Younger also rents a portion of her land to Chinamen, who raise strawberries and onions, paying $20 per acre rental, cash in advance every six months. The Chinese raise onions between the rows of young strawberry plants, and last year took 700 sacks of onions off three acres of land, besides a few strawberries. They clear from $350.00 to $500.00 per acre.

SEED, VEGETABLES, BERRIES. Edward Younger also leases his land to Chinese for strawberry culture at $20 per acre, as do all other members of the family. Upon the tracts belonging to Miss Younger and Mrs. Gally the tenants raise lettuce and celery seed, as well as berries. There is a great demand for celery seed, as it is largely used in the manufacture of a number of patent medicinal preparations. From ten acres of this land the Chinese expect this year to clear $4,000. The soil is rich, and most thoroughly utilized. The broad sunshine, rich soil, absence of summer rain, and the presence of and abundance of artesian water for

DANIEL GAMER'S RESIDENCE, NEAR BERRYESSA.

irrigation, is a combination of the most favorable circumstances imaginable. The Chinese, therefore, work incessantly, early and late, and make money. They plant lettuce or some other vegetable, between the rows of raspberry vines. They plant onions between the rows of strawberry vines the first few years. They plant vegetables between the rows of fruit trees, and utilize every foot of space. The owners of the land offer no objection as the plant food in the soil seems to be inexhaustible. The contract with the Chinese requires that fertilizers are to be furnished by them when necessary. Fertilization, however, has never been deemed necessary.

Of course any white man could take the same land and net nearly as much as the Chinamen do, even hiring white help. Few white men care to do it, however, as the work is very exacting. There is always difficulty in securing white men who will perform the work, and many land owners, therefore, lease their land.

The Younger property is all of the richest garden soil, and is located most conveniently near the city.

DANIEL GAMER'S ORCHARD. In 1889 Daniel Gamer purchased 34 acres of land about three miles east of San Jose, near Berryessa. The entire place is now in fruit trees. Cherries thrive here remarkably. Of these he has 1,400. He has, also, 1,400 prunes, 300 Muir peach, and 260 Blenheim apricot trees. The place is adorned with a modern six-roomed cottage, with bath, and hot and cold water throughout.

Mr. Gamer's orchard is especially well located, as it is near the Union fruit dryer, and is within a little over a mile from the town of Berryessa. The Pala school house is less than a mile distant. The Alum Rock Park motor road passes within three-quarters of a mile of the place, and trains pass connecting with San Jose every two hours during the day, the fare being but ten cents.

Mr. Gamer has extensive interests also in Montana, where he is interested in silver and copper mines, and other property.

The land is a rich loam, and the fruit trees show a remarkably thrifty and healthy growth. The ground is carefully cultivated, the trees are shapely, showing proper pruning. A pretty lawn in front of the house, with roses and bright flowers ever blooming, makes this an ideal home.

THE LIGHTHOUSE FARM.

The Extensive Orchard and Garden Tract Near Alviso, Which Has Been Improved by Andrea Malovos. Silty Soil in the Artesian Well District.

AS a rule, orchards in Santa Clara County are comparatively small, as ten acres of fruit trees in full bearing will support an average-sized family in good style. Again, the proper cultivation of ten acres, with the gathering and marketing of the fruit, will furnish occupation for one man most of the time, whereas, if more land is cultivated, additional help is usually required. Occasionally large companies own orchards of from 100 to 500 acres, but individuals, seldom.

The Lighthouse Farm, on the Alviso road, about five and a half miles north of San Jose, owned by Andrea Malovos, is an exception to the rule. Mr. Malovos secured 260 acres of land, on Coyote Creek in 1870, and at once commenced to improve it. The soil was exceedingly rich and fertile, as it consisted almost entirely of silt deposited by the waters of Coyote Creek, which in winter time formerly spread over the land. Mr. Malovos constructed a levee along the bank of the stream, at great expense, from thirty to forty feet wide at the base, and from ten to fifteen feet in height, for a distance of more than a mile. The work was done most thoroughly, and the levee is safe for all time. Mr. Malovos then sank four artesian wells, varying from 225 to 475 feet in depth. He thus secured an ideal orchard tract—one containing rich soil, with plenty of water, in a locality where there is an abundance of sunshine to ripen and give to fruit its choicest flavor.

Subsequently Mr. Malovos purchased 100 acres more. There are two artesian wells upon this tract, and a fine twenty-five-horse-power engine was purchased at a cost of $2,300, with which to propel a Byron Jackson rotary pump. With this plant, 2,000 gallons per minute are pumped into an irrigation canal which leads to all portions of the vast orchard tract, supplying abundant water for irrigation purposes, just when and just where it is needed.

Mr. Malovos now has a large orchard, and the trees are all very thrifty and bear heavily. There are 22,000 prune trees, 3,000 peach, 3,000 apricot and 2,500 cherry trees. They are planted from 20 to 24 feet apart, the

FAN PALM, R. D. NORTON'S YARD, SAN JOSE.

average number of trees for the entire orchard being 108 per acre. Sixty acres are devoted to asparagus. This is one of the most profitable tracts on the farm. In years when the prices are good, the profits are in advance of those secured from prunes; and are always great. Twenty-eight acres are devoted to strawberries. The profits vary with the season and market price, but are always satisfactory. Twenty-five acres are in pasture for horses and cows.

Mr. Malovos leases about 60 acres to a nursery company. The nursery stock is heeled in between rows of young fruit trees.

Mr. Malovos has supplied a thorough and extensive system of drainage for the entire farm. Thus, with water supplied by artesian wells, and that furnished by the steam pump, he is enabled to supply the land with all needed moisture, and with the drainage canals can at any time remove an excess of moisture.

Mr. Malovos has a large two-story residence, containing sixteen rooms and bath, a large basement, hot and cold water piped throughout, and sewers connecting with the main sewer, which leads to the bay from San Jose. Water is raised from artesian wells to tanks above the house by hydraulic rams. There are also two large barns, and a house for employes.

Mr. Malovos' neighbors, in every direction, are pleasant and intelligent people.

All of Mr. Malovos' children have received good school advantages. Most of the boys have attended the Santa Clara College, while several of them have completed a course at the Garden City Business College. The younger children are now attending the district school.

Mr. Malovos' residence is surrounded by a beautiful flower garden, flowers growing here most luxuriantly.

The residence is connected with San Jose and San Francisco by a long-distance telephone.

Mr. and Mrs. Malovos have ten children, all of whom, except a married daughter, Mrs. B. N. Trubock, wife of the commission merchant of San Francisco, reside at home.

A MALVOS' LIGHTHOUSE FARM, NEAR ALVISO.

The Young Prune Orchard.

The Apricot Orchard.

The Apricot Orchard.

Malovos' Family and Residence.

The Cherry Orchard.

The Apricot Orchard.

A. MALOVOS' LIGHTHOUSE FARM, NEAR ALVISO.

Pumping Plant and Peach Orchard.
Young Prune Orchard and Irrigation Canal.

The Nursery and Young Prune Orchard.
Andrea Malovos.
Picking Scene—Peach Orchard.

Picking Scene—Peach Orchard.
The Young Cherry Orchard.

GLEN UNA.

The Largest Prune Orchard Now in Bearing in the World. A Model Farm with Model Accessories. Private Water Works and Electric Light Plant.

IN every line of work there is an ideal or imaginary condition of affairs in which the beauties and perfections seen in individual instances are combined, and everything that is defective or unseemly is excluded. The idea is seldom transformed into the real, as the process generally involves the expenditure of sums greatly in excess of those usually earned as profits in ordinary lines of business.

THE MODEL PRUNE ORCHARD. There is in Santa Clara County, however, what may be called a model orchard—the Glen Una, situated about midway between Saratoga and Los Gatos, and owned by F. G. Hume. The entire tract covers an area of 680 acres, 350 acres of which are prunes, 160 trees to the acre—this being the largest bearing prune orchard in the world. It is not claimed the profit per acre is as great as it is in some other instances, as the owner endeavors to secure quality rather than quantity, With this end in view the trees are carefully pruned, and all the small and imperfect fruit removed. This decreases the output but insures choice fruit. The income, however, is from $100 to $125 per acre, though some of the trees are not yet in full bearing.

IDEAL ARRANGEMENTS PROVIDED. Everything about the place is kept in perfect order. The trees are carefully cultivated and pruned, the roads are kept in good condition, the engine room is as clean as a parlor, and the fruit wagons are resplendent with bright paint and artistic lettering. The draft-horses are all large, sleek and fat, and the carriage horses are neat-limbed, and of noble lineage. Water is piped from springs upon the mountain side, several hundred feet above, to every building about the place, under a pressure of 150 pounds to the square inch. A hose cart is provided for protection in case of fire.

THE J. T MURPHY FARM, NEAR MOUNTAIN VIEW

ELECTRIC LIGHTS, BELLS, TELEPHONES. The buildings and various portions of the farm are connected with the engine room by electric alarm bells. The residence and packing house are connected with Los Gatos, and all the principal towns in the State, by long distance telephone. A private electric plant furnishes both arc and incandescent electric lights for residence, packing house, stable, and other buildings. The fifteen acre plat used as a drying ground is also supplied with electric lights, and all work involving the handling and packing of the dried fruit is done at night, in order to avoid the settling upon the fruit of the minute particles of dust set in motion by men and horses.

Near the residence there is a grove of live oak trees. From their branches depend a number of electric lights, and scattered about among the trees are a number of rustic seats. Near at hand there is a large cement plunge bath, supplied with a spring board and other accessories. A grape arbor and trailing vines furnish grateful shade, and the pool is supplied with running water from mountain springs.

LABORERS WHO WORK SYSTEMATICALLY. Twenty-five men are employed upon the place the year round, and from seventy-five to a hundred in the fruit season. Every company of men works under its own foreman, each foreman reporting to the superintendent, and he in turn to the proprietor.

PACKING PRUNES AT NIGHT. The packing house is two stories high, 55 feet in width by 185 feet in length, and is supplied with the latest and most improved machinery. It has also an elevator. The ground floor is of cement, and is kept scrupulously clean. The machinery is all propelled by steam power. The engine is a Putnam 60-

THE GREAT GLEN UNA PRUNE ORCHARD.

A Glimpse of Fruit Drying Trays.

In the Engine Room.

Rustic Seats in a Live Oak.

A View of a Portion of the Prune Orchard.

The Stacks of Fruit Drying Trays.

horse power. It was built to order, and is a most beautiful piece of machinery. It is kept as neat and clean as the furniture in a parlor, and is housed in an expensive and model building.

In another room of the engine house there is a 55-horse power engine, which propels two dynamos, one of which is a Thomson-Houston 600-light alternator, and the other an Edison 250 light direct current. The former furnishes light for the residence, stable, and other buildings at the upper place, and the latter supplies light for the packing house and drying grounds.

In the upper story of the packing house the prunes are packed. As they are all extras they are packed exclusively in boxes. The room is 55 x 185 feet, and there are two rows of incandescent lamps the entire length of the building.

THE FRUIT DRYING GROUNDS. A tract of fifteen acres in a little valley about a hundred feet below the packing house, is used as a drying ground, and here are sometimes spread as many as 18,000 white wood fruit trays, each four by eight feet, where they are allowed to remain until the fruit has been thoroughly cured by the warm rays of the sun. At intervals all about the grounds are arc lamps upon electric light poles, to furnish light for the men engaged in attending to the drying fruit. Steel tracks extend to all parts of the grounds, and long trains of flat cars, loaded with stacks of fruit trays, are hauled to and from the various sections by horses. A railroad also extends from the drying ground in the little valley directly up the steep hill to the packing house on the plateau above, and this is operated by a cable from the engine house. All parts of the packing house and drying grounds are connected with the engine house by electric wires and alarm bells, so that signals may be given for the stopping and starting of the machinery.

IMPLEMENTS AND MACHINERY. All fruit wagons, carriages and farming implements are kept in perfect condition, and freshly painted every year, a shop supplied with every requisite having been provided for this purpose. The farm has its own blacksmith shop also, which is supplied with lathes, forges, band and buzz saws, drills, emery wheels, and all other necessary machinery, power being supplied by a Pelton wheel, propelled by water from springs in the mountains above. In winter, when the water supply is ample, the Pelton also drives a 150-light C. and C. dynamo, which supplies light for the residence and grounds.

SANTA CLARA COUNTY CHESTNUT TREES.

THREE ORCHARDS IN ONE. The Glen Una orchard includes the three tracts formerly owned by Geo. Handy, A. P. Chrissman and David N. Coey. The first contained 450 acres, the second 90, and the third 160. The property was purchased by George W. Hume, the well-known owner of Pacific Coast salmon canneries, and by him presented to his son, F. G. Hume, who at once improved it, and has since made it the model orchard of the United States. The annual income now ranges from $35,000 to $43,750. The proprietor, who is 24 years of age, was married in 1892 to Miss Una Handy, and they have one child, a babe one year old. The farm was named Glen Una, in honor of Mrs. Hume, whose given name was Una.

The family orchard contains about 250 trees, including oranges, lemons, chestnuts, cherries, walnuts, figs and pears.

As the place lies against the foothills, several hundred feet above the valley, the view is grand, including as it does the entire valley and the mountains to the east. To the north the bay of San Francisco stretches away, and to the south rise the Santa Cruz Mountains.

THE GREAT DUNNE RANCHO. Choice fruit land in the Santa Clara Valley is cheaper at $200 per acre than the best corn land in the Middle States is at $50 per acre, because ten acres of land here in full-bearing fruit trees will produce more than fifty acres of corn land will in the East. It is not at all an uncommon thing for our orchardists to realize a net income of from $50 to $100 per acre. Land that brings a net return of $100 per acre, is paying 10 per cent interest on a valuation of $1000 per acre. Yet there is land in the county which can be had for from $100 to $125 per acre which will grow fruit trees that will as certainly bring in $100 per acre when in full bearing, as other land in the county does. The usual price of such land, unimproved, is from $150 to $250 per acre. It often pays better to secure land at $150 an acre than to buy that which may be had for $10 an acre. In one case crops may be raised which will aid in paying for the land, and in the other no very remunerative crops can be grown. One of the last of the great Spanish grants in Santa Clara County was the great Catherine Dunne ranch of 18,000 acres. This is now being sold in lots of 6, 10, 20 and 40 acres, by Burbank & Devendorf, of San Jose. Prices range from $25 to $125 per acre, one-fourth cash, balance in six equal payments, with interest at 7 per cent., the mortgagee to pay the tax.

SCENES ON THE CATHERINE DUNNE RANCH—NEAR GILROY.

HORTICULTURAL INTERESTS.

Climatic Conditions Favorable to Fruit Growing. Details of the Business from Nursery to Market. Varieties of Fruit and Profits therefrom. Interesting and Reliable Statistics.

CALIFORNIA is the greatest fruit-growing State in the union, and Santa Clara County is the most important horticultural district in the State. This fact is widely known, but comparatively few are familiar with the factors which combine to produce the result.

THE JAPAN CURRENT. One of the most important is the climate. Upon it successful and profitable horticulture very largely depends; climate in turn, depending upon the contour of the country and its relation to those influences which control meteorological conditions. The climate here is determined principally by the Japan current, which brings the heated waters of the Indian Ocean across the Pacific and sweeps our shores from north to south. New England shores are swept by cold currents from the Arctic, which bring from the frozen north great icebergs which chill the waters. The Straits of Behring, on the other hand, are too narrow to allow the introduction into the Pacific of any considerable amount of water from the Arctic, and there is not enough current to carry icebergs very far south. The Japan stream, therefore, has full sway, and currents of air from this warm water flow over California, modifying the heat of summer and the cold of winter.

CONTOUR OF THE COAST. Another factor which influences the climate here is the contour of the coast and the typographical features of the mainland. The Sierra Nevada and Cascade Mountains bend like a great arm around the country from Alaska to Mexico, shielding it to a great extent from the cold waves from the East, and forming a barrier which effectually prevents the warm air of the Japan current from spreading over the plains of Nevada. This reserves its full influence for California. The conditions are unique, and the resulting climatic effects are not duplicated elsewhere.

MOORPARK APRICOTS, JOSEPH SCHUPP'S ORCHARD.

LOCAL CLIMATIC CONDITIONS. Local conditions are also peculiarly favorable. The valley is protected from harsh sea winds on the west by an unbroken range of mountains. The Coast Range on the East protects us from the cold winds which in winter sweep from off the snows of the Sierra. Under the lee of the high ranges which form a barrier in Santa Clara County, a warm temperature prevails. The cool winds which are deflected toward the lower end of San Francisco Bay and into the valley are moderated and greatly softened by the warmer air that rises from intervening vales. Thus we have higher summer and higher winter temperature than some localities not fifty miles distant.

The chief characteristics of the Santa Clara Valley climate are: first, freedom from extremes of low temperature; second, an abundance of sunshine; and third, an atmosphere with a low percentage of humidity. All these are favorable to fruit growing, as it has been shown that perfect development of fruit depends upon heat, light and a certain aridity of atmosphere, with a proper moisture of soil.

REQUISITES FOR FRUIT GROWING. In fruit growing a temperature above a certain minimum is found necessary for germination, another for chemical modification, a third for flowering, a fourth for ripening of seeds, a fifth for the elaboration of the saccharine juices, and a sixth for the development of aroma. Not only is heat a requisite, but a long-continued sunshine as well. Without light there can be no fructification, though heat be given. The actinic rays are necessary to produce chemical changes. The cloudless skies and almost uninterrupted sunshine which prevail here are important factors in the development of fruit. The absence of clouds insures sunshine, and sunshine insures a higher and more uniform temperature. Uniformity is desirable. Extreme temperatures are fatal.

SANTA CLARA COUNTY FRUITS.

Crawford Peaches.

Early Madeline Pears.

German Silver Prunes.

Royal Ann Cherries.

Moorpark Apricots.

French Prunes.

IN FLUENCE OF DRY AIR. In the East the percentage of humidity of atmosphere is high in summer. In Santa Clara County it is low. Dry air favors access and action of light and heat. Sheets of vapor are in a great measure absorbent of both. The average cloudiness in the East is more than twice as much as in the Santa Clara Valley. The heat, continuous sunshine and dry air, with the extreme length of our growing season, combined with a rich soil, insures the characteristic excellence of our fruit.

PRICE OF LAND. The price of land in Santa Clara County varies considerable, as it is influenced by numerous local conditions. Land in the middle Western States that is level varies but little in price, as the soil is usually of a uniform quality, and is affected by the same meteorlogical conditions. In Santa Clara County, however, the climate is influenced by altitude and the contour of hill and dale. The soil, too, varies greatly. Its location, surroundings, altitude, and distance from market affect the price also.

Land within a radius of three miles from San Jose suitable for fruit growing commands from $200 to $600 per acre, unimproved. Similar land from three to ten miles from the city may be had for from $150 to $300 per acre. Valley land still further from the city, $75 to $150 per acre. Near Gilroy there are some very choice fruit and garden lands that command from $200 to $300 per acre, and some not so good that may be bought for from $100 to $150. Land adjacent to Palo Alto commands a little more than similar land in some other other localities because of its proximity to the Stanford University. Foothill lands vary from $40 to $100 per acre, while timber and grazing lands further back in the mountains may be had for from $5 to $40 per acre. There is a little government land to be had, but it is rough and inaccessible.

PLOWING AND PLANTING. In preparing the land for planting it is, when practicable, plowed thoroughly and deeply in the fall, and the surface left unharrowed and exposed to the desiccating influences of the air during the winter. This adds to the fertility of the soil. More properly speaking, it makes the plant food more available. In laying off an orchard it is desirable to have it symmetrical, to economize the land

RASPBERRIES, MRS. J. A. GALLY'S FARM.

and to provide for facility in future use and care. There are various methods of aligning trees, each method having its own peculiar advantages. The principle forms are the square, the quincunx and the hexagonal. The two first are the ones most commonly used.

By the square method, if the trees are twenty feet apart, 108 trees are planted to the acre. This is one of the handiest forms for an orchard. By the quincunx method the number of rows are doubled and a tree planted in the centre of every square. At twenty feet apart, by this method, 199 trees may be planted per acre. The hexagonal system makes the trees equilateral—equally distant one from the other in every direction. Six trees form a hexagon and inclose a seventh. By this method, at twenty feet apart, 126 trees are planted to the acre.

The distance at which trees are planted in orchard row varies considerable, but the method usually followed in planting peaches, prunes and apricots is to allow a space of twenty feet between trees, which gives 108 trees to the acre. The trees grow so thriftily here, however that the limbs often intertwine and and make cultivation difficult. In many of the orchards planted recently the trees are twenty-five, and in some, thirty feet apart.

PRICE OF YOUNG TREES. The price of nursery stock varies so much that it is difficult to quote. Trees of the several varieties have in some seasons commanded from 25 to 30 cents each, while in others they fell to 8 and 9 cents. The general average price of good trees during the past ten years has been from 12 to 15 cents, new and choice varieties, ruling a little higher. Last year good good prune trees on Myrobolan stock could be had for 7 cents, and on peach stock, 4½ to 5 cents. Apricots were 15 cents and peach trees 10 cents.

THE COST OF CULTIVATION. The cost of cultivation varies. Usually, parties will take contracts to plow shallow, for $2 per acre; deep $3 per acre. The digging of holes and setting of trees costs from 5 to 7 cents, according to soil It is within range to have orchards planted, trees twenty feet apart, at the following figures: Plowing and harrowing, $3; 108 trees at 7 cents, $7.56; staking, digging and planting, $7.56; total cost per acre, $18 12.

Parties often take contracts to plow, harrow and prune young orchards for from $7.50 to $10 per acre per season. For hilly land which cannot be worked except at a disadvantage, as high as from $10 to $12 per acre is charged. When a cultivator is used, the ground is usually worked from four to ten times in a season, according to the nature of the soil. Orchards are never seeded to grass here, as they are in the east. This constant stirring of the soil adds greatly to its productive powers—probably by exposing the plant food to the action of the sun and air, and bringing about chemical changes which makes it more easily assimilated by the tree. The cost of this cultivation is often noted by those who have grown fruit in the East, where this system is not followed. The work costs but 50 cents per acre each time, however, or from $2 to $3.50 per acre per season, and the increased yield makes the work remunerative.

THE COST OF PRUNING. The cost of pruning varies according to the size and variety of trees. Prune trees are not now pruned very much. They are as a rule, merely thinned out to let in the air and sunshine, and allowed to grow, with very little if any cutting back. Peach and apricot trees, however, are cut back heavily, in order to avoid the growth of too much wood and too great a weight of fruit. Notwithstanding the heavy pruning, however, peaches are always thinned after the crop sets, and even then the branches must often be propped to prevent them from being broken by the heavy weight of fruit. The conditions vary so much that each orchard must be figured upon separately by those taking the contracts to prune. Contracts range about as follows: First year, prunes, 25 cents per 100; second year, prunes, 40 cents to 50 cents per hundred; third year, prunes, $1 per hundred; fourth year, prunes, $3 per hundred; fifth year, prunes, $5 per hundred The price for older prune trees ranges as high as $9 per hundred. Apricots and peaches cost more after after the second year, being 2 cents per tree for trees two years old, 5½ cents per tree for trees three years old, and after that about as many cents per tree as the tree is years old, up to twelve.

THE COST OF SPRAYING. Fruit-growing, although it is more profitable here than in any other State in the Union, is attended with difficulties and annoyances, as elsewhere, except, perhaps in a less degree. We never have the severe weather here that prevails in the East, but even in the Santa Clara Valley, noted for the mildness of its climate, and known as the garden spot of the world, our fruit crop is occasionally injured by frost. The greatest drawback, perhaps, is the scale, and other insects which infest the fruit trees. These, however, may be kept in check by using proper sprays. Pear and apple trees are attacked princi-

LEMONS FROM F. H. BABB'S ORCHARD.

pally by the codlin moth. The crop is materially injured unless sprays are used. Paris green is the spray generally used for codlin moth. An average of one pound to 150 gallons of water is a good strength for general purposes. The poison is first made into a thin paste in a small quantity of water, and powdered or quick lime added in amount equal to the poison used to take up the free arsenic and remove or lessen the danger of scalding. The trees are usually sprayed about four times, and the cost per acre averages about $1.50. The brown scale has been almost annihilated by the Australian ladybird. The San Jose scale is also scarce. Prune trees are now seldom sprayed as they are not affected by scale.

COST OF IRRIGATION. Trees always bear better when irrigated, except in the heavier loams, which are usually too moist. Most fruit trees thrive better in a soil that is porous. If trees are irrigated too freely the fruit grows too large and is too soft. If water is applied in proper quantities, however, and at the proper time, the quality of the fruit is improved It is scarcely possible to give reliable figures concerning the cost of irrigation, as there are so many factors which bear upon the matter. Many of our orchardists secure water from streams for irrigation, at small cost. In the artesian belt an abundant and permanent supply is secured from flowing wells. Where the water must be pumped from wells, centrifugal pumps are usually used, operated by steam or gas engine. Plants capable of irrigating a large orchard cost from $2,000 to $3,000, but their use always brings about an increase in the output sufficient to pay for the plant within a few seasons.

WHAT FETILIZERS COST. Fertilizers have been used but little, but the results clearly indicate that fertilization pays if the elements are supplied in which the particular soil is deficient. Bone dust is good, but costs $30 per ton. Gypsum, from San Benito County, is now largely used, as it furnishes necessary plant food, and can be had, in carload lots, at $10 per ton. About 600 pounds per acre is applied usually, but more or less according to requirements. Manure may generally be had for the hauling, and some fertilize with it. The greater proportion of our orchardists, however, use no fertilizers of any kind.

HOW THE FRUIT IS DISPOSED OF. Some varieties of fruit, such as cherries, pears and apples and the berry fruits are sold largely for immediate consumption. A portion of the crop, however, finds its way to the canneries. A large part of the apricots, peaches, pears and plums also are preserved by the canneries; the remaining portion being dried. Prunes are universally dried. In drying prunes, two to two and one-half pounds of green fruit make one pound of the dried product. Of peaches it requires between five and seven pounds (according to variety) of green to make one pound of dried fruit. About six to one is the ratio for drying apricots.

THE COST OF DRYING AND SACKING. In the following table the cost of sacking dried fruit, including sacks, labor of sacking and loading, and in the case of prunes, boxing and grading, so computed as to show the cost per green ton, is shown in the first column, and the entire cost of sacking and drying, per green ton, is shown in the second column.

	Cost of Sacking	Total Cost Sacking and Drying
Apricots	.46	$5 91
French Prunes	1.17	3.29
Silver Prunes	.67	2 67
Egg Plums	.52	2.52
Washington Plums	.42	9 44
Pears	.45	5.87
Early Peaches	.42	5 78
Muir "	.49	5 26
Cling "	.39	6.55
Salway "	.47	5.68

THE COST OF GRADING FRUIT. Apricots, peaches and prunes may be accurately graded by machinery at a cost of from 25 to 40 cents per dry ton. To do the same work has heretofore cost the company as much as $10 per dry ton, for apricots and peaches. With the aid of other improved machinery the crop will this year be handled at a materially reduced cost.

GRADES OF FRUIT. Dried apricots, peaches and prunes are graded into various sizes. Apricots and peaches are, of course, cut into sections before being dried. All sections of apricots 1 inch in diameter or less, constitute the grade termed "prime;" more than 1 inch and up to 1¼ inches, "standard;" more than 1¼ and up to 1½ inches, "choice;" more than 1½ inches, "fancy."

Dried peaches are graded so that all fruit up to 1¼ inches in diameter is termed "prime;" more than 1¼ and up to 1½ inches, "standard;" more than 1½ and up to 1¾ inches, "choice;" more than 1¾ inches, "fancy."

Dried prunes are graded into six sizes, as follows: The largest size, from 40 to 50 prunes weigh a pound; the second size, 50 to 60; third, 60 to 70; fourth, 70 to 80; fifth, 80 to 90; sixth, 90 to 100. Prices are quoted for each size, the best price being paid for the largest size.

PEAR TREES, MRS MARGARET OGIER'S ORCHARD.

THE VARIETIES RECOMMENDED. California has a monopoly on apricots, as they will not grow except in very few other localities, while here they reach their greatest development. Each of four varieties of fruit has some peculiarity about it which causes it to be selected by some orchardists as the best for certain localities. The varieties most satisfactory and profitable in Santa Clara County are prunes, peaches, apricots and cherries.

THE PROFITABLE PRUNE. Prune growing is here the most extensive, and usually the most profitable fruit industry. The prune grows well in most any portion of the valley, though it thrives best in soil which is not too heavy. It is easily cultivated and readily handled. As the fruit is dried, it does not have to be marketed immediately, and does not come under the head of "perishable." The trees are as a rule planted twenty feet apart, which means 108 trees to the acre. They commence bearing the fourth year, sometimes in the third, and are in full bearing by the seventh. The yield will average 100 pounds to the tree, and the green fruit brings from a cent and a half to two cents per pound. The gross income, therefore, ranges usually from $165 to $200 per acre.

THE GOLDEN APRICOT. Next in importance, both as to acreage and profit, is the apricot. The culture of this favorite fruit is limited exclusively to the Pacific Coast, and only reaches perfection in California. This is one instance in which the climate of California does a perfect work; for while the apricot will grow elsewhere, it does not thrive elsewhere, and while it grows in nearly every section of the State, there is but one section which can compete with the Santa Clara Valley. Apricots grow best in the rich sedimentary soils. In this valley they commence to bear the third year, and the fourth year the crop pays a little more than expenses. Thereafter the crops are usually large. This fruit is always in demand, and the demand is increasing as the delicious flavor of the fruit is becoming better known. Either dried or canned, it is beyond comparison as a table fruit. It is dried in the sun, and when dried brings from five to twelve cents per pound. The fourth year from planting an orchard will generally produce five tons of fruit to the acre, and the green fruit sells for from $15 to $30 per ton. The average price last season was 1¼ cents per pound, or $25 per ton. This year the price was $30 per ton.

SANTA CLARA COUNTY FRUIT.

Walnuts.   *Almonds.*   *Rose of Peru Grapes.*

Chestnuts.   *Apples.*   *White Figs.*

canned, it is beyond comparison as a table fruit. It is dried in the sun, and when dried brings from five to twelve cents per pound. The fourth year from planting an orchard will generally produce five tons of fruit to the acre, and the green fruit sells for from $15 to $30 per ton. The average price last season was 1¼ cents per pound, or $25 per ton. This year the price was $30 per ton. The income ranges from $75 to $350 per acre.

PEACHES AND PROFITS. Peaches may be grown in nearly every State in the Union, but they like a warm climate, and only reach perfection in California. All the favorite varieties of this delicious fruit ripen here in the full perfection of sweetness and flavor, but the early Crawford is a prime favorite. Three years after planting the trees yield a good crop, and thereafter the crop is usually so heavy that props must be used to keep the trees from breaking down. Generally the fruit must be thinned out, and it pays do this, as the fruit is larger, and has a better flavor. Peaches thrive best in the lighter and warmer soils. They are as a rule nearly as profitable as apricots, and occasionally net even more. The earliest ripen in May and find a ready sale at high figures. One variety succeeds another throughout the summer, and peaches may be had as late as November. The returns are between $75 and $300 per acre.

THE CHERRY CROP. California cherries, like all other fruit products of the State, are remarkable for their size, flavor, and beauty of appearance. The cherry tree likes a rich, arable, silty soil. Cherries do not come into bearing before the seventh year, but after that will yield largely, and choice cherries always command a good price. The first ripe cherries appear in May, and the later varieties in June, July and August. The principal varieties raised here are the Royal Anne, Napoleon Bigarreau and Black Tartarian. The price ranges from 6 to 20 cents per pound, with the average about 8 cents. The yield per acre ranges from $200 to $1,000, and the average is about $300 gross.

PEARS AND PRICES. The pear adapts itself to a diversity of soil and climate more readily than most any other fruit tree grown. Yet the Bartlett, which is one of the choicest varieties known, only reaches perfection in certain sections. It requires a deep, moist, rich soil and a warm climate. There are several varieties grown here, each presenting some quality which makes it desirable. The pear here commences

to bear the third year, but is not in full bearing until the seventh. The choicest pear-growing sections are the silty lands along water courses, and where water can be had for irrigation. Only the best varieties, with the most favorable surroundings, produce the largest crops, but with the best conditions, pears produce crops worth from $100 to $1,000 per acre, depending upon the market and the variety grown. The price per ton varies considerable. Last year pears were in good demand at $30 per ton.

THE FRUITFUL OLIVE. Olive growing is one of the most profitable industries, but the greatest returns are secured by manufacturing the olives into olive oil, and that requires improved machinery and technical knowledge. The trees do not bear heavily until several years of age. They are long-lived, however, and will in the future be more extensively grown. The price of pure olive oil is now $8 per gallon, and the gross income per acre ranges from $75 to $1000 according to variety and age of trees.

GRAPES AND SOILS. Grapes may be grown in nearly any section of the county. Table grapes like a heavy loam, while other varieties acquire a better flavor in the red gravelly and chalky soils of the foothills. Ordinary varieties are not very profitable, as the area in which they may be grown in California, is extended. The shipment of choice table grapes in refrigerator cars to the East is profitable, but fruit trees bring greater returns.

THREE PROFITABLE BERRIES. Strawberries here yield prolifically, especially along the bay, and in the artesian district, which is one of the choicest strawberry-growing sections in the United States. The yield is usually from $200 to $750 per acre gross.
Blackberries yield well also, and thrive over an extended territory. In the artesian basin, north and north-west of San Jose, however, they bear through a more extended period, and return larger crops than in any other locality. The profits do not average as much as from strawberries, but range from $150 to $300 per acre.
Raspberries are more easily gathered than blackberries, and command a higher price, as the area of greatest production is not so extensive.

THE KINGLY ORANGE. Oranges thrive in the foothills at elevations ranging from 600 to 1,800 feet. They are gross feeders and require a rich and friable soil, containing plenty of moisture. The

FOUR-YEAR OLD APRICOT TREE—JOSEPH SCHUPP'S ORCHARD.

red lands of the foothills give good, perhaps the best results. The oranges grown here are large, sweet and free from scale. They only reach perfection in localities most free from frost, cold winds and sudden changes of temperature. There are but few sections in the county which combine all the various advantages requisite to the most profitable culture of the orange, but some possess them in an eminent degree. The choicest variety is the Washington Navel, which ripens here nearly a month earlier than in the choicest orange-growing districts in the South, and early fruit commands fancy prices. Profits range from $175 to $750 per acre.

APPLES AND OTHER FRUITS. Apples grown in the valley reach a very large size, especially in the silty soils along Los Gatos Creek, Coyote and Guadalupe. They lack the flavor and keeping qualities, however, which characterize apples grown in the mountains, and are not usually as profitable as the stone fruits, though they have been grown very profitably near Alviso.

There are various other fruits and berries which are grown to some extent, usually for home consumption, though occasionally for profit. Of these, quinces, plums, figs, crab-apples, almonds, walnuts, currants and gooseberries may be mentioned. Most anything that will grow anywhere in the temperate or semi-tropic zones will grow here, and many trees and plants only here reach their greatest development. We have treated those which are the most profitable.

WHAT DRIED FRUIT BRINGS. The Santa Clara County Fruit Exchange, the orchardists' co-operative institution, sold dried fruit last season at the following prices: Silver prunes brought from 5½ to 7½ cents, net cash. Some pears sold as low as $1.20 per hundred pounds. A few choice sold for 13 cents per pound, and the average was from 5½ to 6½ cents a pound. For good pitted plums from 6½ to 7 cents was realized. The pitted Hungarian prunes take on a beautiful red color when sulphured, and present a very nice appearance. They sold for from 9½ to 10 cents per pound Dried cherries have not been introduced to any great extent, but the Royal Anne brought from 8½ to 9¾ cents per pound in boxes, delivered. Governor Wood and Black Tartarian do not sell well. For egg plums, pitted, the grower realized 4 cents per pound, net cash. Almonds were last year very low. For some 8½ cents per pound was realized, but the average price was 3½ to 5½ cents. Dried peaches sold from 8 to 19 cents per pound.

THE COST OF TRANSPORTATION. Fast fruit trains, with ventilated cars, leave San Jose every evening at 5:65 o'clock, via Sacramento and Ogden, making the run to Chicago in 127 hours. The rate on canned fruit is 50 cents per 100 pounds to Chicago, New York or any common point. Dried fruit in bags, $1.20 per hundred pounds to New York or any intermediate point east of Denver. Dried fruit in boxes, $1.00 per hundred pounds to Chicago, New York, or intermediate points. Wine

in wood, carload lots, 50 cents per hundred pounds, to New York, or New Orleans, Chicago or other central points east of the Missouri River. The rate on green apples from San Jose to Montana, and Chicago, Cincinnati, Pittsburg and New York is $1.00 per hundred, with minimum carload of 30,000 pounds. Canned goods, 65 cents per 100 pounds to Chicago, Pittsburg, Cincinnati, and intermediate points. Sweet and Irish potatoes to Denver, 75 cents per 100 pounds.

The minimum weight for a carload is 25,000 pounds. The freight rates on the Santa Fe and Southern Pacific are identical, one company always meeting any reductions made by the other. The rate on green fruit from San Jose to London is $3.00 per 100 pounds.

THE HORTICULTURAL COMMISSIONER. The Legislature of California has wisely provided means of protecting and fostering the horticultural interests of the State. The Board of Supervisors of several counties are authorized to appoint a Horticultural Commissioner, whose duty it is to prevent the introduction of fruit tree pests, to investigate and treat diseases of trees, to conduct experiments in the domain of horticulture and to

E. M. EHRHORN.
Horticultural Commissioner.

advise fruit growers concerning improved methods of fruit growing, the cure of diseases and the eradication of pests. The advantages accruing to the fruit industry by this sort of legislation is most beneficial, and Santa Clara county is particularly favored in having as commissioner one eminently qualified by experience and education to perform the duties of the office. The commissioner is Edward M. Ehrhorn. He is a native of California and was educated in Europe, spending eleven years in various colleges, his course of study being of a scientific nature. In addition, he took a special course at Stanford University under Professor Comstock, studying scale and parasytic insects. In 1890-1 he was Deputy Quarantine Officer and Assistant Entomologist of the State Board of Horticulture. He was elected Horticultural Commissioner of Santa Clara County in 1892 and served one and a half years. The office was, in 1895, made a permanent one and he was again elected to the same position. He has all the necessary facilities for conducting experiments and has secured much valuable information for the benefit of the fruit-growers of the county, who appreciate the services he has rendered.

THE FIRST FRUITS. The first fruits of the several varieties ripen in the Santa Clara Valley as follows: Strawberries, March; loquats, April; currants and cherries, May; apricots, peaches, pears, plums, apples, blackberries and raspberries, June; prunes, grapes, figs and nectarines, July; quinces and pomegranates, August; persimmons, October; oranges, December. Generally the earlier varieties to ripen are not as good as the later ones. Cherries are most prolific in June, apricots in July, peaches, plums, prunes and pears in August, figs and grapes in September, October and November. Strawberries, apples, oranges and lemons have all seasons for their own.

SAN JOSE FRUIT PACKING COMPANY.

The Pioneer Packers of Extra Fruits in California, and the Largest Fruit Cannery in the World. The New Vacuum Perfection Process of Sealing Jars.

GENERAL VIEW OF SAN JOSE FRUIT PACKING COMPANY'S PLANT.

THE market for California fruit grows in direct ratio with the spread of knowledge concerning its merits. Consumers are learning that the long continued sunshine of California gives to fruit a flavor that cannot be secured in any climate where the presence of excessive moisture will not permit the actinic rayes of the sun to do perfect work.

The best and freshest fruit can only be packed by firms whose establishments are situated in the midst of orchards, or near enough to them to insure the securing of fresh fruit, fully ripe. If fruit is picked before it is ripe the full flavor is not secured. If it is picked when fully ripe, and shipped any great distance, it becomes too ripe before it can be placed in the cans.

With these facts in view the San Jose Fruit Packing Company located their cannery at San Jose, in the center of a great fruit growing district. Thus they are enabled to select the best fruit from hundreds of orchards. The resulting quality of the pack is indicated by the fact that they have never failed to take the highest prize wherever fruits packed by them have been exhibited. They early recognized the opportunity to supply the demand for extra goods, and commenced to put up table fruits, preserves and jams of extra quality. The size and flavor of the fruit enabled them to, in a great measure, displace goods packed in Europe.

Uutil last season the bulk of the pack was placed in tin. There will always be a demand for a certain quantity in tin, as when thus packed it may be more advantageously shipped on long voyages. For domestic use, however, and especially for first-class trade, glass jars are preferable. The fruit presents a better appearance, and the jars, after the contents have been removed may be added to the permanent store of the housewife.

In 1895 Manager W. H. Wright went to Europe, and there learned of an invention for sealing cans and jars by the extraction of air. It is known as the vacuum perfection jar. The lid is a simple tin cap, and is pressed in place, fitting over a round rubber band or cord encircling the neck of the jar, and is securely held in place while the fruit is being processed by a spring steel clamp which adjusts itself automatically, permitting the air and steam to escape until a partial vacuum has been formed by the exclusion of the air and gas from the jar while the fruit is being cooked. The remaining air is extracted with an air pump. The jar is opened by simply piercing the cover with any sharp pointed instrument, when the pressure is relieved, and the cover may be easily removed without the aid of can opener, key or other device. This season a specialty will be made of the packing of dessert fruits in glass jars by the vacuum process. Heretofore the Company has packed from 200,000 to 275,000 cases of twenty-four cans each, per annum, in tin. In future the bulk of the fruit will be packed in glass jars and the firm will enter into the business on a very extensive scale. It is already the largest fruit cannery in the world, and frequently ships in the busy season from five to twenty carloads of canned fruit per day, while as high as twenty-seven carloads have been shipped out in one day. The officers of the Company are: Col. Herman Bendel, Pres.; W. H. Wright, Man. and Treas.; K. H. Plate, Sec.

SAN JOSE FRUIT PACKING COMPANY'S PLANT.

The Labeling Department   *Manufacturing the Cans.*

The Jelly Room   *Soldering Cans.*

THE FLICKINGER CANNERY.

The Growth of an Immense Establishment with an Output of One Million Cans Yearly. Preserving the Fruit in the Orchard Where it is Grown.

A few years ago the only fruit canning plants in the State were located in San Francisco. and to these fruit was shipped from all over the State. As a result, much of the fruit was necessarily picked when it was green. That which was allowed to remain on the trees until it was thoroughly ripe was entirely too ripe by the time it reached the cannery. It was then made into jams, which were unfit for food.

J. H. Flickinger was at that time a wholesale dealer in cattle and sheep. He noted the difficulties experienced by the cannerymen, however, and at once planned to obviate them. His first proposition was that instead of taking fruit to the cannery, the cannery should be taken to the fruit. He decided also that only the best varieties should be used, and of these varieties only the most perfect fruit. He accordingly purchased 500 acres in Santa Clara County, which seemed to recommend itself as the choicest fruit-growing section, selecting a tract near Berryessa. Having first determined which varieties were the most suitable for canning purposes, he selected and planted them. The growth of each tree was carefully noted and the tree was shaped with a view of securing a strong and healthy development.

The ground was from the first thoroughly cultivated and close attention given to pruning. All fruit in excess of what the tree should bear is removed, in order that the remainder may be properly ripened and developed. In order to insure this it is often necessary to remove nine-tenths of the crop. The fruit is constantly watched as it develops. If the orchard is invaded by insects they are promptly exterminated. If after the first thinning the tree is still overloaded, more fruit is removed. If a tree shows any evidence of disease it is at once attended to. Trained employes watch the fruit constantly. When it is thoroughly ripe it is gathered and taken direct to the cannery, the same day. At 4 o'clock in the afternoon the fruit gatherers cease work, in order that no fruit may be left over night uncanned. In this way only the ripest and choicest fruit is canned. There are no long hauls, the cannery being located in the orchard. The fruit, therefore, is left on the tree until it has attained its full size and best flavor. Again, the fruit is carefully assorted by hand after it reaches the cannery and only the choicest is used for canning. All fruit that has been bruised or is too small or not of the proper ripeness for canning is at once cut and put on trays for drying. The fruit may be just as good, but if lacks even in appearance it is dried instead of being canned. Thus nothing is canned but extras. There are no seconds or standards. An idea of the fruit that is canned may be gained when it is stated that the smallest aperture in any can used here is $2\frac{7}{8}$ inches in diameter and that many of the pears and peaches have to have parings taken from them before they can be inserted in the cans. These parings are subsequently dried. The Flick-

THE J. H. FLICKINGER COMPANY'S CANNERY.

inger Company raises tomatoes also for canning, growing them without irrigation, as they are much firmer and sweeter than those supplied with too much water.

The Flickinger Company manufactures all its own cans and uses only resin as a flux. Thus any possible danger from poison acids is averted. All cans are tested under powerful pressure in order to discover any possible leaks. Over 1,000,000 cans per year are manufactured. Thirty barrels of sugar is used per day during the fruit season, or a total of about 400,000 pounds.

ORCHARDS AND CANNERY OF THE J. H. FLICKINGER COMPANY—NEAR BERRYESSA

The J. H. Flickinger brand, which consists of the letters J, H, and F joined, is now widely known, as millions of cans of fruit bearing it have been sent out. It originated in an interesting manner. In 1851 Mr. Flickinger was in the cattle business and had a brand made combining the initials of his name, which brand he used for thirty years. In 1880 he commenced to plant an orchard, and in 1885, when the orchard business superceded the the cattle business, the J. H. F. brand was transferred from hides to boxes and is now known throughout the United States and in some parts of Europe. The Flickinger orchard contains 50,000 fruit trees of the best varieties, including Yellow Crawford, Lemon Cling and Salway peaches, Moorpark and Hemskirk apricots, Royal Anne and Black Tartarian cherries, Bartlett pears, Egg and Green Gage plums and French prunes.

The Flickinger cannery is one of the largest in the world, and is supplied with the latest improved machinery. This is driven by two engines, one twenty and one sixty horse power. The company has its own electric light plant and the buildings are lighted with 150 incandescent lamps. One hundred men are employed the year round; about 500 during the fruit season. The drying ground is kept clean and neat and the fruit is dried on clean white pine trays. Everything about the place, in fact, is kept perfectly neat and clean, and all work is performed systematically. The fruit is all packed by white men and women, who are required to exercise care that neatness and cleanliness shall characterize all their work.

In 1893 the business reached such proportions that Mr. Flickinger formed a corporation known as the J. H. Flickinger Company, with a capital stock of $1,000,000, $500,000 of which is paid up. The officers of company are: President, J. H. Flickinger; Vice-President and General Superintendent, L. F. Graham; Secretary, H. A. Flickinger; Treasurer and Attorney, Joseph R. Patton; Assistant Superintendent, Charles Flickinger.

NURSERY OF R. D. FOX, NEAR SAN JOSE.

THE J. C. AINSLEY PACKING COMPANY. In 1891 J. C. Ainsley started the business of fruit packing in a small way at Campbell. The business has steadily grown until the output of canned goods reached last season nearly half a million of cans. It is probably the only factory in the United States which preserves fruit exclusively for the English market. It is well located for packing a fine class of goods, as it is in the midst of the orchards. The fruit is picked fresh from the trees, is placed in the cans without any delay while perfectly ripe, and thus the product possesses a flavor which cannot be excelled. That the business is a success is shown by the following figures, which gives the pack each year since the commencement: In 1891, 1,100 cases of 24 cans; in 1892, 2,400 cases; in 1893, 4,300 cases; in 1894, 8,300 cases; in 1895, 17,000 cases. An illustration of the factory of J. C. Ainsley Co. is given on page 103.

RELATIVE VALUE OF PRUNES. The following table shows the relative values of the different grades of dried prunes, reckoned with reference to quotations applicable to the four sizes. It was prepared by F. M. Righter, President of the Campbell Fruit Growers' Union:

BASIS PRICE FOR THE FOUR SIZES.		3c	3¼c	3½c	3¾c	4c	4¼c	4½c	4¾c	5c	5¼c	5½c	5¾c	6c	6¼c	6½c	6¾c	7c	7¼c	7½c	7¾c	8c
Sizes of prunes—that is, the number required to make one pound.	30 to 40	5¼	5½	5¾	6	6¼	6½	6¾	7	7¼	7½	7¾	8	8¼	8½	8¾	9	9¼	9½	9¾	10	10¼
	40 to 50	4¾	5	5¼	5½	5¾	6	6¼	6½	6¾	7	7¼	7½	7¾	8	8¼	8½	8¾	9	9¼	9½	9¾
	50 to 60	4¼	4½	4¾	5	5¼	5½	5¾	6	6¼	6½	6¾	7	7¼	7½	7¾	8	8¼	8½	8¾	9	9¼
	60 to 70	3¾	4	4¼	4½	4¾	5	5¼	5½	5¾	6	6¼	6½	6¾	7	7¼	7½	7¾	8	8¼	8½	8¾
	70 to 80	3¼	3½	3¾	4	4¼	4½	4¾	5	5¼	5½	5¾	6	6¼	6½	6¾	7	7¼	7½	7¾	8	8¼
	80 to 90	2¾	3	3¼	3½	3¾	4	4¼	4¼	4¾	5	5¼	5½	5¾	6	6¼	6½	6¾	7	7¼	7½	7¾
	90 to 100	2¼	2½	2¾	3	3¼	3½	3¾	4	4¼	4½	4¾	5	5¼	5½	5¾	6	6¼	6½	6¾	7	7¼
	100 to 110	1¾	2	2¼	2½	2¾	3	3¼	3½	3¾	4	4¼	4½	4¾	5	5¼	5½	5¾	6	6¼	6¼	6¾
	110 to 120	1¼	1½	1¾	2	2¼	2½	2¾	3	3¼	3½	3¾	4	4¼	4½	4¾	5	5¼	5½	5¾	6	6¼

THE SOROSIS FRUIT PACKING COMPANY.

A Two Hundred and Fifty Acre Orchard, the Produce of Which is Preserved Fresh From the Trees. Extra Care Taken to Maintain a High Standard of Excellence.

SOROSIS RESIDENCE AND ORCHARD.

THE superiority of the dried fruit product of Santa Clara County is largely due to the fact that many of the packing firms either own orchards or are directly interested in them. This mutual interest insures the packing of good fruit, in the best possible manner. The Sorosis Fruit Company, for instance, owns an orchard of 250 acres. The fruit is picked fresh from the tree and canned the same day, and hence is fresh and clean. The packing house is situated in the orchard, on the Saratoga road, a few miles from Santa Clara. The orchard was planted with a view of securing a supply of choice varieties for canning and drying. Of the 250 acres the trees on 209 acres are six years old, and those on the remaining 41 acres are four years old. The Foster peaches, five years old this year, are yielding from two to three forty-pound boxes per tree. The peaches and prunes are planted twenty-five feet apart. As prunes do not come into bearing as early as peaches or apricots, the two latter are planted alternately in the center of spaces. They came into bearing quite young, and as a result three crops of peaches and apricots have been secured while the prunes have been coming into bearing. When all varieties are in full

bearing that one which seems to be the most satisfactory and profitable will be allowed to remain, and the others will be cut out. The various varieties grown are peaches, prunes, pears, plums, apricots and cherries. The fruit is dried or canned, according to the condition of the market. When the cannery is in operation the output per season is from 18,000 to 20,000 cases, each case containing two dozen cans. The company has an extensive plant, consisting of three very large buildings and all the necessary machinery for an increased output. Ten men are employed the year round and from 50 to 100 hands during the busy season.

LOAD OF FRUIT FROM SOROSIS PACKING COMPANY.

SOROSIS FRUIT PACKING HOUSE.

The packing season sometimes lasts from August till April. The business is constantly increasing, and last year the company purchased from other orchardists and packed 300 tons of prunes.

The Sorosis process of manufacture insures good, clean fruit, packed in a choice manner. This always commands a good price in the market. Eastern dealers frequently specify that they must have the Sorosis pack, and better prices are received right along than is paid for fruit from the southern portion of the State. Fancy dried peaches, sold last year for 8 @ 9 cents.

INTERESTING FRUIT STATISTICS. Fruit trees in bearing in Santa Clara County were assessed this year at from $50 to $60 per acre. Fruit trees in California are not included with land in the assessment, but are assessed as improvements.

Santa Clara County produces about three-fourths of the total amount of prunes raised in the State.

There are 4,457,761 fruit trees in Santa Clara County, according to the Assessor's report in 1895.

GREAT DRYING ESTABLISHMENTS.

Benefits of Drying and Selling Fruits Co-operatively. Experiments Showing the Ratio of Green Fruit to that Which Has Been Dried. Cost of Drying, Sacking and Selling.

EARLY in the horticultural history of the county it became evident that the financial success of the fruit-grower depended as much upon his ability to properly market the product as it did upon the selection of varieties and the localities in which they should be grown. Orchardists for years produced fruit and entrusted the sale of it to commission men who were interested in securing their commissions, rather than in widening the market or intelligently supplying its demands. As a result, the markets in some cities were often over-supplied, while those of larger cities were not supplied at all. In the case of green fruits, which were perishable, this often resulted in forced sales and a demoralization of prices. At the same time the same fruit would have been gladly received in other cities, where good prices could have been obtained.

THE REMEDY SUGGESTED. Our fruit-growers from time to time held meetings to discuss the situation and suggest remedies. As a result of these meetings, in 1891, the West Side Fruit Growers' Association was formed. Among the objects to be attained was the securing of more economical methods of fruit-drying, and more careful methods in the marketing of the product. Both were accomplished.

The success achieved by the West Side organization led to the establishment, in June, 1892, of the Campbell Fruit Growers' Union. The projectors at once inaugurated a series of scientific experiments. These resulted in the discovery of methods whereby fruit could be more economically dried, showed the exact ratio of the dried product to the green fruit, and the exact state of ripeness when fruit should be gathered. It has been demonstrated that the shrinkage of prunes is less when the fruit is allowed to drop to the ground than it is when the fruit is shaken from the tree.

SANTA CLARA COUNTY MOORPARK APRICOTS

DRYING AND GRADING. A more uniform grading was also insured, with a corresponding increase in the price of the product. When the grower cured his own fruit, some was taken from the trays before it was sufficiently dry, and in other instances was left until it became too dry. Other growers neglected to remove imperfect fruit. Buyers were quick to discover it, and refused to rate the product as choice goods, even though the bulk of the fruit was faultless.

The fruit was also graded more cheaply co-operatively than individually, as the result of improved and costly machinery. The fruit was likewise sold to better advantage. Individuals had become, however unwillingly, competitors of each other, and excessive competition brought low prices, and entailed a state of worriment and unrest. The Union held the fruit as a whole, and could afford to hold it until the best possible price was secured, while if the fruit had remained in the hands of individual growers, many of them would have been forced to sell, thus depreciating the price.

CURING AND PACKING. The expense of curing, packing, grading and marketing was also materially reduced and the temptation of some dealers to sell "short" was removed, as the bulk of the product was in the hands of the Union, and could not be manipulated to suit the purposes of the bears. The concentration of fruit in large quantities commanded the attention and respect of legitimate buyers, and gave a firmer tone to market quotations.

The Union supplied the market carefully, and thus was enabled to avoid contributing to markets already over-supplied.

It has also advertised the fruits of this county and endeavored to increase the demand for the product, calling special attention to its excellent qualities.

PLANT OF THE CAMPBELL FRUIT GROWERS' UNION, CAMPBELL.

A Glimpse of the Drying Ground, Showing Peach Trays.

In Front of the Packing House

The Sulphur Houses.

View of a Portion of the Drying Ground, Showing Trays of Prunes.

RATIO OF GREEN TO DRIED. The Campbell Fruit Growers' Union tests each lot of fruit delivered to it, in order to determine how many pounds of green fruit are required to make one of dried. To each lot of fruit is attached a tin tag, and it is kept separate until it is dried, graded and weighed. Thus each grower is assured of receiving the exact amount to which the weight, grade and dignity of his fruit entitles him. If he picks his fruit before it is fully ripe, the loss just evaporation of the water of vegetation will be greater than if he had allowed it to reach its greatest development. If he has irrigated his fruit too freely the loss by evaporation will be correspondingly great. The returns, therefore are gauged entirely by the quality, size and quantity of his fruit.

The knowledge gained by the experiments and tests which have been made here is of great practical value, not only to members of the Union, but to fruit-growers throughout the county. One of the results of these tests has been the determination of the loss in pounds by evaporation; while the fruit is being dried, or sun-cured. This loss is known locally as "shrinkage." The shrinkage is always greatest in years in which there is excessive rainfall, and in cases where the trees have been too freely irrigated. The following table shows what the shrinkage has been during the past several years in prunes, pears, peaches and apricots, illustrated by the number of pounds of green fruit to make one of dry:

	1892.	1893.	1894.	1895.
Apricots....	5 15	5 54	5 53	5 53
Prunes	2 12	2 54	2 55	2 55
Pears	5 16	6 88	....	....
Early peac's.	5 40	6 97	....	....
Muir "	.3 65	4 7:	....	....
Cling "	.5 35	6 63	....	....

STRAWBERRY FIELD, JOHN SELBY'S FARM.

that he is highly esteemed by his colleagues and that they are abundantly satisfied with his management. The authorized capital stock of the Union is $1,000,000, and the stock is entirely owned and controlled by fruit growers. The value of the plant is $30,000.

CAPACITY OF THE PLANT. The plant has facilities for curing about 7,000 tons of fruit per annum. It is provided with two engines, graders, dippers, bleachers with a capacity of bleaching twenty-five tons at a time, and a double line of steel railway connecting with the most distant portions of the seventeen-acre plat used for the spreading of the fruit upon the trays for sun-curing. The brick warehouse is 50x80 feet, two stories and a basement, with a cement floor. The building is supplied with elevators, graders, scales and other necessary machinery.

The present officers of the Fruit Growers' Union are: President, F. M. Righter; Vice-President, Frank Waldo; Secretary, S. G. Rodeck; Treasurer, Garden City Bank and Trust Company. These, with G. T. Duncan and W. W. Turney, constitute the Directors.

START AND MORRISON. Start & Morrison, of Alum Rock Avenue, near Capital Avenue, operate one of the largest fruit-drying plants in the county. The firm at first dried only the fruit from their own 140-acre orchard, but the business was rapidly extended, and they now dry large quantities. Last season they cured 1,400 tons of French prunes, 150 tons of peaches, 150 tons of apricots and 50 tons of miscellaneous fruits. They have sold and shipped the entire product at good prices. During the fruit drying

ELECTION OF DIRECTORS. The method adopted by the stockholders of the Campbell Fruit Growers' Union in the election of directors and other officers is probably the most just ever devised. Blanks are sent to each stockholder, who expresses thereon his preference for each officer to be elected. The canvassing committee then counts the votes, and by proxy casts ballots electing those who have received the preference. This is practically a secret ballot, and the fact that F. M. Righter has been successively elected President unmistakably indicates

season, which usually lasts from the middle of July till the latter part of October, about fifty men are employed regularly and about fifty more are hired by the day. In 1894 the following amounts of fruit were handled: Prunes, 1,200 tons; peaches, 300 tons, apricots, 600 tons; plums, 300 tons. Messrs G. H. Start and W. S. Morrison have been associated four years. Previous to that the business was carried on by Mr. Start. The demand for apricots and peaches this year for canning purposes makes the price so high that but few of them will be dried.

START & MORRISON'S FRUIT DRYING PLANT.

Prune Grading Machine.

General View of Drying Grounds

A Glimpse of the Fruit Drying Grounds.

The Packing House.

THE SANTA CLARA COUNTY FRUIT EXCHANGE.

much personal sacrifice, but he retains the confidence of the association.

WEST SIDE GROWERS' ASSOCIATION. The West Side Fruit Grower's Association was incorporated in 1891. Its object was to receive green fruit from its stockholders, dry, grade and sell it. It is located in a good fruit growing district, and in 1893 received from its stockholder contributors 3,650 tons of prunes, apricots and peaches. This amount tested the capacity of preparation made for such work and demonstrated the propriety and necessity of such institutions to prevent individual competition among growers and to make uniform products in large quantities. This is the pioneer institution of its kind among fruit growers. Colonel Philo Hersey has been president since its organization till the present season, when he

COLONEL PHILO HERSEY.

SANTA CLARA COUNTY FRUIT EXCHANGE. The Santa Clara County Fruit Exchange was incorporated in 1892. It had for its object grading, packing and selling dried fruit for its stockholders; capital, $100,000; par value of shares, $10. It commenced business in 1893, in which season it built a warehouse, furnished it with all necessary machinery, and during the fruit season received into and shipped from its warehouse over 6,000,000 pounds of dried fruit, and sold over 8,000,000 pounds, for which it received and distributed among its stockholder contributors $430,000. Since 1893 it has built an additional warehouse and is now able to properly handle 600 carloads, or 15,000,000 pounds, which it anticipates for this year of 1896. This exchange has over 500 stockholders, all growers of fruit. It is really a farmers' institution, established and maintained in the farmers' interest. It is a place exciting great interest and curiosity and has been visited by persons from every civilized country, as well as from every State and Territory in the Union. It has the largest and best plant in the world for its purpose, and itself, with its influence, is hailed as the salvation of the fruit industry, both as to production and distribution. Its methods and grades have become the "standard" with the trade and has a reputation for honesty and responsibility. Colonel Philo Hersey was one of the prime movers of this important enterprise, was the first subscriber to stock and has been its president and manager since its inception. His work has been a difficult one, accompanied with

RECEIVING FRUIT—SANTA CLARA COUNTY FRUIT EXCHANGE.

WEST SIDE FRUIT GROWERS' ASSOCIATION PACKING HOUSE AND FRUIT DRYING GROUNDS.

View Showing Several Thousand Fruit Trays.

General View of the Drying Grounds.

The Packing House.

The Fruit Elevator.

declined re-election. His son, R. W. Hersey, was manager for four years and by intelligent work in the production of uniform goods of excellent quality won for the institution an enviable reputation in the market. He has since been made manager for the sale of the entire product of this and three other institutions of like character. This association at one time had forty-two acres covered with trays filled with fruit for sun drying. Accompanying pictures give a very good idea of the work in progress as well as its magnitude.

J. B. HERBERT'S FRUIT DRYER. In 1887 J. B. Herbert commenced to dry the product of his young orchard, on Mabury road. He then found a few hundred trays sufficient for his needs. He subsequently commenced to purchase fruit from surrounding orchards to dry. The business has since grown to such an extent that he shipped last season seventy-six carloads of dried fruit. Mr. Herbert is a practical fruit grower. His own orchard of fifteen acres is one of the most profitable in the county, which is indisputable evidence that he understands the business in all its details. He knows what good fruit is, how it should be packed and what the market demands. He deals with Feron & Ballou, of Chicago, who place the goods in the East. He is constantly advised of the condition and demands of the market, and can, therefore, pay as much for fruit as any drying establishment in the county. The sales last year were largely of the sizes running from 40 to 50 and 50 to 60. The average for the season was 50 prunes to the pound. Mr. Herbert packs all his prunes under the brand: "Santa Clara Valley Prunes, dried and packed by J. B. Herbert" In each box is placed a recipe for preparing the fruit for the table. Mr. Herbert employs during the packing season about thirty hands, the number being augmented to sixty while peaches and apricots are being gathered. Mr. Herbert has enlarged the capacity of his plant since last season and is better prepared than ever before to handle the increased product of neighboring orchards. He has done much to establish the reputation of Santa Clara fruits in Eastern markets.

THE RUCKER FRUIT DRYER.

SHIPPING GREEN FRUIT EAST. Whether it pays best to dry fruit or ship it green depends upon the quality and variety of the fruit. The quality, in turn, depends upon the soil in which the fruit is raised and the climatic conditions by which it is surrounded. As a rule, fruit raised in the mountains has better keeping qualities than that which is raised in the valley. The quality of fruit, however, depends upon so many things that it is not possible to definitely associate it with altitude.

Shippers claim that cherries produced in the Santa Clara Valley keep better than those from any other section of the State. This claim, however, may have to be modified when cherries are more extensively grown in our mountain districts. Our cherries are now shipped in refrigerator cars to New York, Boston, Chicago and nearly all principal cities in the East. Santa Clara County is also noted for the excellency of its fall and winter pears. There are other districts which send out Bartlett pears that are equally as good, both as to flavor and keeping qualities, as those raised here, but our fall and winter pears are in great demand. When picked at the proper state of ripeness, they will keep from four to six weeks without refrigeration. Shippers often send them through to the East in ventilated cars, and there place them in cold storage, where they keep through the winter and till as late as March and April. Thus they are in market at a time when the season for other fruits has closed, and, as a result, bring high prices.

Good table grapes are shipped East profitably in refrigerators. The varieties that are the most satisfactory for this purpose here are the verdel, muscat and cornichon, and as a rule those exhibiting the best keeping qualities come from that portion of the county known as the Santa Cruz Mountain district. Some of the cornichons grown in the valley keep well enough for Eastern shipment, and all of the best table varieties may be profitably grown for the San Francisco market.

As a rule, the fruit that may be most profitably shipped to the East green are cherries, grapes, plums and pears. The profits realized depend,

J. B. HERBERT'S FRUIT DRYING PLANT.

View of the Drying Grounds.

In the Boxing Department.

In the Grading Room.

View of the Warehouse.

of course, upon the quality of the fruit, the condition of the market and the care exercised in properly supplying the demand. If the grower deals with some well-known agent, he gets all that the fruit will bring in the Eastern market, after the freight is paid, less the 7 per cent. commission.

J. Z. Anderson, of the J. Z. Anderson Fruit Company, who has been shipping green fruit for many years, furnishes the following figures concerning commission, freight and charges for refrigeration: His company charges a commission of 7 per cent. for selling the fruit. They pay all the commissions charged by the Eastern dealer, and see that the fruit is properly iced by the refrigerator company before it starts. The grower sometimes loads his own fruit in the cars and braces the boxes at the following rates: Cherries, 1 cent per box; plums, peaches and grapes, 1½ cent per box; pears, 2 cents per box. Freight rates on green

fruit from San Jose to Eastern cities are usually quoted per carload. With a view of securing greater detail, the rate is here given per box for the several varieties of fruit that are shipped green, in refrigerator cars, the freight and refrigeration charges in each instance being included. Cherries are always shipped in ten-pound boxes, pears in forty-pound boxes, and plums, peaches and grapes in twenty-pound boxes.

From San Jose to Kansas City or Omaha, cherries, per 30-pound box, 19 cents; pears, per 40-pound box, 83 cents; plums and grapes, per 20-pound box, 41½ cents; peaches, per 20-pound box, 33⅓ cents.

From San Jose to Chicago, St. Paul or Minneapolis: Cherries, per box, 19⅓ cents; pears, per box, 84 cents; plums and grapes, per box, 42 cents; peaches, per box, 33½ cents.

From San Jose to St. Louis: Cherries, per box, 19¾ cents; pears, per box, 86 cents; plums and grapes, per box, 43 cents; peaches, per box, 34½ cents. From San Jose to New York and Philadelphia: Cherries, per box, 24 cents; pears, per box, $1.07; plums and grapes, per box, 55½ cents; peaches, per box, 42¾ cents.

From San Jose to Boston: Cherries, per box, 26¾ cents; pears, per box,

$1.12; plums and grapes, per box, 56 cents; peaches, per box, 44¾ cents.

From San Jose to New Orleans: Cherries, 22¾ cents; pears, 98½ cents; plums and grapes, 49¼ cents; peaches, 39½ cents.

From San Jose to Denver: Cherries, 18¾ cents; pears, 82 cents; plums and grapes, 41 cents; peaches, 33 cents.

In case the orchardist prefers to sell rather than to ship on commission, the Anderson Fruit Company always buys, offering the best prices which the market rates prevailing in the East will at the time warrant.

At present the most successful and satisfactory method of shipping green fruit great distances is refrigeration. The price of freight will not be higher and will probably be lower, within the next few years. The freight to San Francisco is low. It sometimes pays better, however, to ship East.

HOW TO COOK DRIED FRUIT.

The value of dried fruit as a food and its acceptability to the palate are largely determined by the manner in which it is cooked. In the process of cooking, the flavor, the texture and even the nutritive value may be either preserved or almost entirely destroyed. In too many cases the latter result is successfully attained.

The three rules given below, if followed, will keep any one from going very far astray:

1. All dried fruit should be soaked in clear water until the moisture lost in drying has been nearly replaced.

2. Dried fruit should not be boiled. Steam or simmer only.

3. All sugar used should be cooked with the fruit.

A convenient way to prepare dried fruit is as follows: Rinse it well in warm water, letting it stand in the water five or ten minutes, stirring it well, if the fruit is at all dusty or "sugared," to make it entirely clean. Put it now into the cooking vessel—preferably of porcelain—with just enough water to cover it and let it stand several hours. Put in needed sugar, more water and let simmer till quite tender.

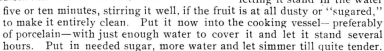

THE J. Z. ANDERSON FRUIT PACKING COMPANY, SAN JOSE.

SANTA CLARA COUNTY ORCHARD SCENES.

F. H. Holmes' Fruit Grader.

Mrs. E. B. North's Foothill Orchard.

W. Ainsworth's Packing House.

J. H. Postlethwaite's Orchard.

FRUITFUL ORCHARDS.

A List of the Profitable Fruit Farms of Santa Clara County. Individual Instances of a Competence Gained by Fruit Growing and Homes Secured Among the Trees.

THE Souvenir was published largely with a view of furnishing to those who reside elsewhere reliable information concerning Santa Clara County and its resources. Fruit-growing is our principal industry, and concerning it, no doubt, will information most be sought. The practical man wants to learn of practical things. He does not want to hear of extraordinary crops, but of ordinary crops. He wants the names of orchardists, their postoffice address and facts and figures concerning average crops in a sufficient number of instances to enable him to form estimates that will be reliable. For the purpose of supplying such information the following facts are given concerning fruit growing in Santa Clara County:

C. M. HATCHER'S TWELVE-ACRE ORCHARD. As a fair example of what may be considered a good investment and average crops one year with another, we may refer to the twelve-acre orchard on the Homestead road, about five miles west of San Jose, which belongs to C. M. Hatcher. The house, barn, windmill and other buildings occupy a little space, so that there are not quite twelve acres of fruit trees. There are upon the tract, however, 1,200 trees, nine years of age, apportioned as follows: Prunes, 520; apricots, 420: Bartlett pears, 260.

The average annual income for these 1,200 trees during the past three years has been $1,300 gross, or a little more than $100 per acre. Assuming the twelve acres to be worth $6,500, which is about the price asked for similar land, Mr. Hatcher secures nearly 20 per cent. per annum upon the value of his orchard. In California, where agriculture and horticulture are more profitable and interest higher than in the East, such an income from such an investment attracts no particular attention. In other States it would be considered a very good investment. The value of an orchard depends upon the interest it pays upon the investment.

PRUNE TREES IN BLOOM, ORCHARD OF C. M HATCHER

JOSHUA COZZENS' ORCHARD. While Santa Clara County is most widely known for its great number of small orchards, supporting a large population, there are orchards hundreds of acres in extent. Such an orchard is that situated on Dry Creek and Kirk roads, leased by Joshua Cozzens. Standing at the intersection of these two roads, as far as the eye can reach, one sees for a mile in both directions a magnificent orchard of 500 acres. About 50 are planted to apricots, nearly 150 bear peaches, and the remaining 300 acres are in prunes. All the trees are now in full bearing, the youngest being five years old, and producing good crops. Last year's yield netted 1,800 tons, and with the trees bearing to their full capacity it is expected that the output will reach 3,000 tons of green fruit. This great orchard is all the work of the lessee, Mr. John Cozzens, who has been in charge of it fourteen years and planted every acre.

ORVIS STEVENS' ORCHARD. Orvis Stevens, whose farm is on Coyote Creek, about a mile from Coyote Station, owns 108½ acres. But a small portion of this is in orchard, most of the hilly portion of the land being used for pasturage. The orchard contains a variety of trees, as Mr. Stevens believes in variety there is safety. He argues that if the orchardist raises but one variety, some unforeseen difficulty may cause a heavy loss, whereas if several are raised, a more uniform income is insured. Most of Mr. Stevens' trees are from eleven to twelve years of age. The apricots, of which there are about 648 trees, produce from five to six tons of green fruit per acre, or a total of from forty to fifty tons. There is a section of this tract containing one and one-half acres which is irrigated. This produces eight tons per acre, which is an exceptionally large crop.

There are 425 Bartlett pear trees, planted seventy five to the acre. These produce on an average 200 pounds per tree, or 15,000 pounds to the

JOSHUA COZZENS' ORCHARD AND DRYER.

Glimpse of the Drying Grounds.

Loads of Fruit Coming In.

In the Packing Shed.

View of the Orchard.

acre. The price is occasionally as low as $15 per ton. Last season it was $30 per ton. Dried pears sold for 6 cents per pound.

There are two acres of peaches, or 215 trees. The average product is twelve and one-half tons per acre. One year the output was fifteen tons per acre. The price per green ton this year averaged about $20. Mr. Stevens dried his peaches and sold them for 6½ cents per pound.

The apple orchard contains 400 trees. The choicest fruit is sold at an average price of one cent per pound, and the seconds are used for manufacturing vinegar. There are more seconds than firsts, because of the codlin moth. Mr. Stevens manufactures from 6,000 to 10,000 gallons of vinegar per annum, using not only fruit from his own orchard but the product of several adjoining, paying from $4 to $5 per ton for seconds. For the vinegar he receives 12 cents per gallon, or a total of from $720 to $1,200.

There are four acres of vines, consisting of muscat, rose of Peru and malvoise. The product sells for from $8 to $12 per ton. Mr. Stevens has forty swarms of bees also, and from these he secures an average of thirty-seven and a half pounds per hive, or a total of 1,500 pounds, which he sells in the comb at from 10 to 12 cents per pound.

Mr. Stevens has a large fruit drying plant and dries not only the product of his own orchard, but purchases and dries the product of other orchards. He dried last year a total of five carloads of 12,000 pounds each, or thirty tons He does not dry the entire product of his orchard, as he occasionally finds it more profitable to ship the fruit East green.

The farm is supplied with a large number of buildings, including a commodious residence, barns, cider factory, fruit houses, etc. Steam power is supplied with which to run the cider mill, fruit grader and other machinery.

Mr. Stevens owns, in addition to the home place, two ten-acre tracts on the Monterey road, on each of which there are 750 trees, consisting of apples, peaches, cherries and apricots. These he leases to other parties on shares.

SHAW'S REMARKABLE ORCHARD. J. W. Shaw owns a twenty-acre orchard only a quarter of a mile west of Berryessa, in the center of the Berryessa district, which is one of the best of the many good

RESIDENCE OF ORVIS STEVENS, COYOTE CREEK.

ones in that section. Mr. Shaw's right hand was injured last summer, and he decided to lease his orchard. It includes 1,200 prune trees, 300 apricot trees and 580 Salway peaches. It was leased for a term of three years, one of which has expired, by Francis de Fiore, who pays a cash rental of $1,430 per annum, or $70 per acre, which is 7 per cent. interest on a valuation of $1,000 per acre.

CAPTAIN D. H. BLAKE'S ORCHARD. Captain D. H. Blake, of the West Side, owns 53 acres. He has 20 acres of prunes, 10 acres are divided between apricots, peaches and cherries and 20 acres in vines. The trees yield five tons per acre; the grapes average four tons.

CAPTAIN WHEELER'S ORCHARD. E. A. Wheeler of West Side was born in Connecticut in 1830 and followed the sea until 1855, when he engaged in business in San Francisco, continuing in that occupation until four years ago, when he removed to his orchard home, of which he had been the owner for seven years. At the time of purchase the land was used as a wheat field. French prunes occupy 20 out of the 30 acres; five acres are in peaches, and pears and cherries cover 2 acres. Two acres and a half are in use as a drying ground. Forty Washington navel orange trees supply not only the family and friends, but a number of boxes to be sold.

THE HOLMES BERRYESSA ORCHARD. F. H. Holmes leases an orchard a mile and a half northeast of Berryessa. There are in the tract 160 acres, of which amount 100 acres are in prunes, 25 in peaches, 20 in apricots, 10 in cherries, and 5 acres are used as a drying ground. The trees vary in age from two to twelve years. About 120 acres are now in bearing. Mr. Holmes irrigates his orchard, and as a result gathers large crops. His apricots and peaches produce from five to twelve tons per acre.

The irrigating plant consists of a forty-horse power engine and a Byron Jackson centrifugal pump, and cost $3,000. With it 1,200 gallons per minute are raised. This will irrigate thoroughly from three to four acres per day. Mr. Holmes not only irrigates his own orchard, but sells water to other orchardists, the rate charged being $2 per hour for 72,000 gallons

ORCHARDS AND DRYING GROUNDS.

F. H. Holmes.

D. H. Blake

John W. Shaw.

E. A. Wheeler.

per hour. Mr. Holmes has had the place nine years. He employs from seven to eight men the year round, and more in the busy season, and always employs white people.

BERNAL'S FRUIT AND VEGETABLES. Ygnacio Bernal owns, on the Monterey road, about nine miles southeast of San Jose, 395 acres of land. The soil here is exceedingly fertile, as it consists largely of silt washed down from the surrounding hills. In this vicinity were located immense cattle and slaughtering pens, and the great pits where the refuse meat was thrown. Here hundreds of tons of bones have been mouldering for more than half a century, and bone dust is one of the richest fertilizers known. Here Ygnacio Bernal planted his orchard. He could scarcely have found a richer spot, and his trees show a remarkable growth. The peach trees, now but three years old, are about ten feet in height, and bore this year a large crop, considering their age. The prune trees are much larger than ordinary trees of their age also, and bore a few prunes last year. Mr. Bernal has about 400 prune trees, 100 peaches and 100 apricots.

Mr. Bernal utilizes the space between the rows of trees by planting corn, peas, beans, melons and pumpkins. The pumpkins produce on an average ten tons to the acre. The price received for them varies with the season. The lowest price is $1.50 per ton in the field, the highest $5 per ton delivered in San Jose, and the average price about $2.50 per ton. The peas raised are the Spanish garvanzas, or soup peas. The product ranges from ten to fifteen 100 pound sacks to the acre. The price is usually low, but last season rose to $4.75 and $5 per hundred pounds. The corn averages twenty sacks, or 2,000 pounds, per acre. Lowest prices received, $1.50 per hundred; highest, $2 per hundred. Muskmelons sell for $3 to $5 per hundred. The usual crop of hay upon Mr. Bernal's valley land is two tons per acre; upon the hillsides, less. The price of hay varies from $8 to $20 per ton, the average being about $12.

About 300 yards from Mr. Bernal's residence a strong spring of water gushes out from beneath a ledge of slate. It is about seventy-five feet higher than the house and the water has been piped to the house, barn and garden. At the spring a reservoir has been built in the rocks which holds 35,000 gallons. Mr. Bernal was born upon the farm which he now owns, as was his father. The land was formerly owned by his grandfather, who came from Mexico.

ARNOLD MOS' ORCHARD. One of the thriftiest of the orchards yet too young to be in bearing is the tract of nineteen and a half acres on the Alum Rock road, about three and a half miles from San Jose, owned by Arnold Mos. The future development of a tree is indicated in some degree by its growth when young, and Mr. Mos' orchard certainly loaks very thrifty. The soil is composed principally of a dark loam consisting of clay and silt that have been washed down from surrounding hills and is therefore fertile.

Mr. Mos purchased nineteen and a half of acres of unimproved land in 1892, paying $250 per acre. He planted 2,200 trees, divided as follows: French prunes, 650; Robe de Sargent prunes, 400; apricots, 150; assorted varieties, including nectarines, peaches and plums, 100. Last year a few of the apricot trees commence to bear. This year he will harvest a few prunes, and hereafter the crop will rapidly increase until the trees are in full bearing. Mr. Mos might have secured some additional income by planting corn or beets between the rows of trees, but he thinks such crops consume plant food that is necessary to the proper growth and development of the trees. A number have offered to plant crops in his orchard on shares, but he has steadily declined and his trees promise to bear accordingly. Land here, as elsewhere in the valley, is slowly but steadily increasing in value, and since Mr. Mos purchased for $250, land in the vicinity has been sold for $300. He is so well satisfied with the present appearance of his orchard that he says $650 an acre would not tempt him to part with it. This is in excess of prices at present ruling, yet land within less than a mile and a half in full bearing sold several years ago for $500 an acre, and within three years Mr. Mos' trees will easily pay 10 per cent. interest on a valuation of $1,000 per acre.

VIEW OF YGNACIO BERNAL'S FARM, MONTEREY ROAD.

SANTA CLARA COUNTY ORCHARDS

Ygnacio Bernal.

Thomas Derby.

John Shaw.

Mrs. von Kaathoven.

Mr. Mos has a comfortable four-roomed cottage, barn, windmill, tank and all accessories. He is a great lover of fine stock and has two very promising colts, one a yearling Hambletonian and the other a two-year old Belmont. His poultry is thoroughbred Plymouth Rock.

The Citizens' Water Company, which recently purchased the Fiacro Fisher Lake, near Coyote Station, paying therefor $111,600, has surveyed a canal through Mr. Mos' orchard. If water for irrigation is brought through here it will greatly enhance the value of the property. The land fronts on the great Alum Rock road, directly east of San Jose, and the cars of the Alum Rock railroad pass in front of the door at short intervals during the day. The distance to the business center of the city, three miles and a half, is made in about twenty minutes.

GOULTER'S WEST SIDE ORCHARD. W. A. Coulter for many years practiced law in Washington, D. C., and still has several important cases there on appeal, though he has retired from general practice. In the early part of 1894 he came to Santa Clara County, and in June of that year purchased a fifty acre prune orchard near the Lincoln school house, about nine miles west of San Jose, paying therefor $600 an acre. Twenty-five acres are in prunes ten and twelve years of age, and therefore in full bearing. The trees on the remaining twenty-five acres are five years of age and have just come into bearing. From the fifty acres he last year gathered 157½ tons of prunes, or 3.15 tons per acre. These he could have sold in a green state for $30 per ton, or $4,725, equal to a gross income of $94.50 per acre. He had a large storehouse, however, and drying grounds, and decided that he could market the fruit in a dried state more profitably. It dried 2.62 to 1, or, in other words, 2.62 pounds of green fruit were required to make one of dried. The dried fruit he graded and sold at an average of 5 cents per pound, or a total of $6,000, equal to $120 per acre gross, though twenty-five acres, or one-half the tract, has just come into bearing. Thus he secured an income last year representing nearly twenty per cent of the amount invested. Mr. Coulter pays particular attention to the grading of his fruit. He not only grades it in its green state, but after

THE ARNOLD MOS YOUNG PRUNE ORCHARD, NEAR SAN JOSE.

it is dried, as well. Of the sixty tons of dried prunes, eighteen tons, or nearly one-third of the entire crop, went thirty to forty prunes to the pound. The average of the county is about fifty to the pound.

MRS. HELENA WRIGHT'S FARM. November, 1852, William Wright, with a partner, purchased 160 acres of land six miles west of Santa Clara. The following year he purchased his partner's interest and subsequently acquired adjoining property. Five years ago Mr. Wright died, and since then the property, consisting of 220 acres, has been managed by his widow, Mrs. Helena Wright. The soil is exceedingly fertile and consists largely of a fine silt, mixed with gravel, which was undoubtedly deposited by the overflow of some creek. There are yet upon the place scattered sycamore trees, which seldom grow in California except along water courses.

Such uniformly large crops of wheat have been grown that until last season fruit trees were not planted, except enough to supply fruit for the use of the family. However, the four-acre plot, which includes apples, peaches, pears, prunes, cherries, persimmons, walnuts, chestnuts, quinces, nectarines, almonds and figs, now produce so much that the product as a whole is sold, enough only being reserved for home use.

The income has been gained by what may be termed general farming, rather than by attention to a specialty. Wheat is raised, and the several fields are then used for pasturing hogs, horses and cows. The refuse and remnants from orchard, vineyard and vegetable garden, with corn and pumpkins, are used as food for poultry, hogs, etc. Thus the stock is raised almost without cost, and the increase adds largely to the farm revenue.

Last year Mrs. Wright's son, W. T. Wright, put out eighteen acres in prunes, apricots and peaches, on his tract of twenty-five acres, and this year planted two acres more. The land here is so fertile that it is a common practice to plant vegetables between the rows until the trees come into bearing. Mr. Wright planted yellow corn, and it grew in a way that was wonderful. The average height is between eight and nine feet, while

SANTA CLARA COUNTY COUNTRY RESIDENCES.

James R. Judge.

W. A. Couiter.

Theodore Hersey.

Randolph Hersey.

much of it is from twelve to fourteen feet. It bore a heavy crop, the ears being unusually large and long. Corn on the cob weighs on an average 72 pounds per sack. This will just make a good bushel of 56 pounds when shelled. It usually sells in California for more than any other cereal. From $1 to $1.15 per cental is not an unusual price. At present yellow corn is down to 90 @ 85 cents per cental, which is very low. The average crop in Santa Clara County is 50 sacks of 72 pounds each on the cob, equal to 2,800 pounds shelled, per acre, At the present price the gross income per acre averages $23. This, it should be understood, is raised between the rows of young fruit trees before they come into bearing.

The soil on Mrs. Wright's farm is all porous and friable and just such as is well suited to the growth of peaches and apricots. Of course all varieties of fruits and vines thrive, but the two mentioned reach unusual size. The county road from Santa Clara to San Francisco passes through the farm, leaving 140 acres on the south of the road, 80 of which belongs to Mrs. Wright's daughter, Mrs. M. P. Gibson, of Santa Clara. This tract of 140 acres will probably be sold. Mrs. Wright's farm is about two and a half miles southeast of Mountain View, nine miles from San Jose, six miles west of Santa Clara, and eight miles from the Leland Stanford University.

MRS. WATSON'S ORCHARD. On the West Side one of the thriftiest orchards is owned by Mrs. Elizabeth L. Watson, who in 1881 purchased a wheat field and unaided except by the labor of a sixteen-year-old son, planted it with fruit trees. The plat contains twenty-six acres, 22 of which are in prunes and 4 in apricots. The trees are now in full bearing. Mrs. Watson one year gathered 100 tons of prunes from 22 acres. Her net income that year was $3,500, while the lowest income any year since the orchard has been in bearing was $1,200. The product of the orchard is dried and prepared for market upon the place, ample facilities having been provided for that purpose. Mrs. Watson years ago retired from active participation in work of any kind, and yet she exercises a personal supervision over all work done upon the orchard.

Mrs. Watson is a polished speaker, having a rare gift of language and a personal address that is charming and at once wins her audience. She preached in Metropolitan Temple every Sunday for four years, excepting an interval of six months spent in Australia, and always had audiences ranging from 500 to 1,500 people. She often addresses audiences under the great oak tree known as Temple Oak, upon her Sunny Brae farm. Susan B. Anthony and Miss Anna Shaw have also held services here.

The residence is a very beautiful building and is surrounded by lawns and flowers. Rose hedges align the driveways, and beds of carpet gardening, Mrs. Watson's own handiwork, are numerous. The furnishings and furniture of the house are palatial and exceedingly artistic. The whole property is attractive and is visited annually by thousands. Mrs. Watson and her daughter reside alone, but the house is rarely without guests, as Mrs. Watson is known throughout the United States. Miss Lucretia Watson has just finished her third year at Berkeley. After graduating from the California University she will take a two-years' divinity course at Harvard.

PRATT'S ILLAWARRA ORCHARD. In 1887 G. W. Pratt purchased the twenty-acre orchard now known as Illawarra, on the Hostetter road, near Berryessa. The trees were at that time five years of age. There are twelve acres of apricots, six acres of prunes and two acres of cherries.

Mr. Pratt holds that the greatest average of profit is secured when one has several varieties of trees. There is scarcely any variety which bears heavily continuously, and if the orchardist has several varieties he is almost sure to get a good crop of some kind.

Mr. Pratt also advocates irrigation. He purchases water from a neighbor who has an irrigating plant, paying therefor $1.50 an hour for a flow of 800 gallons a minute. He turns the water on early in May, when the fruit is about half grown. He allows the 800 gallons per minute to flow ten hours a day for seven days. This costs but $105, and the increase in the size of the crop more than compensates for this.

Mr. Pratt's apricots are Moorparks, a variety which does not everywhere bear regularly. Upon his land, however, he finds it a very satisfactory fruit, and thinks that apricots will continue to be a safe crop to raise, as they cannot be grown successfully in any other State in the Union. From the twelve acres Mr. Pratt last year gathered ninety tons, or seven and one-half tons per acre. This was, of course, an unusually large crop.

MRS. HELENA WRIGHT'S CORNFIELD.

REPRESENTATIVE SANTA CLARA COUNTY COUNTRY RESIDENCES.

Mrs. Helena Wright.

A. H. Upton.

George W Pratt.

Mrs. E. L. Watson.

During the past five years the crop from the twelve acres has ranged from forty-five to fifty tons. The best tree on the place yields regularly from twelve to thirteen forty-pound boxes, while from it one year were gathered twenty-two boxes. One year 7,000 apricots were removed from this tree, by actual count, in order that the tree might not have to bear an excessive crop.

Mr. Pratt also finds cherries profitable. The crop from the two acres sold last year for $400. One year the yield was unusually large and the price unusually high and he sold the crop from his two acres of cherries for $800. From the six acres of prunes, when the trees were five years old, he sold $800 worth of fruit, and he received about the same amount the succeeding year. Since then the crop has, upon the whole, been steadily increasing, though sometimes less in one year than another. The largest gross income from the six acres in any one season was $1,500, or $250 per acre.

Mr. Pratt thinks he made a good investment when he purchased his twenty-acre tract, and says nothing less than $900 an acre would tempt him to part with it.

ATTORNEY UPTON'S ORCHARD. A. H. Upton, the attorney, who, by the way, is a graduate of the law department of the noted university at Ann Arbor, has eleven acres of full-bearing orchard on Stevens Creek road, about three and a half miles west of San Jose. This orchard is in some ways a remarkable one. There are about four and one half acres of apricots, four and one-half acres of prunes, one acre of cherries, and a few trees of other varieties to supply fruit for family use. Most of the trees are about fifteen years of age, and are, therefore, in full bearing.

Mr. Upton has owned the place three years. In 1893 the crop from the ten acres aggregated eighty-one tons. This was an extra large crop. The house, barn, lawn and roads occupy about one acre, leaving but ten acres in fruit. When a very large crop is borne one year, the crop is always below the average the succeeding year. In keeping with this rule, the crop for 1894 was but twenty-five tons. In 1895 the trees began to recover from the excessive demand made upon them two years previously and the crop amounted to forty-five tons.

The average price of the crop, as a whole, during the three seasons, including the prunes, cherries and apricots, was $25 per ton. This made the gross income in 1893 $2,015, or $202.50 per acre for the ten acres; in 1894 $625, or $62.50 per acre; in 1895 $1,125, or $112.50 per acre. The average per acre for the three seasons was $125.83. Of the one hundred

GARDEN SCENE, HOME OF O. M. BOYLE.

cherry trees seven are of the Napoleon Biggarreau variety. These Mr. Upton finds quite profitable. as they pay each season from $7 to $10 per tree. Mr. Upton's other varieties of cherries, however, are much less profitable, though they bring a gross income of $1 per tree per annum, equal, at 100 trees to the acre, to $100. Twelve almond trees usually produce about $10 worth of nuts. This year the crop sold for $15.

Mr. Upton has one lot of prunes, consisting of 140 trees, which have been remarkably thrifty, and which, during the past fifteen years, have never suffered from any disease, and not one of the number has been lost.

In 1893 Mr. Upton harvested from a little less than five acres of prunes fifty-eight tons of fruit. This was more than eleven tons per acre, which was a remarkable crop. Mr. Upton preserved the warehouse receipts for the benefit of doubters.

Mr. Upton values his place at $1,000 an acre, which is not surprising, considering that his gross income from the orchard is more than 12 per cent. interest on such valuation.

THE EMERSON TRACT. The missionaries and other early settlers in California had their choice in the selection of land, and naturally selected the choicest. S. B. Emerson, nearly four decades ago, selected a tract of more than 900 acres, two miles south of Mountain View, near the foothills. It was a magnificent tract, covered with groves of large and beautiful oak trees. Two young men once said in his presence that they would like to have some land. He at once told them that if they would plant eighty acres with fruit trees and care for them until they were a certain age he would give them one-half of the land. They accepted the offer, and when the time was up he made them a present of the entire tract. He preserved the remainder intact, however, until his death, in 1889, when it was learned that he had willed it to his relatives, C. B. Emerson and C. P. Berry. The former subsequently died, willing his share to his wife, Mrs. O. A. Emerson, and his children, E. L. Emerson, F. L. Emerson and Grace Emerson. The land was at that time used for grain growing, and could, of course, be handled by one person. When the fruit-growing era was inaugurated, the value of the land grew so rapidly and the amount of work and capital involved was so great that a few acres were enough for each owner. A tract of 400 acres was accordingly set aside to be sold in ten and twenty-acre lots, the Emerson heirs retaining 240 acres and Mr. Berry a like amount. The land was offered at $200 per acre, with a clause in the contract providing that the land should be planted with fruit trees. As a result there are now upon the tract offered for sale a number of young

SANTA CLARA COUNTY ORCHARDS AND VINEYARDS

A. H. Upton's Prune Orchard—in Winter.

Residence of W. Postlethwaite

Orchard and Vineyard of Dr. E. O. Cochrane.

Under the Oaks—C. P. Berry and Family.

and thrifty orchards. The wood secured in clearing the land was quite an object, as live oak stove wood commanded $6.50 per cord, on the ground, and white oak $5.50. The remainder of the tract offered will probably soon be covered with orchards also. Most of the larger ranches and grants in the valley have now been subdivided. The property is well situated, being but two miles from the postoffice and depot at Mountain View, six miles from Stanford University and twelve from San Jose.

S. R. JOHNSON'S ORCHARD. S. R. Johnson owns 360 acres on the Bollinger road, all of which is in fruit and vines except twenty acres. After putting out 200 acres in French prunes, the remaining acreage was planted to apricots, peaches, cherries and almonds in divisions of about twenty acres each. Sixty acres are also in bearing vines. Twenty acres are reserved for raising hay, and this plot is also used as a drying ground. The trees are all now five years old and upward and are producing excellent crops. No irrigation of any kind is done.

THE TANTAU FARM. Frederick W. Tantau owns, on the Bollinger road, about seven and a half miles southwest of San Jose, 136 acres. There are 100 acres in prunes, only 20 acres of which are in bearing. From the latter he last year gathered 100 tons of fruit, or five tons per acre. The product sold for $30 per ton, or $3,000 for the crop from the twenty acres. There are five acres of apricots, only a few of which are yet in bearing. The remaining thirty-one acres are devoted to hay and pasturage. The hay field generally yields two tons of wheat hay per acre. The farm is well supplied with buildings, the residence and barn both being especially large and well appointed. Mr. Tantau has built and furnished for the amusement of his two little girls a play house which is a complete counterpart of ordinary residences. The building is handsomely finished inside and out—redwood within and rustic without. It is also thoroughly furnished and is a complete establishment, with dishes, cupboard, fine furniture and a good stove. The little girls are here learning the routine of the household.

Mr. Tantau came to California in 1853, when he was but four years old, and has resided in Santa Clara County continuously since.

He is one of the pioneers who have been active in developing the State of California, and has made a success of life.

Besides his magnificent orchard property he has valuable business property in San Jose which yields a substantial income.

EVELYN AND MABEL TANTAU'S PLAY HOUSE, WEST SIDE.

MRS. NELLIE ARQUES' FRUIT LAND. When the Martin Murphy estate was divided, the six heirs, B. D. Murphy, J. T. Murphy, Patrick Murphy, Mrs. M. Taafe, Mrs. Nellie G. Arques and Mrs. R. T. Carroll, each received 820 acres. Mrs. Arques was given that portion of the land nearest to the town of Mountain View. Much of it was formed of sediment deposited by Stevens Creek, and is therefore unusually fertile. It has been used largely for grain growing, but within the past few years its peculiar adaptability as a soil for apricots and peaches has been demonstrated, and the demand for good fruit land in the vicinity caused the subdivision of several large tracts. These were sold at prices ranging from $200 to $250 per acre. Mrs. Arques owns 910 acres of land near Tres Pinos, in San Benito County, which is now leased. She owns also 225 acres north of Lawrence Station, besides an interest in San Jose business and residence property. She therefore placed in the hands of Walter A. Clark, of Mountain View, a few hundred acres of the Mountain View property, which has been placed on the market at from $225 to $250 per acre. The land lies about a mile east of Mountain View, between the main highway from San Jose to San Francisco and the railroad.

The facilities for shipping at Mountain View are excellent, as there are several shipping points, or landings, on sloughs which put in from San Francisco Bay, from a mile and a half to a mile and three-quarters north of town. The freight on hay from Mountain View to San Francisco by the railroad is $1.80 per ton and by schooner $1 per ton. A large portion of Mrs. Arques' land on the northern side of the railroad is covered with groves of oak trees, giving it a park like appearance which is very beautiful. Her land extends to tidewater in Guadalupe Slough. Upon the land south of the railroad water may be obtained at a depth of from forty to seventy feet. Upon the land north of the railroad artesian water may be obtained most anywhere. The railroad is the boundary of the artesian belt on the south. At Mountain View the water barely flows over the top of the well-casing an inch. As one goes north the flow increases in volume until the bay is reached. All of the land in the artesian belt is choice garden land; that south of the railroad is a lighter and more porous soil, particularly adapted to peaches, prunes and apricots. In fact, it is adapted to the raising of any kind of fruit, berries or vegetables. Irrigation is not necessary on this land except for berries and vegetables, and as artesian water can be obtained, makes the property valuable. Illustrations of Mrs. Arques' property may be found on page 75.

SANTA CLARA·COUNTY ORCHARDS.

A Portion of the Emerson Tract   S. R. Johnson.

C. P. Berry.   Mrs. Van Kaathoven.

EDEN VALE ORCHARDS. Eden Vale is a station on the Southern Pacific Railroad, about seven miles south by southeast of San Jose. Here is located the great Hayes-Chynoweth mansion, with its extensive grounds, luxuriant flower gardens and magnificent groves of oak. A church is located upon the property and near at hand there is a public school. Adjoining the Hayes-Chynoweth orchards and grounds on the south there is a tract of orchard land containing 3,000 acres, which has recently been put upon the market by Frank C. Ensign, the real estate agent of San Jose. As indicative of the price of good fruit land, it may be stated that this tract is offered at from $250 to $285 per acre in five and ten-acre lots, half cash, balance in one and two years at ruling rates of interest. Water, an abundant supply, is obtained at a depth of sixty feet. The main county road from San Jose to Gilroy and Monterey passes in front of the property. Mr. Ensign is engaged in a general real estate and insurance business in San Jose, where he has resided the past nine years.

J. P. SCHEUER'S ORCHARD. J. P. Scheuer owns a fifteen acre orchard on the corner of Plummer avenue and the Foxworthy road, a few miles southwest of San Jose. It consists mostly of prunes and peaches, though he has some apricots, pears, plums, cherries and apples. During the past two years Mr. Scheurer irrigated his orchard, he thinks profitably. He came to Santa Clara County seven years ago and purchased ten acres. Two years ago he purchased an additional tract of five acres.

J. B. HERBERT'S REMARKABLE ORCHARD. J. B. Herbert, whose home is on the Mabury road, a few miles east of San Jose, has one of the best and most profitable orchards in the county. In 1887 he purchased fifteen acres, which is now all in fruit except the space occupied by the house, barn, roads and creek. There are three and three-fourths acres of apricots, four acres of peaches, six acres of prunes and about three fourths of an acre in apples, pears and cherries. Last year he gathered from the three

and three-fourths acres of apricots seventeen tons. They were sold for $510, making the income from the apricots $153.84 per acre. The product of the entire orchard of fourteen acres sold in 1892 for $3,200, or $228.57 per acre; in 1893 for $2,600, or $185.71 per acre; in 1894 for $2,700, or $192.85 per acre; in 1895 for $2,000, or $142.85 per acre. In May of last year Mr. Herbert was offered $16,500, or $1,100 per acre, for his orchard, but declined to sell

THE PARR PROPERTY. When Vancouver visited the Santa Clara Valley in 1892, he was impressed with the magnificent groves of oaks and the park-like appearance which they lent to the landscape. Most of them were long ago removed. One of the few groves which yet remain may be seen upon the Oakhurst farm, a few miles south of Campbell, on the road to Los Gatos. Here remain some of the grand old oaks in all their original beauty.

The farm, consisting of sixty acres, belongs to Mrs. W. J. Parr, of Los Gatos. Forty acres are in fruit trees, and the twenty-acre plot enclosing the grove of oaks is used for raising hay. The majority of the fruit trees are prune, though there are apricots, almonds, peaches, figs, walnuts and cherries It is an attractive place of residence, where the surroundings are beautiful and pleasant. It is maintained as a property for the children rather than as a source of revenue, as Mrs. Parr has extensive interests elsewhere, including the Parr block in Los Gatos, residence property in Los Gatos for rental, business property in Santa Cruz, and unimproved land in the fruit district near Saratoga and elsewhere. Mrs. Parr resides in Los Gatos with her son and two daughters, where she has a fine residence.

EDENVALE ORCHARDS AND GROVES.

MRS. NORTH'S FOOTHILL FARM. About four miles west of Saratoga, in the foothills, is a farm known as Idlewild. Here there is a large fourteen-roomed house which the former proprietor kept as a summer resort. It is located on a sunny southern exposure just

WEST SIDE COUNTRY RESIDENCES.

S. R. Johnson.

Nathan Hall.

F. Tantau.

J. C. Merithew.

below the crest of a hill, commanding a very extended and beautiful view of the valley. There is an abundance of small game in the vicinity, such as quail, doves, squirrels and rabbits, and Stevens Creek, a mile west, is a good trout stream, though perhaps not better than Campbell Creek, two miles south. Less than a mile away is located the Azule Mineral Springs, the water of which is noted for its medicinal qualities, and is bottled and sold throughout the State.

About 100 acres have been cleared. This is all good fruit land, and is especially well suited to vines, though it is at present used for raising hay and for pasturage. About 60 acres are covered with chaparral and oak, from which hundreds of cords of wood could be cut.

A number of fruit trees, such as apples, pears, prunes, peaches, apricots, oranges, lemons and walnuts are upon the place. The Idlewild farm now belongs to Mrs. E. B. North, of San Jose.

JOHN McALISTER'S ORCHARD. John McAlister owns 38 acres on Bascom avenue, west of the Fair grounds, three-fourths of a mile from Santa Clara, and about two miles from San Jose. Sixteen acres are in prunes; 10 acres in apricots; 2 in pears; 2 in cherries, and 8 in peaches, almonds, walnuts, oranges and other fruits. This orchard is sheltered from wind by tall blue gums, allowing the

LATE RESIDENCE OF JOHN M'ALISTER, BASCOM AVENUE.

AT THE GATE, JOHN M'ALISTER'S FARM.

orchard to receive the full benefits of the ripening rays of the sun, with the result that all the fruit ripens very early. The soil is rich and loamy, and highly productive, all the trees bearing freely and yielding good crops. Last year from the sale of one acre of cherries, $750 was realized. Recently his beautiful residence was destroyed by fire, but will be rebuilt more beautiful than before.

DR. LUSSON'S SUNNYWOOD ORCHARD. Sunnywood orchard, the property of Dr. and Mrs. Lusson, is very pleasantly situated in the foothills on the west side of the valley, five and a half miles west of Santa Clara, and four miles south of Mountain View on the Southern Pacific railroad. It is within an easy drive from Stanford University. The place contains 55 acres of land, about 45 acres of which are in fruit trees, now in full bearing. The orchard includes peaches, pears, prunes and apricots. The output varies, of course, according to the season and prevailing prices. The average gross income for the past several years has been $6,000, or $133 33 per acre. The soil produces fruit that has an excellent flavor. The location is most healthful and picturesque, being on high ground at the foot of the hills, which add to the landscape a romantic beauty, while the Santa Cruz mountains in the background shelter it from the fogs and wind. The climate

SANTA CLARA COUNTY COUNTRY RESIDENCES.

W. Ainsworth.

Mrs. E. B. North.

Dr. E. O. Cochrane.

Dr. Pedro Merlin Lusson.

approaches perfection, as the heat in summer is not extreme, and frosts in winter are extremely rare. The most delicate flowers bloom in the open air throughout the year, making it one of the most charming localities in the county.

WESTON'S PEAR ORCHARD. A good illustration of the profits secured in Santa Clara County in pear culture is furnished by B. F. Weston, whose orchard is on the Kifer road, about two miles and a half northwest of Santa Clara. The pear orchard is a side issue with Mr. Weston, as he secured it through a trade, and only resides here because of the healthful climate and natural beauty of the country. His principal investments are in timber in Calavaras and Tuolumne counties, and in lands in Los Angeles and San Diego counties.

The crops and income for each year since the orchard came into Mr. Weston's possession have been as follows: In 1890 the trees bore a few scattering pears, the entire output of the orchard aggregating but one ton, which was sold for $55; crop of 1891, 50 tons, which sold for $45 per ton, or $2,250; crop of 1892, 75 tons, which sold for $40 per ton, or $3,000; crop of 1893, 100 tons, which sold $30 per ton, or $3,000; crop of 1894, 185 tons, which sold for $20 per ton, or $3,700; crop of 1895, 190 tons, which sold for $30 per ton, or $5,700. Mr. Weston's is probably the best pear orchard in the county. Fruit buyers are unanimous in the opinion that it will, when in full bearing, produce 400 tons of fruit.

The trees are all of the Bartlett variety, and are now eleven years of age. They were well planted, have been well cared for, and are perfectly clean, harboring no scale or codlin moth. The land is in the artesian belt, and there are upon the place three artesian wells, averaging 500 feet in depth. The land was formerly in strawberries, and the water was used for irrigation. Mr. Weston does not irrigate the pear orchard, however, and the wells are capped.

Mr. Weston was born in Somerset County, Maine, in December, 1849. He resided in Whitehall, Muskegon, County, Michigan, until he came to California. In 1883 he was united in marriage to Miss Abbie May Bunker, also a native of Maine, and shortly thereafter removed to the Golden West.

E. P. REED'S 100-ACRE ORCHARD. On the east side of the valley, on the corner of the White and Story roads, is located the orchard of E. P. Reed. At this point the land gently rises from the level plain to meet the foothills and the average altitude is about one hundred feet higher than the center of the valley. On this account the location is an ideal one, as there is no danger from frosts. The soil is a dark loam, very rich and easily worked. The trees show evidences of the extreme fertility of the soil by the abundant green foliage and general thriftiness. The tract was originally a portion of the great Pala Rancho of 4,400 acres. In 1852 it was owned by Charles White, who died in that year. For many years thereafter it was a subject of litigation and for twenty years Mr. Reed had charge of the estate. He was familiar with every acre of the tract and after the distribution he selected and purchased a tract of 240 acres, which he conceived to be the choicest part of the ranch. Out of this he conveyed to his three sons, George, Edward and Henry, 140 acres, reserving 100 acres for himself, which he set out to fruit. All of the trees are from five to ten years old and are in full bearing, producing bounteous crops every year. Recently Mr. Reed sold fifteen acres for the price of $350 per acre. Of the remaining 85 acres 10 are devoted to hay, 31 are in apricots, 13 acres in prunes, 3 acres in cherries, 14 acres in pears, 6 acres in peaches and 5 in plums. The other improvements consist of a house, barn, sheds, house for laborers, windmill and tank-house, a fruit cutting-house, fruit store-house, etc. There are complete appliances for handling, drying and packing the entire product of the place, and it is one of the most complete and best arranged fruit ranches in the county.

GENERAL VIEW OF E. P. REED'S GREAT ORCHARD.

Mr. Reed is one of the pioneers of the State, coming here in 1850. He has prospered in this land of sunshine, and besides his fruit interests he has a tract of 97 acres of land near Milpitas and another of 425 acres in Santa Cruz County. He also owns valuable property on Market street in San Jose, where he has a large residence surrounded by beautiful grounds.

E. W. CONANT'S FARM, MERIDIAN ROAD. The wealth of flowers, fruits and vegetables that may be produced upon a few acres in some of our choice districts will ever be beyond the comprehension of all except those who have seen the land and its products. Where water can

SANTA CLARA COUNTY ORCHARDS.

F. L. Emerson.

B. F. Weston.

Thomas Derby.

J. P. Scheuer.

be had for irrigation, various crops may be grown in one season, and the product per acre is truly wonderful.

On the Meridian road about two miles south of San Jose, is a representative orchard of twenty six acres, the property of E. W. Conant. Prunes occupy about fifteen acres. There are one hundred and sixty-three cherry trees, and a peach orchard, the remaining space being devoted to almonds, walnuts, figs and olives. Prunes, peaches and cherries form the bulk of the crop, other trees being grown simply for ornament, variety and family use. The orchard is irrigated from Los Gatos creek.

The fertility of the soil is such that space is utilized to a remarkable degree. A small patch of raspberries, perhaps a hundred feet in length, planted between two rows of trees furnishes more than one family can use, as the bushes reach a height of from seven to ten feet, and bear prolifically. Likewise a few blackberry bushes furnish all that is needed in that line. Grapevines clamber up the side of the tank house twenty feet, with bunches of grapes everywhere peeping from beneath the leaves. Roses trail along the side of the house, each stem bearing a separate variety, as the result of Mr. Conant's enthusiasm in budding. An almond tree, whose trunk is perhaps two feet in diameter, bears immense quantities of nuts. A walnut, walnuts; an olive, olives.

A little plot between the house and barn shows green peas in luxuriance: strawberries rich and ripe. Flowers grow in profusion all about the house, which is a beautiful residence of six rooms and bath. Finely-bred Partridge Cochins and Buff Leghorns sing in the neat wire fenced plot beneath the fruit trees. Sleek-coated carriage horses, through whose veins courses the blood of Almont Patchen, who has trotted a mile in 2:08¾, look out from padded stalls, and carriages, buggies and carts are seen through an open doorway. A bicycle, also, for one may with it reach the heart of the city in twenty minutes. Twenty-six acres in this section furnishes a handsome income, and Mr. Conant has a wife and two children to help him enjoy it.

A. H. HARTEVELT'S ORCHARD. A. H. Hartevelt is a native of Holland and was attracted from the mother country by the renown of the Garden Spot of the World. He arrived in 1888. His orchard

RESIDENCE OF WARREN COTTLE, MONTEREY ROAD.

contains twenty acres, all in French prunes. It is now nearly six years old and is one of the most promising. In addition to the orchard Mr. Hartevelt is the owner of a 100-acre ranch in Tulare County.

A FERTILE SIX-ACRE ORCHARD. Mrs. Jane H. Smith owns, on the Meridian road, about a mile from the Alameda, an orchard of six and a half acres, which is one of the thriftiest and most profitable in the county. The trees were well planted, have been well cared for and even among the many thrifty orchards of the vicinity attracts attention by reason of the size and appearance of the trees and the crops borne. The orchard contains cherries, peaches, apricots and apples. Mrs. Smith's residence is one of the most beautiful, architecturally, in the county.

JOHN VANDER WENS' ORCHARD. John Vander Wens owns, about five miles south of San Jose, an orchard of 55 acres. There are 35 acres of prunes, 12 acres of peaches, 7 acres of cherries and 1 acre of apricots. Mr. Vander Wens purchased the orchard in 1890. It is now eight years old and produces on an average 250 tons of fruit per annum. Two water rights were secured with the land and the orchard is irrigated. The soil is extremely fertile and is tilled scientifically, with a view of stimulating the growth of the trees without impairing their vitality. The trees are pruned, so that they can bear their loads of fruit without breaking, and care is taken so that they will not overbear and shorten the life of the tree. It is one of the best cultivated and most fruitful orchards in the county, and the returns it brings its owner is an evidence that fruit growing pays.

P. G. GOODMAN'S PEACHES AND PRUNES. P. G. Goodman, of the Senter road, for many years raised grain in San Joaquin County. He farmed on an extensive scale, cultivating several thousand acres. The uncertainty of the market, however, often resulted in the loss of all that had been made in years previous. In 1879 Mr. Goodman came to Santa Clara County and purchased a tract of twenty-five acres on the banks of the Coyote Creek, near San Jose. In 1881 he planted several acres to fruit trees, and has each year added a few of those varieties which proved profitable. The entire twenty-five acres is now in fruit, though some of the

REPRESENTATIVE ORCHARDS AND HOMES.

E. W. Conant.

John Vander Wens.

A H. Hartewelt.

Mrs. Jane H. Smith.

trees, recently planted, have just come into bearing. He now has 1,200 apricot trees, 550 peaches, 550 prunes, and 20 trees of assorted varieties, such as apples, pears, figs, cherries and plums.

The soil is composed of a fine silt, apparently deposited by overflows from Coyote Creek in ages past before the channel had reached its present depth. This silty soil is about twelve feet in depth and is the very choicest soil for peaches, apricots and cherries. Mr. Goodman has kept a strict account of his income since 1890, and furnishes the following figures of the gross income for each year subsequent: 1890, $1,600; 1891, $2,100; 1892, $2,600; 1893, $3,500; 1894, $3,800; 1895, $4,000. Mr. Goodman has kept account of the various varieties, also, and of individual trees, with a view of learning which were the most profitable. The average gross income of the prune trees has been $300 per annum. The twelve acres of apricots have averaged $3,000 gross for the past five years. This year the price is better than usual and the income will be a little larger. The fruit from the twenty pear trees usually bring from $70 to $80. One year the fruit from 140 apricot trees netted $1,300, though that was a large crop and the price was higher than usual. One cherry tree, a large one, produces from 700 to 900 pounds per annum. The fig tree bears large crops. The fruit is sold to Townsend, the San Francisco candy manufacturer, who preserves it by the glace method. The tree one year produced fruit which sold for $34, figs having brought that year 4 cents per pound. In 1894 Mr. Goodman's prunes produced 500 pounds per tree. Last year the crop was considerably lighter. The income from one plot of 360 prune trees has ranged from $800, the lowest, to $1,600, the highest.

Mr. Goodman dries all his own fruit and thus saves the working capital. He dries fruit also for neighbors, the plant having capacity for drying from 200 to 300 tons per annum. Mr. Goodman's orchard is four miles from San Jose and one mile from the end of the First Street electric car line.

Mr. Goodman has demonstrated by his careful business management, that fruit growing is a profitable industry.

C. E. WHITE'S ORCHARD, NEAR ALUM ROCK PARK.

HARVEY SWIGKARD'S FARM. It is a common saying in California that it takes a smart man, with a big tract of land, to make money raising wheat. In order that the force of this statement may be understood by residents of other sections, it may be stated that most land in California is too valuable to profitably raise wheat upon. As a rule, wheat must be grown extensively in order to be grown cheaply. If the ground is perfectly level and the soil is light and friable, and may be plowed, sowed and harrowed with a traction engine and the crop harvested with a combined header and thresher, the cost is reduced to a minimum.

Even under such circumstances the land must be assessed at a low figure to insure profit at the prices which at present prevail. If the land is unusually fertile, is thoroughly and carefully tilled and as carefully harvested, wheat may be grown at a profit, even on a small scale.

The most favorable conditions must have prevailed on Harvey Swickard's farm, for he certainly has made money raising hay and wheat. It should be stated, however, that he has resided here twenty-three years, and has not depended entirely upon wheat farming, but has raised a few horses and cattle, besides poultry and other stock, and gradually made investments along other lines that are now yielding a profit. He farmed, too, when prices were higher and wheat growing more profitable. Mr. Swickard's home place is on the Senter road, a mile and a half east of Eden Vale, and contains 320 acres. Here he has a very large and comfortable dwelling and numerous barns and farm buildings and a young orchard of twelve acres, including prunes, peaches, apricots, cherries and apples, none of which are yet in bearing. He owns also 262 acres on the Monterey road, but two miles from the home place, and this he devotes also to hay and grain raising, cutting the crop, as at home, for either hay or grain, as the condition of the market at the time may seem to warrant.

WM. MATTHEWS' PRUNE ORCHARD. On the northwest corner of the Senter and Tulley roads there is one of the most remarkable orchards in the county. It is owned by William Matthews, the

234

HOMES AMONG FRUIT TREES AND FLOWERS.

Harvey Swickard.

O. M. Boyle.

William Matthews.

P. G. Goodman.

retired lawyer, who takes pride in keeping it in perfect condition. The farm contains 104 acres, 47 acres of which are in fruit trees. The prune trees were planted thirty feet apart. Twenty feet apart is the usual distance, but Mr. Matthews finds that the fruit is larger and his trees bear more heavily, the output averaging from six to eight tons per acre, notwithstanding the smaller number of trees per acre. Prunes do not bear each year alike. If an extra large crop is borne one year, the crop next year will not be so great. The present season is an unfavorable one, yet the crop will average, in Mr. Matthews' orchard, six tons per acre. The product commands $30 per ton, making the gross income of the prune orchard $180 per acre. Mr. Matthews takes a great interest in botany, and he has a tract of six acres which is devoted entirely to the growth of rare trees and shrubs. They were apparently planted in the most uneven manner, but were in fact arranged in accordance with carefully made plans, so that wherever one stands a vista between the trees may be obtained. Here are gathered trees and plants from nearly every country on the globe. Among the varieties may be mentioned: Umbrella tree, Eastern maple, pinus ponderosis, magnolia, petisphorum, funeral cypress, dwarf Jayanese maple, Brazilian pine, linden, Chilian pine, silver-leaved poplar, Tasmania gum, Virginia poplar, madrone, sequoia gigantea, loquat, Maden Von Roup, hawthorne, cut-leaved weeping birch, Japanese cypress, ash, Norway spruce, Canada pine, bamboo, Austrian pine, golden barked oak, live oak, Irish yew, Aleppo pine of Palestine, sacred tree of Buddhas, deodar cedar, Italian cypress, English ash and California redwood.

The residence contains a number of rooms of unusual size, all being richly furnished and filled with antique furniture and bric-a-brac. The drawing-room is finished in California woods, such as curly redwood, white oak, etc. The library contains a large collection of rare and costly volumes.

SCENE ON CAPTAIN T. J. SENNETT'S FARM, NEAR SANTA CLARA.

CAPTAIN SENNETT'S ORCHARD. Captain James Sennett owns, on Bascom Avenue, near Santa Clara, 50 acres. There are 25 acres in prunes, 20 acres in pears, and the residence, barns and grounds occupy five acres. The 20 acres of pears are of the Winter Nellis, Glout Morceau and Easter Buerre varieties and produce an average of five tons per acre, or 100 tons for the plot. The 25 acres of French prunes yield on an average a little less than 200 tons of fruit. Mr. Sennett is an old sea captain, having formerly been a Commodore in the Hudson Bay Company's service. He is now the English stevedore of San Francisco, and goes to the city each morning, returning in the evening.

G. L. BEAVER'S ORCHARD. One of the most beautiful orchards in the Moreland school district is located on the San Tomas Aquino road, one mile south of the Moreland School House and belongs to G. L. Beaver, who bought it in 1881 as a grain field, and in 1882 planted it with various varieties of trees and vines. The wine grapes did not prove profitable, and they were uprooted. The entire tract was subsequently planted, from season to season, with fruit trees.

The farm contains 85 acres, of which 77 are in fruit and 3 acres in table grapes. There are 15 acres in apricots, of which 5 acres are of the Royal variety, 7 acres are Moorparks, 3 Large Early and 1 acre Blenheim. Mr. Beaver considers the Royal the best all-around apricot. It is not so large as the Moorpark, but is a heavy, steady bearer and it ripens evenly. It yields from 75 to 150 pounds to the tree, while the Moorpark ranges from 30 to 180 pounds per tree.

Mr. Beaver says that in his locality Bartlett pears are not always a profitable crop. He sold his pears this year green at $30 per ton. The average price is $25 per ton. Last year they were hauled to a co-operative dryer and only netted $7 per ton. This year they paid 15 per cent. on $500 per acre.

Silver prunes bear here remarkably, and Mr. Beaver always finds them a profitable crop. In 1894 118 trees produced $163; in 1893, $310 per acre; in 1895, $250.

Cherries did not bear well last year, and Mr. Beaver harvested only 40 pounds per tree, which sold at 6 cents per pound, or $204 per acre.

Of the 3⅓ acres in table grapes 1⅓ are white muscats, 1 acre verdel and ⅔ of an acre Hamburgs and muscats. Prices of these varieties were depressed last year and they were not shipped.

The French prune trees, of which there are 13 acres, produced 6.3 tons per acre, or a total of 82 tons. These were sold for $31.50 per ton, or $2,583, which is equal to $198 per acre, gross.

SANTA CLARA COUNTY COUNTRY RESIDENCES.

G. L. Beaver.

Mrs van Kaathoven.

J P. Scheuer.

Henry Farr

The farm is 832 feet wide and seven-eighths of a mile long. This fact led to the adoption of the name by which the farm is designated—Long-acres.

MRS. MARY SCOTT'S TEN-ACRE ORCHARD. Mrs. Mary A. Scott's farm on the Quito road, a few miles northwest of Los Gatos, contains fifty-nine acres, forty-five of which are in fruit trees and fourteen are devoted to the growing of wheat for hay. Of the forty-five acres in orchard, but ten acres are in bearing. From this tract, however, the income during the past few years has averaged $1,500 per annum, or $150 per acre. This indicates what the orchard may be expected to produce when the remaining thirty five acres come into bearing.

The peaches sold last year for from $11 to $20 per ton, according to variety, and the prunes sold for $30 per ton. Besides the main orchard Mrs. Scott has a number of trees of various varieties, including apples, pears, figs and olives, which furnish fruit for family use.

Mrs. Scott has recently erected a handsome cottage, at a cost of $1,200, which is surrounded by a beautiful flower garden, well cared for. The farm is well supplied with farming implements, barns, windmills, etc., and Mrs. Scott manages the property carefully, giving it her individual attention.

PRUNES, APRICOTS, CHERRIES. Herman Hoeft came to the Pacific Coast from Michigan in 1893 in search of a good climate. After having visited Oregon, Washington, Idaho and Montana he decided to locate in California. In Oakland he heard of Santa Clara County as an educational center, and brought hither his four youngest children that they might avail themselves of the advantages offered. After his arrival he purchased a 20-acre orchard on the Stevens Creek road, about two and a half miles from San Jose.

Mr. Hoeft had for many years owned a general merchandise store in Michigan, had been extensively engaged in getting out railroad ties and was also interested in a line of steamboats plying on Lake Huron. He placed his interests there in charge of his eldest son and prepared to enjoy life upon his Santa Clara fruit farm. The trees are now from ten to twelve years old, and are mostly prunes, of which there are twelve acres. There are four acres of apricots, two acres of cherries and two acres of young prune trees,

ORCHARD OF JOSEPH SHUPP, NEAR BERRYESSA.

the latter not yet in bearing. Some fruits are biennial. That is, if they bear very freely one year the succeeding crop will be light. This peculiarity is more marked, perhaps, in the case of Moorpark apricots than in any other fruits, but is noticeable in all varieties. The past two seasons have not been counted seasons of average production. Last year Mr. Hoeft took from the twelve acres of prune trees fifty-three tons, which he sold for $28 per ton, or $1,484, making the gross income of the prune orchard $123.66 per acre. In seasons when the trees bear heavily the crop is from 80 to 100 tons of prunes for the twelve acres. In 1894 180 trees bore eighteen tons. The apricot crop last year was light. The crop was sold for $26 per ton.

In 1893 the two acres of cherry trees brought a gross income of $420. In 1894 the crop was sold on the trees, net, for $600. Last year the crop was very light. The Black Tartarians were sold for 3½ cents per pound and white cherries for 5 cents per pound, The two-acre tract produced $300 worth of fruit.

Mr. Hoeft paid for his place $15,000, or $750 per acre, in 1895. Orchards in the vicinity in full bearing are now held at $1,000 per acre. Upon this valuation they are paying from 8 to 10 per cent. interest.

RESIDENCES, URBAN AND SUBURBAN. Nothing more directly reflects the wealth or poverty of any locality than the character of the residences. Handsome and commodious homes indicate wealth and taste upon the part of the owners. For this reason, particularly, in this publication attention has been given to residences, urban and suburban. One of the representative orchard homes shown is the residence of Sylvester Newhall, on Lincoln Avenue, just south of Los Gatos Creek. Mr. Newhall was one of our pioneer nurserymen. He naturally engaged in fruit-growing, and now owns seven orchards, aggregating over two hundred acres, prunes being the principal crop. Of these he raised and dried over four hundred tons last season. He also raises cherries, peaches, pears and apples, all of which in the Willows section are particularly profitable. Mr. Newhall has been a resident of the county thirty-nine years, and he has done as much as any one to develop the horticultural interests of the county and State. An illustration of his handsome residence will be found on page 241.

SANTA CLARA COUNTY RESIDENCES.

Mrs. John Tully, near Evergreen.

M. D. Phelps, Fifth and Reed Sts., San Jose.

Mrs. Mary A. Scott, Quito Road, near Los Gatos.

C. Meyerholtz, Homestead Road, West Side.

HON. I. A. WILCOX, A PIONEER. In the upbuilding of the great State of California the constructive work was performed, in a great measure, by the early pioneers, who faced dangers and carried the burdens of hardships heroically self-imposed, to the end that their children and their children's children might live with the advantages of an advanced civilization. Many of these pioneers made successes of their lives and lived to enjoy the fruits of their earlier labor. One of these who is entitled to distinguished mention is Hon. I. A. Wilcox. He is a descendant of Edward Wilcox, a pioneer of Rhode Island, who was a partner of Roger Williams. His father, of Herkimer County, was a farmer, merchant, manufacturer and banker. In 1848 he was a Free Soil member of the State Legislature. I. A. Wilcox was born in 1822. He received such education as the times afforded, in connection with the business training acquired by association with his father. Among his schoolmates at Clinton Liberal Institute were the late Senator Stanford, Chancellor Hartson and Hon. N. J. Colman, Secretary of Agriculture during Cleveland's first administration. Mr. Wilcox taught school, served as Superintendent of Schools and then studied law in the office of Judges Loomis and Walton, at Little Falls. He assisted in copying the New York Code, formulated by Judges Loomis, Graham and Field.

Close application to study affected his health, to regain which he came to California, arriving in San Francisco in 1852. He mined in Nevada County for awhile and then located in Alameda, where he assisted in the surveying of the town and became a property-owner. At this place he became a pioneer in the growing of wheat and vegetables, and he was also engaged in the business of nurseryman and fruit-growing, having an interest in some of the first fruit trees brought to the State. Later he established a commission house in San Francisco, and among his sales were strawberries at $3 a pound. He became a member of the Vigilance Committee of 1856, helped organize the Republican party and became otherwise prominent in public affairs. In 1858 he "took in" the Frazier river excitement, but did not remain long. He returned to Fruitvale, Alameda County, and to his fruit farm, where he built a cottage, married and settled down to nursery work and fruit growing. About thirty years ago he gave up all other affairs and bought a portion of the Morrison

RESIDENCE OF HON. I. A. WILCOX.

rancho, near Santa Clara. A large part of this he still owns. Here he has lived and here the greatest successes of his life have been achieved. As one of the pioneer horticulturists of the State, he has rendered valuable work in developing that industry which has made this State such a great commonwealth. Mr. Wilcox was the first to engage in the growing of berry fruits, and had sixty acres of berries of selected varieties which he obtained in the East. His place became known as Experimental Gardens, and he has been a recognized authority upon all matters appertaining to berry culture, and has written many standard articles concerning the same. He was instrumental in building up a market for small fruits. In late years he has grown an orchard with a garden between the trees. He has a beautiful home, surrounded by trees and flowers, with fountains playing in the sunlight.

Mr. Wilcox is a member of the State Horticultural Society and of the Patrons of Husbandry; also of the I. O. O. F. and several fruit organizations and co-operative enterprises. He was a representative of the State at the New Orleans Exposition in 1884-5; also was a member of the Legislature in 1877-8. Thus he has had an eventful and successful life, doing good work in building a great State, respected by his neighbors and honored by the public and deserving of just and liberal reward.

FRUIT FARM OF GEO. H. BRIGGS. Another of the pioneers who have been instrumental in making California the Garden of the World, and Santa Clara County the Garden Valley of the State is George H. Briggs. He came to this State in 1852 and located a quarter section of land about four miles west of Santa Clara. It was a fertile tract, covered, as was most of the valley, with gigantic oak trees and under the spreading branches of which he built his squatter's cabin. Some of these primitive oaks still remain upon his land, retaining all their pristine beauty. For many years Mr. Briggs devoted himself to raising hay and grain, but when the era of fruit growing set in he planted a large portion of his land to orchards, which are now in full bearing, and sold another portion to others who desired to raise fruit. At present he has ninety acres of as rich orchard land as can be found in the valley, and of this twenty acres are in orchard and twenty acres in vineyard. The trees are prunes, peaches, pears and cherries, and the grapes are of the choicest wine

SUBURBAN ORCHARD HOMES.

B. F. Weston, near Santa Clara.

G. B. McAneny, near Lawrence Station.

S. Newhall, Lincoln Avenue.

Mrs. A. C. Fessler, Tully Road.

varieties. Mr. Briggs is prepared to dry his own fruit, using special care to produce a high standard of excellence, and which always finds a ready sale. His grapes he sells directly to the wineries. His orchard presents a thrifty appearance and the trees are vigorous, showing excellent care and cultivation. The returns have been all that could be desired. Mr. Briggs has a neat residence surrounded with flowers, where he enjoys life with his wife and children. He is a prominent member of the Society of Pioneers and has contributed much historical matter of interest to the records of the association.

A PIONEER ORCHARDIST. Alexander Coil was born in Oneida County, New York, in 1830. He came across the plains to California in 1850 and settled in the northern part of the State, where he was engaged in sheep raising. After a residence of twelve years in that section he moved to Santa Clara and settled on a fruit ranch south of town. A year later he sold this place and bought a fifty-acre ranch at West Side, five acres of which were planted in French prunes. The remainder he soon planted to various kinds of fruits. As a fruit grower he has been very successful, having in one season raised forty-four tons of prunes on five acres of six-year-old trees. Part of this place was at first planted to grapes, but as there was so little profit in them, he decided to put in prunes, and never had reason to regret it. After a residence of ten years in this delightful section of the valley, Mr. Coil sold his beautiful home and moved to the Garden City, where he now resides. Not being satisfied with city life alone after ten years of successful prune raising, he purchased forty acres of vacant land within sight of his old home and

FORTY-ACRE PRUNE ORCHARD OF A. COIL.

planted it also in French prunes, expecting some day to build and make it his permanent residence Mr. Coil has a home at 156 North Fifth street in the city of San Jose, where he lives at peace with the world, contented with the fact that the labors of his life have brought a fair measure of reward.

ONE OF THE SHOW PLACES OF THE VALLEY. One of the most attractive orchards in the Willows is that owned by O. M. Boyle. Situated as it is in the heart of the prune belt of this valley, his returns from his forty-acre tract are simply marvelous. Mr. Boyle conducts his business upon scientific principles and one can see upon his model orchard what results can be attained by strict attention to the smallest details. A practical horticulturist, he is ever on the alert for enemies of the orchard. A drive through his place is a revelation, even to old-time fruit-growers. In connection with his orchard he has a drier with a capacity for handling some seven or eight hundred tons of fruit, besides that which he raises. Mr. Boyle takes the safe middle ground in most questions upon which there is such radical differences of opinion among fruit men, such as pruning, irrigating, spraying, etc. He has no less than three or four sources open to him by which, in dry seasons, he can cover his land with water. Bounded on the east by Guadalupe creek, his orchard is rich in deep

RESIDENCE OF A. COIL.

alluvial soil and his prunes are richer in saccharine matter than is generally found even in our favored valley. Mr. Boyle, a life-long newspaper man, seems to be happy and contented in his new sphere, and well he may be, for truly his is one of the show places in this Garden of Eden.

A COSY NOOK IN THE FOOTHILLS. One of the most picturesque locations to be found in Santa Clara County is found in the home of F. H. Babb. It is on the east side of the valley, and is in fact a little valley by itself as a ridge of high ground on one side and high mountains on the other completely shut it in from the outside. A living stream of water finds it way down from the canyons above and flows through the tract, giving water for irrigation and adding to the beauty of the place. The farm contains 220 acres, half of which has been planted in orchard and the remaining portion is used for grain, pasturage and the raising of vegetables. Shut in as it is from any cold winds which may blow from the north and being

HOMES AND ORCHARDS OF SANTA CLARA VALLEY.

Residence of Mrs. E. L. Watson.
View of the Orchard of O. M. Boyle.

Oak Tree on Farm of George H. Briggs, Covering 7,000 feet of Ground.

Residence of George H. Briggs.
Fruit Drying Grounds of W. A. Coulter.

several hundred feet above the level of the valley, frost is unknown and tropical plants here find a luxuriant growth. A large banana tree, the largest in this part of the State, grows in front of the house as evidence of the absence of cold. In fact, there are many other rare tropical plants and flowers about the place, and Mr. Babb, who is an enthusiast in horticulture and floriculture, has a collection which is not excelled in Northern and Central California. There is no fruit that can be possibly grown in a semi-tropic climate but what can be here found, including oranges, lemons, figs, persimmons, walnuts, almonds, chestnuts and rare Japanese plums and strange fruits from other countries. His flower garden is a thing of beauty, and here are seen masses upon masses and bed upon bed of geraniums, gladioli, fuchsias, begonias, cannas, dahlias, and other bright-hued and showy blossoms. He gets every new plant and flowers that promises to be interesting and his collection is a wonder and delight to all beholders. Mr. Babb, however, does not neglect the more profitable side of horticulture. His orchards are in fine condition and yield heavy crops. There are thirty acres of prunes and the same area of apricots, twenty-five acres of peaches, twenty of almonds, ten of olives, a few acres of grapes and a variety of other fruits. He dries all of his own fruit and markets it through the exchange. He resides with his parents and sister. The place was originally purchased by his father, Rev. C. E. Babb, shortly after the latter's arrival in California in 1873. Mr. Babb, the elder, is a Presbyterian minister and succeeded Henry Ward Beecher when the latter left Indianapolis to go to Brooklyn. Later he performed editorial work on the *Herald of Presbyter*, one of the leading religious journals of the country, and he is still a contributor to that paper.

HOME OF MARSHALL POMEROY

THE FLOWER EMBOWERED RESIDENCE OF F. H. BABB.

MARSHALL POMEROY'S ORCHARD. Marshall Pomeroy owns 120 acres of rich fruit land on the San Francisco road, two miles west of Santa Clara. Seventy acres of the tract are in prunes and five acres are in apricots, pears, etc. Upon his place is a magnificent grove of eucalyptus trees covering four acres. Many of the trees are two feet in diameter and have attained a height of one hundred and sixty feet. From this grove Mr. Pomeroy secures all the firewood necessary for home consumption and the raising of eucalyptus trees is not an unprofitable investment. There are several such groves in the valley, and they add a picturesqeness to rural scenes which is appreciated by all lovers of art in nature. Mr. Pomeroy has about forty acres which is devoted to hay and grain. He is a lover of fine stock and has a number of fast horses with good pedigrees. The place is scientifically cultivated and indicates that the owner understands his business. It is one of the nicest home places in the valley.

J. H. POSTLETHWAIT'S FRUIT FARM. One of the most productive fruit farms in Santa Clara County is that owned by J. H Postlethwait. It is situated on the San Francisco road near Lawrence station and comprises a tract of thirty acres, which is completely covered with bearing fruit trees eight and nine years old. The fruits produced are apricots, peaches and prunes, and immense crops are raised, for the soil is dark, deep and of exceeding richness. Moreover, the trees are given the best possible cultivation and the ground is kept soft and mellow by constant stirring and not a weed is allowed to appear upon the surface. The trees are scientifically pruned and the surplus fruit is always carefully removed to

SANTA CLARA COUNTY FARM AND ORCHARD SCENES.

View on M. D. Kell's Farm.
View on Theodore Hersey's Farm.

View on J. J. Bergin's Farm.
Young Orange Trees, Randolph Hersey's Orchard.

preserve the life and to make the fruit large and of extra quality. Mr. Postlethwait gives his orchard his personal attention and thus makes a success of horticulture and realizes substantial returns. He is prepared to dry all of his fruit and has all the appliances necessary therefor, but he frequently finds it profitable to sell his fruit to the canneries and dryers.

A FERTILE TRACT OF COUNTRY. One of the most productive sections of Santa Clara County is that which lies near the center of the valley, midway between the stations of Coyote and Madrone. Here the soil is deep and rich, drainage is all that can be desired and facilities for irrigation unsurpassed. The Coyote creek flows through the land, which by past overflows has deposited the washings of the hills, making it rich in the elements necessary to plant life, and its waters may be now taken from its channel and used for irrigation. For many years the land in this section was used for the production of grain, and it is yet the greatest grain producing section of the valley, producing bounteous crops. The grain area has, however, been invaded by orchards, and hundreds of acres of thrifty and wealth-producing trees cover the once-golden grain fields. These orchards are among the finest in the valley, demonstrating the fact that this section is perect for the production of fruit.

THE FARM OF JOHN FITZGERALD. In the center of the land referred to in the foregoing paragraph is located the farm of John Fitzgerald. It comprises 326 acres extending from the Monterey road to the foot hills on the

A GAME OF TENNIS.—ORCHARD OF J. H. POSTLETHWAIT.

east side of the valley. It is three miles north of Madrone and the same distance south of Coyote station. The land is very rich and a number of large oaks are dotted over the tract. The Coyote creek flows through the center of the tract and its waters can be used for irrigation. There are, besides, two large springs of water on the land, sufficient for household and stock purposes and to irrigate a large vegetable garden. Most of the land has been devoted to the raising of hay and grain and for pasture, for Mr. Fitzgerald has given his attention to agriculture and dairying, and at present keeps a number of dairy cows and produces a large amount of butter which finds a ready sale. The tract, however, is an ideal one for an orchard and will be only a short time until some enterprising horticulturist will take hold of it and set it in fruit. Mr. Fitzgerald would have planted it in orchard before this, but the fact that he is not as young as he used to be, deterred him from undertaking a work which would bring him additional labor with its many new and unfamiliar details. The price asked for this land is extremely low, $100 per acre, and it will not be long before Mr. Fitzgerald will retire from active work with a snug competence. He is one of the early settlers of the valley and has resided on his present place since 1862.

THE RANCH OF GREGORY FITZGERALD. Lying alongside of the ranch of John Fitzgerald is that of his brother, Gregory Fitzgerald. It fronts on the Monterey road and is two and a half miles from the village of Madrone, and comprises 308 acres of as rich land as can be found in Santa Clara Valley. It is all capable of irrigation from the Coyote creek which flows through the tract and which adds to its worth, making it extremely valuable for orchard purposes. At present

PEAR PACKING SCENE, ORCHARD OF CAPT. JAMES SENNETT,

SANTA CLARA COUNTY COUNTRY SCENES.

Orchard and Farm near Evergreen—F. Knowles'.
Twin Boulders, on Road from San Jose to San Felipe Valley.

Foothill Land, near Azule Springs—Mrs. E. D. North's.
Wheat Land, near Mountain View—W. F. Wright.

Mr. Fitzgerald is engaged in raising hay and grain and live stock and has done well. He has a comfortable home situated in a grove of big oaks and the surroundings are those of picturesque beauty. The land is situated in such a way as to make it available as a town site and when it is subdivided and put upon the market, as will soon be done, the smaller tracts will be eagerly sought for and an important town is more than likely to occupy a portion of the tract. There are at present many thrifty orchards in the immediate vicinity and it has been demonstrated that the fruit here raised is of superior quality. Mr. Fitzgerald is one of the pioneers of the county, having resided here since 1862. He is a man of sterling integrity and is highly respected by his neighbors.

MOUNTAIN HOME OF V. PONCELET. Not only are the mountains which surround the Valley of Santa Clara to a large extent adapted to the growing of fruit trees and vines, but there are many spots among them which nature has fashioned in a rude and rough, but withal an artistic way, intended to attract and charm the eye of man. In the deep seams of the hills furrowed by the rushing waters of ages past, brooks flow clear and noisily and in the deep pools overshadowed by the willow and alder, trout hide waiting for the enticing fly cast by the adept angler. Along the bushy streams and in the chaparrel-covered hillsides the toothsome quail live and breed in countless numbers, affording in lawful season rare sport to the hunter and his dogs. Higher among the hills where the forest is unbroken and the habitations of men are few, is the haunt of the deer, and here the deer-slayer can find pleasure and excitement to his heart's fondest desire. One of the favorite

PONCELET'S MOUNTAIN HOME.

resorts in Santa Clara County is located on a beautiful mountain stream called the Llagas, which flows down the side of the Santa Cruz mountains about twenty miles from San Jose. Here Victor Poncelet has 320 acres of land, a part of which has been cleared and planted to trees and vines. He has fifteen acres in grapes and 1000 fruit trees. Most of the remainder is in a state of nature, covered with native trees affording a shady and quiet retreat for those who admire nature's handiwork. The Llagas flows through the place and furnishes good fishing for a distance of ten miles. In the fall there is excellent quail shooting and it is the headquarters for all the deer-hunting parties that frequent that section of the country. He has accommodations for many guests and many campers pitch their tents in the vicinity. It is a charming place and is visited each season by many hundreds from San Jose, San Francisco and other cities. Mr. Poncelet is an agreeable host and all who visit his delightful mountain resort speak in the highest terms of his hospitality.

SCENE ON FARM OF GREGORY FITZGERALD.

THE FARM OF P. MARTIN. A typical grain ranch of Santa Clara County is that owned by P. Martin. It is situated at the base of a low range of hills that jut out from the main range into the valley about ten miles south of San Jose, on the Monterey road. The tract comprises 670 acres, of which 140 acres is hill land and is used as pasture for stock, the remaining portion being level valley land, and is devoted to raising grain. This season Mr. Martin had 420

V. PONCELET.

248

FARM AND GARDEN SCENES IN SANTA CLARA COUNTY.

View of the Ranch of John Fitzgerald.

A General View of the Farms of John and Gregory Fitzgerald.

Garden Scene, H. Hoeft.

Grove of Eucalyptus Trees, Place of M. Pomeroy.

General View of the Farm of P. Martin.

acres in grain, about one-half wheat and one-half barley. The yield of these grains has always been abundant, wheat producing from 13 to 15 centals per acre, or 22 to 25 bushels. Of barley the yield is about 16 sacks per acre. A considerable portion of the grain is cut before it is ripe and made into hay. The yield of hay is from two to three tons per acre and is worth from $9 to $10 per ton, according to quality. The land of Mr. Martin is well adapted to fruit culture, and there are several thriving orchards on adjoining tracts. He has a handsome residence, surrounded by flowers and fruit trees, which produce sufficient to supply the household needs. He keeps about fifty head of horses and cows. Mr. Martin is a pioneer resident of the county, and has resided on his present place since 1853.

J. F. PYLE'S ORCHARD AND CANNERY. One of the pioneers of California is J. F. Pyle, who came here in 1846. In 1852 he purchased the place which he now owns at the corner of the King and Mabury roads, about three miles from the center of San Jose. The tract embraces 84 acres, of which 60 are in orchard, the trees being from one to four years old. Upon most of the remaining portion is grown vegetables, and in addition twenty-three acres are leased, which are devoted to raising rhubarb and tomatoes. Between the rows of young trees beans have been planted and the whole place is cultivated with a thoroughness not often seen. A year ago Mr. Pyle experimented with canning string beans and tomatoes, with a view of supplying the trade with these vegetables, and succeeded so well that this year he erected a building to be used as a cannery, and has now entered into the

J. F. PYLE'S ORCHARD CANNERY.

business extensively. This season his output will be 400 cases of string beans and 1000 cases of tomatoes, each case containing two dozen two-and-a-half pound cans. Those who have used his product pronounce it excellent, and there is no doubt but that he will build up a good trade in this line. The name of his brand is "Twin Walnut Farm," so called because the cannery is shaded by two gigantic walnut trees which were planted by Mr. Pyle when he was a young man. Mr. Pyle is assisted in his enterprise by his two sons, Frank G. and Harry F., and his daughter, Ethel M. Pyle.

FISHING SCENE ON THE LLAGAS.

F. FISHER OF LAGUNA SECA. Elsewhere in this volume is described at some length the history of the Rancho de Laguna Seca, one of the large Spanish grants of the State which was purchased by William Fisher for a small sum and which is now extremely valuable. Fiacro Fisher is a son of William Fisher and succeeded to a portion of his father's estate and he now owns 2,600 acres of the Laguna Seca ranch. It comprises a part of the most fertile portions of the rancho and is distant twelve miles from San Jose on the Monterey road. Most of the land is capable of producing bounteous crops of any kind and was for many years one of the most productive grain ranches in the valley. Much of it is yet devoted to hay, grain and pasture, but Mr. Fisher has also a large orchard, the soil being well adapted to the growth of trees. Mr. Fisher was born in this valley in 1850 and was educated in the public schools and at Santa Clara College. He is one of the successful agriculturists of the valley, and is prominent in his section of the country.

ORCHARDISTS AND FARMERS OF SANTA CLARA COUNTY.

I. A. Wilcox.	Joshua Cozzens.	Ephriam Hatch.	Herman Hoeft.	Alexander Coil.
Gregory Fitzgerald.	E. W. Conant.	John Fitzgerald.	P. Martin.	Fiacro Fisher.
J. H. Flickinger.	J. F. Pyle.	F. H. Babb.	P. G. Goodwin.	E. P. Reed.

THOMAS DERBY'S ORCHARD. The orchard of Thomas Derby is located on McLaughlin avenue, one-half of a mile south of the Tully road and about four miles from the business center of San Jose. It is situated on the banks of Coyote creek and the land is composed of alluvial soil that has been deposited from overflows of the waters of the creek. It is rich and friable and easily worked and contains a large quantity of nutritious elements necessary to sustain plant life. The tract embraces 150 acres, 100 of which are in orchard. and the trees are mostly prunes from four to seven years old. The trees are exceedingly thrifty and show a marvelous growth. The crops consist of fruit of unusual size and the orchard is one of the noted ones in the county in this respect. There is none finer in the county.

MRS. A. R. SCOTT'S VINEYARD. Mrs. A. R. Scott is the owner of 320 acres of rich land in Santa Clara County about four miles west of Santa Clara. All excepting 60 acres have been planted in the best varieties of wine grapes, which are in full bearing. The varieties embrace savignon, cabernets, charbano, riesling, medoc, etc. There are two large wineries upon the property, one an immense brick and stone structure four stories high, shown in the accompanying engraving. The combined capacity of the two wineries is 550,000 gallons. Most of the wine is matured in the cellar before being sold and is of high grade. At the Midwinter fair held in San Francisco in 1894 Mrs. Scott was awarded first premium gold medals for the best petit pinot and zinfandel. One hundred and fifty thousand gallons are produced annually and finds a ready sale at good prices.

SCENE IN FRONT OF RESIDENCE OF THOS. DERBY.

DISTILLERY OF MRS. A. R. SCOTT.

The winery is in charge of a competent and experienced winemaker and the vineyard is superintended by a man who understands the science of viticulture. In addition to manufacturing wine a distillery is also run and 2,000 gallons of pure brandy are produced each year.

BEAUTIFUL HOME OF W. H. ROBERTS On the Stevens Creek road, one mile west of Saratoga avenue, is the orchard home of W. H. Roberts. The place consists of sixteen acres, fifteen of which are planted in prunes. Eight acres of trees are six years old and the remainder are two years old. Those that are in bearing produce bounteous crops, for the place is situated in the prune belt and the crops raised in the vicinity are extremely large. Mr. Roberts purchased the place in the fall of 1895, and has just completed a handsome residence of eight rooms. It is of modern style of architecture and is supplied with all the conveniences necessary for comfort and enjoyment, including a gas machine, hot and cold water, etc. In another year, when the flowers and shrubbery which have just been planted become more mature, he will have as pretty a home as can be found anywhere. Mr. Roberts is a native of Mercer County, Penn., but has resided in Santa Clara County for twenty-three years.

J. P. BUBB'S WEST SIDE HOME. The place of J. P. Bubb, located on the western edge of the valley, a few miles north of Saratoga, is part valley land and part hillsides. The residence is picturesquely situated a hundred feet or so above the valley, affording an incomparable view of the country

VIEWS OF SANTA CLARA COUNTY HOMES.

W. H. Roberts.

C. W. Holaen.

Reservoir on Place of J. P. Bubb.

J. P. Bubb.

Family of J. P. Bubb.

north, east and south. Beside the house are giant oaks and in front are large orange and lemon trees, with their dark green leaves affording a beautiful contrast for the golden fruit with which the trees are constantly laden. All around are choice shrubs and fragrant flowers, rare plants nurtured in a conservatory near at hand, indicating that nature finds here enthusiastic devotees. The hills that rise above are covered with grape vines and almond trees, while stretching out in front down the gentle slope are the orchards of prunes, peaches, apricots and other fruits. The place is a large one, comprising 230 acres and a portion of a 500-acre tract purchased by Mr. Bubb thirty years ago. For many years he devoted his place to raising grain and stock, but about 15 years ago he commenced to grow fruit extensively and disposed of a portion of his land. There are now 100 acres devoted to wine grapes and another hundred in trees. He manufactures about 50,000 gallons of wine annually and has a complete winery with a capacity of 75,000 gallons. He produces clarets exclusively and produces an excellent article. The place is abundantly supplied with water from living springs which gush out from the hills above. For the purpose of irrigation and also to supply the neighbors with water for domestic use, Mr. Bubb has just completed an immense reservoir, capable of storing a million gallons. Mr. Bubb is a pioneer of the State, coming from Missouri in 1849.

SANTA CLARA VALLEY FRUIT CO. This is a company which has for its object the purchasing of green fruits, drying them and selling the same. It purchases fruit of the neighboring orchardists, paying cash on delivery, and being located in the Willows fruit district, it is a convenience to the growers

FRUIT DRYING GROUNDS OF E. E. THOMAS CO.

WINERY OF MRS. A. R. SCOTT.

and at the same time an abundant supply of the raw material is secured. This establishment makes prunes its principal output. The drying ground includes about twelve acres, upon which can be dried at one time 600 tons of prunes. The probable output of the drier will approximate 1,000 tons this year, besides which the company will purchase large quantities of fruit which may be dried by individual growers. The entire shipment of prunes by this company will probably reach 100 carloads this year. The prunes are running very large this year, in some instances eight trays of first grade being secured to one tray of second grade. This company handles Santa Clara Valley prunes only and buy only the best grades of fruit, for they received a gold medal for fine fruit at the World's Exposition at Chicago, and they aim to maintain the excellent reputation with which their goods stand accredited in the East. This company does a strictly f. o. b. business and makes no consignments, which enables them to pay cash to growers. Important improvements have been made to the plant this season, and its capacity has been doubled, so that 100 tons of green fruit can be handled daily. D. D. Brooks is the manager of the company. Feron & Ballou Co. have established their brand of fruit throughout the United States and Europe and are their sole selling agents.

THE GEO. N. HERBERT COMPANY. This company is a firm composed of George N. Herbert and J. W. Raines. Their business is that of buying, drying and packing fruit, making a specialty of prunes. The establishment is located at the junction of Lincoln and Moorpark avenues, and is in the midst of the Willows fruit district. It is equipped with all the modern appliances and im-

VIEWS OF FRUIT DRYING ESTABLISHMENTS.

Drying Grounds and Dryer of

Geo. N. Herbert Co.

Drying Grounds and Dryer of

Santa Clara Valley Fruit Co.

provements for the rapid and economical handling of green fruit, including abundant steam power and a large grader. It has a capacity of producing five carloads
of dried fruit daily and is supplied with an abundance of room for storing and
packing. The drying grounds are of such an extent as to permit the drying of
about 600 tons at one time. Last season the firm handled 1,500 tons of green fruit
and shipped seventy-five carloads of dried fruit. This season it is expected that
the output of the drier will reach 500 or 600 tons of dried fruit, besides which they
will purchase from individual dryers as much more, so that the total shipments will
reach 100 carloads. They do strictly an f. o. b. business and pay cash on delivery
for all the fruit which they purchase. This is an important advantage to the seller.
They make a specialty of large sizes and purchase all their fruit with a reference
to its size and quality. Thus they have established a reputation for putting on the
market goods of high grade and excellent quality, realizing in consequence a high
price. They have been in the business for ten years and are familiar with every
detail of drying, packing and shipping. As men of business they have earned a
reputation for integrity and fair dealing, which they are careful to maintain and
which is a guarantee that whatever representations they make are founded on facts.

E. E.
THOMAS
FRUIT CO.

One of the oldest establishments in the county engaged in the
general business of buying green fruit, drying, packing and
selling it is that conducted by the E. E. Thomas Fruit Co. A
large building, three stories in height, located on the corner of Race street and the
Stevens Creek road, was erected for packing and storage purposes and is one of the
most complete of the kind in the world. The machinery is specially adapted to the
rapid and economical handling of fruit, and much of it has been designed by Mr.
Thomas as the result of years of experience in this business. The drying grounds
are extensive and a thousand or more tons of green fruit may be in process of drying at one time. Mr. Thomas is thoroughly posted as to all the details of
the business and keeps well informed as to markets, prices, etc., and is enabled to pay the highest possible price for fruit. His reputation as a business man
is above reproach and his integrity is unquestioned.

DRYER OF E. E. THOMAS CO.

SANTA CLARA COUNTY ON WHEELS.

SANTA CLARA
COUNTY
ON WHEELS

Has been known as California Introducing Co. It is a
train of cars built especially for introducing goods and is
traveling in the East, under the indorsement of the San
Jose Board of Trade, demonstrating and introducing Santa Clara County products, dried fruits, etc. Mr. Leak, the manager of this train, as an advertiser
has no superior, and we doubt if his equal can be found in the United States.
Mr. Leak's office is with S. T. Fish & Co, No. 189 South Water Street,
Chicago. Wm. B. Hayford, No. 12 North First Street, San Jose, is Pacific
Coast Manager.

FISH,
FLESH AND
FOWL.

The market prices for meat in San Jose, retail, can be stated to
be about as follows: Porterhouse, or short loin, 15 cents per
pound; sirloin, hip, 12½ cents; rib steak or roast, 10½ @ 12½
cents; chuck steak, 8 cents; round steak, 8 cents; rump steak, 6 @ 8 cents;
shoulder, 6 cents; navel, 5 @ 6 cents; plate, 5 @ 6 cents; flank, 5 cents; breast,
4 @ 5 cents; neck, 4 cents; leg, 2½ cents; shin, 2½ cents. Mutton—Stews,
3 cents per pound; roasts, 7 @ 8 cents; chops, 8 @ 10 cents. Veal for stew-
ing, 6 cents; roasts, 8 @ 10 cents; cutlets, 12 cents. Poultry—Hens, 35 @ 75
cents; turkeys, 15 @ 20 cents per pound. Fish—Herring, flounder, rock cod,
halibut, sea bass, 10 cents per pound; smelt, mackerel, striped bass, 12 cents.

WEST SIDE VINEYARDS AND WINERIES.

Grape Arbor, Richard Heney's Vineyard

Henry Farr's Vineyard.

Isabella Regia Grapes, Mrs. C. O. Wilcox's Vineyard.

J. C. Merithew's Winery.

SANTA CLARA COUNTY VINEYARDS.

Where Most of Them Are Located, the Product Per Acre, and What the Crop Sells for Per Ton. Which Soils and Varieties of Vines Are Most Suitable.

THE history of wine-making in California dates back three-quarters of a century, when the Mission Fathers cultivated a single variety of the grape known at present as the mission. From this they produced a light-colored, heavy wine of questionable flavor. Later, however, the best European varieties from Hungary, Germany and France were introduced, and in California they found a climate and soil suitable to their growth and full development. At the present time California takes a prominent place among grape-growing and wine-making countries of the world and furnishes within its area so many different soils and climates that nearly every kind or variety of grapes will flourish here. With our long dry summers the grape is brought to a state of perfection not equaled in its native habitat in Europe, and it is possible to produce a quality that for taste, bouquet and flavor equals, and in some instances surpasses, the best produced in the countries of the old world.

KNOWLEDGE OF WINE-MAKING. In the earlier stages of wine-making in California ignorance as to the proper methods of production prevailed and an inferior wine was the result, but ignorance has now given way to a knowledge gained by experience and a study of the processes used in Europe, until we have improved all former methods, with the result that we are producing a high class of wines which sells readily in Europe in competition with the wines of that country, and at the same time bringing a higher price. It is a fact that a large part of the California wine shipped abroad finds its way back to this country and is sold under a French label.

HIGH-GRADE WINE PRODUCED. Santa Clara County is one of the best wine-producing sections of the State. The soil, especially along the base of the mountains and upon the foot-hills, is admirably adapted to the growth of the finest of wine grapes. It is here that is

manufactured some of the choicest wines in the world and which experts have declared cannot be surpassed. We have here some of the most expert wine-makers, who value the reputation of their wines and refuse to put upon the market anything that is not absolutely pure and of high grade. The following pages are devoted to a description of some of the leading vineyards of the county.

RICHARD HENEY'S VINEYARD. Richard Heney, of the West Side, was for sixteen years a furniture dealer in San Francisco. His place of business was in the Bancroft building, on Market street, where, notwithstanding a rental of $1,320 per month, he amassed wealth. In 1882 he sold his furniture business and purchased 100 acres of land on the heights of Cupertino, overlooking the Santa Clara Valley, about eight miles west of San Jose. This he has since named Chateau Ricardo vineyard. At that time much of it was covered with brush. This Mr. Heney removed and at once proceeded to procure and plant the choicest varieties of wine grapes, and now has 50,000 vines in full bearing. He erected a concrete and brick winery at a cost of $30,000, and expended $10,000 more for cooperage, most of which is oak. He has several tanks which hold 30,000 gallons, the

C. P. HOWE'S VINEYARD, NEAR MOUNTAIN VIEW.

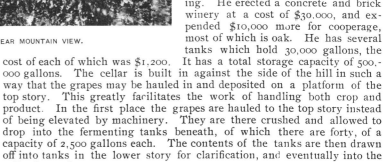

cost of each of which was $1,200. It has a total storage capacity of 500,-000 gallons. The cellar is built in against the side of the hill in such a way that the grapes may be hauled in and deposited on a platform of the top story. This greatly facilitates the work of handling both crop and product. In the first place the grapes are hauled to the top story instead of being elevated by machinery. They are there crushed and allowed to drop into the fermenting tanks beneath, of which there are forty, of a capacity of 2,500 gallons each. The contents of the tanks are then drawn off into tanks in the lower story for clarification, and eventually into the cellar for ageing.

RICHARD HENEY'S VINEYARD AND WINERY.

The Great Wine Tanks.

A Glimpse of the Cellar

Vineyard and Residence.

The Crushers.

Residence and Driveway.

General View of Cellar, Winery and Residence.

The walls of the cellar are three feet thick. The floors between stories are of tongued and grooved lumber and tarred felt is laid between the floor and the heavy plank ceiling beneath to prevent possible leakage and dripping into tanks in the cellar. The winery is provided with hot and cold water, piped to every part of the building. Water is brought in cement pipes from springs, and a thousand feet of two-inch hose has been provided, so that in case of fire the cellar could be promptly drenched with water. In fact, it is one of the finest maturing cellars in the world.

Mr. Heney uses no artificial methods of ageing and never allows the product of his vineyard to be marketed until it is properly aged. He marks all his cooperage plainly, so that visitors can see at once the date of vintage and the price of the wine. His greatest product is a Cabernet, for which he charges $1 per gallon. The Chateau Ricardo he charges $5 per gallon for. Mr. Heney figures that it costs him 6¼ cents per gallon to age his wines. The laws of France, by the way, allow 8 per cent per annum for the natural law of evaporation.

There are stored in Mr. Heney's cellar 200,000 gallons of wine. His eldest son, William J., is now in New York, where he has established an agency. He will also visit Boston, Philadelphia, Baltimore, Richmond, New Orleans, Cincinnati and Chicago, where he will establish other agencies.

The product of the vineyard is hauled for shipment to the railroad at Mountain View, four miles, or to Rengstorff's Landing, on San Francisco Bay, six miles.

Mr. Heney's choicest brand, the Chateau Ricardo, is bottled at the vineyard and is sealed under the law of the State of California. It is sold in glass only, and there is no finer imported. Mr. Heney justly claims that he produces as fine a wine as there is on earth. Mr. Heney sees in the future a great development of the wine industry and prophesies that California wines will be recognized as the best in the world.

LABEL, WINERY AND VINEYARD OF THE CHATEAU RICARDO.

J. J. BERGIN'S FARM AND VINEYARD. One of the numerous vineyards along Permanente Creek is owned by J. J. Bergin. The residence, which is a large and comfortable house of two stories, is situated near the brook and is surrounded by many beautiful trees and flowers. The climate in the foothills is even more equable than that of the valley, and the orange and lemon trees which adorn the lawn are very heavily laden. From one orange tree as many as 2,000 oranges have been gathered. This is equal to about ten boxes.

The farm contains 195 acres, of which 80 acres are in vines, 25 in orchard and 70 acres in hay and pasture land. The remaining ten acres are occupied by the house, barn, lawns and gardens. The vineyard consists of wine grapes exclusively, the varieties being Mataro, Grenache, Charbono, Carignan and Malvoise. They produce on an average four tons of grapes per acre, and the entire product is made into wine. One ton of grapes makes from 140 to 150 gallons of wine. The orchard, twenty-five acres, contains a variety of trees, including 800 apricots, 300 prunes, 300 Bartlett pears and 80 peaches, the remainder being apples and cherries. The gross income of the orchard averages $1,500 per annum, or $60 per acre.

JOHN SNYDER'S PROPERTY. One of the most extensive land-owners on the West Side is John Snyder, whose home farm is on Permanente Creek, four miles south of Mountain View. He gained most of his property by hard labor and close attention to details and the remainder by careful investments. He arrived in the county in 1849, and purchased from owners of Spanish grants, subsequently adding thereto other property purchased from the railroad company, until he owned land aggregating 850 acres. This is the home

SANTA CLARA COUNTY VNIEYARDS AND WINERIES.

J. J. Bergin, near Mountain View.

John Snyder, near Mountain View.

D. M. Delmas, near Mountain View.

Richard Heney, West Side.

place, which he still retains. Most of the land is used for grain-growing and pasturage, though there is a sixteen-acre vineyard and a small orchard. The farm is supplied with a large and comfortable residence, barns and other necessary buildings, all of which are supplied with water piped from a spring on the property 700 feet above. Such a fall would furnish a tremendous pressure, and the water is therefore led to a reservoir 275 feet above the buildings in order to reduce the pressure. The spring is a mile and a quarter from the residence and runs at the lowest stage three miners' inches. The elevator, and all machinery about the place, is propelled by Pelton water wheels.

Mr. Snyder also owns eighty acres about three miles from the home farm, which is all in wine grapes, the varieties being Mataro, Carignan, Grenache and Zinfandel. The crop varies from four to five tons per acre. The price for wine grapes last year ranges from $12 to $13 50 per ton. Last year the net income was $30 per acre. As an outside investment Mr. Synder purchased 160 acres of timber land just over the summit in Santa Cruz County. It is all virgin redwood forest, not a tree having yet been felled. As redwood is becoming scarce, the land each year increases in value.

Mr. Snyder also owns 160 acres of land in the artesian belt, along the shores of San Francisco Bay, north of Mountain View. It is rich garden land, almost exactly like that upon which Morse & Co.'s seed farms are located, several miles east, and artesian water may be had upon any portion of the tract. It is at present however, used for growing wheat and barley for hay. It produces about two and a half tons per acre. Hay ranges in price according to the season, from $6 to $8, $10 and $12 per ton.

The subdivision of the Emerson tract offered an opportunity for investment also, and Mr. Snyder two and a half years ago purchased forty acres there, planting cherries on twenty-five acres and prunes on the remaining fifteen acres.

Several years ago Mr. Snyder purchased also 300 acres of land in Monterey County. Two hundred and fifty acres are used in grain growing and the remaining fifty-acre tract is covered with a heavy growth of live oaks. the entire tract containing scattered groves

Mr. Snyder also owns 320 acres a few miles north of Sanger, in Fresno County. It is used for growing grain and alfalfa. An irrigation canal passes through the property, and most of it can be irrigated.

The home place, on Permanente Creek, is four miles from Mountain View, eight miles from Stanford University and twelve and a half miles from San Jose.

HENRY FARR'S VINEYARD. Two miles and a half northwest of Saratoga and one mile west of the Lincoln schoolhouse, on the Prospect road, Henry Farr owns 343 acres. Of this tract 45 acres are in vines, of the Cabernet, Mataro, Burger, Zinfandel and Riesling varieties, nearly all of them fourteen years of age. Mr. Farr's vines give evidence of careful pruning and attention. In fact, evidences are seen in the flower garden, vegetable garden and all around the farm of Mr. Farr's watchful care and ability as a farmer, gardener and vineyardist.

It may be stated here for the benefit of Eastern readers that vines are never trained on trelises here, as in the East, but are pruned closely each year, only a few short branches being left on the trunk of the vine. Vines here grow so thriftily that branches are thrown out each season from four to eight feet. Instances occur where this length is greatly exceeded, lengths varying from ten to thirty feet sometimes being reached. Close pruning, therefore, is practiced almost universally.

Upon 200 acres of this land Mr. Farr raises hay. It is all choice vineyard land, but he finds that forty-five acres in vines calls for considerable attention, and he has, besides, eighteen acres in prunes. Eighty acres are entirely unimproved, being at the present time used for pasture.

Mr. Farr takes a great interest in everything that pertains to farm work and has one of the richest vegetable gardens on the West Side. Flowers are grown around the house and lawn in great variety and profusion. The family orchard contains peaches, pears, apples and olives. The olives are as healthful and bright as any in the county, the soil and climate of this locality seeming to present a combination particularly suited to their culture. Mr. Farr has a plot on the hillside where he raises alfalfa.

HENRY FARR'S HOME, WEST SIDE.

SELENGER'S WEST SIDE VINEYARD. Fifteen years ago L. Selenger, of San Francisco, purchased 176 acres of unimproved land on Stevens Creek. His vineyard now covers 70 acres. The varieties represented are: Matero, 6 acres; cabernet, 6 acres; zinfandel, 6 acres, and charbono, 52 acres. The product last year was 60,000 gallons of wine. In 1894 Mr. Selenger sold the output of the vineyard as a whole for 12½ cents per gallon. Mr. Selenger also has 35 acres in prune trees, which have just come into bearing. He has the crop dried by C. W. Proctor, a neighbor, paying one-fifth of the crop for the service. Last year Mr. Selenger received for the remaining four-fifths of the crop from 4½ to 5 cents per pound, or a total of a little less than $3,000. The trees are not yet in full bearing. They are planted in very rich soil, which is a silt deposited by overflows

WEST SIDE VINEYARDS.

L. Selenger.

C. A. Baldwin.

Henry Farr.

Mrs. Mathilde Portal.

from Stevens Creek. The remaining 71 acres of the farm consists of hay land and pasture land, about equally divided. Along the creek and in the pasture there are yet many trees and some undergrowth. This land is being cleared as opportunity offers. Stove wood commands such a good price, however, that the work is done at a profit. Oak stove wood sells on the ground for from $4 to $5.50 per cord, and for from $5 50 to $7 per cord delivered in San Jose.

The residence contains twelve rooms and bath and is handsomely finished and furnished throughout. It is located on a plateau, or table land, the creek sweeping around from the southern to the eastern side, furnishing most excellent drainage. Every room is supplied with hot and cold water. Seven sewers lead from the house to the creek. The kitchen is supplied with a French range, and in fact everything that would add to the comfort and convenience of the family has been provided.

There are a number of other farm buildings, including a large wine cellar, barns, shops. residence for foreman, etc. The wine cellar contains cooperage for 60,000 gallons. Stevens Creek, a most beautiful stream which rises in the Santa Cruz mountains, flows through the farm from south to north and furnishes royal sport to lovers of trout fishing, while the brushy hillsides are alive with quail and other small game.

When the well was sunk, a number of years ago, within a few yards of the house, a flow of petroleum was struck at a depth of a little over 100 feet and it became necessary to abandon it and sink another. Within a few hundred yards of the house rises a high bluff showing a mass of chalky clay. This contains clam shells and other marine fossils. With it are beds of a dark colored silt.

RESIDENCE AND VINEYARD OF L SELENGER

The farm is but two miles from the postoffice at West Side and is within five minutes' walk of a telegraph office. San Jose is ten miles away and the nearest railway station is Mountain View, six miles north. In addition to the home place Mr. Selenger owns 545 acres in Calaveras County. The average annual income of the Stevens Creek property he places at $6,000 to $8,000. Mr. Selenger is a Veteran of the Mexican War and also a Veteran Fireman of San Francisco.

C. A. BALDWIN'S VINEYARD. One of the most beautiful vineyards in the West Side district is that located on the Stevens Creek road, near Cupertino Creek, belonging to C. A. Baldwin. and known as Beaulieu. Mr. Baldwin owns 70 acres, situated on a high plateau, made by a gravelly deposit left by Cupertino Creek. Its situation and the general qualities of the soil closely resembles the conditions which prevail at Medoc, near Bordeaux, and efforts are here made to reproduce the finer growths of that locality. To that end the finest varieties, notably Cabernet, Sauvignon and Cabernet Merlot, which are those entering most largely into the higher grades of Bordeaux wines, have been imported from Chateau La Fitte.

The cellar was built underground, thus insuring even temperature and humidity, which are so essential to the proper development of wine. It was built of stone and has a capacity of four vintages, and wines are here stored in barrels corresponding to the Bordeaux barriques, where they remain under constant care till the moment of bottling or export. This is the only vineyard in the county where the plan of ageing in small packages is adopted. All wine is kept three years before being bottled, and some four years. The wines of the Beaulieu vineyard are sent to New York, London and Central America, where they have met with a flattering reception in competition with the wines of France.

MRS. WILCOX'S VINEYARD AND WINERY. Santa Clara valley land is noted throughout the State as choice fruit and vine land. There is good land in nearly every county, and much that for horticultural purposes is rated as choice. There is, however, comparatively little of equal fertility that is under the influence of a similar climate. In order that readers at a distance may better understand the situation it may be stated that climate varies in California according to the topography and altitude and may differ widely in two sections not more than fifty miles apart. As the years go on and the superiority of our climate is more clearly demonstrated, the price of land increases.

In 1880 L. W. Pollard purchased a tract of 160 acres of unimproved land on the San Francisco road, four and a half miles west of Santa Clara, paying therefor $37 50 per acre It had been plowed and sowed to grain, but all such land is here quoted as unimproved. There is very little in the immediate vicinity that is now used for grain growing, and it commands from $180 to $350 per acre, while land planted with vines commands from $350 to $450 per acre.

The property reverted upon his death to his widow, now Mrs. C. O. Wilcox. Ninety acres of the place, which is called the Eskimo vineyard, are now in vines. eighty acres of which are wine grapes and ten acres table grapes. The wine grapes, which are planted seven feet apart, produce

WEST SIDE VINEYARDS AND WINERIES.

C. A. Baldwin.

Nathan Hall.

J. C. Merithew.

Mrs. C. O. Wilcox.

from three to eight tons per acre, the average being about five tons. The varieties grown are Matero, Grenache, Charbono and Malbec.

Mrs Wilcox has a winery, with cooperage enough to make 100,000 gallons per annum, and in order to work it to its full capacity purchases grapes from others. Mrs. Wilcox does not attempt to age her wines, but sells them from year to year.

The table grapes, of which there are ten acres, produce from five to eight tons per acre, or a total of from fifty to eighty tons. The choicest of these Mrs. Wilcox packs in boxes and ships to San Francisco, making wine of the remainder. The quantity marketed usually ranges from 3,000 to to 4,000 twenty-pound boxes. The varieties are Muscat, Rose of Peru, Malvoise and Cornochon, and the price per box varies from 30 to 75 cents. This is $45 per ton, or a gross income of from $1,350 to $1,800 from the ten acres of table grapes, besides the remaining product of from twenty to fifty tons, which is otherwise utilized. It should be stated, however, that Mrs. Wilcox uses extra care in the packing of her grapes, and therefore receives good prices. The bloom upon the grape is never disturbed, and all imperfect berries are carefully removed with scissors. They are then packed in new boxes, and as only the best grapes are marketed, they always present an attractive appearance.

Mrs. Wilcox has also thirty acres in orchard, of mixed varieties, including peaches, pears, cherries, apples, apricots, silver prunes, French prunes and English walnuts.

Mrs. Wilcox employs three men the year round, ten in the busy season, and for a short time, also, fifteen grape-pickers.

THE
MONTE VISTA
VINEYARD.
Several miles west of Santa Clara, on the Saratoga and Mountain View road, M. D. Phelps has a vineyard of ninety acres. The vines are all of the Bordeaux and Burgundy types, and are twelve years of age. They yield from five to eight tons of grapes per acre, according to the season. The product of the vineyard is hauled for shipment to Mountain View, a distance of five miles.

THE
KNOWLES
VINEYARD.
The Knowles ranch is situated on the San Felipe road, two miles from the postoffice and telephone office at Evergreen, an hour's drive from San Jose, and adjoins the well known Lomas Azules vineyard, the property of William Wehner. It consists of over 400 acres, in part pasture, but comprising 200 acres of level land, which the present owners have partly planted in trees and vines,

which planting they are engaged in extending. One view presented in this book shows a fine stretch of land backed by the foothills, and it is on this table or bench land they are carrying on the work of planting. The hills in the background constitute a source of perennial moisture and afford excellent never-failing streams for irrigation purposes, besides supplying good pasturage and quantities of fire-wood. This section boasts immunity from frosts and freedom from fogs. The house and other buildings are prettily situated and are surrounded with eucalypti, coniferæ and other ornamental trees and shrubs.

THE
PORTAL
VINEYARD.
A vineyard which has the reputation of producing high-class wines is the well-known Burgundy Vineyard of Mrs. Mathilde M. Portal. It is located on the north side of the Stevens Creek road, six miles west of San Jose. A number of years ago Mr. Portal, after a careful examination of the soil, the average mean and extreme temperatures of various parts of the Santa Clara valley, selected the present site of the vineyard as the most suitable for the reproduction of the finest types of French wines. The soil is calcareous and situated in the warm belt and at a moderate elevation. The estate consists of over 200 acres, substantially fenced, of which nearly that number are planted with vines, all of which are in full bearing. The varieties are the choicest that France produces. The Portal cellars have an unexcelled reputation for Medoc Clarets, Burgundies and Sauternes.

The capacity of the crushing and fermenting house and its cooperage is 250,000 gallons. Besides the buildings devoted to wine-making the permanent improvements consist of two large barns, houses for the foreman and employes, blacksmith shop and general workshop,

WINERY OF MRS. MATHILDE PORTAL.

windmills, steam engines, two tank-houses and tanks and two inexhaustible wells. The residence of Mrs. Portal is a two-story Eastlake villa of eighteen large rooms, with all modern conveniences and an illustration of which will be seen on page 7. The superintendent and manager is Mrs. Portal's son, Mr. S. E. Portal, who has by experience and education especially fitted himself for the responsible position. The Portal label has been established in the East and in London and is a guarantee of high quality.

VINES
AND
WINES.
A. Zichovich, who owns a forty-acre vineyard on the West Side, furnishes the following facts concerning wine-making: The average crop ranges from three to five tons of grapes per acre, the smaller and choicer varieties producing the

VINEYARDS AND WINERIES.

C. A. Baldwin's Wine Cellar.

Nathan Hall's Vineyard.

Wine Grapes, Mrs. C. O. Wilcox's Vineyard.

M. D. Phelps' Vineyard.

former amount, and the larger and more common varieties the latter. In seasons when the rainfall is usually abundant and when it falls just as needed, the crop ranges from five to ten tons per acre, varying, of course, in different localities. Only those grapes showing twenty-two or twenty-four degrees by the saccharometer are used for wine, those showing less being made into brandy. One ton of grapes makes from 135 to 160 gallons of wine, according to the variety of the grape. The wine-makers last season paid from $12 to $16 per ton for grapes, and wine of last year's vintage sold for 15, 18 and 20 cents per gallon, according to quality. Wine sold early last season for 12 cents per gallon.

WINERY AND VINEYARD. J. D. Williams has near West Side a winery where he manufactures from 160,000 to 200,000 gallons per annum. His own vineyard contains but twenty-five acres of Cabernet, Mataro, Sauvignon Verte and Zinfandel. He buys most of the grapes used from surrounding vineyards, and last year paid from $12.50 to $13.50 per ton. The average crop of wine grapes in the vicinity is between five and six tons per acre. One ton of grapes, on an average, makes 150 gallons of wine. Some vineyardists prefer to have their grapes made into wine on shares, and Mr. Williams in such cases gives 100 gallons of wine for each ton of grapes, retaining 50 gallons for his work. As wine is selling for 12½ cents per gallon, it amounts to $12.50 for 100 gallons, the amount manufactured from one ton of grapes, which would sell for $12.50.

LOS GATOS CO-OPERATIVE WINERY. This association is made up of grape growers who own stock in the corporation. Its business is to purchase grapes of its stockholders and also from growers who are not stockholders, manufacture wine and sell the same at wholesale. For this purpose it has a complete plant at Los Gatos which was constructed at a cost of $50,000. It consumes about 3,000 tons of grapes annually, producing from 450,000 to 500,000 gallons of wine. All kinds of wine are manufactured, white, red, sherry, port, angelica, etc. It operates an electric plant, that work may be conducted day and night, and is otherwise arranged for the economic and rapid handling of grapes. The idea is to produce a class of wine of standard quality, and no difficulty is found in securing a ready market for its entire product at good prices. The directors of the corporation are: John Cilker, president; W. B. Rankin, secretary and manager; W. A. Riggs, Dr. S. G. Moore and C. Schofield.

Mr. Rankin, in addition to superintending the work of the Los Gatos

WINERY OF A. ZICOVICH.

Co-operative Winery, leases the Pacific Winery, the largest establishment in the county and one of the largest in the State. It has a capacity of 1,000,000 gallons annually, producing dry wines exclusively.

DR. E. O. COCHRANE'S VINEYARD. In California many professional and business men purchase land and plant orchards or vineyards in order that they may have not only property which will insure a steady income, but a pleasant home in the country. In Santa Clara County such instances are frequent. Here doctors, lawyers, editors, teachers and professional men of all kinds may be found enjoying life in magnificent country homes, surrounded by all the comforts of modern life. As a rule they have the daily papers delivered at the door every morning before breakfast. Many of them have their residence connected with cities throughout the State by telephone, and all of them may reach a town or city within a few moments over well-kept roadways.

In 1883 Dr. E. O. Cochrane, of San Francisco, purchased fifty eight acres three miles west of Santa Clara, on the San Francisco road, and subsequently planted forty-five acres with the choicest varieties of wine grapes, such as cabernet sauvignon, charbono, pinot, alacanta bouchet, semillion, tannat, sauvignon verte and muscatel de Bordelaise. He also planted 3 acres of prunes, 1½ acres of apricots, 1 acre of cherries, 1 acre of Bartlett pears and a few apples and nectarines. Mr. Cochrane subsequently purchased 20 acres on the north side of the road, about 19 acres of which are planted to grapes, making a total of 64 acres of grapes. The yield varies from 4.37 to 5 tons per acre. From these varieties 125 gallons of wine can be made from one ton of grapes. The minimum price for wine of last year's vintage was 12 cents per gallon. A few acres of orchard were planted for family use, but as in many similar instances, produces much more than is needed, and the overplus is sold. Dr. Cochrane is a very successful dentist in San Francisco, where he has a large practice.

DR. DUDLEY'S CONDENSED GRAPE MUST. On the Almaden road, five miles from San Jose, Dr. J. P. Dudley has a beautiful place of 140 acres. Here he has practiced experimental agriculture and horticulture for many years and at the same time has made a success of it, viewed from a business standpoint. His genius for experiments has led him to seek to obtain from the fruits which he grew a knowledge of their special qualities which would render them of great value as life-sustaining elements. In pursuit of this knowledge he discovered that a particular

SANTA CLARA COUNTY VINEYARDS.

Dr. J. P. Dudley.

J. D. Williams.

Mrs. Mathilde Portal.

Los Gatos Co-operative Winery, W. B. Rankin, Manager.

kind of grape, treated in a certain manner and used as food possessed high nutritive and medicinal properties. The particular kind of grape is one having a peculiar degree of acidity of the Rose of Peru type, and the treatment to which it is subjected is the cundensation of the juice by a process of evaporation. Thus is obtained in a convenient form an abundant supply of tartrate of potash, which, when taken into the stomach as food, is converted into an alkaline carbonate. To obtain the proper quantity of this tartrate, the grape must be grown on a soil having a clay base. The action of the alkaline carbonate upon the human system is to dissolve the uric acid, and therefore the concretions, and to stimulate every gland to healthy action. The medicinal qualities of tartrate of potash have long been known to eminent physicians of this country and Europe, but the idea of obtaining it from the grape in a form convenient for use originated with Dr. Dudley, and his success is due to years of study and experimental work. That Dr. Dudley's Evaporated Grape Juice is all that is claimed for it, actual use by a large number of neighbors and friends of the Doctor will readily testify. It is a specific for all scrofulous complaints, as well as for rheumatism, gout, liver and kidney affections and other diseases. Last year was the first that Dr. Dudley has manufactured this article on a scale sufficient to meet the demands of the trade, a demand that has become more than local and promises to become world-wide in proportions. Five acres of the Dudley farm is devoted to the cultivation of the variety of grape that produces the Evaporated Grape Juice of medicinal and nutritive worth.

VINEYARD OF C. MEYERHOLTZ. On the Homestead road, west from Santa Clara, is located the orchard and vineyard of C. Meyerholtz. He is a pioneer of the State, having come from New York to California in 1850. He purchased forty acres of his present place in 1880, afterwards adding twenty more. His vines are now fifteen years old and his trees fourteen. He has a winery, the capacity of which is 100,000 gallons, and he has made his own wine since 1887. His vineyard and orchard has paid ever since it came into bearing. He is independent, owes no man and is contented. He has a substantial residence of seven rooms, surrounded by flowers evergreens, and other improvements. His vines are mostly ... ...arbonos and mataros, and his grade of wine ranks high.

THE LONE HILL VINEYARD. One of the largest in the county is the Lone Hill Vineyard, owned by J. H. Freyschlag. It consists of 275 acres and is located on the Los Gatos and Almaden road and is eight miles distant from San Jose. It is one of the oldest vineyards in the county and there are some vines on the place of the mission variety that are forty years old. Mr. Freyschlag has been in possession of the place for four years past, succeeding to the interest of his uncle, C. Freyschlag, now dead. In the vineyard are about thirty varieties of table grapes and half a dozen kinds of wine grapes. The largest portion of the area, however, is given to wine grapes. The winery has a capacity of 200,000 gallons, and the annual production is about 150,000 gallons. It is equipped with an elevator, presses and improved machinery, which permits of the economical handling of the wine. Mr. Freyschlag has made many improvements and contemplates others, among which are a handsome residence to be located on the summit of Lone Hill. His wines are of the standard quality, which he sells at wholesale. He manufactures both red and white wine, his special pride being a fine Riesling, which, when properly matured, possesses a delicate flavor and charming bouquet. The soil of this locality is adapted to grape growing, being a light gravel, and is exposed to the warm sunlight which is so necessary in bringing the grape to its highest state of perfection.

MRS. ANNIE MUNIER'S VINEYARD. One of the prettiest foot-hill vineyards in the West Side district is that owned by Mrs. Annie Munier. In 1882 it was wild land, covered with a heavy growth of brush and native grasses. In that year the entire 80 acres was purchased for $1,000. Of the 80 acres about 35 are now in trees and vines. There are about 8 acres in fruit, of which amount 2 acres are not yet in bearing. The fruits represented are prunes, peaches and apricots.

SOME VITICULTURAL FACTS. Santa Clara County produced in 1895 about 5,000,000 gallons of wine. The prices at which wine grapes were sold in 1895 ranged from $11 to $15 per ton. This year (1896) they will be several dollars per ton higher. The wine men will do well this year. The grape pomace from the wineries is generally sold to manufacturers of cream of tartar. San Jose has a factory of this kind.

ON THE ROAD TO DR. J. T. DUDLEY'S FARM.

IN THE WEST SIDE VINEYARD DISTRICT.

Mrs. Annie Munier.

J. H. Freyschlag.

Mrs. Annie Munier.

M. D. Phelps.

REPRESENTATIVE COUNTRY RESIDENCES.

John Snyder.

M. D. Phelps.

J. C. Merithew.

E. A. Wheeler.

PROMINENT SANTA CLARA COUNTY VINEYARDISTS.

T. B. Kerwin.	J. H. Freyschlag.	John Snyder.	Richard Heney.	A. Zicovich.
Daniel Sutherland.	J. C. Merithew.	A. L. Williams.	Henry Farr.	M. D. Phelps.
L. Selenger.	S. E. Portal.	A. H. Wood.	J. D. Williams.	C. Meyerholz.

THE BENCH AND BAR OF SAN JOSE.

The Evolution of Local Jurisprudence. Some Men Who Have Made Their Mark in Temples of Justice and Mastered Broad Principles of Law.

IT was forty-nine years ago that old John Burton sat in the adobe juzgado administering a very rude and simple sort of justice and constituting Bench and Bar of San Jose. Half a century is not so long, after all, and there are men still living who remember that primitive Court of the Alcaldes, and who there plumed their young professional pinions for the wilder flights of later years. They have seen the Bench and Bar of San Jose from this small beginning grow and increase with the expanding institutions and increasing population of the State of California until it takes rank to-day among the most notable legal forums of the Pacific Coast.

During all of its history the Bench and Bar of San Jose has been remarkable for the importance of its causes, the ability of its judges and the learning and eloquence of its advocates. The four decades which have passed, and the one which is passing in the history of our Bench and Bar, have each been distinctive in the character of its litigation and the quality of its judges and lawyers. During the fifties the County and District Courts were organized, and superseded the old Mexican tribunals. Over the County Court during that decade presided in turn Judges Redman, Allen, Buckner and Moore, while the District Bench, during the same period, was occupied by Judges Watson, Hester and McKee. Before these courts came the best lawyers which the young State contained, to argue great causes and do battle for their clients' claims. Among the lawyers of that time were Rufus A Lockwood, Col. E. D. Baker, Edmund Randolph, William T. Wallace, A. L. Rhodes, Lawrence Archer and William Matthews. These are but a few of the great advocates who adorned our early Bar. It would require a volume to relate the history of that epoch of great causes and brilliant men. It was the era of the adjustment of the validity and boundary of the Mexican land grants and of the consequent legal warfare between the claimants and the squatters over their respective rights.

The growing value of the fertile plains of the Santa Clara Valley, its rapid increase in population and its propinquity to San Francisco, caused its legal forum to be sought by the brightest minds and keenest intellects of the State.

The era of the sixties saw the beginning and the growth of what may be termed "commercial litigation." The villages of San Jose, Santa Clara and Gilroy enlarged to towns; a railroad or two crept down into the Santa Clara valley from the north; the farming industry of the county became organized and important, and the character of its litigation changed.

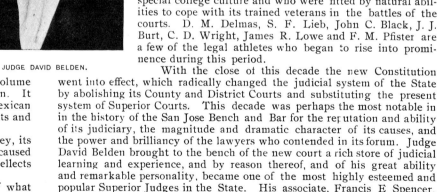

JUDGE DAVID BELDEN.

During this period the County Court was presided over by Judges John H. Moore, Isaac N. Senter and Lawrence Archer, while Samuel Bell McKee remained District Judge during the decade. The leading lawyers of the time, in addition to those who had survived from the former decade were C. T. Ryland, P. O. Minor, S. O. Houghton, John Reynolds, J. Alexander Yoell and Thomas Bodley, while coming rapidly to the front in their profession were such men as Francis E. Spencer, Thomas H. Laine and D. W. Herrington. The seventies saw yet other changes in the complexion of the local Bar and in the character of its litigation. This was the epoch of partition suits of the great ranchos, affecting the finest portions of the county, and involving many persons in the meshes of the law. The County Court was, during the larger portion of this period, presided over by Judge D. S. Payne, who occupied its bench until the change in judicial systems caused by the adoption of the new Constitution in 1879. Judge McKee was succeeded by Judge David Belden upon the bench of the Twentieth Judicial District formed by the Legislature in 1872, and comprising the counties of Santa Clara, Santa Cruz and Monterey. To the bar of this era came an accession of younger men who had received the advantages of special college culture and who were fitted by natural abilities to cope with its trained veterans in the battles of the courts. D. M. Delmas, S. F. Lieb, John C. Black, J. J. Burt, C. D. Wright, James R. Lowe and F. M. Pfister are a few of the legal athletes who began to rise into prominence during this period.

With the close of this decade the new Constitution went into effect, which radically changed the judicial system of the State by abolishing its County and District Courts and substituting the present system of Superior Courts. This decade was perhaps the most notable in in the history of the San Jose Bench and Bar for the reputation and ability of its judiciary, the magnitude and dramatic character of its causes, and the power and brilliancy of the lawyers who contended in its forum. Judge David Belden brought to the bench of the new court a rich store of judicial learning and experience, and by reason thereof, and of his great ability and remarkable personality, became one of the most highly esteemed and popular Superior Judges in the State. His associate, Francis E Spencer, came to his side upon the bench not less richly endowed with ability and legal learning, and during their united service the bench of Santa Clara County was considered the best equipped in the entire State. In 1888 Judge Belden died, and was succeeded by Judge John Reynolds, who had long adorned the local bar, and who has since administered justice in Department Two of the court with great ability and fairness and with much satisfaction to the people of Santa Clara County. Upon the voluntary retirement of Judge Spencer from the bench in 1890, Judge William G. Lorigan was elected to succeed him and, although one of the younger members of the bar, speedily showed that he possessed the necessary qualities of mind and purpose to maintain the quality of the bench at the high mark of excellence and reputation to which it had been elevated by his predecessor.

During the past fifteen years the Bar has had many accessions, both in the way of young men who, having passed through the various schools and colleges of the Santa Clara Valley, have come to regard it as the ideal place for residence and business, and in the way of older men who have come westward from States less favored than our own. Of the former class may be mentioned W. G. Lorigan, J. H. Campbell, Joseph R. Patton, John E. Richards, C. F. Wilcox, V. A. Scheller, P. F. Gosbey, D. W. Burchard, H. V. Morehouse, H. D. Tuttle, Nicholas Bowden, Jackson Hatch, William P. Veuve, W. C. Kennedy, W. A. Beasley and many others. Of the older men who have located in San Jose and taken place at the bar may be noted such names as Noble T. Biddle, A. W. Crandall, W. L. Gill and others. It is impossible to enumerate all of the present members of the local bar. The list is too long for individual mention, and our sketch must draw to a close with the biographies of a few among the many deserving members of the profession.

Superior Judge John Reynolds is a native of New York, having been born in Westchester County in 1825. He was educated at Union Academy, at Bedford, and studied law at Sing Sing, in the office of his brother, S. F. Reynolds. Upon his admission to the bar he commenced the practice of law in his brother's office and continued for one year. He came to California in 1853 and opened an office in San Francisco, where he practiced successfully until the fall of 1871, when he came to San Jose. In 1888 the death of David Belden created a vacancy in the office of Superior Judge, and the Governor appointed Mr. Reynolds. A few months afterward the appointment was ratified and the wisdom of the appointment confirmed by the people at the election, Judge Reynolds

RESIDENCE OF MRS JUDGE BELDEN, SAN JOSE.

being elected for the unexpired term of the office. In 1890 he was again elected, this time for the full term of six years. Judge Reynolds served as a member of the Assembly in 1881 and rendered important services in that connection. As a lawyer he has been engaged in many important cases. One of the most extensive legal undertakings was the partition of the Las Animas Rancho. This ranch covered the City of Gilroy, and thousands of acres of outside lands. This had to be divided among two thousand persons, some of whom were entitled to a small fraction of an acre. Years of labor were devoted to this matter, and so successfully was the work done that there was no flaw in the record, and all the parties received their just dues and were satisfied.

For five years past the administration of justice in Department One of the Superior Court of Santa Clara County has been in charge of Judge William G. Lorigan. The parents of Mr. Lorigan, in 1852, removed from Cincinnati, Ohio, to the gold fields of Australia, and it was while they were temporarily residing there, in 1855, that the subject of this sketch was born. Seven years later his parents returned to America, settling in Santa Clara, and there Mr. Lorigan passed his youth and early manhood until he took up his residence in San Jose in 1884, except for a short period when he was attending school in the East. Hie education was obtained at Santa Clara College and at St. Vincent's College at Cape Girardeau, Missouri. He studied law with Moore, Laine, Delmas & Leib, and after a thorough course of preparation he was admitted to practice by the Supreme Court in 1879. He immediately engaged in active practice and it was not long until he established himself as one of the best lawyers of the city. In 1890 he was elected to the position of Superior Judge, an office which he has filled with grace, dignity and learning. As a judge he has been impartial in his rulings, justly exacting regarding the conduct of the lawyers in his court, yet treating all with a gentleness and courtesy which has won for him the universal respect of the members of the bar. The Supreme Court has generally sustained the views of Judge Lorigan in matters of law which have been appealed, and he has established a reputation as one of the prominent judges of the State.

PROMINENT SAN JOSE ATTORNEYS.

Jackson Hatch.
W. P. Veuve.
D. W. Burchard.

Victor A. Scheller.
Judge John Reynolds.
S. A. Barker.

D. M. Delmas.
S. M. Shortridge.

J. C. Black.
Judge W. G. Lorigan.
J. B. Kerwin.

C. F. Wilcox.
Judge J. W. Gass.
W. L. Gill.

PROMINENT SAN JOSE ATTORNEYS.

W. C. Kennedy,   Nicholas Bowden.   W. A. Bowden.   D. V. Mahoney.
H. V. Morehouse,   Judge L. Archer.   S. F. Leib,   Judge A. L. Rhodes,   C. T. Bird,
J. R. Patton.   I. S. Thompson,   James H. Campbell.   N. H. Castle,   C. D. Wright,

The judicial arm of the city is represented by John W. Gass, whose title is that of City Justice of the Peace and Police Judge. Upon him falls the responsibility of punishing the violators of the city's ordinances, and he has done so fearlessly and impartially that he is feared by all evil doers. Mr. Gass is a native of Illinois, and is 52 years of age. He served with distinction in the civil war and was permanently disabled in 1864 and received an honorable discharge. He came to San Jose in 1887 and in 1890 was elected to his present position, to which he has been twice re-elected by large majorities and once, in 1892, without opposition. He had previously held similar judicial positions in the East, and his experience as a magistrate covers a long period of years.

For more than forty years Judge Lawrence Archer has been identified with the bench and bar of Santa Clara County, and is justly entitled to be considered the nestor thereof. He was born in South Carolina in 1820. He attended the University of Virginia, and later studied law in the office of Armisted Burt, a prominent lawyer of Abbeville, South Carolina. The educational advantages which he received were largely secured by his own efforts and paid for by his own earnings. He removed to Mississippi in 1841, and was there admitted to the bar. He practiced law for two years in Yazoo County, but his health failing, he removed to St. Joseph, Missouri. There he continued his practice with success for eight years, for a part of which time he acted as District Attorney. Continued ill health caused him to resign and migrate to California. He first located in Sacramento, but two years later, in 1853, he came to San Jose, where he has since resided. Judge Archer has been honored and has honored the county and the State in many official positions. Once, in 1867, he was County Judge; twice he was a member of the Legislature, once in 1866 and again in 1875. During the session of the latter year he made the memorable fight against the railroads of the State for reduced freights and fares. The Archer Bill was the first chapter in the history of the struggle for lower freights and fares in California. He was twice Mayor of the City of San Jose, once in 1857 and again in 1877.

Conspicuous among the names of the leaders of the bar of the State is that of D. M. Delmas. He is a native of the south of France and was born April 14, 1844. Ten years later he came to San Jose. In 1858 he matriculated at Santa Clara College, an institution famous for its thorough educational methods. In 1862 he received the degree of Bachelor of Arts, and continuing his studies one year later received the further degree of Master of Arts, carrying off the honors of his class. He immediately commenced the study of the law and entered the law department of Yale University. From this institution, in 1865, he received the degree of Bachelor of Laws. He at once engaged in the practice of his profession in San Jose. In 1867 he was elected District Attorney, which position he held two years. Thereafter, and until 1876, he was a member of the firms of Moore, Laine & Delmas, and Moore, Laine, Delmas & Leib. In 1879 he was admitted to the Supreme Court of the United States. He continued to practice in San Jose until 1883, when he removed to San Francisco. His residence, however, always has been and still is in this county, and he has a beautiful home near Mountain View.

In the month of January, 1894, D. M. Delmas, formerly of San Jose, but of late years one of the leaders of the San Francisco bar, who has attained a national reputation as an advocate, and Samuel M. Shortridge formed a copartnership for the practice of law. The members of this copartnership have gained a high reputation as leading lawyers, and the large interests intrusted to their care as attorneys-at law become more extensive year by year. S. M. Shortridge was born at Mount Pleasant, Iowa, in 1861, and with his father came to California in 1876, settling in San Jose. He attended the public schools and graduated from the San Jose High School with distinguished honors. Thereafter, for four years, he taught school in Napa County, and as a teacher took prominent rank among the popular and notable instructors of the State. He commenced his legal studies in the office of his present partner, Mr. Delmas, in 1883, and went through the junior course in the Hastings Law College. He was admitted to the bar by the Supreme Court in 1885, and shortly after commenced practice. As a student of Shakespeare he has few equals. Politics early claimed his attention, and in the campaign of 1884 he made a brilliant record as an orator and thinker, and the sobriquet of "Boy Orator" and the "Henry Clay of the Pacific Coast" were freely bestowed upon him. As a lawyer and an advocate he has achieved a signal success. His bright intellect and keen perception enable him to see the salient features of a legal contest, and to lay bare iniquity by searching questions to a witness. He has conducted some of the most important cases in the State in a manner to call forth encomiums from the bench and bar.

H. V. Morehouse is a native of Elkhart, Indiana, and was born April 1, 1849. He came to this State when young, and received his education in the public schools and at Sotoyome Institute, in Sonoma county. For seven years he taught school, and at the same time applied himself to the study of the law, and in 1874 he was admitted to the bar. From 1874 until 1890 he practiced law at Salinas, in Monterey County, removing in the latter year to San Jose, where he has established himself prominently in his profession. Mr. Morehouse has been connected with a vast amount of important litigation, and there is scarcely a county in the State that has not been visited by him in a professional capacity. One of the noted murder trials of the State was that of the People vs. Prewett. After four long trials, in which every available juror in San Benito County had been summoned, Mr. Morehouse secured the acquittal of the defendant. At present Mr. Morehouse is engaged in the celebrated Barron will case, a matter involving millions. He has been honored by the people, having been District Attorney of Monterey County and a member of the Board of Education for eight years. In 1892 he was a Presidential elector upon the Republican ticket.

Joseph R. Patton is a native of Santa Clara County, and was born in 1861. He received his education in the public schools of the county, and later graduated from the University of the Pacific, receiving his degree in 1879. Thereafter he taught school six months and then entered the law department of Michigan University at Ann Arbor. He completed the prescribed course in 1882, returned to San Jose, and for a time continued his studies in the office of Hon. T. H. Laine. In 1883 he established himself at San Louis Obispo and successfully practiced there four years. In 1884 he was elected District Attorney of San Luis Obispo County, and served in that capacity two years. In 1887 he returned to San Jose and has since occupied a prominent place among the members of the profession. For a number of years he was a member of the firm of Wilcox & Patton, and at present is the partner of H. D. Tuttle.

One of the oldest practitioners at the bar of Santa Clara County, in length of service, is John C. Black. It has been an honorable service, with many triumphs and few defeats, a service that has brought with it the confidence of his clients and the respect of the community. Mr. Black was born in Butler County, Pennsylvania, in 1834. He was educated at Wilmington and Allegheny Colleges. He came to California in 1855. Shortly after his arrival he studied law and was admitted to practice in 1863. He first located at Marysville, and was Deputy District Attorney of Yuba County in 1864 and 1865. In the latter year he removed to San Jose, where he has since remained. In 1871 he was elected and served a term as District Attorney. One of the incidents of his public career was that he endeavored to compel the railroad company to pay its taxes. After a protracted legal struggle Mr Black was victorious and every cent of the tax claimed was paid into the treasury. Mr. Black has been engaged in many notable cases, one of which is that of Nicholas vs. Dunphy, which has been the leading California case on the law of the road. Famous also was the case of the People vs. Cooper Cummings. The charge was murder, and after a hotly contested trial Mr. Black secured a verdict favorable to his client, the defendant.

D. W. Burchard is by birth a Missourian. He left Burton County in 1858, when a few months old, and came with his parents to California. Mr. Burchard has lived in several places in California, among them being Stockton, Santa Rosa, Oakland, Hollister and Gilroy. Most of his life has been spent in this county. He received the best education afforded by the public schools, coupled with an instruction received at home of more than ordinary value. He studied law in the office of Henley & Johnson, at Santa Rosa, and was admitted to practice in all the courts of the State in 1879, a few days after he had attained his majority. He commenced the practice of his profession at Hollister, and remained there three years, during which time he was City Attorney. He came to San Jose in 1883, and at once attained prominence in his profession. In 1885 he entered the District Attorney's office as a Deputy. The knowledge he acquired in that position qualified him for higher honors, and in 1888 he was elected District Attorney, which position he occupied two years. In 1891 he formed a partnership with ex-Judge F. E. Spencer, which continued until 1894. Mr. Burchard has been connected with many important cases and has been eminently successful.

Jackson Hatch is a native son of California. He received his education in the public schools and completed the course when he was 17 years of age. At 19 he taught school and continued two years, at the same time studying law. At the age of 21 he was admitted to the Supreme Court and entered into practice. In 1875 he was elected District Attorney, and served until 1880, when he resigned, and at once acquired a large criminal law practice. Between that time and 1874 he defended twenty-one murder cases, the most important of which was that of Miller, who was charged with the murder of Dr. J. H. Glenn. After practicing four years at Red Bluff, during which time he was engaged in many important cases, among which was the one involving the removal of the county seat of Shasta County, he removed to San Francisco, where he was appointed First Assistant United States Attorney. In 1890 he came to San Jose and has since resided here. In 1890 he was named as one of the Democratic candidates for Judge of the Supreme Court; the entire ticket, however, was defeated at the election. In 1894 he was mentioned as a prominent candidate for Governor, but refused to have his name placed before the convention. During his residence in San Jose he has been engaged in many important cases, some of which are still pending in the courts.

W. C. Kennedy was born in Philadelphia in 1847 and came to California with his parents when he was four years of age. He was educated in the public schools of Santa Clara County and at the College of Santa Clara. From that famous institution he graduated in 1865, receiving the degree of Bachelor of Arts. He studied law at Carson City, Nevada, and was admitted to practice by the Supreme Court of that State in 1870. He returned to San Jose in 1871, and has pursued the profession of the law here ever since with pronounced success. He has been concerned in many important cases and in the Supreme Court has won notable triumphs, as, for instance, in the case of the People vs. Sepulveda, where he secured the discharge of the defendant, after a conviction in the lower court; also the cases of Root vs. Root, Weibald vs. Rauer, and Wood and Brown vs. Blaney. Mr. Kenneday has many important cases still pending in the Supreme Court and in the Superior Courts of Santa Clara and adjoining counties. He is a zealous advocate and enters into a case with an ardor and determination to secure a full measure of justice.

James H. Campbell has received a State-wide reputation by reason of his connection with the estate of the late multi-millionaire, James Lux. He is a native of Massachusetts, and was born in 1850. He came to Nevada County, California, in 1857, and remained there until 1867, since which time he has been a resident of San Jose. In 1871 he graduated from Santa Clara College, and in the year following he commenced to study law. He pursued his studies successfully and was admitted to practice in 1874. Almost immediately ne was appointed Assistant District Attorney, and served two years. In 1879 he was elected District Attorney, being the only candidate upon his ticket elected. He was re-elected in 1882. During his term he was called upon to prosecute the murderers of Renowden (Majors, Jewell and Showers) which he did successfully. For several years past his attention has been, in a great measure, engrossed by his duties as attorney for the heirs of the great Lux estate, and litigation with Henry Miller, as survivor of the firm of Miller & Lux, in which many of the leaders of the bar of the State are directly or indirectly engaged.

S. A. Barker is a native of Kennebec County, Maine, and was born July 26, 1833. He was educated in his native State, and studied law in the office of Judge Josiah H. Drummond, who was a very prominent lawyer. Mr. Barker was admitted by the Supreme Court of Maine in 1857, and practiced very successfully ten years and held several minor judicial offices.

In 1867 he came to California, located in San Jose, and continued the practice of law. He has confined himself as nearly as possible to probate and commercial cases and matters involving the title to lands. His sound judgment and knowledge of the law has brought him a large and lucrative practice. Mr. Barker is the attorney for the Board of Trade, which position he has held since its organization.

C. D. Wright was born in Watertown, New York. For nearly thirty years he has been actively engaged in his profession, and has attained a high rank in the legal fraternity. He came to San Jose when a youth of 15 years, and shortly afterward became a student in the office of Hon. S. O. Houghton. Mr. Wright was admitted to practice in 1868. At one time he was very prominent in politics, and contributed much in the way of valuable services for the success of his party, but never sought any position of emolument or honor. Of late years he has been too busily engaged in the work of his profession to concern himself in matters political. Mr. Wright has been connected with many of the important cases that have been tried in the courts of the county, and of neighboring counties, and has been uniformly successful in securing decisions and verdicts favorable to his clients.

John B. Kerwin is one of the rising younger members of the bar. He was born on a farm on the west side of the valley, and is now in his 31st year. Owing to the fact that his services were greatly needed in the cultivation of the farm, his early education was meager, and much of his study was done at home. However, he managed to spend two years at Santa Clara College—years the value of which is inestimable to him. He was devotedly fond of books and always had an ambition to become a lawyer—an ambition that he could gratify only by hard work and making many self-denials. He studied as opportunity presented itself. In 1893 he was appointed a deputy clerk, and this gave him an opportunity to study law and learn the ways of actual practice in the courts. In January, 1895, he was admitted to practice by the Supreme Court, and at once opened an office in San Jose. He has already been intrusted with many important matters, which he has given faithful attention, and is rapidly establishing a lucrative practice.

Victor A. Scheller's primary education, received in the public schools, was followed by a complete course at Santa Clara College, where he received the degree of A. B in 1886, after which he entered Hastings Law School in San Francisco, graduating with honors in 1889. The following year he was elected District Attorney, which office he filled satisfactorily. Many noted criminals are now serving terms in prison as a result of his successful prosecutions. By his kindliness, courtesy, honesty and unquestioned ability he ingratiated himself so thoroughly into the hearts of the people that in the year 1892 he was re-elected by an overwhelming majority. In spite of earnest solicitations he refused to have his name considered in connection with further nomination for the office in 1895. Since retiring from his official duties he has devoted himself assiduously to his private practice, and has already attained eminence in his profession.

D. V. Mahoney was born in Dublin in 1861, and came to America when a lad of seven years. Shortly afterward his parents died and he was obliged to make his own living. He was about fifteen years old when he came to San Jose, and he at once set about securing an education. By studying nights he fitted himself to enter the University of the Pacific, from which he graduated. Following that he studied shorthand and became an expert in that line and he has been one of the official reporters of the Superior Court. He studied law four years in the District Attorney's office, and was admitted to practice in 1889. By reason of his position as court reporter he has been able to acquire a thorough knowledge of practice, and that further important essential in a lawyer, the art of trying causes in court. He has been trusted with many important matters and the trust has been faithfully discharged.

C. T. Bird is a native of Alabama and was born at Montgomery in 1841. He came to San Jose with his parents in 1851 and has resided here since. His education was mainly secured in that famous educational institution of early days, Gates' San Jose Institute. He commenced the study of law in 1872 and made considerable progress therein, but at that time did not intend to practice the profession and did not then apply for admission to the bar. Later, however, he had occasion to use his legal knowledge, and underwent an examination and was admitted by the Supreme Court in 1882. Since then he has applied himself with a zeal and earnestness that has brought him success. Though Mr. Bird has an extensive general practice, he has gained a wide reputation for his knowledge of street law. He is recognized as an authority on matters concerning street improvements, and his counsel is sought outside of this county. Mr. Bird is a Commissioner of the United States Circuit Court of this district, and for the faithful performance of the duties of this office received the compliments of the late Circuit Judge, Lorenzo Sawyer.

I. S. Thompson was born near Santa Clara, in this county, in 1861. His father was and yet is a prominent citizen of the county, and has been identified with its progress since its infancy. Young Thompson attended the public schools and graduated from the San Jose Normal School. In October, 1885, he entered Michigan Law School at Ann Arbor, and graduated in 1887, receiving the degree of Bachelor of Law. He was admitted to practice by the Supreme Court of Michigan in 1886, which was prior to his graduation. He commenced the practice of his profession immediately upon the completion of his legal studies, locating in San Jose. For two years he assisted James H. Campbell. He has been very successful and for several years has enjoyed a fair share of the litigation which has occupied the attention of the courts. He has been intrusted with many important and complicated matters, and has succeeded in securing justice for his clients. He is identified with the interests of the county and owns the Union Hotel property at Gilroy, and valuable residence property in Santa Clara. Besides being prominent in his profession, Mr. Thompson is an active member of several fraternal societies, particularly the Odd Fellows and Knights of Pythias.

Among the most active members of the San Jose bar is William A. Bowden. Although a comparative young man, being only 30 years of age, he has established for himself a practice and a reputation which might well be the envy of many older practitioners. He is a native of New York. He came West in 1869, and after remaining a few years in Indiana, located in San Jose in 1876. He attended the public schools of the city and afterward was a student at Santa Clara College. Later he was employed in a real estate office, and in connection with his labors, and during spare hours, read law books. Undergoing a thorough examination by the Supreme Court, he was admitted to practice in 1887. From this date until 1891 he served as a deputy in the County Clerk's office and thereby became familiar with practice and the manner of conducting trials. Since 1891 he has been actively engaged in the practice of his profession. Mr. Bowden acts as attorney for some of the banks of San Jose and has been somewhat prominent in politics.

Charles F. Wilcox came to California with his parents from Illinois in 1857, when five years of age. He lived a few years in Sierra County, then a few years in Solano County, finally coming to this county in 1865. He attended the public schools and afterwards Vacaville College. He then entered Santa Clara College, from which he graduated in 1871. He at once commenced the study of the law in the offices of B. P. Rankin and Judge F. E. Spencer. He was admitted to the bar in 1875, and entered into a successful practice, becoming associated with his former instructor, B. P. Rankin. For twenty years Mr. Wilcox has been engaged in practice and he has acquired a reputation as a careful and safe counsellor, so much so that he is the legal adviser of the Commercial and Savings Bank, the Safe Deposit Bank of Savings, and the Commercial Bank of Los Gatos. He has also been intrusted with the management and settlement of many large estates, and has performed the duties of these trusts with strict fidelity. Among such estates can be named those of Martin Murphy, deceased; John Auzerais, deceased; Mrs. E. E. White, deceased, and G. W. Rutherford, deceased. Each of these estates inventoried over $100,000.

William P. Veuve was born under the shadow of the old juzgado, or town hall, situated on the Plaza of the Pueblo de San Jose, in the year 1853. In his youth he attended the public and private schools of the city, and afterwards completed a course in Santa Clara College, graduating therefrom with honor in 1874, with the degree of Bachelor of Arts. Thereafter he studied law in the office of Thomas H. Bodley, one of San Jose's leading practitioners, and was admitted to the bar by the Supreme Court in 1877. In 1880 he was elected City Justice and Police Judge, and served so acceptably that he was re-elected in 1882. From 1890 to 1894 he was City Attorney for Los Gatos, and rendered important services in that connection. He has been favored with a large and increasing practice, and has been concerned in much of the important litigation that has transpired in this vicinity. At present he is devoting much time in the settlement of a controversy involving the title to the Guadalupe Quicksilver mine and thousands of acres of land in the vicinity, valued at a million of dollars. The proceedings and suits involving the above subject of controversy are pending in several courts of the State and in the United States Land Office.

N. H. Castle was born in San Francisco in February, 1863. He received good educational advantages there and in 1880 entered Yale College. He completed the classical course in 1884, and received the degree of Bachelor of Arts. Shortly after his graduation he commenced the study

of law in Hastings Law School. While attending this school, in 1886, he was admitted to practice by the Supreme Court, and afterwards was admitted to practice in the Federal Courts. He came to San Jose in November, 1886, and formed a copartnership with Hon. J. B. Lamar, which continued until the latter's death, in 1892. He has been the San Jose representative of the San Francisco Board of Trade, and also represents a large number of large mercantile houses of the same city having extensive dealings in San Jose. His legal practice is largely mercantile and commercial. He is also familiar with insurance law and matters appertaining to land titles, and has had a number of cases involving the law of street improvements.

Nicholas Bowden was born in Ireland forty-four years ago, and came to America with his parents in 1853. His father, Pierce Bowden, and the family, soon after arrival settled at Cooperstown, New York, where the subject of this sketch spent his early youth. Here he attended the public schools, and subsequently the Cooperstown Seminary, leaving the latter at the age of 15 to perfect his education by practical experience in the great world of action which he then found it necessary to enter. In 1869 young Bowden located at Evansville, Indiana, where for several years he filled responsible positions as business manager and accountant for two large commercial houses. Subsequently he entered the field of journalism, and in 1875 assumed the management of the Evansville Daily Courier, one of the leading Democratic papers of the State, and took an active part in local and State politics until the Spring of 1877, when ill-health forced him to seek a milder and more congenial climate. After visiting Colorado and several points in California, he came to San Jose. A few months stay in in the Garden City brought good health and convinced him that the climate and social conditions of the Santa Clara valley were as nearly perfect as it was possible to find. Pleased with the surroundings and prospect, he concluded to make San Jose his permanent home. In October of the same year he took charge of the Daily Herald of this city and conducted the paper with great skill and vigor for about three years. In the winter of 1880-81 Mr. Bowden took up the study of the law, and finished his reading in the office of Hon. Lawrence Archer, and was admitted to practice in the Supreme Court in 1882. Immediately after his admission he formed a partnership with Judge Archer, which continued until the end of 1892. On October 4, 1883, Mr. Bowden married Miss Sallie Trimble, daughter of the late John Trimble. They have four children, three sons and one daughter. While Mr. Bowden has always been a consistent Democrat and taken great interest in the political questions of the day, he is in no sense a politician and has never been a candidate for office. In 1888 he was one of the Presidential electors on the Democratic ticket, and for many years has been prominent in the councils of his party. During the fourteen years of his practice Mr. Bowden has been engaged in many of the leading and important civil and probate cases, not only in this county, but elsewhere throughout the State, and has achieved marked success in his profession. He enjoys a large and lucrative practice, has been for many years the legal representative of several of the largest banking institutions and corporations in this part of the State, and is recognized as one of the leaders of the bar.

SANTA CLARA COUNTY MEDICAL SOCIETY.

Some Prominent Physicians of the Old School. Men Who Are Skilled in Modern Methods, and Who Have the Moral and Financial Support of the Community.

THE representative medical body of this city is the Medical Society of Santa Clara County, which was organized May 9, 1870, by nine of the foremost physicians of San Jose. Since the date of its inception the society has increased in numbers and influence until it now includes forty active workers—many of whom are medical practitioners of rare ability and exceptional mental power. Like other organizations of its class, its purposes are manifold, its broadest aim being, of course, the alleviation of human snffering by stimulating its members to an exercise of their utmost endeavors in acquiring and perfecting medical knowledge. With this object in view meetings are held on the second Tuesday of every month, at which time papers appertaining to the medical sciences are read and discussed, histories of obscure cases recounted and commented upon, interesting patients presented and examined, and such other business transacted as will lead to the unity, harmony and advancement of the medical fraternity. In this latter respect the efforts of the Society have been exerted with a view to securing the passage of stringent State laws to regulate the practice of medicine, and this end has been accomplished largely through this Society acting in unison with similar organizations throughout the State. The qualifications now required to enable one to practice in California are of the most commendable character, and should reflect credit on those who lent the moral and financial support which secured their adoption.

The work of the Society in this regard, however, is not yet ended. Itinerant quacks, charlatans and mountebanks still flourish and impose on credulous human nature. This condition of affairs, however, must be ascribed to laxity in the enforcement of existing laws, rather than to an inherent defect therein. To correct this evil the energies of the members will be directed, in part, toward stimulating a more vigorous prosecution of all pretenders to medical knowledge. When this work is accomplished the society will have richly earned the thanks of the community, for all must realize how much it will redound to the welfare of the people to have their health and lives intrusted to none but men of scholarly attainments, ample experience and strict moral probity.

It was also through the instrumentality of this Society that the City Board of Health came into existence, and it has already accomplished much good in matters appertaining to public hygiene. The Society does not, however, leave the full burden of this work to fall upon the Board of Health, but by means of special committees aids the Board in exposing

DR. ELIZABETH GALLIMORE.

unsanitary conditions which menace the public health and demand attention and abatement.

The officers for 1895-6 are; President, A. C. Jayet; First Vice-President, Thomas Kelley; Second Vice-President, J. W. Thayer; Secretary, J. Underwood Hall, Jr.; Treasurer, H. J. B. Wright.

The pioneer physician of San Jose was Dr. Benjamin Cory, the first to locate in the place, which was then known as the Pueblo de San Jose de Guadalupe. It was in 1847 that he saw the few adobes clustered around the plaza, and believing that time would witness a material growth in the population and business of the town, at once established himself in his profession. He witnessed a transformation of the valley and the State, and his most extravagant dreams of its future growth in wealth, in adornment and all that accompanies an advanced civilization were more than realized.

Dr. Cory was a native of Ohio, and the date of his birth was 1822. He graduated from Miami University in 1842, and then commenced the study of medicine with his father, who was a prominent physician. Later he attended the Medical College of Ohio at Cincinnati, and received his degree in 1845. For two years he practiced medicine with his father, and then started across the plains to the Pacific Coast. He arrived at Portland, Oregon, and from there he went to San Francisco, and then came directly to San Jose.

He has performed much faithful public service. He was a member of the first Legislature of the State, and was also a member of the City Council for for years, and served a like term as a member of the Board of Education. Later he served ten years as a Trustee of the State Normal School, making a total public career of twenty years. He died last February.

Dr. Frederick W. Hatch was born in Kenosha, Wisconsin, December 4th, 1849. He came to Sacramento, California, in 1853. He was educated in the schools of Sacramento and later entered Jefferson Medical College, Philadelphia. From this institution he graduated in 1873, and then returned to Sacramento, where he engaged in hospital and private practice until March, 1879, when he accepted a position as Assistant Physician at the State Asylum for the Insane at Napa, in this State. There he remained until December 1, 1889, on which date he took charge of the State Insane Asylum at Agnews, having been elected its Medical Director two months previously. For the past six years he has retained that position and has given evidence of his eminent qualifications therefor.

J. Underwood Hall, Jr., M. D., a son of Dr. J. U. Hall, Sr., was born

SAN JOSE PHYSICIANS OF THE REGULAR SCHOOL.

Dr. William D. McDougall.
Dr. H. C. Brown
Dr. John S. Potts.

Dr. A. C. McMahon.
Dr. George W. Seifert.
Dr. Chauncey Rea Burr.

Dr. Benjamin Cory.
Dr. Pedro Merlin Lusson.

Dr. J. McMahon.
Dr. J. U. Hall, Jr.
Dr. Richard Henry Burke.

Dr. F. W. Hatch.
Dr. Thomas Kelley
Dr. J. R. Curnow.

February 9, 1868, at Gold Hill, Nevada. In 1884, after graduating from the High School, he commenced his medical education by taking a course in pharmacy at the University of California, after which he served as assistant to the mining surgeon at New Almaden. Two years later he entered Cooper Medical College, San Francisco, where he acted as assistant to Dr. C. C. Lane, Professor of Surgery and President of the College. Upon leaving San Francisco he entered the Jefferson Medical College of Philadelphia, from which he graduated in April, 1889. Upon his return to California he was appointed resident physician and surgeon for the Quicksilver Mining Company of New Almaden, which position he held for five years. After his retirement from the service of the company he again visited the East, where he studied at Chicago under Dr. Nicholas Senn, the foremost American surgeon, and with Dr. Charles McBurney, Rosevelt Hospital, New York.

In 1894 he located in San Jose, and on December 27th of that year married Miss Grace Spencer, daughter of Judge F. E. Spencer. He is a member and Secretary of the Santa Clara County Medical Society, a member of the California Medical Society, of the San Francisco Microscopical Society and of the American Medical Society.

Dr. Pedro Mellin Lusson was born in Cuba, and is of French and German descent, his parents having been owners of large coffee plantations on the island. When very young he was sent to France to be educated, and after his return he entered the College of Santiago de Cuba. In 1857 he went to Philadelphia, where, after learning the English language, he began the study of medicine in the University of Pennsylvania, graduating in 1864. After taking post-graduate courses at the Bellevue Hospital, New York, he attended the Pennsylvania Hospital for over three years and practiced until failing health compelled him to take a rest. He came to California in 1873, and finding his health much improved, located at San Jose, where he has since successfully practiced. The Doctor has always had great confidence in the future of Santa Clara County, and has shown such confidence by making large investments in real estate. Dr. Lusson is one of the ex-

presidents of the Santa Clara County Medical Society, ex-first vice-president of the State Medical Society, and is also a member of the American Medical Association.

Chauncey Rea Burr, M. D., was born at Portland, Maine, October 16, 1862. He was educated in the public schools of Portland and at Dartmouth and Yale Colleges. From the latter institution he received, in 1884, the degree of Bachelor of Philosophy. He attended the medical department of Harvard University and graduated with honorable mention in 1888. In the same year he married Frances Brewerton, sole surviving daughter of the late Major-General James Brewerton Ricketts, U. S. Army. Prior to this, however, he had spent the summer of 1887 in the study of his profession at Heidelberg, Germany, and after his graduation from Harvard again went abroad and was appointed interne pupil at the Rotunda Hospital, London, and was also connected with other famous hospitals of the world's metropolis. After a year's work there he returned to Boston, and became a Fellow of the Massachusetts Medical Society, district physician to the Boston Dispensary, physician to the department for nervous diseases, and a member of the Boston Medico-Psychological Society. He was also connected with the Boston City Hospital and the Children's Hospital. He has contributed numerous articles to medical journals and societies, some of which have received favorable comment abroad. In 1893 he removed to this Coast with his family, and in 1894 located in San Jose. He is a member of the County Medical Society.

One of San Jose's leading lady physicians is Dr. Elizabeth Gallimore. She is a native of Santa Clara Valley, and has always regarded this as her home. She attended the public schools of the county, and later graduated from the University of the Pacific. Thereafter she attended Cooper Medical College in San Francisco, from which she received her diploma in 1887. For fifteen months thereafter she was a resident physician at the Children's Hospital in San Francisco, and following that she took a post-graduate course at the New England Hospital for Women and Children at Boston, Massachusetts.

RESIDENCE OF J. H. CAMPBELL, SAN JOSE.

Late in 1889 she returned to San Jose. For three years she was associated in practice with the late Mrs. E. S. Meade, M. D. Dr. Gallimore is a member of the Santa Clara County Medical Society, of which she was last year the Secretary.

Though a native of Maine, Dr. H. C. Brown was reared in the State of Michigan, where he attended the public schools and graduated from the High School of Muskegon. He attended Rush Medical College, Chicago, and received his diploma from that famous institution in 1887. Returning to Muskegon he practiced there, and for a time was Health Officer of the city. In 1890 he came to San Jose. Dr. Brown is now the County's physician at the Almshouse. He is an active member of the County Medical Society and also of the National Medical Society.

Dr. John S. Potts was born in Missouri, September 12, 1840. He attended the public schools when a youth, and at the age of 17 years he entered the University of Missouri at Columbia. He would have graduated from this institution in a few months, but the breaking out of the civil war interrupted his studies by the suspension of the university. He rendered military service during the war and at its close commenced the study of medicine, first in the St. Louis Medical College and later in the College of Physicians and Surgeons at Keokuk, Iowa, where he received his degree. Afterward he attended lectures at Bellevue Hospital and the College of Physicians and Surgeons, New York. He returned to Mexico, Missouri, in 1869, and entered upon the practice of his profession. In 1875 he came to California for the benefit of his wife's health, and finding the climate of Santa Clara valley healthful, and its people hospitable, he settled here and has since established a successful practice. Dr. Potts has been prominently identified, not only with his profession, but with public works. He was active in organizing the Board of Trade, and largely through his efforts the Hotel Vendome was erected. He was the first president of the Hotel Vendome Company. He has been a member of the Masonic fraternity for over thirty years. He is a member of and one of the organizers of the Santa Clara Medical Society, of which he served a regular term as President. He is also a member of the State Medical Society, and of the American Medical Association. At the present time he holds the position of President of the Board of Directors of the Waldeck Sanitarium, a leading private hospital of San Francisco.

Among the physicians whose practice in San Jose extends over a period of more than twenty years is Dr. A. McMahon. In 1875 he came to San Jose from Marysville, where he had resided for five years previously. Prior to that he had practiced in New York City and Pittsburg. Throughout the war, from 1861 to 1865, he served as a surgeon of volunteers in the Union Army, and was honorably discharged with the rank of Lieutenant-Colonel. Dr. McMahon was educated at Bargetown, Kentucky, Literary College, and is a graduate of the Ohio Medical College at Cincinnati, and received his diploma therefrom in 1857. In the interval between his grad-

LEONARD E. RICE, M. D.

uation and his enlistment in the army he practiced in Cincinnati. He was elected Coroner of Santa Clara County in 1876 and served as County Physician in 1878 and 1879.

Dr. J. McMahon is a son of Dr. A. McMahon, and is associated with him in the practice of medicine at San Jose. He received his education at Jefferson Medical College, Philadelphia, and received his diploma therefrom in 1881. Upon his graduation he located in San Francisco and practiced there four years. He then came to San Jose and has followed his profession at this place ever since. He is a prominent member of the Santa Clara County Medical Society

Dr. Leonard E. Rice was born in Canada in 1866. He attended the public schools, and in 1883 the High School at Woodstock, Ontario. At the age of 16 he obtained a teacher's certificate. From 1884 to 1886 he taught school, and then entered Trinity Medical College, Toronto, resuming his teaching during vacations. He graduated from Trinity University and Trinity Medical College in 1890 and later from the College of Physicians and Surgeons at Toronto. He located at Atwood, Ontario, where he soon acquired a large practice. In November, 1894, he was appointed resident surgeon in the Post-Graduate Hospital of Chicago. After holding this position for some time he resigned and located in San Jose. Dr. Rice devotes himself to his specialty, which is that of diseases of women, and surgery.

Dr. Thomas Kelley is a native of Illinois, and was born in 1836. He received a good common school education. The outbreak of the civil war found him eager to enlist for the preservation of the Union, and for four years he rendered faithful service, receiving promotion from the ranks to that of first lieutenant. After the war he studied medicine, and in 1871 received his diploma and degree from Rush Medical College of Chicago. He immediately came to San Jose, where he has since remained in the practice of his chosen profession. He has been President of the County Medical Society, and is a member of the State and National societies. He was appointed postmaster at San Jose during the term of President Harrison, and served nearly four and a half years. As a public official he rendered efficient and faithful service.

Dr. Richard Henry Burke has been a resident of and a practicing physician in the City of San Jose since 1888. During his youth he resided in Wisconsin, and graduated from the College of the Sacred Heart, Watertown, Wisconsin. Thereafter he attended that renowned institution, Rush Medical College of Chicago, from which he graduated in 1883, receiving the degree of M. D. He practiced there five years and until he came to the Golden State. He ranks high among the medical fraternity and is a member of the State Medical Society and the Medical Society of Santa Clara County.

The present Health Officer of the City of San Jose is J. R. Curnow, M. D. He is a native of England, but came to this country when very young. His youth was spent in the mining districts of Nevada County, where he attended the public schools. Later he attended the University of the Pacific, from which institution he graduated. For a time he studied medicine in the office of Drs. Potts and Caldwell, and afterward took the scientific course at Columbia College. He spent some time in Bellevue Hospital, completing his course of study, and graduated in 1882. For twelve years he has been a member of the medical fraternity of San Jose. He has devoted much time to studying and improving the sanitary condition of the city, and largely through his efforts was brought about the establishment of the Board of Health.

William D. McDougall is a son of Rev. Allen McDougall, and was born in Niagara County, New York, in 1857. He was educated in the public and private schools of New York and Canada. Afterward he attended the Medical Department of the University of Buffalo, from which he received his degree and diploma in 1882. He practiced five years in Monroe County, New York, and in 1887 came to San Jose, where he continued the practice of his profession. Soon after his arrival here and during the small-pox scare in 1887-8 he was appointed small-pox physician. Later, and for three years, he was the physician of the County Hospital. Dr. McDougall is the retiring president of the Santa Clara County Medical Society, and is also a member of the State Medical Society.

George W. Seifert, M. D., is a native of Santa Clara valley, having been born in the town of Santa Clara thirty-five years ago. His father was one of the early argonauts, and was also a practicing physician. The subject of this sketch is a graduate of that famous institution, Santa Clara College, and received the degree of B. S. Upon his graduation he attended the Medical Department of Jefferson College, Philadelphia, from which he graduated in 1883, with the degree of M. D. Thereafter he served an interne of one year and a half at St. Mary's Hospital, Philadelphia, at the expiration of which time he returned to Santa Clara and practiced his profession four years. During 1889-90 he pursued a post-graduate course in Vienna. For five years past he has been a practicing physician in San Jose. He is a member of the State and County Medical Societies, also of the Board of Health, and is physician for the Sanitarium.

THE SANITARIUM, SAN JOSE.

A HOME AND HOSPITAL. Among the many institutions of the State dedicated to uses of a sanitary character, the Sanitarium at San Jose stands eminent. This institution was erected in 1888-9 by Judge and Mrs. M. P. O'Connor, and by them was donated to the Sisters of Charity of St. Vincent de Paul, under whose auspices it is now conducted. During the first six years of its establishment this sanitarium has admitted and cared for 1,500 patients, the number in constant attendance being between fifty and sixty. The building is located on Race street, in the southwestern part of the city. It is a large structure of brick and sandstone, and contains about thirty-five private rooms and several wards, the entire house being neatly and tastefully furnished, well heated and lighted and provided with all modern conveniences. The grounds are spacious and laid out in the latest style of landscape art, with trees, flowers, lawns and pleasant walks, the whole, building and surroundings, being arranged with a view to the comfort and ease of the patients.

It is something more than a hospital, for besides the sick the aged can here find a home, where they can pass their declining years in quiet restfulness and obtain peace of mind and body. Arrangements have been made by many such, who find it a cheerful home and at the same time an economical mode of living.

THE BOARD OF HEALTH. The Board of Health was organized in 1889, and Dr. J. R. Curnow was chosen Health Officer, which position he has filled ever since. Through the instrumentality of the Board 2,000 connections have been made with the city's sewer system, and a corresponding number of private vaults and and cesspools have been abated. So thoroughly has the work of drainage been done that typhoid fever, diphtheria and other zymotic diseases have been practically eliminated from the city. Besides it has abated nuisances which were a menace to the public health, and condemned impure food products. In doing this it has materially reduced the death rate.

DEATH RATE PER 1,000 IN UNITED STATES.		DEATH RATE PER 1,000 IN CALIFORNIA CITIES.	
New York......24.19	Cincinnati........18.89	San Francisco.....18.33	Los Angeles......15.82
Philadelphia......17.17	Milwaukee.. 15.85	Sacramento.. 16.78	Stockton 15.33
Boston 20.37	Richmond, Va 20.10	Oakland..... .. 14.45	Alameda......... 13.40
Baltimore........ 20.31	Savannah 33.75	San Diego....... ..10.88	San Jose. 11.78

TWO WELL=KNOWN SPECIALISTS.

Physicians of the Regular School Who Have Made a Specialty of Diseases of the Eye, Ear, Nose and Throat. Brief Sketches of Their Professional Careers.

AMONG the eminent specialists of the Pacific Coast is Dr. W. A. Gordon, of San Jose. He was born at Watkins, New York, in 1834. His early education was acquired in a private school of his native town and in the public schools of Chicago and Waukegan, Illinois. Later he attended Lind (now Northwestern) University, and also Rush Medical College, from which he graduated in 1856. In 1857 he located at Wausau, Wisconsin, and soon became a prominent surgeon. He was three terms County Superintendent of Schools. While taking a post-graduate course in Will's Eye Hospital, Philadelphia, in 1862, he received a commission as Assistant Surgeon of the Tenth Wisconsin Infantry. This he accepted, and became attached to the Army of Kentucky. His executive and professional ability was immediately recognized and he was made surgeon in charge of the U. S. A. General Hospital, No. 15, at Louisville, and subsequently was promoted to the chief surgeonship of several of the most important hospitals at the base of the Army of the Cumberland. He was recommended for further promotion and accordingly ordered by the Surgeon General at Washington to report to the U. S. Medical Examining Board for examination as to his qualifications. He demonstrated his worthiness by the honor conferred, his

W. A. GORDON, M. D.

commission being approved by the Senate and the signature of President Lincoln promoted him to the corps of Surgeons of the United States Volunteers. He was again directed to report to the field of active military operations in the West, and was ordered on duty as assistant to the Superintendent and Medical Director of the U. S. A. General Hospital, with headquarters at Louisville, Kentucky.

Before the close of the year he was appointed by the Surgeon General at Washington to the position of Secretary of the United States Medical Examining Board for the Armies of the Cumberland, Tennessee and Kentucky. At the close of the war he located in Chicago, but ill health compelled him to seek a milder climate and he established himself at Hannibal, Missouri, where he resided twenty years. His habit has been to take a post-graduate course every five years, either in Chicago, Philadelphia or New York. In addition to the diploma of his alma mater he holds diplomas

from the Chicago Opthalmic College and from the New York Post-Graduate Medical College. He has been an active member in several medical and scientific societies in the East and is a member of the American Medical Association. Dr. Gordon's specialty is diseases of the eye, ear, nose and throat. For three years past he has been a resident of San Jose.

Dr. F. B. Eaton, who is associated with Dr. W. A. Gordon in the treatment of diseases of the eye, ear, nose and throat, was born in Chicago, Illinois. He received his literary education at Columbian University, Washington, D. C., and his scientific and professional education at Cornell University, the medical department of Columbian University, Cooper College, San Francisco, and in the eye, ear, throat and nose clinics of New York, London, Paris and Vienna. In 1877 he was appointed surgeon in the United States Army, and served in the campaign against the hostile Nez Perces Indians, being attached to the command of troops L and E. First Cavalry, which, by forced marches, intercepted and turned back the Nez Perces Indians, under "Young Joseph" in May, 1877, thus saving the settlers in the Wallowa Valley. Later in the Nez Perces war he served in the field under Surgeon (now Surgeon-General) George M. Sternberg. In 1878 he had medical charge of Fort Stevens,

F. B. EATON, M. D.

Oregon, and Fort Canby, Washington, during the Bannock war. In 1878 Dr. Eaton left the army and began the practice of his specialty in Portland, Oregon, where, during the eighteen years of his residence he built up a large and lucrative practice. From 1883 to 1887 he was professor of diseases of the eye and ear in Willamette University, and in 1877 was appointed to the same position in the medical department of the University of Oregon, which he held until his removal to San Jose. In 1883 he was appointed eye and ear surgeon to the Good Samaritan Hospital, which position he held until his departure from Portland, and was also occulist and aurist to the Union Pacific Railroad and Oregon Railway and Navigation Company since 1889. Dr. Eaton has had a long and extensive practice in the treatment of diseases of the eye, ear, nose and throat, both in private and hospital practice. Being obliged to leave the humid climate of Oregon on account of his wife's health, Dr. Eaton came to San Jose in 1896.

ASYLUM FOR INSANE.

The Great Institution at Agnews and Its Importance Commercially. One Hundred and Thirty Thousand Dollars Spent in the Community Annually.

AMONG the public institutions located in Santa Clara County, the great asylum for insane, located at Agnews Station, five miles north of San Jose, is one of the largest and most important. This magnificent building is three stories high in the main, while the administration building is four stories, and the entire structure is built of

The reservation includes 276 acres, and the land is all utilized, either for orchards, gardens, hay fields or pasture. A large herd of cows is kept for the purpose of supplying the institution with milk, and a sufficient number of horses are kept to properly till the ground.

There are now 915 patients, of whom 340 are women and 575 are men.

THE GREAT ASYLUM FOR THE INSANE, AGNEWS STATION, SANTA CLARA COUNTY, CALIFORNIA.

stone and brick. It has a frontage of 750 feet, and presents a most imposing appearance. The building cost in round numbers $750,000. The original structure was completed in 1888, and has since been added to as necessity required.

The asylum, aside from its main purpose, is of great commercial benefit to the county, as local merchants secure many of the contracts for furnishing supplies. The contracts aggregate over $100,000 per annum, and the pay roll amounts annually to $35,000, making a total of $135,000, a large proportion of which is expended in the county.

The cost per capita for maintaining the patients varies from 38.62 cents to 48.6 cents per day, the average being about 40 cents. Water for the entire plant and for all uses about the establishment and farm is supplied by artesian wells, of which there are eight, varying in depth from 201 to 580 feet.

The trustees, appointed by the Governor, are: Isaac Upham, of San Francisco; O. A. Hale and J. R. Curnow of San Jose, Edward White, of Watsonville, and Frank H. Gould. They serve practically without pay, receiving but $130 per year.

REPRESENTATIVE SAN JOSE RESIDENCES

H. W. Edwards.

L. Archer.

C. A. Armstrong.

Dr. H. C. Brown.

SANTA CLARA OIL WELLS.

Location of the Oil Belt and Product of the Wells. History of the Moody Gulch District. The Great Brea Fields and Tar Springs Near Sargents Station.

ONE of the greatest resources the world has ever known is petroleum. It not only occupies an important position in domestic economy, but enters largely into the arts and sciences, and the demand for it increases as chemists find new ways of utilizing its various products.

THE MOODY GULCH FIELD. There is within Santa Clara County an oil belt that is known to be both extensive and valuable, which has, nevertheless, been but partially developed. With the exception of the work at Moody Gulch very little has been done toward developing the field. Here there are nine wells in sight, with perhaps others which are piped but not easily located. This locality is about two miles southwest of Alma and about a mile west of the railroad. The surface in the vicinity of the lowest wells is about 1,100 feet above the level of the sea, while the upper wells are 1,325 feet above sea-level. In a canyon on the east side of Los Gatos Creek there are five wells. Oil from both localities is piped to the railroad, and there transferred to the regular oil-car tanks.

Oil was first discovered in small quantities floating upon the water in Moody Gulch and in adjacent springs. A well which was sunk at the old Half-way House at the mouth of Moody Gulch was made useless by the petroleum which gathered upon the surface of the water. This led to the search for and development of the oil field.

Every precaution is taken to prevent the public from acquiring information concerning the wells and their output. Notices warn people not to trespass, and hunters have been repeatedly ordered from the premises. It is known, however, that the sandstone and shales in the vicinity of the oil wells strike north 60 degrees west, and dip 65 degrees south. The oil is green and about 40 degrees Baume.

OIL WELLS AND DERRICKS IN MOODY GULCH.

The Moody Gulch property is owned by David B. Moody, Addie M. Hubbard and Martha J. Moody, and a lease is held by Charles S. Ellis and C. C. Iver, who give one tenth of the product for the right to extract the oil. The product has, for reasons best known to the lessees, been for some time held at 160 barrels per month. The oil sells for 2.40 per barrel of forty-three gallons. Two barrels of oil when used for fuel equals one ton of coal.

FORMATION AND INDICATIONS. Most of the sand strata are overlaid with a hard, quartzose shale. Some gas is usually struck in boring at Moody Gulch, and this is burned under the boilers to keep up steam with. East of Los Gatos and extending as far as the Guadalupe Quicksilver mines, the oil formation is exposed at numerous points along the foothills. In the country rock at the New Almaden mines a peculiar black substance is found which seems to be a compressed bitumen, resembling ozocerite.

THE SARGENT TAR SPRINGS. The belt seems to be fairly well defined all the way from Moody Gulch to the brea fields upon the farm of J. P. Sargent, near Sargents Station. Here petroleum oozes from the ground in several hundred places. These tar springs cover an area of about sixty acres. The crude petroleum in many places forms springs, varying in diameter from six inches to six feet. From these the oil overflows and trickles down the hillside, soon to become hardened into brea by the sun. The springs look exactly like caldrons of tar.

NATURAL GAS AND ASPHALTUM. Small quantities of natural gas are noticeable when the springs are agitated, and in the engraving which accompanies this article the natural gas will be seen as tiny

half of a barrel to flow in less than twenty minutes. Several charges were subsequently exploded, which caused petroleum to flow temporarily. The well was never pumped. In March, 1890, a cut of twelve or fourteen feet deep was made in the serpentine on the opposite side of the ravine to tap one of the tar springs. Heavy petroleum flowed at the rate of a barrel a day until the cutting caved. A company shipped considerable bitumen from the larger spring further up the canyon during 1890 and 1891. Petroleum was gathered from various springs, also, and sent to Oakland to be refined. In July, 1890, a well was sunk at the principal outcrop of bitumen. Sand and shale, much impregnated with bitumen, were passed through for seventy feet. At forty feet a body of gas was struck which discharged with a roaring sound for two or three days, when surface water filled the boring, and gas ceased to rise. At a depth of seventy feet a hard, siliceous rock was struck, upon which the drill failed to make any impression. A gelatine torpedo was then exploded in the hole. This broke the shell, which was between three and four feet thick. Boring was continued about ten feet further, in bituminous rock, when the work was abandoned. The well is now filled to within a few feet of the top with petroleum. Wells sunk further up in the hills, in the anticlinal axis, ought to secure a good flow.

THE GREAT BREA FIELDS, FARM OF J. P. SARGENT.

silvery bubbles, attempting to free itself from its coat of tar. There are thousands of tons of asphalt in the vicinity of the main springs, consisting of hardened petroleum mixed with sand. It is much sought for in this State for street-paving purposes. All the main streets of San Jose are paved with similar material, and it makes a smooth, beautiful and durable pavement. It forms a comfortable cushion for the horses' feet and presents no crannies for collection of dust.

EXPERIMENTAL CUTS AND WELLS. No systematic effort has ever been made to develop this oil field At the Little Tar Springs, which are only about a mile from the railroad station and can be reached by wagon road, the petroleum exudes from a serpentine formation on a hillside facing south. On the opposite side of the ravine a well was bored in 1886 to a depth of 900 feet, when some of the machinery broke and the parties who had secured permission from Mr. Sargent to drill the well abandoned it. In 1890 an open cut was run into the side of the hill, tapping the pipe about ten feet beneath the surface of the bitumen. A four-inch pipe was then put in, through which twelve barrels of heavy petroleum flowed in two days. The flow then ceased. A charge of giant powder was subsequently exploded in the bottom of the well, and this caused a

TAR SPRING ON THE FARM OF J. P. SARGENT.

HOMEOPATHIC PHYSICIANS.

Prominent Santa Clara County Disciples of Hahnemann, Who Have Graduated at Well-Known Colleges and Have Held High Positions.

DR. R. E. FREEMAN, of Los Gatos, graduated from the Hahnemann College of Philadelphia in March, 1886. He had previously taken a two-years' course in the Pennsylvania Hospital, under such men as Gross, Da Costa, Agnew, Hutchinson, Pancoast, Packard and Bartholow. He also took a post-graduate course in the Homeopathic Medical College of Chicago, and a course under A. H. Pratt of the Lincoln Park Sanitarium. He practiced first in Philadelphia, and subsequently in Lynn, Massachusetts In 1888 he was called to California by a telegram announcing the serious illness of his mother in Santa Clara. He was attracted by the broad sunshine, and while visiting Los Gatos he decided to make it his home, though to do so meant to relinquish a lucrative practice in Lynn. Here he soon gained a wide reputation as a surgeon. He was uniformly successful, having never lost a case, though he performed many capital operations. With a view to securing to patients the perfect rest and quiet which are always such potent aids to recuperative powers, he secured a fine property at Fair View, in Los Gatos, where the air is pure, drainage perfect, and there is no noise more unpleasant than the singing of wild birds in the green copse on the hillside. This he named the Fair View Sanitarium. It was not intended for a hospital, but for the care of patients requiring surgical operations, and it is never without occupants, as the doctor has a large practice, his skill in orificial and abdominal surgery, and in fact, general surgery, being well known. Dr. Freeman is a member of the American Association of Orificial Surgeons, and also of the American Institute of Homeopathy.

Dr. William Simpson has resided in San Jose since 1881, previous to

DR. FREEMAN'S FAIRVIEW SANITARIUM, LOS GATOS.

which time he was for thirty-five years a resident of New York. He is a graduate of Long Island College Hospital, at Brooklyn. After a severe competitive examination he was chosen the first resident physician of the Brooklyn Children's Aid Society at the Children's Seaside Home at Coney Island. When his term of service at the Seaside Home ended he engaged in general practice in New York for a period of three years. After taking special courses at the New York Ophthalmic Hospital and the Metropolitan Throat and Charity Hospital, he came to San Jose, being the first specialist to locate in the city, and has established a successful and lucrative practice, paying particular attention to diseases of the eye, ear, nose and throat. He concerned himself in the organization of the Board of Health, compiled its ordinances, was the first Secretary of the Board, and Health Officer of the city. He is still a member of the Board, and has given much time and study to the sanitary improvement of the city, and his efforts in this connection have been productive of beneficial results. Dr. Simpson was twice unanimously elected President of the State Homeopathic Medical Society, and is now Professor of Sanitary Science and Hygiene in the Homeopathic College of San Francisco.

Dr. Leonard Pratt came to San Jose three years ago from Chicago, where he held for years the chair of Clinical and Medical Surgery in the Hahnemann Medical College, and afterwards, in the same institution, that of Special Pathology and Diagnosis. Dr. Pratt is a native of Pennsylvania, and was born at Rome, Bradford County, in 1819. After the usual preparatory study he entered Lafayette College, at Easton, Penn. He then studied medicine with Dr. L. C. Belding, and attended the first

PROMINENT HOMEOPATHIC PHYSICIANS.

Dr. C. A. Goss.   Dr. P. G. Denninger.   Dr. C. A. Wayland,   Dr. Howard B. Gates.   Dr. J. M. Bowen.
                   Dr. F. H. Bangs.   Dr. William Simpson,   Dr. R. E. Freeman.
                                            Dr. Leonard Pratt.

course at Jefferson Medical College, Philadelphia. He then became a convert to homeopathy and practiced for a time at Towanda. Thereafter he attended a course of lectures at the Homeopathic Medical College at Philadelphia, and received a diploma. After practicing his profession for eight years in Bradford County, Pennsylvania, he located in Illinois, and during his years of practice there was Treasurer, Secretary and President of the Illinois State Medical Association of Homeopathy and contributed articles to various medical journals. He was, in 1869, appointed to the chairs in the college first above mentioned, and was connected therewith nine years. Since then he has been Emeritus Professor in Chicago Homeopathic Medical College. Dr. Pratt is a member of the American Institute of Homeopathy, the oldest national medical organization in America, of the California State Homeopathic Medical Society, and also of the American Association of Orificial Surgeons.

Dr. Charles A. Wayland was born in Monterey County, California, in 1865. He received his education at Hahnemann Medical College of Homeopathy, Philadelphia, and his diploma in 1891. Immediately upon his graduation he returned to San Jose and has practiced here ever since. For two years he was the physician in charge of the County Infirmary. He is a member of the American Institute of Homeopathy, and also of the State Homeopathic Medical Association.

Dr. F H. Bangs was born in Jackson, Michigan, and is now 36 years of age. He acquired an education in the common schools of his native State, and also at the Agricultural College of Michigan. He entered the Medical Department of the University of Michigan, and nearly completed the course. Then he studied at the Cleveland Hospital, where he received a degree, and later took a course at the College of Physicians and Surgeons at Chicago, from which he graduated in 1880. He came to California in 1882, and for eight years practiced in Arcata, Humboldt County. In 1990 he established himself in San Jose. In 1893 he established a sanitarium on Third street for the treatment of chronic diseases. This institution has grown remarkably. Dr. Bangs is a member of the State Homeopathic Medical Association.

Howard B. Gates was born in San Jose in 1867, and is a son of Professor Gates, who was the principal of Gates' San Jose Institute, which was considered one of the leading private educational institutions of the State. He received the advantages of a good education, which included one year at the University of the Pacific, a preparatory course under the tutelage

DR. BANGS' SANITARIUM, SAN JOSE.

of P. R. Boone at Berkeley, and a course in the State University, earning the degree of Ph. B. He then took up the study of medicine, and spent two years in Cooper Medical College, San Francisco. Going East he continued his studies in the York Homeopathic College and Hospital. From this institution he graduated and received his final degree as Doctor of Medicine. Following his graduation he took a course in the New York Post Graduate Medical College, and thereafter he returned to his old home at San Jose, and at once entered into the practice of his profession.

Dr. P. G. Denninger is a native of Berlin, and was born in 1848. He came to this country with his parents in 1862, and located in Wisconsin. He attended the Northwestern University at Watertown, Wis., and in 1869 entered the Hahnemann Medical College at Cleveland, O., and later graduated from Hahnemann Medical College, Chicago. He practiced in Minnesota and for ten years was located at Faribault, where for some time he was the physician to the State institutions for the deaf, dumb and blind. In 1889 he returned to Berlin and pursued his special studies under the tuition of Dr. Hirschberg and other eminent specialists. He came to San Jose in 1890 and has established a successful practice. From time to time he has taken post-graduate courses in prominent medical hospitals, and has thus kept in touch with the advancement of science. Dr. Denninger's specialty is the eye, ear and throat.

Dr. C. A. Goss is a native of Massachusetts, but has been a resident of California since 1878. It was in this year that she graduated from the Chicago Homeopathic Medical College and immediately came to Santa Cruz, where she practiced successfully for three years. For a period of a year following she was resident physician at St. Luke's Hospital, San Francisco, and thereafter she located at Sacramento, where she remained seven years, gaining a very large practice. Six years ago she removed to San Jose, where she has since resided and has acquired prominence in her profession. She is a member of the State Homeopathic Society.

Mrs. J. M. Bowen, M. D., is a native of Iowa, but has resided in San Jose since 1861. She is a graduate of the New York College and Hospital for women, and has pursued post-graduate studies at the Hahnemann Hospital, San Francisco. She is associated with her daughter, Dr. Amy G. Bowen, with offices at 1425 California street, San Francisco, and much of her time is spent in that city, two days each week being devoted to her San Jose practice. Dr. Bowen is a member of the State Homeopathic Medical Society, and has acquired prominence in her profession.

REPRESENTATIVE SAN JOSE RESIDENCES.

R. D. Norton.
Mrs. Catherine Dunne.

M. D. Green.
Dr. C. R. Burr.

THE SHERIFF AND HIS DEPUTIES.

The Men Who Guard the People's Interests and Preserve Peace. Something of Their History, Character and Accomplishments. Their Names and Rank.

MR. JAMES H. LYNDON, the Sheriff of Santa Clara County, has proven himself to be a safe guardian of the public interests and worthy of the honor and trust which the people have confided to him. He has been a resident of Los Gatos for more than twenty years, and during a greater part of that time was engaged in the lumber business, in which he still retains an interest. During the administration of President Harrison he served as Postmaster of Los Gatos.

Mr. Lyndon made a wise appointment when he selected Sandford G. Benson Under Sheriff, for Mr. Benson has had a wide experience with the world's affairs and is a man of judgment and integrity. He is a son of Dr. H. C. Benson, and was born in Indiana in 1845. He came to Santa Clara Valley with his parents in 1852. Mr. Benson was educated in the public schools and at the University of the Pacific. He served two years as Clerk of the Board of Supervisors, and later was Secretary of the Board of Trade and the San Jose Agricultural Society.

Frederick W. Tennant is serving in the position of head deputy. He has been a resident of this county for thirty-six years. When a youth he attended Gates' Institute at San Jose, and later spent three years at San Augustin College at Benicia. Mr. Tennant has had previous experience in the line of his duty, having served for two years as deputy under Sheriff Bollinger.

Mr. Lyndon's outside deputy is Edwin A. Kennedy, who is a son of

THE SANTA CLARA COUNTY SHERIFF AND HIS DEPUTIES.

J. N. Black.   F. W. Tennant.   C. M. Gardner.
C. T. Smith.   J. H. Lyndon.   E. A. Kennedy.
                S. G. Benson.

J. F. Kennedy, a pioneer citizen of the county, who was Sheriff at the time of his death in 1864. E. A. Kennedy was born in Philadelphia in 1850. He received his education in the public schools of this county and at Santa Clara College. For two years he was County License Collector under Treasurer McComas.

Charles M. Gardner has charge of the County Jail. He is a native of San Jose and is 29 years of age. Most of his life has been spent at Gilroy. In 1889 he was elected City Marshal of Gilroy, and later was elected constable. These positions he continued to fill up to the date of his appointment to his present position.

John N. Black, who acts as assistant jailer, is a son of the well-known attorney, J. C. Black, and is a native of San Jose, having been born in 1871. He was educated in the public schools, Normal School and University of the Pacific. With a natural aptitude for detective work, he, in 1892, associated himself with D. W. Campbell, a constable, and succeeded in making an enviable record as a peace officer.

Charles T. Smith is the bailiff of the Superior Courts, in which capacity he has served since 1880. Mr. Smith is a native of Illinois and is 47 years of age. He came to California in 1852, and enlisted in 1864 and served in the Union army until the close of the war, being stationed at Fort Point. He engaged in stock raising in this State and Nevada until 1875, and then settled in San Jose.

THE SAN JOSE POLICE FORCE.

C. J. Nolting.	A. F. Allen.	E. A. McClintock.	E. C. Gould.	J. F. Prinaiville.	C. Shannon.	J. Monahan.
T. Hughes.	J. A. Monroe.	G. E. Pickering.	J. A. Kidward.	E. W. Bateman.	R. A. Anderson.	
	J. Horn.	E. Evans.		D. W. Campbell.	J. Humburg.	J. F. Haley.
		C. Pfau.	Thomas Vance.	V, L, E. Bache.		

SOME PROMINENT INDIVIDUALS.

Men in Business Who Assisted in the Development of the County. Pioneers and Others, Some of Whom Have Passed Away, and the Part They Have Taken in Life.

A FEW lines at this time and place are appropriate to set before the readers of this book of some of the individuals who are engaged in business in San Jose, and who by their efforts have advanced the interests of the community. A description of the county would not be complete without the mention of their names.

THE MOUNT HAMILTON STAGE COMPANY. The great Lick telescope annually attracts to Mount Hamilton thousands of tourists. Aside from the Observatory and the many attractions there, the wonderful road and grand views of the valley create impressions which cause each visitor to ever after advertise to the world the beauties of the trip. It was one of the conditions of the Lick bequest that the county should build a road to the summit that should be wide and of uniform grade, not to exceed in any place six and one-half feet to the hundred. This required a road twenty-eight miles in length, though the distance from San Jose in an air line was but thirteen miles. The road, as a result, is one of many broad curves and winds in and out of canyons and around jutting points in such a way that there is a great variety of charming scenery. The safe and speedy transportation of travelers to and from the observatory requires costly and well-made coaches, strong, well-bred horses, and careful drivers. The main stage line, carrying the tourists brought by Cook & Son and the Raymond Company, is owned by F. H. Ross & Sons, who conduct the Vendome Livery Stables, connected with the Hotel Vendome. Ross & Sons have been in the transportation business many years, and understand it thoroughly. They raise horses upon

F N. ROSS & SONS' VENDOME STABLES.

their farm in Stanislaus County especially suited to the purpose—roadsters with just enough of the Directum, Nutwood and Electioneer in them to give them style. Ross & Sons have a large number of elegant vehicles, including, carts, drags, surreys, buggies, two-seaters, three-seaters, four-seaters and coaches, and can furnish fifty conveyances—enough to take to the Observatory a large number of visitors. They maintain a stage station at Smith Creek and change horses coming and going. The care used in selecting horses, coaches and drivers is evidenced by the fact that the Mount Hamilton Stage Company has never had an accident since the line was established, eight years ago.

The distance between stations, the time occupied in travel and the elevation of points along the road are given in the following table:

	TIME.	ELEVA-TION.	MILES
Leave San Jose	7:30	80	
Leave Junction House	8:10	400	5
Leave Grand View	9:0	1450	11
Leave Halls Valley	9:35	1200	15
Leave Cape Horn	10:30	2500	19
Leave Smith Creek	11:00	2000	21
Leave Water Tank	12:0	3100	24½
Leave Brick Yard	12:30	3650	26
Arrive at Observatory	1:00	4200	28

RETURNING.

Leave Observatory	2:15
Leave Smith Creek	3:10
Leave Halls Valley	4:10
Leave Grand View	4:50
Leave Junction House	5:25
Arrive at San Jose	6:00

SATURDAY SPECIAL.

Leave......12:30 P. M.   Return.. 12:30 A. M.

The company is incorporated, and the stock is held by F. H. Ross, his sons and daughters.

IN THE REAL ESTATE BUSINESS. A. K. Whitton was for seventeen years the court reporter of the local Superior Courts. For eight years he was captain of Company B, Fifth Regiment of the National

REPRESENTATIVE RESIDENCES OF SAN JOSE AND SUBURBS.

J. Q. A Ballou.
Mrs. Annie E. C. Backesto,

A. K. Whitton.
J. R. Patton.

Guard, in this city, then Major of the Regiment, and now its Lieutenant Colonel. He recently entered into partnership with C. M. Wooster in the real estate and insurance business. He owns an orchard and is associated with the Trimble Orchard Company.

MODERN ARCHITECTURAL FEATURES. The various engravings presented herewith make prominent the fact that architecture has reached a degree of development in this county far in advance of that shown in many localities in the East. Among the most striking may be mentioned the Hall of Records, the Asylum at Agnews, the Hotel Vendome, the Alice, the Louise block, the Rucker building, the Doerr building. They were all designed by a local firm of architects, Jacob Lenzen & Son, of San Jose.

JACOB LENZEN.

THE ANGORA INDUSTRY OF CALIFORNIA. C. P. Bailey of San Jose, Cal., has made a specialty of Angora goat breeding for the past thirty years, and is a most earnest promoter of the mohair industry. He exhibited 42 head of Angoras at the Chicago World's Fair in 1893 and took all the first premiums. He also took first premium on all of his entries of Angora Goats at the New Orleans World's Fair in 1885, and has taken most of the first premiums at the California State Fair for the past twenty years. He has sold over $100,000 worth of goats for breeding purposes and still owns about 10,000, 1,000 of which are pure bred. He has for the past ten years raised more mohair than the combined product of any four goat raisers of

ANGORA GOAT—C. P. BAILEY'S.

the United States. The average fleece of a pure bred goat is from four to six pounds, but frequently eight to ten pounds have been taken from choice animals The best mohair is now worth 55 cents per pound, five times as much as ordinary California sheep's wool. The average price of mohair for the past thirty years has been 60 cents per pound. Pure bred bucks are now worth from $25 to $50 per head. Only one-tenth enough mohair is raised in the United States for home consumption. Angora goats are longer lived, more hardy, live on poorer and less range, are freer from all kinds of disease, and are less trouble to take care of than sheep. California alone ought to raise a

WHITEHURST & HODGE'S SAWMILL, NEAR GILROY.

million of goats, that will yield five million pounds of mohair annually. What are stock raisers thinking about?

FOSS & HICKS, DEALERS IN REAL ESTATE. In order to buy real estate intelligently one must be acquainted with local conditions. In California a difference of a few hundred feet in altitude may mean a difference of $50 or $100 an acre in the price of land, especially if land is sought that is suitable for orange or lemon culture. Those who are not acquainted with the

RESIDENCES OF MODERN ARCHITECTURE—BY JACOB LENZEN & SON.

Mrs. Carmichael, Locust and San Fernando Sts., San Jose.

J. T. McGeoghegan, Chapman and Emory Sts., San Jose.

Leopold Strauss, 142 South Second St., San Jose.

Mrs. D. J. Murphy, Milpitas Road.

Gustave Lion, Third and Julian Sts., San Jose.

conditions which here affect horticulture occasionally pay $200 an acre for land upon which to grow olives, while they might secure soil more suitable for $25 an acre. Likewise they purchase pear land upon which to raise apricots and apricot land upon which to raise pears. When buying land all things which affect its value should be taken into consideration, notably transportation facilities, the kind and quantity of water obtainable, roads, distance from market, schools, churches and stores. Owing to the diversity of opinions, and often to circumstances beyond human control, tracts of land may always be found that are for sale. They are well acquainted with property, both in the city and throughout the county, and are competent to judge of the real value of land placed in their hands for sale. It has taken them years to acquire this knowledge. They give customers the benefit of their experience. Office, San Jose.

THE BOARD OF TRADE BUILDING. One of the prominent young business men of San Jose is William Moir. He has large property interests here and owns the Board of Trade building on North First street, which was erected at a cost of $40,000. He is a Director of the Board of Trade.

W. L. WOODROW, UNDERTAKER. To acceptably perform the duties of a funeral director requires more than mere experience. To enter the house of death, where sorrow prevails to the exclusion of all else, and there perform the last kindly offices, requires that he who performs the duty shall be possessed of a gentle, sympathetic nature, one who knows what sorrow

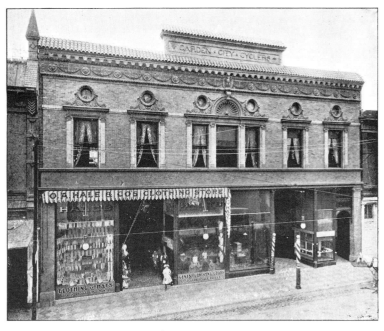

O. A. HALE & CO.'S CLOTHING STORE, SAN JOSE.

SAN JOSE BOARD OF TRADE BUILDING. OWNED BY WILLIAM MOIR.

means to those who mourn, and who is capable of helping to assuage grief. Until the sad hour has come, few can appreciate how necessary are the services of one who is experienced to lift the burden of direction and administer tenderly and understandingly the last sad rites. For twenty-five years past W. L. Woodrow has performed the duties of funeral director in this community and has proven to be possessed of the qualities of mind and heart necessary to acceptably serve in that capacity. Those who have had occasion to employ Mr. Woodrow can bear witness to the superior manner in which he has always performed every duty connected with his business. His parlors at 117 South First street are models of taste and elegance and are complete in every detail. His goods are of the best, his hearses are of the finest and his services conscientiously rendered. Mr. Woodrow is a member and an ex-President of the State Funeral Directors' Association.

SAN JOSE MEAT COMPANY. This company was incorporated in 1893 by John A. Woodward, formerly of Marysville, Cal., and E. J. Bennett, formerly of Gilroy, who are President and Secretary, respectively, of the company, and its principal stockholders. They established markets equipped with Gurney refrigerators and all the latest improvements for the successful handling of fresh meat. The finest, most juicy and most tender meat is not that which is freshly killed, but that which has been given a certain age. This improves the meat and makes it more suitable for food.

REPRESENTATIVE SANTA CLARA COUNTY COUNTRY RESIDENCES.

F. H. Holmes
W. W. Montague.

Mrs. W. J. Parr.
Mrs. S. L. Winchester.

This chemical change is brought about by refrigeration. The San Jose Meat Company employs the most improved system of refrigeration. The retail price of meat is less here than in the East, and an exemption which we enjoy is that no slop-fed cattle are raised in the State. The fat of our cattle is the product of the nutritious grasses of our hills and the grain of the fertile valleys.

GREEN'S LUMBER YARD. An important business enterprise is that conducted by M. D. Green on the corner of Fifth and St. John streets. Here can be found a complete line of building material, comprising redwood and Oregon pine, doors, sash, shingles, etc.

Mr. Green came to San Jose in 1870, and for nearly twenty years was engaged in the business of contracting and building. Among the structures erected under his supervision are the Beach building, on the corner of Santa Clara and Second streets, and the Lux residence, in East San Jose. In 1878 Mr. Green

E. J. Bennett.

purchased an interest in the lumber business of Charles McKiernan, and later, after the death of that gentleman, he purchased the remaining interest from the heirs. The business has continued under his sole management since. Mr. Green gives his personal attention to every detail of the establishment, and being a practical builder, understanding just what his customers expect, supplies them with the best in the market. In this way he has secured a good trade, which is rapidly increasing. Mr. Green has a beautiful home on North Sixth street.

THE WOOLEN MILLS. The San Jose Woolen Mill is one of the largest in California. Here are manufactured the finest quality of cassimeres, flannels and blankets. The latter have the reputation of being the finest blankets in the world and are extensively sold in the East. The cloth produced is largely manufactured into men's clothing and has a large local demand. The knitted underwear of this establishment is of the highest excellence.

THE SAN JOSE MEAT COMPANY   *John A. Woodward.*

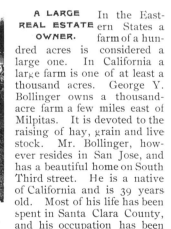

A REAL ESTATE FIRM. One of the most widely and favorably known men in Santa Clara County during his lifetime was James A. Clayton, and the real estate firm of J. A. Clayton & Co. was likewise known throughout the State. Mr. Clayton came to California in 1850, and to Santa Clara County in 1853. He conducted a photograph gallery for thirteen years. In 1861 he was elected County Clerk and re-elected in 1863. In 1867 he established a real estate office, and it is the oldest established office in the City of San Jose. As his sons grew to maturity he associated them with him in business. Upon his death, in April, 1896, they succeeded to his business, and the firm is now composed of Edward, Willis and John Clayton. At the time of his death he was President of the First National Bank, and had extensive property interests. He was known as an upright, public-spirited and liberal man. His sons succeed to the good name, as well as to the business of their father, and are well posted as to land values in the county and the value and safety of all kinds of investments. The firm has for sale orchards, vineyards, unimproved land and city lots; they also act as agents in making any kind of a business investment.

A LARGE REAL ESTATE OWNER. In the Eastern States a farm of a hundred acres is considered a large one. In California a large farm is one of at least a thousand acres. George Y. Bollinger owns a thousand-acre farm a few miles east of Milpitas. It is devoted to the raising of hay, grain and live stock. Mr. Bollinger, however resides in San Jose, and has a beautiful home on South Third street. He is a native of California and is 39 years old. Most of his life has been spent in Santa Clara County, and his occupation has been that of horticulture and farming. In 1892 he was elected Sheriff and served two years. His conduct of the office was satisfactory and he displayed all the qualities which should be found in a public officer and a conserver of the public peace. Possessed of sound judgment, he was cool in all emer-

REPRESENTATIVE SAN JOSE RESIDENCES.

Property of C. E. White and Mrs. M. E. Staples.

Nicholas Bowden.

D. F. McGraw.

The Martin Murphy Residence.

RESIDENCE OF GEORGE Y BOLLINGER.

FRANK
V.
WRIGHT.
The Secretary of the San Jose Building and Loan Association is Frank V. Wright, who is also Assistant Cashier of the Union Savings Bank and Past President of the California State League of Mutual Building and Loan Associations.

JUDGE
J. R.
LEWIS.
Judge Joseph R. Lewis, ex-Chief Justice of the Territory of Washington, is a native of Ohio and was born in 1829. He was educated in the public schools of his native State and for five years followed the profession of school teaching. He then studied law and was admitted to the Supreme Court of Ohio in 1854. He established himself in the practice of his profession in Washington County, Iowa, and in 1856 was elected prosecuting attorney for the county and served in that capacity until 1859. Thereafter he engaged in private practice until 1869, when he was appointed Associate Justice of the Supreme Court of Idaho Territory by President Grant. This position he held until 1871, when he was appointed Associate Justice of the Territory of New Mexico, which honor he declined. In 1872 he was appointed Associate Justice of the Supreme Court of Washington Territory, which position he filled until 1875, when he was appointed Chief Justice of the Supreme Court, with his residence at Seattle. He served until 1879, when he engaged in private practice, and he was concerned in most of the

gencies and brave on all occasions when bravery was needed. It is not improbable but that Mr. Bollinger will be called to fulfill similar or other public duties in the future.

THE
STAR
BAKERY.
P. F. McGettigan is the proprietor of the Star Bakery, which is situated on the corner of Park avenue and Sunol street, San Jose. The business was first established twenty-five years ago by Mr. McGettigan's father, and has grown constantly ever since. There are two ovens, and five wagons are required in the distribution of bread. A large trade is done in supplying the large vineyards and ranches during the season of harvest. In the busy season ten barrels of flour are consumed daily and twelve men are employed. All kinds of bread and pastry are manufactured and the highest grades of flour are used. The greatest care possible is taken to have the product uniform and of excellent quality.

THE PRESIDENT
OF THE
WATER COMPANY.
Edward Williams was born in 1823 in Somersetshire, England. In 1846 he came to America, settling in Troy, New York. In 1850 he came to California by way of the isthmus, and engaged in mining in Nevada County, where he remained until 1871. In 1873 he removed to San Jose, and became a stockholder in the old Savings Bank, and was one of the original incorporators of the Commercial and Savings Bank, of which he has since been a director. He was also President of the San Jose Water Company nearly twenty years, resigning less than a year ago.

M'GETTIGAN'S STAR BAKERY, SAN JOSE.

306

YOUNG MEN WHO ARE PROMINENT IN BUSINESS AFFAIRS

John J. Clayton.	James T. Rucker.	Samuel Rucker.	Joseph H. Rucker.	Charles W. Fay.
F. M. Stern.	Charles Lux.	John W. Ryland.	Martin Murphy.	J. E. Fisher.
E. J. Richardson.	F. C. Ensign.	Charles W. Coe.	John Shaw.	Daniel Chapman.

JUDGE J. R. LEWIS.

important litigation of the Territory. In 1883 he identified himself with many business enterprises which carried with them the development of the country. In 1890 he came to San Jose and located here. Believing that the fruit industry afforded a safe field for investment he has recently purchased a tract of 120 acres near Eden Vale, which he intends to plant in fruit at once.

HON. F. C. FRANCK. Hon. F. C. Franck came to California in 1852 and mined successfully in the placer gold fields near Columbia several years. In 1855 he came to Santa Clara county and in 1856 settled in the town of Santa Clara, where he has since resided. He now has extensive property interests. From 1871 to 1874 he represented his district in the Assembly, and in 1894 was elected State Senator. Mr. Franck was a delegate to the National Republican Convention that nominated Harrison.

CYRUS P. BERRY. Cyrus P. Berry was born in the town of Sweden, Maine, September 26, 1842. He was educated in the public schools, graduating from Biddford High School in 1857. He worked at the machinist trade until the breaking out of the civil war, when, on the 27th day of April, thirteen days after the firing on Fort Sumpter, he enlisted in Company B, Fifth Regiment of Maine Volunteer Infantry, and took part in all of the principal battles in which that regiment was engaged. On the expiration of his first term of service in 1864 he re-enlisted and remained until the close of the war. After returning home he went to work at the machinists' trade. He was elected by the Republicans as city clerk of Biddford in 1873 and 1874, and also in 1877 and 1878. He served as Assistant Postmaster of Biddford during 1875

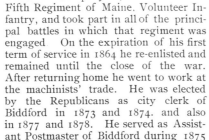

F. C. FRANCK.

NIGUEL D'OYLEY.

and 1876, and was inspector of customs at Portland from 1880 till 1886. He worked at his trade as machinist till October, 1889, when he came to California, locating at Mountain View, where he is engaged in farming and fruit growing. He was elected Assemblyman of the Fifty-fourth District at the last election. In politics he is a Republican.

CAPT. NIGEL D'OYLY. Capt. Nigel D'Oyly was a native of France and was born in 1835. He came to America when a lad of nine years and was educated in Virginia. He had a fondness for the sea, and at the age of 15 years he commenced his sea-faring career. When the civil war broke out he enlisted in the volunteer navy of the United States and received the title of acting master. He soon rose to the command of vessels, and rendered valiant service in many engagements, and was instrumental in capturing vessels from the enemy and also those engaged in running the blockade. Owing to sickness he was compelled to resign from the navy in 1863, and upon his restoration to health he re-entered the merchant marine service and for ten years he was recognized as one of the most competent ship-masters on the sea. Having gained a competence, he retired from the sea in 1874 and removed with his family to San Jose, where he resided until his death, October 7, 1894. He belonged to the Military Order of the Loyal Legion of the United States, to which he was devotedly attached.

THE LATE S. A. BISHOP. One of the most active and energetic men and one who did as much toward fostering a progressive public spirit in the community as any other citizen was Samuel A. Bishop. He was a native of Virginia, but at an early age followed the star of empire in its westward way and for a number of years lived in Missouri. In 1849 he came to California. Here he found an ample field for his restless energies and engaged in various enterprises, mining, mer-

C. P. BERRY

S. A. BISHOP.

REPRESENTATIVE RESIDENCES OF SAN JOSE.

Mrs. A. H. Burrell.
William Buckley.

Louis Rothermel.
Mrs. S. A. Bishop.

DR. O. A. HOOKER, DENTIST.
Washington Block, San Jose.

chandising, contracting, road building, etc. In 1867 he came to San Jose, and in the following year he constructed the first street railroad in the city, one which connected the two towns of San Jose and Santa Clara. He also became interested in various other enterprises and was prominent in the social, business and political life of the community. In the year 1889 he converted his horse railroad into an electrical one, being the first one of its kind in California. He was known as a generous and genial man and possessed of many endearing traits of character.

His death occurred June 3d, 1893.

J. P. BACKESTO, M. D. John P. Backesto was born in Lancaster, Pennsylvania, November 1, 1831. Three years later he moved with his parents to Ohio, settling near Mansfield, and it was here that he received his early education and entered on the study of medicine. After a thorough preparatory course he entered the Cincinnati Eclectic College, from which he graduated, with high honors, in 1852. He soon after started west in search of a location and chose Germantown, Indiana, where he remained until 1855, when he removed to St. Louis, Missouri,

DR. J. P. BACKESTO.

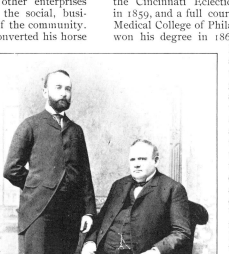

J. D. AND JAMES PHELAN.

where his kind and genial nature soon won for him a host of friends and a lucrative practice. After five years of close application to business he concluded to spend a year in travel and study, after which he took a post-graduate course at the Cincinnati Eclectic Medical College in 1859, and a full course at the Eclectic Medical College of Philadelphia, where he won his degree in 1860. Returning to Indiana, he located at Indianapolis, where he soon gained for himself a good practice, warm friends and a lovely home, but, after a few years, the health of his wife led him to seek the more genial clime of California.

DR. D. F. M'GRAW, DENTIST.
36 South First Street, San Jose.

Here he again won warm friends and a large practice. In 1875 he became a member of the Eclectic Medical Society, of which he was Vice-President for several terms, and he was also a member of the Board of Examiners of the Eclectic Medical Society of California. By close application to business and judicious investments he soon gained a competence, and in 1880 he gave up the practice of his profession to enjoy the quiet retirement of his beautiful home, on North First street, surrounded by many rare shrubs, trees and flowers, where he died March 17, 1890.

A PROMINENT DENTIST. One of the prominent men of his profession in San Jose is G. F. Nevius, D. D. S. He is a native of Ohio and a graduate of the Philadelphia Dental College. He was a member of a class which received the highest credits of any which had graduated from the institution up to that time, and the doctor was specially honored by the faculty in the presence of his class for his very high attainments. He has been a resident of San Jose since 1887, and has secured a very large and lucrative practice. His work has the reputa-

DR. F. G. NEVIUS.
Safe Deposit Building.

SANTA CLARA COUNTY PIONEERS.

W. L. Woodrow.   Abram King.   J. P. Sargent.   James A. Clayton.   Freeman B. Gates.
M. D. Keil.   Thomas Rea.   Harry Bee.   Cuthbert Burrell.   George B. McKee.
                                             Arrived in the County in 1830. Now a resident of Milpitas.
George H. Briggs.   C. T. Ryland.   I. M. Davis.   William Matthews.   Dr. B. F. Headen.

tion of being of a high degree of excellence. His office is in the Safe Deposit block. Dr. Nevius is a member of the State Dental Association.

CUTHBERT BURRELL, A PIONEER. Cuthbert Burrell was born in Wayne County, New York, in 1834. In 1835 his father removed to Illinois. In 1846 Cuthbert Burrell came to California across the plains, enlisting under General John C. Fremont. In 1860 he engaged in farming and stock raising in this county. In 1874 he was married to Mrs. Addie Adams, of San Jose. He died on August 7, 1893. His wife and three children, Varena J., May and Luella, survive him, and reside on the corner of Third and William streets, San Jose.

ISAAC M. DAVIS. Isaac M. Davis is enjoying the quiet evening of a well-spent life in his handsome mansion on the corner of Third and William streets, San Jose. He was born in Smithfield, Jefferson County, Ohio, in 1823. His parents were James and Elizabeth (Stayman) Davis, both natives of Pennsylvania. Mr. Davis remained at home until he was 16 years of age, when he was engaged to teach school. He continued to teach most of the time till 1846. He then began mercantile life as a partner in a general merchandise business at Middletown, Ohio. In 1848 he sold out and went to Smithfield, where he carried on a store until 1855. In that year he transferred his business to Pomeroy, Ohio, where he engaged in business until the year 1870, when he sold out

RESIDENCE OF L. L. ARGUELLO.

and removed to the Pacific Coast. He remained three years at Virginia City, Nevada, where he transacted business for the Virginia and Truckee railroad, and dealt in stocks. In the fall of 1872 he brought his family to San Jose, and when he had settled his business affairs in Virginia City, in 1873, he joined his family here, where he has since resided. Mr. Davis was married in 1847 to Miss Susanna K. Sharon, of Smithfield, Ohio, sister of the late Hon. William Sharon, ex-Senator of Nevada. Mr. and Mrs. Davis have six children living: Clara J., wife of Charles L. McCoy, of Oakland; Ida M., wife of Judge J. M. Allen, of Menlo Park; Lily, wife of J. C. Kirkpatrick, of San Francisco; William S., of Fresno County; Rosabel Hildreth and Charles H., of San Jose. William S. Davis was married in 1886 to Miss Susan Stone, of San Jose. Living, as Mr. Davis did, upon the border land between the North and South during the rebellion, he saw much active service. He joined the Ohio National Guard in 1863, and for four months, in 1864, was constantly under fire in the Kanawha Valley, West Virginia. Both of Mr. Davis' grandfathers fought in the revolutionary war under George Washington, and his father in the war of 1812 under General William Henry Harrison.

I. M. DAVIS' SUMMER HOUSE AND FLOWER GARDEN, SAN JOSE.

LOUIS L. ARGUELLO. A descendant of one of the first families in California is Louis L. Arguello. His grandfather was the first Governor of California under Mexican rule, and his father was one of the leading landed proprietors of early days. He was born in Santa Clara in

L. L. ARGUELLO

312

REPRESENTATIVE RESIDENCES OF SAN JOSE.

C. J. Owen.
Jackson Hatch.

L. J. Pfau.
I. M. Davis.

CHARLES WEHNER'S RESIDENCE, SAN JOSE.

married in Milwaukee in 1868 to Miss Lena Garrecht. Their son, George Rothermel, is now in the Security Savings Bank, of San Jose.

Joseph Schupp, whose thirty-acre orchard is situated at the junction of Julian and White roads, was born in Baden, Germany There he received a thorough college education, subsequently devoting several years to the study of languages, including French, Latin and English, studying the latter language with a view of future residence in the United States. Having heard that America was a prosperous land, he decided to make it his home, and embarked in 1851. He went to Buffalo, N. Y., removing shortly afterward to Toledo, Ohio, where he remained several years. In 1858 he went to Stillwater, Minnesota, of which State he may be called pioneer. At Stillwater he engaged in the mercantile business, building up a lucrative trade in the wholesale grocery line. His health became seriously impaired by the rigorous climate, and in 1888 he, with his wife and three children, came to San Jose, and purchased property at 647 East Santa Clara street, where he built a comfortable and modern house. What was then a bare lot is now a beautiful lawn, adorned with palms and many rare shrubs and flowers. Mr. Schupp has been an extensive traveler, having taken extended annual trips for health and pleasure. He has visited more than once every State in the Union, and Canada. as well as Mexico and Central America. In 1894 Mr. and Mrs. Schupp took a trip to Europe, to visit once more the old home they left forty-three years ago. They traveled through France, Switzerland, Italy, Austria and Germany. They found localities where the climate was very pleasant, but think that even Italy does not quite compare with the Santa Clara valley.

1867 and was educated at Santa Clara College and St. Mary's College, San Francisco. He married Miss Arcadia Spence, and their home is in Monterey. However, besides having large interests in Monterey County, Mr. and Mrs. Arguello have property in San Jose and in Santa Clara County. They own a beautiful residence on the Alameda, shown in the accompanying engraving.

SOME WELL-KOWN MEN. One of San Jose's most substantial business men is Louis Rothermel. He was born in Fuerth, Hessedarmstadt, Germany, February 1, 1824. In 1847 he came to America and shortly thereafter started a store in Chicago, which

H. W. EDWARD'S RESIDENCE, SAN JOSE.

he carried on until 1850, when he came across the plains, landing in Sacramento in August of that year. There he started a furnishing store, but was soon drawn to the gold mines. He cleared $2,000 there and then bought a farm and remained upon it five years, after which he commenced to buy and sell stock. In 1867 he had a wholesale slaughter house in Montana. He removed to San Francisco, but shortly came to Santa Clara County in search of a better climate. He at once invested in real estate in San Jose. He now owns four business houses on First street, besides several residences. He also owns several business blocks in the town of Tulare, in Tulare county, and owns stock in Tulare and Santa Cruz banks. He was

NICHOLAS BOWDEN'S RESIDENCE, ON THE ALAMEDA.

SAN JOSE RESIDENCES.

CITY OFFICIALS OF SAN JOSE.

Citizens Who Have Been Entrusted with the Management of Municipal Affairs. A Government Which Has Been Administered with Economy and in the Interest of the People.

THE municipality of San Jose is governed by a Common Council of eight members, two from each of the four wards into which the city is divided. The chief executive officer is the Mayor, and the other executive officers are a Chief of Police, a Street Commissioner, City Assessor and Clerk, and Treasurer. The Council has also provided for a City Attorney and City Engineer. A Board of Education has charge of school affairs and consists of eight members, two from each ward. This board elects a Superintendent of Schools, who has supervision over all the schools of the city.

The Mayor of the City of San Jose is Valentine Koch. He is a native of Germany and came to this country in 1864, when 14 years old. He learned the trade of harness-maker in New York, and in 1868 came to California and located in San Jose. He worked at his trade for thirteen years, when, in company with Peter Keiser, he established a business for himself. The firm of Keiser & Koch, dealers in carriages and harness, conduct one of the largest establishments of the kind in the city. Mr. Koch has therefore demonstrated his ability as a successful man of business. His public career embraces four years as Councilman of the city and four years as trustee of the Agnews Insane Asylum. In April, 1896, he was elected Mayor as an independent candidate. His administration has been highly satisfactory.

The duties of the City Assessor and Clerk are numerous and exacting. The work of assessment is a most important one. The clerical duties are also very important, for the office of clerk includes that of Anditor. He keeps account of the finances of the city, draws the warrants, computes the taxes and writes the receipts therefor. J. W. Cook holds this important

THE ALUM ROCK PARK COMMISSIONERS.

Valentine Koch.
H. B. Alvord.
B. D. Murphy.
L. G. Nesmith.
A. T. Herrmann.

position. He has been a resident of San Jose twenty years. He has held the office six years. In 1884 he was elected a member of the Legislature, and made an honest and conscientious official.

The City Treasurer, besides being the custodian of the city's money, is also the collector of taxes and licenses. His responsibilities are great, and he is obliged to furnish a heavy bond for the faithful performance of his duties. The present Treasurer is J. N. Ewing, who was elected in 1894. Previously he had held responsible positions in the County Treasurer's office, having been license collector for two years. Mr. Ewing is a native of Indiana, and was born in 1833. He is one of California's pioneers, having come to the State in 1853. He has resided in San Jose since 1879.

The work of the Commissioner of Streets is constant, exacting and of a nature demanding the exercise of sound judgment and the application of business qualities of a high order. Colonel A. G. Bennett served throughout the war and rose from a private in the ranks to the command of a regiment. He has been a member of the Board of Education, Common Council and Legislature, and in each position earned promotion. He came to California in 1875.

The Police Department consists of a Chief of Police and twenty patrol men, inclusive of the captains. One of the most responsible positions within the municipality is that occupied by James A. Kidward, at the head of the Police Department. His administration has brought great credit to him. He is a native of Ohio, is 33 years of age and has been a resident of Santa Clara County fourteen years.

316

SUP'T SCHOOLS

STREET COMMISSIONER

CITY ENGINEER

MAYOR

CITY ATTORNY.

TREASURER

CLERK.

SAN JOSE CITY OFFICIALS.

C. M. Barker

F. P. Russell.

Valentine Koch

A. G. Bennett.

J. R. Welch.

J. N. Ewing.

J. W. Cook.

Frank P. Russell has held the office of City Superintendent of Schools for the past eight years, and was recently elected to serve four years more. He has been engaged in educational work for the past twenty years. He is also a Vice-President of the State Teachers' Association.

The City Attorney is J. R. Welch. He is a native of Illinois, where his father was a prominent citizen and highly connected in the Masonic fraternity. He came to this State when a youth and received his education largely in the schools of this county. He graduated from the University of the Pacific in 1887 and at the present is one of the trustees of that institution. He was admitted to the bar in 1888, since which time he has been actively engaged in practice and has reached a prominent position among the members of the bar. He was elected City Attorney in January, 1896, and has discharged the duties satisfactorily and conscientiously. Mr. Welch is 36 years of age.

The City Engineer prepares all plans and specifications for street work, sewers and river improvements, establishes grades and superintends all constructive work. The City Engineer is Curtis M. Barker, a native of Detroit, Mich. He attended the State University at Ann Arbor, and prior to coming to California did surveying in Colorado for various mining companies and for the South Park Railroad Company. He came to California in 1885 and for seven years was assistant engineer in the construction of the Stanford University. He was also on the location and construction of the Coast division of the Southern Pacific railroad. He was chosen City Engineer in February, 1896.

The members of the Common Council are: First ward, T. C. Hogan and W. T. Nolting; Second ward, A. H. Mangrum, and J. P. Fay; Third ward, George B. Dittus and E. P. Main; Fourth ward, J. P. Jarman and Julius Kreig.

The members of the Board of Education are: First ward: T. O'Neil and J. R. O'Brien; Second ward, E. H. Wemple and F. W. Moore; Third ward, Charles Kenyon and W. C. Hamilton; Fourth ward, J. Koenig and M. J. Graham.

THE ALUM ROCK RAILROAD. One of the pleasures which the people of San Jose are free to enjoy at any time is a trip to that delightful resort, Alum Rock Park. Recently, for the convenience of pleasure-seekers, there has been constructed a railroad to the park, connecting with the electric road at East San Jose. It is a very pleasant trip to take, as the road runs under the shade of large trees along the main avenue for over a mile and then turns aside through orchards and grain fields to the canyon of the Penetencia, thence around jutting points up the narrow gorge, with high hills on either side until the reservation is reached. The road is five and one-half miles long and is under the management of H. Center. Mr. Center has been active in improving the road and recently a new steam motor was purchased and several new cars added to the rolling stock.

A PROMINENT CONTRACTOR. For fifteen years past Charles Wehner has been the leading contractor in San Jose in the line of street improvements and sewer work. He constructed the outlet for the main sewer of the city near Alviso, and a large portion of the street pavements were laid under his supervision. That the work has been well done goes without saying. He has all the tools and machinery necessary for excavating, grading and constructing streets, street railroads, sewers, etc.

ALFRED C. EATON. This Souvenir was printed by Alfred C. Eaton, of San Jose. The excellence of the work is apparent upon every page. There is no printing establishment in the State that could have insured better results, and very few indeed that could have produced work of equal merit. No work of equal magnitude has ever been published in which half-tone engravings have been brought out more clearly. Alfred C. Eaton is prepared to do all kinds of printing, including books, newspapers and job printing, and guarantees good work, fair prices and complete satisfaction.

ANDREW P. HILL. Andrew P. Hill, the photographer of the Souvenir, is also well known as an artist. He was educated at Santa Clara College, studied art at the School of Design in San Francisco, and later was associated with L. O. Lussier. Together they painted

ALUM ROCK MOTOR ROAD

CHARLES WEHNER.

REPRESENTATIVE RESIDENCES OF SAN JOSE.

J. Z. Anderson.
Mrs. Ann Faull.

R. Hoelbe.
J. H. Rucker.

pictures of the ex-Governors of Nevada, which were purchased by the Legislature of that State in 1879. In 1877 Mr. Hill made an exhibition at the State Fair of animal, portrait and landscape paintings, receiving the Society's gold medal for the most meritorious display of oil paintings. In 1878 he again made an exhibit, taking the gold medal the second time. He did not again exhibit his work at the fair until 1890, when the State medal for the best landscape painting, won over sixty-five competing artists, was awarded to him on a large painting entitled "The First Emigrant Party Ascending to the Summit from Donner Lake,"—the Murphy party. Mr. Hill also painted Senator Stanford's noted horse Electioneer, and was employed by him to photograph his thoroughbred stock.

Mr. Hill has been in the photographic business in San Jose since 1889. At present he is located in the Porter block. Mr. Hill is also interested in fancy poultry, and at 313 Willow street, in co-partnership with William H. Yeaton, conducts a regular poultry brokerage, all kinds of thoroughbred fowls being bought and sold on commission. They have, especially, many fine Black Spanish and Plymouth Rocks.

J. D. BEGGS OF LOS GATOS. One of the prominent young men of the county is J. D. Beggs, of Los Gatos. He is a native of Pennsylvania, but has been a resident of California for over twenty years. His father, J. J. Beggs,

A. P. HILL'S PEN OF FAMOUS PLYMOUTH ROCKS, SAN JOSE.

J. D. BEGGS.

owns a beautiful place of forty acres in the hills above Los Gatos, which is much frequented in the summer by visitors from the cities and is a favorite summer resort. Mr. J. D. Beggs was in business in Los Gatos for several years, and was appointed Justice of the Peace in 1893 and elected in 1894. During the incumbency of the office he studied law and has been admitted to the Supreme Court. As a lawyer he promises to be a prominent member of the bar, as he has the education, the habit of study, the perseverance and the other qualifications necessary to make him a successful practitioner. In the conduct of his office he has been impartial and just and has earned a reputation for sterling integrity.

THE NEWSPAPERS OF SAN JOSE. The oldest newspaper published in San Jose is the MERCURY. It was established as a weekly in 1861 by J. J. Owen and has been in existence ever since. The same year the DAILY MERCURY was first issued, but was discontinued the following year. In 1869 it was again issued and its publication continued for a year, when another suspension occurred. In 1872 it appeared once more and since that time it has been an important factor in moulding public opinion and shaping the destinies of the community. In 1877 it was incorporated under the style of the Mercury Printing and Publishing Company, Mr. Owen holding a majority of the stock. In 1876 the present proprietor of the MERCURY, Charles M. Shortridge, became first connected with the paper. His connection was that of general utility boy. Working in this capacity he familiarized himself with the details of the newspaper business. He worked his way into the business office, into the subscription and mailing department, and finally went upon the local staff. In 1883 he severed his connection and with the aid of several prominent business men and capitalists who had faith in his capacity and integrity, he established a paper of his own named the *Times*. In 1884 he purchased a controlling interest in the MERCURY and merged the two papers into one. The career of the paper has been a highly successful one, and in its conduct Mr. Shortridge won a high and wide reputation as a newspaper man. In 1895 he purchased the San Francisco *Call*, which he personally conducts, and has made it one of the leading and most influential papers of the country.

The other papers published in San Jose are:

The *Herald*, an afternoon paper, of which H. H. Main is the manager and W. M. Webster the editor; the *News*, also an afternoon paper, of which C. W. Williams is the publisher.

The weekly papers are the *Democrat*, by P L. Barrington; the *Report*, by Mrs. J. K. de Jarnett; the *New Charter*, by M. W. Wilkins; the *Letter*, by F. Hichborn; the *California*, by Schmidt & Currlen; the *Pioneer*, by A. P. Murgotten. There are several monthly publications issued viz: The *Poultry Fancier*, the *Tree and Vine*, and the *Santa Clara Magazine*.

EL MONTE HOTEL, LOS GATOS. When Los Gatos evolved from a village to a city, which it did in a marvelously short period of time, a necessity arose for a first-class hotel. It was needed not alone as a convenience to the traveling public, but from the further circumstances that the climate at this place was highly beneficial to invalids and the surroundings were sufficiently attractive to induce many to seek the locality in pursuit of rest and pleasure. So the Hotel El Monte was erected as a hotel and health and pleasure resort and a beautiful and convenient structure now adorns the main street, only a few minutes' walk from the depot. It was constructed in 1890 and in 1892 it was leased by Captain S. S. Austin, under whose management it has acquired a wide reputation as being a strictly first-class hotel.

The hotel is constructed with a view of supplying all modern conveniences to travelers and pleasure-seekers. The rooms are all large, airy and sunny, there being no inside or dark rooms in the house. The parlors and dining rooms are spacious and handsomely furnished. Wide verandas encircle the building, and these are shaded by masses of trees and vines. The service is excellent and the class of patrons is of the best. Captain Austin is a native of New York and is a retired sea captain. His voyages brought him to California, and he thus became impressed with the beauties of the State and the healthfulness of its climate, so that when the opportunity came he located here and selected Los Gatos for his home because of its attractiveness and because the air was curative of asthma, from which he was a sufferer. He has had previous experience in the hotel line, having for two years conducted the Coleman House, New York City. His son, Lynn Austin, has the active business management of the establishment, a position for which he is eminently fitted, having been previously connected with the Baldwin Hotel in San Francisco. The hotel is situated to afford attractions and entertainment at all seasons, and is a winter as well as a summer resort. The mountains near at hand offer good hunting and fishing and in every direction are beautiful drives, through mountain canyons or amid the fruitful orchards of the valley. It is an ideal resort and is becoming more and more popular year after year.

VIEWS OF THE HOTEL EL MONTE, LOS GATOS.

A BUSINESS MAN OF LOS GATOS. For forty-six years C. W. Holden has been in the livery business, having first commenced his career in this line in his native State of Vermont. He has resided in Los Gatos for nine years and has one of the best-equipped and well-managed stables in this part of the State. His vehicles embrace every variety from six-in hand coach to a two-wheeled cart. He has about twenty head of horses, which are stylish, gentle and excellent roadsters. His drivers are selected with a view to their habits of carefulness and sobriety, and none are allowed to drink intoxicating liquor. Once a week, leaving Los Gatos on Saturdays, he drives a six-horse coach to Mount Hamilton and returns on Sunday. These excursions are very popular and are liberally patronized. His stable is located near the depot and convenient to the hotels. Mr. Holden has a beautiful residence in Los Gatos and is one of the prominent men of the city.

E. S. WHITNEY OF LOS GATOS. Elijah Skinner Whitney was born at Corinth, Maine, October 4, 1834. He began a mercantile career in 1860 in his native town and continued until 1875, when he moved to Santa Cruz, in this State. He continued at Santa Cruz in the same line of business for ten years, when he came to Los Gatos and engaged in the merchandising and then in the real estate and railway business, being the passenger agent for the Northern Pacific Railway. He is still in the real estate business and has a number of desirable properties for sale, including bearing and income-producing prune orchards. Mr. Whitney has a beautiful home in Los Gatos, a few hundred yards from the business center and situated on an elevation which affords a fine view of the town. He owns ten acres within the town limits, and this tract contains very desirable residence lots. He has other lots for sale which will make suitable villa lots and for which there will be an increasing demand, as the town is rapidly growing in all directions. There are many handsome residences in the vicinity.

Los Gatos is supplied with electric lights, the plant having been installed in June, 1896. The light is furnished by T. D Hume from his country place.

RESIDENCE OF E. S. WHITNEY, LOS GATOS.

HOLDEN'S LIVERY STABLE, LOS GATOS.

THE NEW PRINCIPAL OF THE NORMAL SCHOOL. Since the time at which the pages herein relating to the State Normal School went to press there has been a change in the management of that institution. On July 26th, the Board of Trustees of the Normal School elected Prof. A. H. Randall as principal for the ensuing year. In January, 1884, he began his work in the Normal School which has won for him the position to which he is now elected. During all these years he has shown himself earnest, faithful and efficient in any work demanded of him. In the somewhat difficult position of Vice-Principal, which he has held for the past year, he has shown marked executive ability, winning the hearty respect and esteem of students and teachers. Professor Randall brings to the discharge of the new duties that will devolve upon him wide experience, ripe scholarship and a strong determination to make the Normal School at San Jose the best, not only in the State but among the best in the country. The school has been re-opened auspiciously under his management. A reorganization was accomplished without friction and in a manner which demonstrates his executive ability and good judgment. Prof. Randall was born at Livermore, Maine, and was educated in the public schools and graduated from the Maine Wesleyan University. He has since taught in his native State, and in the high schools of Stockton and Santa Cruz.

PROF. A H. RANDALL.

322

EXECUTIVE FORCE AND EMPLOYES OF THE SAN JOSE MERCURY.

D. M. Foltz.
C. L. Degelman.   J. T. Waldorf.
        F. L. Foster.
C. A. Wolfolk.   J. J. Adel.
                H. J. Alexander.

Mrs. M. A. Carroll.
        Miss Edith Coalman.
        C. J. Owen.
                E. J. McManimon.
        J. E. Harris.

                J. J. Owen.
        Charles M. Shortridge.
                M. E. Gilbert.

                        Rollin Caughey.
Miss May Driscoll.
        John T. Wallace.
        H. S. Foote.
                        F. L. Dennis.

                        H. A. DeLacy.
David J. Gairaud.   Clifford Gage.
                        H. E. Boothby.
        E. J. Whipple.   M. J. Graham.
                        A. P. Hill.

Union
Photo Engraving
Co.

ALL CUTS IN THIS SOUVENIR
WERE MADE BY THE

UNION PHOTO ENGRAVING CO.

523 MARKET ST.

SAN FRANCISCO.

A · L · CRANE
President

G · O · WATKINS
Treas. & Mgr.

INDEX.

* Deceased.

*Deceased.

* Deceased.